3. T

D1644922

THE BUILDINGS OF ENGLAND
EDITOR: NIKOLAUS PEVSNER
ASSISTANT EDITOR: JUDY NAIRN

BE37
NORTH LANCASHIRE
NIKOLAUS PEVSNER

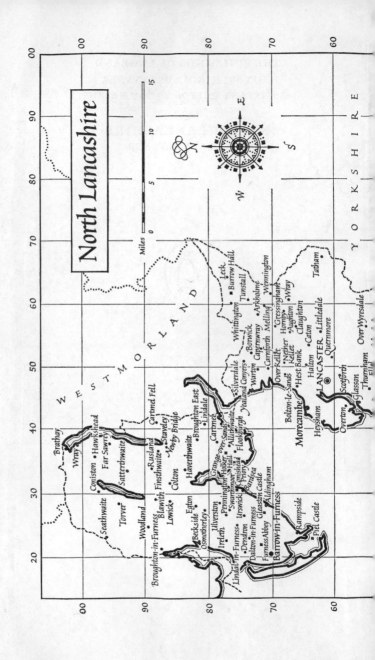

North Lancashire

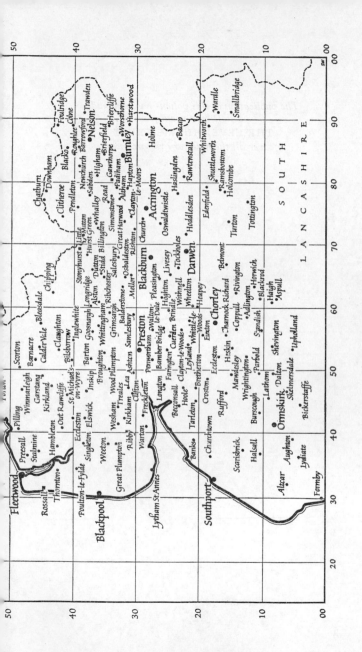

*The publication of this volume has been made
possible by a grant from*
THE LEVERHULME TRUST
to cover all the necessary research work

Lancashire

2
THE RURAL NORTH

BY

NIKOLAUS PEVSNER

★

PENGUIN BOOKS

Penguin Books Ltd, Harmondsworth, Middlesex, England
Penguin Books Inc., 7110 Ambassador Road, Baltimore, Md 21207, U.S.A.
Penguin Books Australia Ltd, Ringwood, Victoria, Australia

—

First published 1969

—

Copyright © Nikolaus Pevsner, 1969

Made and printed in Great Britain
by William Clowes and Sons, Limited, London and Beccles
Gravure plates by Harrison & Sons Ltd
Set in Monotype Plantin

CONTENTS

Map References

★

The numbers printed in italic type in the margin against the place names in the gazetteer of the book indicate the position of the place in question on the index map (pages 2–3), which is divided into sections by the 10-kilometre reference lines of the National Grid. The reference given here omits the two initial letters (formerly numbers) which in a full grid reference refer to the 100-kilometre squares into which the country is divided. The first two numbers indicate the *western* boundary, and the last two the *southern* boundary, of the 10-kilometre square in which the place in question is situated. For example Carnforth (reference 4070) will be found in the 10-kilometre square bounded by grid lines 40 and 50 on the *west* and 70 and 80 on the *south*; Leyland (reference 5020) in the square bounded by grid lines 50 and 60 on the *west* and 20 and 30 on the *south*.

The map contains all those places, whether towns, villages, or isolated buildings, which are the subject of separate entries in the text.

FOREWORD

North Lancashire was prepared for me by Mrs Neild, so competently that if there are faults and errors in the gazetteer, they are more likely due to me and to my bad handwriting or to absence of published research than to her work. She was of course greatly helped by the existence of the volumes of the Victoria County History. Mr E. Hubbard, my experienced South Lancashire assistant, also helped, and Giles Clotworthy drove me from place to place with rather more dash than was good for my inside and the peace of my mind, but always ready to do what chores had to be done. My secretary Mrs Tabner toiled away at all the work needed to get such a volume ready for the typing and even seemed to like it, and Miss Dorothy Dorn did the typing once again with uncanny accuracy in the interpretation of my minuscule scrawls. Mr Clotworthy and I enjoyed the hospitality kindly offered us by Father Hoy, the Rector of Stonyhurst, by Russell and Mary Davies in their house facing the sea at Morecambe, and by Paula Quick in her cottage tucked away near Coniston. What a difference the luxuries and warmth and the human friendliness make after all the nights in boarding houses and minor hotels!

My thanks also go out to those who help on all volumes of this series: the National Monuments Record (NMR), though their coverage of Lancashire (57 boxes in all) is not as full as they themselves would like it to be, the Goodhart-Rendel Index (GR) at the Royal Institute of British Architects, Mr Peter Ferriday (PF), who placed his copious index of Victorian church restoration on loan in my office, Mr Edward Hubbard for writing the text of Scarisbrick Hall, Mr Denis Evinson for information on some Catholic churches, Mr Donald Buttress for information on some Anglican churches, Mr Jeffrey Howarth for information on Georgian houses (more alas than I could make use of), Father Clark for information on Stonyhurst, Mr David McLaughlin for information on Rossall, Sir Hugh Wilson for information on Skelmersdale, Mr R. Jolley for information on Edward Sharpe, and the librarians of Accrington (Mr J. C. Goddard), Barrow (Mr F. Barnes), Blackburn (Mr W. W. Yates), Blackpool (Mr F. E. Cronshaw and Mr P. Dunderdale), Burnley (Mr R. Caul), Clitheroe (Mr A. Hanson), Darwen (Mr A. Holden), Lancaster (Mr E. H. Lowe), Morecambe (Mrs J. P. Webb), Preston

(Miss Jane Downton), Rawtenstall (Mr J. Elliott), and Southport (Mr E. G. Twigg). After the libraries the churches and after the churches the houses. Incumbents obliged me generously by answering questions and reading proofs, and owners of houses not only gave me access liberally but also put their knowledge of their houses at my disposal. I owe it them to state here that an account of a house in my gazetteer does not mean that it is open to the public.

The principles on which the following gazetteer is founded are the same as in the thirty-six volumes of The Buildings of England *which precede it. I have myself seen everything that I describe. Where this is not the case, the information obtained by other means is placed in brackets. Information ought to be as complete as the space of the volume permits for churches prior to c.1830 and all town houses, manor houses, and country houses of more than purely local interest. However, I am dejectedly conscious of gaps. There are far too few textile mills mentioned, largely because there was no way of knowing which would be structurally most worth-while. Victorian schools and parsonages are also included less than Victorian churches, and as for Victorian churches, North Lancashire revealed to me for the first time an ominous possibility for the future of this series. In certain areas nearly every church was locked, and to obtain the key for every Victorian church specially would have held up my progress intolerably. Yet I am told that this locking had become a necessity, not because of possible damage by malefactors which an incumbent might be ready to face for the sake of what his conscience tells him ought to be done, but because certain insurance companies insist on locking out worshippers and visitors with the threat of increasing premia otherwise. Let the church authorities weigh up the arguments. If they decide on universal locking, I might just as well give up. Another one of the shortcomings of this volume is that hundreds of dated and even more undated houses of the C17 and C18 exist in North Lancashire which I have not even seen, let alone mentioned. They are listed by the Ministry of Housing and Local Government (MHLG), who always with the same generosity let me travel with their lists. To follow them all up would have made my job impossible. I can only hope that by and large I have picked out the right ones. But it may well be that some generalizations in the introduction to this volume need minor revising in the light of houses which I have overlooked.*

As in the preceding volumes, I have tried to be complete on furnishings in churches, but have not included movable furnishings in houses. The rule in the case of churches does not apply to bells, chests, hatchments, royal arms, altar-tables, and plain fonts. Small Anglo-

Saxon and Anglo-Danish fragments could only be included where they were of special interest, and coffin lids with foliated crosses also only in such cases. Brasses of post-Reformation date are mentioned occasionally, church plate of after 1830 only rarely. Village crosses are omitted where only a plain base or a stump of the shaft survives. As for churches and chapels of after 1830, I had to make a selection, and this is dictated by architectural value or by significance otherwise in the light of architectural history. The same applies to secular buildings of the C19 and C20.

Finally, as in all previous volumes, it is necessary to end the foreword to this with an appeal to all users to draw my attention to errors and omissions.

INTRODUCTION

No county has a greater variety of landscape than Lancashire. From the slums of Manchester to Coniston Water and Winder- 1-3 mere and from the sand-beaches N of Liverpool to the moors towards Yorkshire, from the loudspeakers of Blackpool to the solitude of Bleasdale – the range appears unlimited. Manchester and Liverpool are not to be found in this volume: there is a separate South Lancashire volume including them. The boundary between the two volumes is drawn, admittedly arbitrarily, as follows (from W to E): Ince Blundell S, Formby N – Maghull S, Lydiate N – Rainsford S, Skelmersdale N – Orrell S, Upholland and Shevington N – Wigan S, Standish N – Hindley S, Horwich N – Bolton S, Edgworth N – Bury S, Tottington and Ramsbottom N – Rochdale and Littleborough S, Whitworth and Wardle N. So the largest towns in this volume are Blackpool with 150,000 and Preston with 110,000 inhabitants. Yet the range of landscape and 5 townscape is just as wide. Large cities, it is true, are absent, but industrial conurbations are not. Between Preston and Blackburn, between Blackburn and Burnley there are only a few miles of open country, and between Burnley, Colne, and Nelson there is no visible boundary anywhere. Then there are the industrial villages, the foremost example the group of Haslingden, Rawtenstall, and Bacup also running imperceptibly into each other, and similarly the cluster S of Preston and round Leyland. And of course there is the seaside stretch of 17 miles from Fleetwood by Blackpool to Lytham. But that is about all that can be called urban, except of course for Lancaster, which is factually as 4 well as visually an ancient town. But the vast majority of the acres of North Lancashire is rural. The result, statistically speaking, is that Lancashire, the whole of the county, comes seventh in size (if West and North Riding are counted as two), but first in population (except for London), but that of the area three-quarters belong to this North Lancashire volume, of the population only about one-third. How all this, and geography and social history, express themselves in architecture and building is the subject of this introduction. How the geography of North Lancashire is reflected in geology, i.e. in building materials, will be found on p. 37, how it affected prehistoric settlement on p. 41, and how it affected Roman occupation on p. 43.

Regarding occupation in the MIDDLE AGES, it was scanty, as appears from the scarcity of monuments of art and architecture. ANGLO SAXON ARCHITECTURE has nothing to show but St Patrick's Chapel at Heysham with its reeded door-arch, and some masonry and doorways of the Heysham parish church and of St Mary, Lancaster. ANGLO SAXON SCULPTURE has nothing earlier than the late C9, and very little earlier than the year 1000. The most interesting fragments are those of the Halton Cross and the Heysham Cross (with busts inhabiting what must be meant to represent a building), the Heysham hogback coffin, and a stone with figures at Hornby. Other fragments are at Aughton near Ormskirk, Bolton-le-Sands, Gressingham, Hornby, St Mary at Lancaster, Melling, Urswick, and Whalley.

Nor is the NORMAN PERIOD represented much more excitingly. In parish churches there is nothing of more than local significance: tympana at Altham, at Caton (badly mauled), and, with a runic inscription and the demi-figure of an angel, at Pennington. Doorways are at Aughton near Ormskirk, Beckside, Bispham (Blackpool; nearly entirely re-cut), Gressingham, Out Rawcliffe (also re-cut), Overton, Tatham, Ulverston, and Whalley. Overton originally had an apse, Norman St Mary at Lancaster also had one; Aldingham still has a s arcade. This has waterleaf capitals, i.e. belongs to the end of Norman and the TRANSITION TO EARLY ENGLISH. To this also belong the two major C12 to early C13 monuments of North Lancashire, Furness Abbey and Cartmel, and both are not parochial but monastic.

MONASTIC HOUSES are few, starting chronologically with Furness Abbey which was founded from Savigny at Tulketh in 1123, moved to Furness in 1127, and became Cistercian in 1147. Cartmel followed in 1188, as a house of Augustinian Canons, and Cockersand in 1190 as a house of Premonstratensian Canons, and Whalley, again Cistercian, did not start on this site until 1296.* That leaves only the Benedictine priory at Lancaster Castle, founded in 1094 and the origin of Lancaster parish church, Burscough Priory founded c.1190 for Augustinian Canons, and Upholland Priory founded in 1317–18 for Benedictines.‡

* It had been at Standlaw from the 1170s.

‡ There were also small cells or granges of the Benedictines at Penwortham and Lytham, of the Cistercians at Beaumont, Hawkshead, and Staining near Poulton-le-Fylde, of the Augustinians at Conishead, and of the Premonstratensians at Hornby. The Dominicans started a house at Lancaster before 1260, the Franciscans a house at Preston c.1260.

Of Lancaster we have the former priory church, of Burscough hardly anything, of Upholland most of the church, of Cocker-sand only the beautiful (and neglected) E.E. chapter house, of 14 Whalley and Furness a good deal more, and of Cartmel – a very rare thing – the whole church, though nothing but the gatehouse 25 of the monastic quarters. At Whalley there are two gatehouses, 18 at Furness the remains of one and the *capella extra portas*. As for other important parts of Furness, Whalley, and Cartmel, they will be discussed in their proper context, and the first proper context is now.

Furness has just one detail of the mid C12; most of the rest is late C12. The mid C12 detail, a respond in the claustral w range, is interesting in so far as it consists of a demi-column and two entirely detached shafts, and is one of the first instances of this attractive motif, which appealed especially to the English. A contemporary Late Norman North Country example is in the York Minster crypt. The church of which much of the E parts is still upright has waterleaf capitals, pointed arches, and a fairly 10 consistent Transitional character. At Cartmel the situation is different and at first baffling. There are arches richly decorated 8 in a wholly Late Norman style, but they stand close to, and must belong to the same build as, purely E.E. lancets. There is no escaping the assumption that Norman and E.E. went on at the same time, even if of course so purely Early Gothic a motif as the pointed-arched chancel triforium came later than the elements which belong to the ground level. By about 1230 the E parts of 9 Cartmel must have been complete. Of about the same date, but unhesitatingly E.E., are the chapter house and dormitory at 11–Furness. 13

There is no other EARLY ENGLISH work in North Lancashire (excepting the Cockersand chapter house) which would be worth more than a passing reference: the chancel and the nave arcades of St Mary Whalley, the chancel of Ribchester, the s doorway of Stidd, the inner gatehouse of Lancaster Castle.

CASTLES of the Middle Ages are rare in North Lancashire too. The Lancaster keep was begun before 1102 by Roger of Poitou, to whom the Conqueror had given a large part of Lancashire. There is a wall across inside. No other internal details remain, but the inner gatehouse of Lancaster is Norman too. The only other Norman keep is the very small one at Clitheroe. E.E. are parts of the walls and towers of Lancaster Castle. The mighty outer gatehouse belongs to *c.*1400. All the other fortified places are late too, and most of them are PELE TOWERS. A keep rather

than a pele tower however is Piel Castle (in spite of its name).
The date of the licence to crenellate is 1327. Of the C13 is the
lower part of the pele tower of Hornby Castle (early C16 above).
C14 peles are at Borwick Hall, Broughton-in-Furness, Dalton-in-
Furness, and Gresgarth (Caton; with the typical vaulted basement). Of the C14 also is the large Ashton Hall, which is oblong
with four diagonally projecting towers, and Gleaston Castle,
with four irregular angle towers. Yet later are Turton Tower
(C15), Wraysholme Tower at Flookburgh, and Greenhalgh
Castle at Garstang (late C15), and probably the core of Gawthorpe.

More fruitful is a survey of MEDIEVAL HOUSES. At Warton
near Carnforth is the ruin of a hall of the early C14 and another
fragment of the same time close by. The hall still has its three
service doors. Two service doors, main doorway, and exit survive
at Marholme, Great Harwood. Claughton Hall has a fine oriel of
the late C15, and Little Mearley Hall, Pendleton a gorgeous
early C16 bay window. At Little Mitton Hall the interest is the
interior of the hall with its fine timber roof of the C15, and it is
in fact the carpenters who have produced the most splendid late
medieval houses in Lancashire. In South Lancashire they are
Speke (Liverpool), Ordsall (Salford), and Smithills (Bolton). In
North Lancashire to the family of Ordsall and Smithills belong
30–32 Rufford Old Hall and Samlesbury Hall. They have external and
internal decoration with rows of quatrefoils, and they have a
spere truss to divide the screens passage from the hall proper.
Moreover Rufford has and Samlesbury had a detached screen
31 between the two spere posts, and that at Rufford is a splendid,
gloriously barbaric piece with its pinnacles of thick rope- or shell-
like convolutions. Rufford has a canopy over the high-table end,
and Samlesbury had one. The roof of Rufford has hammerbeams and wind-braces. That at Samlesbury has been treated
unkindly. At Samlesbury incidentally a second campaign of
building went on about 1545, and this involved the use of brick
walling, the earliest dated occurrence of this material in Lancashire. But we are not ready yet for the mid C16 – we have neglected so far all church building later than the early C13.

Not that there is much to report on the late C13 and the
DECORATED. Whalley Abbey is the most important church.
Work began in 1330, and it was complete by 1380. Earlier is the
infirmary of Furness Abbey and the adjoining building. The
date here must be about 1300, and the two-light windows
deserve a sentence to themselves, because they have all arch

shanks straightened out into diagonals. Of about 1300 also is the chancel at Aldingham. The best example of flowing, i.e. maturely Dec, tracery, is the s chancel chapel of Cartmel. Dec also are the[25] tower of Aughton and probably the s tower of Ormskirk.

After that comes the PERPENDICULAR. For the late C14 (though not securely dated) the outstanding church is St Mary[23] Lancaster. Early C15 is Tunstall, with its ornate porch. But most of what one comes across of Perp churches in North Lancashire is Late Perp, i.e. early C16 and later. It often represents the North Country type with squat tower and long, low nave – e.g. at Great Harwood and St Michael's-on-Wyre. Win-[26] dows are mostly straight-headed and have uncusped heads to the lights. Datable buildings are Cartmel Fell of *c.*1505, and Hornby of *c.*1514–24 with its w tower octagonal from the ground and its E end a polygonal apse. The finest piece of decoration is the sedilia of Furness Abbey. What is exceptional and would require[21] explanation from Lancashire religious history is the continuation of the Late Perp type of church, and indeed of church building altogether, AFTER THE REFORMATION had won in the South. At Aughton near Ormskirk we have the dates 1528–48, but can they apply to the round arches ? At Rivington work is documented for *c.*1540; the w tower and probably the s arcade of Ormskirk[24] are of *c.*1540. The w tower of Ulverston is of *c.*1540–5, of St Michael's-on-Wyre of *c.*1549. Broughton-in-Furness was[26] consecrated in 1547. Billington is said to be of *c.*1557, Samlesbury is of 1558, Hawkshead has dates 1578 and 1633, the w[27] tower of Halton a date 1597. But the most important church of the Elizabethan Age is Standish. It has dates 1582–4, though building may well have gone on already in 1539, and/or 1557–8. Externally it is all Perp, as the other buildings or parts of buildings just mentioned are, but internally it has Tuscan columns[33] instead of piers, a motif one might expect in 1620 or 1630, but not in the 1580s.

The problem of Gothic after its own time, as it is posed in these Elizabethan Perp motifs, also arises in the best works of church furnishing of the centuries now under discussion. Here again, and in CHURCH MONUMENTS as well, the Middle Ages have very little to contribute. There are no noteworthy brasses, there are a few stone effigies, the best set at Furness Abbey with two cross-legged Knights of as early as *c.*1250–60, and there is[15] only one outstanding funerary *ensemble*, the Harrington Tomb at[17] Cartmel of *c.*1347 where the usual *pleureurs* or mourners are carved in their procession out of the same block of stone as the effigies, where little bedesmen crouch and read and the badly jumbled-up architectural framework includes statuettes on the buttresses and the top cresting. Nor is there more to enumerate for the Elizabethan Age – really nothing but some Sandys monuments at Ulverston † 1559 and at Hawkshead, formerly dated 1578.

In CHURCH FURNISHING the great example of Gothic *versus*
19Gothic-out-of-time is the stall canopies of St Mary, Lancaster, C14 and highly Flamboyant,* and the stall backs and screen of 42Cartmel, with exactly the same motifs but of *c*.1620. The latter however is undeniably not Gothic Survival but Gothic Revival, and belongs to similar endeavours of the later C17 in County Durham (Bishop Cosin). The stalls themselves at Cartmel are late C14 and have a good set of misericords. So have those of 20Whalley which can be dated *c*.1420–30, and more good miseri-28cords are preserved at Blackburn Cathedral. No other church furnishings qualify for this summary, except perhaps the Cartmel stained glass of *c*.1500 of which large parts have gone to Bowness 29(Westmorland) and to Cartmel Fell.

The latest date so far referred to concerning houses is 1545 for Samlesbury. The next date, and this leads now straight into the much more rewarding topic of the ELIZABETHAN AND JACO-BEAN HOUSES, is 1561. This date is on the gatehouse to Marholme, Great Harwood, and the windows with arched lights go with that date. 1561 and 1565 are also on the exterior of Hoghton Tower. But what does it there represent? The two gatehouses certainly, and they are Perp in their essential elements. Possibly also a mysterious appendix to the hall, with pilasters on corbels, 34but surely not the hall itself. The hall belongs to a group of very grand and rather austere halls in North Lancashire, the supreme example being that of Stonyhurst. Stonyhurst altogether is the most monumental Elizabethan mansion in the county, with its 36gatehouse frontispiece of four tiers of paired columns and its 35inner courtyard with the hall facing the gatehouse. Work began & in 1592, and the hall was done in 1597. At the high table end it has large bay windows to both sides, and several transoms. Stonyhurst is designed round an inner courtyard. The very 37opposite principle of planning is Gawthorpe of 1600–5, which is & 38as compact as it could be made. Gawthorpe has a long gallery on the top floor, and good plasterwork.‡ The more usual stretched

22   * The pulpit at Holme has similar panels.
      ‡ The stucco ceilings of the Diocesan Conference Centre at Rawtenstall go with this, if they are original.

and symmetrical plan is represented by Pleasington Old Hall of 1587, Hacking Hall near Billington of 1607, and Carr House near Bretherton of 1613. Carr House has an inscription recording the building of the house by a London and an Amsterdam merchant. Another inscription, and one unique in English country houses, is on Hesketh End near Chipping, a house of 1582. The inscription runs along the façade and commemorates events from English history from the Romans and Saxons to the time when the house was built. Timber-framing also went on, but nothing Elizabethan is as ornate as one finds it in South Lancashire, though Worthington Hall Standish of 1577 has the kind of decorative timber motifs which the Elizabethans liked. The much more ornate ones which Turton Tower of 1596 displays date from after 1835, and the ranges at the back of Astley Hall, Chorley are quite simple.

The façade of Astley Hall on the other hand, of brick with₃₉ stone dressings, is gorgeous. It is more sweepingly glazed than any other in England. The top floor especially, which is given over entirely to the long gallery, is glazed throughout. The pattern of mullions and transoms makes the whole façade a grid.* But the surprising thing about Astley Hall is its date. Much as the bay windows e.g. resemble Stonyhurst, the date is not the mid nineties of the C16 but the mid fifties of the C17.

The North was indeed exceedingly conservative in the C17. This comes out especially in cottages and minor farmhouses. More of these are dated than in any other county, and so it is possible to follow the development very closely, far more closely indeed than the following lines may give the impression to readers.

There is here a serious shortcoming in this volume to which its author must draw attention. For such minor buildings the prime sources of information are the VCH and the lists compiled by the MHLG. They contain far more buildings than *The Buildings of England* can or should. But how is one to choose what to seek out and what to leave aside ? To visit them all was entirely out of the question. Tatham, to choose one parish at random, has 68 listed buildings. Of these 38 are graded III, 30 are graded II, and one is II.* Claughton near Garstang has 25 II, Halton near Lancaster has 14 II, and so on and so forth. The gazetteer of this volume in such cases cannot afford more than one, two, or

---

* Claughton Hall near Hornby, shifted bodily from the village to the top of the moor, has at the top of its two canted bays also completely glazed lookouts.

maximally three. The descriptions in the MHLG lists give good in-
dications what a visit will show. But that criterion is not infallible,
and it is more than likely that specially good-looking and specially
significant houses have been overlooked. This applies particularly to houses whose dates make them important if one tries to
trace the development from the façade of medieval tradition to
the classical façade. The development as such is clear. It starts
with mullioned windows, the doorway not in the middle, the
hall window singled out by being larger or higher, i.e. provided
with a transom; it goes on to a central doorway, but the hall
window still larger than its opposite number on the other side of
the doorway; it also incidentally moves from individual hood-
moulds to a continuous string-course; it replaces horizontal
mullioned by vertical mullioned or by cross-windows; and it
ends symmetrical with sash windows.

Some dates to illustrate this development are these. First of all,
symmetry of course did exist early in major houses such as
Pleasington of 1587 and Gawthorpe. Classical symmetry appeared first in the brick wing of Rufford Old Hall dated 1662 and in
the Judge's Lodging at Lancaster of 1675. The Judge's Lodging
has a big broken segmental pediment over the doorway, detailed
in a barbaric way. The portal details of Astley Hall incidentally
had also been bewilderingly barbaric. Another early example of
symmetry and cross-windows is Slyne Manor, Hest Bank. The
date is 1681. Scale Hall, Lancaster finally appears with a completely Georgian five-bay front before 1737. But still in 1731
Blindhurst, Bleasdale had mullioned and even mullioned and
transomed windows, and still in 1735 Tongue Hill, Pleasington,
in 1736 Withnell Fold Farm, and in 1746 Lane End Farmhouse
Tatham had not quite symmetrical façades. Yet later, in 1751,
Lane Side, Pendleton uses upright mullioned windows, though
now of square section. Intermediate stages are represented by
Shepherd's Farm, Cockerham of 1705, not symmetrical, but
with string-course and upright two-light windows, Old Malthouse, Melling of 1684, symmetrical, but with mullioned windows, a house at Flookburgh of 1686 the same, Sir Nicholas
Sherburne's range of 1699 at Stonyhurst the same,* Bolton-le-

---

* Sir Nicholas incidentally was also responsible for the Versailles conceit
of the long avenue and the two sheets of water of the approach to the Stonyhurst gatehouse and for the two garden pavilions of *c.*1710 with their concave-
sided pyramid roofs. The impression is of *chinoiserie*, and a Chinaman's face
on the chief keystone is proof that they were meant like that – a memorably
early case of *chinoiserie*.

Sands 1701 the same, Pimlico Farm, Clitheroe 1715 the same, but with mullioned and transomed windows, and Newton Gate, Whittington of 1692 again the same but with stepped mullioned windows.

Such stepped mullioned windows are frequent in the West Riding, and there appear also in more fanciful forms. North Lancashire has a few such too, e.g. five lights with lights two and four as rising convex quadrants (house at Barrowford 1696, Southfield Fold Farmhouse, Nelson)* or with the centre light a40 truncated ogee (Shuttleworth Hall, Hapton). Another Yorkshire speciality which has inspired North Lancashire to a considerable extent is door lintels with rustic abstract patterns. Such lintels are mostly of the later c17, but the latest dates recorded in the gazetteer are 1738 at Whittington and 1770 at Outhwaite near Wray.‡

Something of the same conservatism appears in CHURCH FURNISHINGS of those years, and especially in pulpits; for little else was provided – some benches, all quite simple and some very engaging, and (as in all other counties) a number of fonts. They date from the first years of the Restoration, 1661–7, and are characterized by very elementary geometrical or symbolic motifs (Ormskirk 1661, Warton near Carnforth 1661, Croston 1663,44 Great Harwood 1663, Hoole 1663, Penwortham 1667). As for the pulpits, they keep up the general character of the Elizabethan style, the arabesques and even the carving technique, well beyond the middle of the c17 (Standish 1616, Ribchester 1636, Kirkland 1646, Parbold 1648, Over Wyresdale 1684). It is only with the three-decker at Cartmel Fell that the earlier motifs are given up, and that is dated 1698, and it is only with the glorious woodwork of c.1704 at Churchtown outside Southport that we catch up with48 the metropolitan Grinling Gibbons style, and that is imported from St Peter at Liverpool. Add to this the upper parts of St Anton's Cage at Whalley, dated 1697,§ and the series of brass chandeliers either with Baroque-shaped or with ball-shaped bodies and all with two tiers of arms, and you have exhausted the subject of church furnishings for the whole of the Georgian century (Kirkham 1725, Cartmel 1734, Newchurch 1756, Rufford 1763, Brindle 1792, Downham 1802, Broughton 1817, and many undated ones). 62

* And Old Lodge Burnley demolished c.1900 (NMR).

‡ The latter I know only from the photograph in the NMR. Can the date really apply?

§ If it were not foreign (Belgian?) the gorgeous pulpit of Scarisbrick would45 have to be referred to here.

One would like to make an additional check on North Lancashire conservatism and scarcity of worth-while works of art in churches by going to CHURCH MONUMENTS, but there the surprising experience is an almost total absence. Edward 43Wrightinton † 1658 at Standish is the only noteworthy C17 piece – alabaster, with recumbent effigy, and of excellent workmanship. Of the C18 and C19 hardly anything needs a reference – perhaps the Lowthers († 1700, 1705, 1745) at Cartmel, certainly the 49Fleetwood at Churchtown († 1717) and certainly the Watt by 64*Bacon Jun.* at Standish (1806). In addition names such as *Nollekens, Flaxman, Westmacott,* and, among North Country 63artists, the *Fishers* of York do occur and can be looked up in the index of artists, but not one of their North Lancashire performances calls for comment. Local sculptors were active too, especially up here *Webster* of Kendal, whom we shall meet later as an architect,* but again more than the name would be superfluous in this Introduction.

So it is exclusively architecture which concerns us for the EIGHTEENTH CENTURY, churches and houses, and admittedly the interior decoration of houses. As it happens the start has to be made in the field of interior decoration; for at the same time as the Judge's Lodging was built at Lancaster with a classical, 46though very provincial, façade, the plasterwork of ceilings and &47the wood-carving of the staircase were done at Astley Hall, also classical and also extremely provincial. The skill of the plasterers was indeed prodigious, but all this playing with almost unbelievably detached flowers, leaves, and figures – replacing the stucco here and there by lead and leather – is yet coarse in the extreme and quite often grotesque. However, this kind of stucco is what in the 1670s London and the Home Counties were doing too, and the same is true of the openwork leaf carving of the staircase balustrade. Just compare with the woodwork from St Peter's Liverpool, and the difference leaps to the eye. Before Astley Hall is left, one more item of interior decoration must be referred to, though it probably dates back to the mid C17: the series of indifferently painted *uomini famosi* in the hall. The iconography is the fascinating thing here; for the painter, no doubt entirely guided by his client, probably Thomas Charnock M.P., has with commendable fairness included among his heroes not only Queen Elizabeth and Drake and Leicester but Philip II, not only Skanderbeg and Tamerlane but also Bajazet I and Mohammed II, and also Alessandro Farnese, and Ambrogio Spinola, who

* And who did more tablets than are even mentioned in the gazetteer.

subjugated the Southern Netherlands for Spain, and in addition Henry IV of France and Gabor Bethlen, the Hungarian, and the explorers Magellan and Christopher Columbus.

Among HOUSES the transition between the C17 and the C18 is Stone Hall, Dalton of *c*.1710, which has only three bays, and still with cross-windows, but each bay flanked by giant pilasters and in the middle a steep pediment. Fully Early Georgian was *Leoni*'s grand Lathom Hall of *c*.1725–30, alas destroyed, except for one large service wing,* and the w range of Townley Hall, Burnley of 1725 with its gorgeous entrance hall which runs 51 through two storeys and has stucco by *Vassali*. It vies with the finest of Gibbs's great halls, and *Gibbs* indeed employed Vassali at Ditchley and other Italian stucco artists at the Radcliffe Camera in Oxford and the Senate House in Cambridge and at the two London churches of St Martin-in-the-Fields and St Peter, Vere Street. The stucco style of Townley Hall is reflected in the equally gorgeous stucco of the Music Room at Lancaster, 52 which must be of *c*.1750 at the latest and has been allowed to fall into decay beyond hope of redemption, and the stucco of Burrow 53 Hall, a house extremely restrained externally.‡ Equally restrained, i.e. fully Palladian, is the exterior of *Carr*'s Lytham Hall of 1757– 55 64, and there also splendid plaster ceilings compensate. Some 54 are mid C18 in style, but others are already purely Adamish. Other Palladian houses in North Lancashire are Parbold Hall, Standen Hall Clitheroe, and the derelict Clayton Hall, which dates from 1772. Broughton Lodge is a good example of the 59 perfectly plain but elegant late C18 house of moderate size. More explicitly Palladian again is the Custom House in Lancaster by *Richard Gillow*, which was built in 1764 for the sea traffic which then began to play an important part in the life of Lancaster. This is the first secular building other than private houses here mentioned. Other C18 examples are the Shireburne Almshouses now at Hurst Green which date from 1706 (and still have cross windows), the Stidd Almshouses of 1728 with their curious arrangement, and the surprisingly large Bushell Hospital at Goosnargh of 1722(?). The Garstang Town Hall was built in 1755–64, and the old Lancaster Town Hall in 58 1781–3. Several smaller places have C18 town halls too (Hawkshead).

---

* *Leoni* also did Bold Hall near Warrington, South Lancashire, but that also is demolished.

‡ By *Gibbs* himself is Bank Hall, Warrington, South Lancashire, now the town hall.

Quantitatively there are probably more GEORGIAN CHURCHES in North Lancashire than Georgian country houses, but qualitatively there is little of any ambition. The best probably are St 56 John at Lancaster of 1754–5 (tower 1784, by *Thomas Harrison*, who also built the fine Skerton Bridge at Lancaster) and St John 57 at Blackburn of 1789. Most of the others are simple oblongs with large arched windows. This incidentally became the pattern also for the Catholic churches which late in the c18 began to appear in towns and villages of this most Catholic of all English counties. It was accepted by the Nonconformists too. As for them, they also produced exceptionally many buildings in Lancashire relatively early on. Among the earliest are the Tunley Presbyterian chapel at Wrightington of 1691 and the Unitarian chapels of Rivington (1703), Dimple near Turton (1713), Preston (1717), and Chorley (1725). Their standard elements are two doorways, flanking a pair of large windows. Yet earlier are the earliest Quaker Meeting Houses. Their dates are as follows: Height near Cartmel 1677 (disused), Swarthmoor and Colthouse near Hawkshead 1688, Yealand Conyers 1692, Lancaster 1708, Crawshaw Booth, Rawtenstall, 1716. Their standard element is the two large windows of the meeting house proper, then the doorway, and then one two-storeyed bay. To return to the c18 churches of the Church of England, the gazetteer, confined to what still stands, refers to fifteen and two w towers: Wood Plumpton deserves a special reference for its w tower and s aisle of 1748, but still in the style of 1730, and Edenfield of 1778 for having an exceptionally unaltered interior.

With the late c18 the volume of building of all kinds began to increase spectacularly, and with it the significance of the buildings. This was due – it need hardly be said – to the INDUSTRIAL REVOLUTION. The Industrial Revolution meant the ironworks of the Wilkinsons at Backbarrow near Haverthwaite, the cotton mills, for spinning, weaving, bleaching, dyeing, such as that near Accrington founded by Sir Robert Peel's father in 1760, the coal mines and the canals, first of course the Bridgewater Canal of 1759–61, but that is in South Lancashire, then the Leeds and 68 Liverpool Canal of 1770–4, and after that the Preston and Lancaster Canal, begun in 1793 and carried on to Kendal by 1819 – and ultimately the railways. All these appear in the gazetteer, in so many words or only implied, and they need no individual comments here. The Wilkinson story is told on p. 168 under Lindale. 65 It ends with the cast-iron obelisk commemorating John Wilkinson who cast the parts of the Coalbrookdale Bridge, the earliest of all iron bridges. The story of Barrow is also an iron, and then a steel story. It is told on pp. 55–6.

Barrow and Fleetwood are the only attempts at planning the pattern according to which the growth of a town should take place. The other North Lancashire TOWNS grew entirely haphazardly, and they grew fast. Here are the figures for 1801 and 1851 for five of them.

	1801	1851
Blackburn	12,000	47,000
Burnley	4,000	21,000
Chorley	4,500	12,700
Preston	30,000	97,000
Southport	2,000*	13,000*

The result, examined today, is a great variety and little to praise. Preston and Blackburn are much like the industrial towns of South Lancashire; Burnley, Colne, and Nelson are smaller individually but have grown into one amorphous whole. They have the advantage of the setting in the moors, as has Chorley. Haslingden–Rawtenstall–Bacup are no more than inflated villages, but again redeemed by the setting. Equally varied is the character of the seaside places: Blackpool a riotous front and rows and rows of suburban brick terraces behind, Morecambe a smaller Blackpool now indistinguishable from Heysham, which is a mixture of Anglo-Saxon and holiday-camp entertainments, Southport a town of some dignity in its own right, with stately churches and the C18 appendix of Churchtown, Lytham a small town, again with an individual existence apart from the sea front, and St Annes the latest and quieter than the big places. In all these seaside resorts there is only one terrace which deserves comparison with St Leonards and Brighton, and only one hotel of comparable scale and dignity. Both are at Fleetwood and both by *Decimus Burton*.

Then the MILLS, and here another fault of this volume must [60] be admitted. Until about ten years ago it was very difficult to come by dates and descriptions of early mill-building. Now several theses, books, and articles have spread out material.‡ But within the limits of the time available for the preparation of the Lancashire volumes of *The Buildings of England* it has proved impossible to follow up this newly revealed material. Moreover,

---

* The figure for 1801 is North Meols only, as there was no Southport. Even in 1851 Southport proper accounts for only 4,500 of the 13,000.

‡ See the bibliographical note on p. 36.

often the mill-owners built terraces of cottages for their workmen, and they also appear only rarely in the gazetteer. Finally, there are the mill-owners' houses. Wherever possible they are referred to, but local research could do far more. Ideally these industrial towns and villages should be treated by mills, owners' mansions or villas, and churches and chapels donated by these mill-owners, and not by churches, public buildings, and perambulations in the routine way. That could be done only rarely, and no more can be said for the present than to express the hope that it will gradually be done locally.* For their strictly architectural interest few mills deserve notice. One is the India Mills at Darwen of 1859–67 with its campanile-chimney and its cyclopean rustica-
93 tion, another the Coppull Mills of 1906 with their Edwardian flourishes. With the first World War the cotton boom was definitely over, and now mills are being pulled down – a whole area of Horrocks's e.g. at Preston – or used by more recent industries. As for the industrialists' and great merchants' houses, they come into the story of architectural development much more, and are in this Introduction treated as part of that development rather than socially.

Once again, the volume of building between the late C18 and say 1830 was enormous, both in churches and houses. In churches this is the period of the COMMISSIONERS' CHURCHES, the churches built with part of the one and a half million pounds granted by Parliament for the building of new churches. The grant was made in two parts. The reasoning behind the grants was summed up by the *Quarterly Review* in 1820: 'The edifices which we have erected are manufactories and prisons, the former producing tenants for the latter. . . . The only way of making the people good subjects is by making them good Christians.' Similarly a memorial sent to the Prime Minister in 1815 had drawn attention to 'the danger to which the constitution of this country . . . is exposed for want of places of public worship, particularly for persons of the middle and lower classes'.

The Commission, aware of the phenomenal growth of popula-tion in Lancashire, provided more churches in the county than anywhere else, a total of 19 before 1830 and 62 between c.1830 and 1856, varying in cost from the £19,948 for Foster's St Martin in Liverpool, no longer extant, to the £1,058 for Sharpe's church at Bretherton. Of the first grant only six of the nineteen were in

---

* Examples where at last I have made efforts are Rawtenstall and Calder Vale.

North Lancashire. Of the second grant much more was spent on North than on South Lancashire. All the Commissioners' churches so far as they still exist will be found in the gazetteers of the two volumes. They are universally characterized by tall side windows, usually of lancets (e.g. *Rickman's* Haigh, 1831–3) or pairs of lancets (*Rickman's* St Paul Preston, 1823–5, and Mellor, 1825–7, *Vulliamy's* Holy Trinity Outer Burnley of 1835–6 and *Sharpe's* Turton, 1839–40, and Holy Trinity Morecambe, 1840–1) or stepped triplets of lancets (e.g. *Sharpe's* St Thomas Lancaster, 1841–4) or with minimum-Perp motifs (*Rickman's* Holy Trinity Darwen, 1827–9, and Clitheroe, 1828–9, Burscough by *D. Stewart*, 1829–31) and by aisled or aisleless interiors with three galleries. Many have w towers, and they are as a rule clumsy. Among architects employed *Rickman* is the best known, and he deserves his reputation. Among nationally unknown architects by far the most interesting turns out to be *John Palmer* of Manchester with the Blackburn parish church (now cathedral) of 1820–6 with tall three-light Dec windows with transom and the Catholic church of Pleasington of 1816–19 with its astonishing 76 façade aspiring to a portal with carving of figures in the jambs and arch as well as in niches above. The skill of the carver was inferior, but the conceit remains interesting, and Palmer was proud enough of it to sign himself on the façade as *architectus*. Another nationally unknown architect worth some lines here is *John Latham*. His churches at Preston are certainly interesting, even if their only virtue is originality. They are Norman such as no Norman church had ever been. They were designed in the late thirties (Christ Church 1835–6, St Mary 1836–8, St Thomas 1837–9), and the great fashion for neo-Norman or sometimes rather neo-Romanesque belongs indeed to the years between 1835 and the late forties. Examples are Brathay, 1836, large, in a joyless brick Romanesque, Out Rawcliffe 1837–8, in a rather Prussian brick *Rundbogen* way, St James Clitheroe and Adlington 1839, Holy Trinity Bacup 1840–1, Sabden 1846, Lumb, i.e. Rawtenstall, 1847–8. This list does not include *Sharpe*, whose interest in the c14 did not prevent him from building Romanesque too. St Mark Outer Blackburn of 1836–8 has the tower over the sanctuary with distressing interior consequences; Cuerden is of the same years, Christ Church Chatburn of 1838, but Scotforth of 1874 is an amazing anachronism. Sharpe was 68 then, and he also returned to a passing early passion for using terracotta instead of stone. So much for Gothic and Romanesque; Grecian is almost absent. The one example in the Church of

England is All Saints Outer Preston of 1846–7, and that is by *Latham* of all people. The Nonconformists, in order not to conform, were readier to be classical, though they soon turned to mixed Italianate motifs. But the Methodist church at Oakenhead, Rawtenstall of 1841–2 is very pure Grecian.

In EARLY NINETEENTH CENTURY HOUSES the situation is different. Although Gothic seems to have dominated more in North Lancashire than in other counties (because the men who commissioned the houses were short of known medieval ancestors ?), the Grecian and otherwise classical contingent is substantial. The common type – and a very dignified type it is – is ashlar-faced, with the windows cut in without any mouldings, and with a porch of four, mostly unfluted Ionic, columns, evenly spaced or, more often, in pairs. More ambitious are *James Wyatt*'s Woodfold Hall, Mellor of 1798, alas gutted, with a giant tetrastyle portico and characteristic tripartite windows, *Lewis Wyatt*'s Cuerden Hall of 1816–19 with the grouped chimneys at 67 the corners like turrets, and *Webster* of Kendal's Read Hall of 1818–25 with detached giant columns round a central bow*; yet 69 more ambitious is Haigh Hall of 1827–40, with a splendid staircase hall. As a rule the interior plasterwork in these houses is decidedly heavy. Excellent interiors also survive in Quernmore 66 Park Hall, 1793 by *Harrison* of Chester, and again the stucco decoration is heavy. What *Sir Jeffry Wyatville* did at Townley Hall, Burnley in 1817 (again heavily stuccoed) is oddly ahead of its date. These large windows look Early Victorian rather than Regency.

Finally, to finish the classical side of Late Georgian, there are the town houses, many individual ones at Lancaster, and a whole 61 quarter at Preston, Winckley Square, undulating and landscaped. It would be an asset even to Dublin.

So to the GEORGIAN GOTHIC and slightly post-Georgian Gothic. The list must start with the additions to Lancaster 70 Castle made in 1788 etc. to designs first by *Harrison*, then by *J. M. Gandy*. The Shire Hall is ornately appointed with much remarkably accurate decorative detail. Among houses typically c18 are Broughton Tower (with ogee-headed windows), the block-shaped castellated house in the Heysham entertainment area, Gresgarth Hall, Caton of c.1805–10, the so-called Boat House at Halton, with two towers and an embattled wall, and 71 Leighton Hall, Yealand Conyers (*Richard Gillow*'s house) c.1810 & 72 and Thurnham Hall as late as 1823, and even Crawshaw Hall,

* *Webster* also did Downham Hall in 1835.

Rawtenstall of 1831–2. Grander, heavier, and much bigger are some Gothic extravaganzas of 1820 and after with castellated and sometimes machicolated towers and usually asymmetrical compositions. Towers incidentally often appeared on their own too, as beacons, as memorials, or simply as FOLLIES. North Lancashire has particularly many of them, from the Rivington Pike of 1733 to Lord Leverhulme's dovecote, close by, of 1905. True memorials are the Barrow Monument above Ulverston of 1850 in the form of a lighthouse, and the 120 ft high monument to Sir Robert Peel above Holcombe of 1851–2. Towers tend to crop up everywhere: Allithwaite, Bardsea, Brindle Lodge, Blacko, Broughton East, Conishead, Dalton, Darwen, Far Sawrey, Newby Bridge, Silverdale. The largest or most conspicuous of the GOTHIC MANSIONS of 1820–50 are Conishead 73 Priory by *Philip Wyatt* begun in 1821, Whittington Hall, Tudor Gothic of 1831 (or later?), Wray Castle near Hawkshead of 75 1840–7 (praised by Wordsworth), Heysham Tower of c.1830–40, Capernwray Hall of 1844 by *Sharpe*, and Hornby Castle of 1849– 74 52 by *Sharpe & Paley*.

When Sharpe becomes Sharpe & Paley and then E. G. Paley alone, the pre-Victorian has become the VICTORIAN STYLE. The dates are as follows, and they need be set down here, because this Lancaster dynasty of architects did more work in the county, and for a time more outstanding work, than any other. *Edmund Sharpe* (1809–77), famous as a scholar of flowing tracery and as the architect of churches built entirely of terracotta (in South Lancashire), took into partnership in 1845 *E. G. Paley* (1823–95). He retired as soon as 1851 and left Paley alone. In 1868 Paley took in *H. J. Austin*, and it was Austin, it seems, who was responsible for the firm's masterpieces. Paley's son joined about 1890, Paley Scn. died in 1895, and the firm then became *Austin & Paley* and operated under that name right into the 1930s.

The change which took place in this one firm in the 1840s is a national one – from a Gothic true only in an associational sense, i.e. with motifs which suggest Gothic, to a Gothic archeologically sufficiently accurate to make at least the layman think he is looking at a real medieval building – a building not in the Perp or the lancet style so far plundered for motifs, but in the Middle Pointed or Second Pointed, i.e. the style which was current from Westminster Abbey to the early C14, the style characterized by geometrical tracery and tracery forms up to but excluding the flowing of the Dec style. This momentous change, not only from

one Gothic phase to another but from associationally to archeologically Gothic, was made at the same time by Pugin for reasons
of fanatical Roman Catholicism and by the Cambridge Camden
Society and its journal *The Ecclesiologist* for reasons of equally
fanatical Anglo-Catholicism. The operative dates lie between
1840 and 1845. *Pugin* himself did only one church in North
Lancashire, St John Kirkham in 1842–5, a rather neutral piece, but
78-he designed Scarisbrick Hall in 1837 with its gorgeous interiors.
81 His son *E. W. Pugin* in the sixties enlarged the building and endowed it with the spectacular tower which appears on the horizon
for miles around Southport. Other early signs of the change in
church architecture were the steeple of Kirkham parish church
by *Sharpe* of 1843–53, All Saints Outer Burnley of 1846–9 by
Weightman & Hadfield and the Catholic St Mary Burnley, 1846–
9 by the same, and St Bartholomew, Whitworth, 1847–50 by
Joseph Clarke.

For the fifties the outstanding churches are three: the Preston
parish church by *Shellard*, 1853–5, without doubt the *magnum
opus* of this minor architect, the Catholic cathedral at Lancaster
by *Paley*, side by side with the slightly later St George at Barrow (1859–61), the *magna opera* of this architect, who, before
Austin joined him, rarely reached such heights, and *Joseph*
82 *Aloysius Hansom*'s St Walburge Outer Preston of 1850–4, a
&
83 church no-one is likely to forget who ever saw its 300 ft high,
excessively thin spire from a distance or entered its long, un-
ecclesiastical nave with the excessively steep hammerbeam roof –
fanatical and unbalanced and for some even sinister. For the
sixties to these three must be added *Clutton*'s Our Lady of
Compassion at Formby (1863–4), with the Italian Romanesque
E end and the interior whose aisles are divided from the nave by
slender columns, two-deep, with shaft-rings, and *E. W. Pugin*'s
St Mary at Barrow (1866–7), his best in North Lancashire,
though not in all Lancashire, and though nothing like as convincing as Scarisbrick. Of the sixties also is an early entirely
High Victorian church by *J. Medland Taylor*, the Liverpool
'rogue', to use the term in Goodhart-Rendel's sense for an
architect who chose to go it alone and who preferred quirks and
deliberate challenges to conventionality. He did Christ Church
Blackpool in 1865–6, and made it as Brutalist as any High Victorian church. His later churches at Bacup (1882–3) and Aspull
(1897) are no less naughty. Naughty certainly is the word for the
Audsley brothers' St Mary Ellel of 1873, bewildering perhaps
the more appropriate word for *Goldie & Child*'s uncouth St

Joseph Outer Blackburn of 1875–7, and both bewildering and naughty are a number of cemetery chapels, notably those of Darwen by *J. Stevens* of 1860. It is hard to understand why it should be such mortuary chapels which roused architects time and again to combine a maximum of variety with a maximum of solecisms.

1868 is the year, it has already been said, when *H. J. Austin* joined Paley, and then immediately the character of the architecture of the firm changed – a nobility and at the same time resourcefulness appeared which had not until then been seen in its products. The first is St James at Barrow, begun actually in 1867, with its beautiful steeple and its arcade arches of brick. It is hard to choose which to single out for *Paley & Austin,* and later *Austin & Paley's, œuvre* – one might even argue that the very best are in South Lancashire – but St Mary, Dalton-in-Furness 84 of 1882–5 is magnificent throughout, and no-one would not admire the mauve and buff flushwork of Pilling (1886–7) and the fertility of ideas in the interiors of Broughton East (1892–4) and of Flookburgh (1897–1900). Large, or small, Paley & Austin could provide something personal and powerful. One would have to search far and search long in England to find village churches to vie with Finsthwaite of 1873–4, Torver of 1884, and Dolphinholme of 1897, with their central towers.

Paley & Austin's services were also sought for county mansions, and there also they shone. Holker Hall, largely rebuilt 85 after a fire in 1871, is their biggest, Elizabethan in style, the smaller range at Leighton Hall, Yealand Conyers of 1870, also Elizabethan, perhaps their most felicitous. Thurland Castle, Tunstall of 1879–85 has a specially happy library. For houses by other architects we must go back a generation. Turton Tower, between *c.*1835 and *c.*1840, received a great deal of ornate Elizabethan half-timber decoration at the hands of a Preston cotton spinner. Ashton Hall in 1856 was given a big Gothic appendix to the medieval tower-house. *Waterhouse's* Domestic-Gothic Crookhey Hall near Cockerham of 1874 is nothing like as satisfying as contemporary Paley & Austin. Abbeystead near Over Wyresdale is by *Douglas & Fordham* of 1886. And finally the Italianate mood *à la* Osborne is represented uncommonly well by Ellel Grange of 1857–9.

Once again for the Italianate one must go to the NONCONFORMIST CHAPELS. Quite a number come into the gazetteer. Here only four examples need be given: the former Methodist church in Todmorden Road Burnley, the Methodist church of 1874 at Wardle, the Green Street Methodist church of 1875 at Morecambe, and the former Methodist church at Clitheroe of 1888.

For CATHOLIC CHURCHES one must first for a moment go back to c.1800. They were then, like Nonconformist chapels of the same time, quite plain boxes externally, with round-arched windows (e.g. Stidd 1789, Samlesbury 1818, and so on to Eccleston 1835). Often (e.g. Lea 1801, Samlesbury 1818) the priest's house was under the same roof with the church. Internally the Catholics already before the Emancipation of 1829 risked a little more display. It took the form of giant columns or pilasters at the E end (Chorley 1814-15, Samlesbury 1818, Aughton 1823, Chipping 1827, Eccleston 1835, St Augustine Preston 1838-40). Pleasington, of 1816-19, already mentioned, was the first granite building and also the first Gothic one. Gothic became more frequent after the Act (Mawdesley 1830-1, St Ignatius Preston by *Scoles* 1833-6, Osbaldeston 1837-8). By far the most ambitious Catholic church of the thirties is – perfectly understandably – *Scoles*'s church for the Jesuits of Stonyhurst (1832-5). The Victorian vicissitudes of the Gothic style among the Catholics from *Pugin* onwards have already come into this survey together with those of Anglican churches. Only a few things need be added. Among the early archeologically accurate Catholic churches one is by *Hansom*: Thurnham of 1847-8. The most frequently used Catholic architect in Lancashire was *E. W. Pugin*. His best church in our area is at Barrow-in-Furness (1866 etc.). The successor firm *Pugin & Pugin* did an outstanding job in 1894 at the Sacred Heart Blackpool. Uncommonly good also is *E. Kirby*'s St Mary Parbold of 1884. But by then a trend began to appear in favour of an Italian style and with more correct and more historically interesting features of the Renaissance, chiefly the Quattrocento. The two examples in North Lancashire are both at Preston: St Wilfrid, 1879-80 by Canon *Scoles* and *S. J. Nicholl*, and St Augustine, 1890 by 77 *Sinnott, Sinnott & Powell*, who as a rule preferred the Gothic. So we are once more back at the Italianate.

Among Victorian PUBLIC BUILDINGS in North Lancashire the Italianate is absent, the Gothic rare, the classical in various more or very much less pure varieties dominant. On the Grecian 86 side the most surprising performance is the Harris Library and Museum at Preston by *J. Hibbert*. It looks a convincing 1835, grand, high, and majestic, and is 1885, or 1882-93 to be precise

– one of the most puzzling anachronisms in England.* The
classical Harris College of Arts had preceded it in 1846–7. The
one major Gothic public building is the Barrow Town Hall by
W.H.Lynn (1882–7). The sweeping and splendid extensions to
Stonyhurst school by *Dunn & Hansom* of 1877–89 are in a free 87
English C17 style, Carolean and later. They are among the most
successful scholastic buildings of their date in England. The
Lancaster Town Hall of 1906–9 by *Mountford* of London is in an 92
Edwardian Neo-Georgian. It was given to the town by Lord
Ashton, the linoleum manufacturer, and he also paid £87,000 to
erect on a hill outside Lancaster the vastest of all follies in 91
England, the memorial to his wife, a domed Baroque pile. The
architect was *Sir John Belcher*, and what more blissful dream
could a knighted Edwardian architect have than to be asked to
design a building on such a scale and serving no function what-
ever?

With almost as much pomp and circumstance ends the church
architecture of the C19. Holy Trinity at Southport is by *Matear*
of the Liverpool Wool Exchange. It was begun in 1903 and completed in 1913 and is also the gift of members of commercial and
industrial families, the Elders for nave, tower, and west front,
J. Mallineaux and F. Dewhurst for the chancel.

A few years earlier the anti-monumental tendency originating
from Morris and Webb and Shaw had erected two of its very
best works in North Lancashire: *Voysey*'s superb Broadleys and 89
his Moor Crag, both on Windermere (*see* Cartmel Fell), and &
90
both of 1898–1900. Ten years later the same, convincedly anti-
formal, anti-symmetrical style appeared in *Greenaway &*
Newberry's Kirkham Grammar School (1909–11). From such 88
buildings, along ways not visible in the county, the style of the
TWENTIETH CENTURY was created. It was created under
English influence on the Continent and in America, and it
ricocheted into England a good deal later – only after 1930.
Early-modern in that sense are *Velarde*'s St Gabriel Outer Blackburn, a blocky brick building of 1932–3, and the same architect's
Our Lady of Lourdes School at Birkdale, Southport, of 1935–6,
Oliver Hill's Midland Hotel at Morecambe of 1932–3, which in 94
its moderateness has aged well, and *Joseph Emberton*'s Casino at
Blackpool of 1938.

Then, after the Second World War, when England had at last
fully accepted this so-called International Modern, schools and
office buildings appeared everywhere, though in North Lanca-

* But it would be at home in Glasgow.

shire perhaps less than in some parts of the country. It is hard
to choose, but Sagar House at Eccleston near Chorley, by
95 *William Field*, the Lancaster Castle School by *Roger Booth*'s, the
County Architect's, Department, and two schools at Preston by
the *Building Design Partnership* may serve as examples. This firm
needs a mention in the Introduction to a volume on North
Lancashire anyway, because it is a Preston firm initially, and it
shows that the days of nationally busy provincial offices have not
entirely gone. The two schools are interesting also in so far as the
96 later one, the William Temple School, is stylistically no longer
of the International Modern, i.e. composed of sheer cubes with
much curtain walling, but has the monopitch roofs and the
generally livelier and more arbitrary appearance which belongs
to the sixties.

The change from the self-effacing neutrality of the thirties and
after came in England in the course of the fifties. It was inspired
by Le Corbusier's change in the same direction, and it affected
churches earlier than secular buildings. Much of what was built
and is being built is just gimmicky and will for later generations
have only the value of curiosities of mood, but there are good
buildings as well, and in North Lancashire one ought perhaps
to single out the County Library at Morecambe by the County
Architect *Roger Booth*, with its hexagonal spaces and its hyperbolic paraboloid roof, All Saints Longton by *Tom Mellor &
Partners* of 1963–5, and *Weightman & Bullen*'s Catholic church
at Leyland (1959–64) with its beautiful abstract glass by *Patrick
Reyntiens*. On the University of Lancaster it is too early to pro-
nounce. At the time of writing little was complete. The Kasbah
skyscape is unmistakably 1960s, but the programme is sound
(*Bridgwater, Shepheard & Epstein*).

FURTHER READING

The standard sources of information are the Victoria County
History (5 volumes, 1906–14) and G. Baines's *History of the
County Palatine and Duchy of Lancashire* (edited by J. Croston,
1888–93). But the book which everyone would like to use side by
side with this volume of *The Buildings of England* and will enjoy
more and no doubt wish to possess is Peter Fleetwood-Hesketh's
Lancashire Architectural Guide (1955). R. Millward's *Lancashire*
in the series The Making of the English Landscape is a good
book too (1955). The most important of the old histories is T.D.
Whitaker's *History of Whalley* (1818). A recent short history of
Lancashire is that by J.J. Bagley (4th ed. 1967). R.H. Cheetham's

volume of the *Little Guides* (1920) is rather old-fashioned, whereas the *Memorials of Old Lancashire* by H. Fishwick and P. H. Ditchfield (2 vols., 1909) still repay attention. The two archeological journals are the *Transactions of the Historical Society of Lancashire and Cheshire* (since 1849) and the *Transactions of the Lancashire and Cheshire Antiquarian Society* (since 1884).

Excellent is the work by H. Taylor on the *Old Halls of Lancashire and Cheshire* (3 vols., 1884). Of histories of individual towns there are quite a number: F. Barnes on Barrow (1951) and J. J. Marshall on Furness and the Industrial Revolution (1958), W. A. Abram on Blackburn (1877), Walter Burnett on Burnley (1946–51, 4 vols.), Carr on Colne (1877), K. Eyre on Lytham St Annes (1960), W. Bennett on Nelson (1957), C. Hardwick on Preston (1857), F. A. Bailey on Southport (1955). Several more books, but on smaller places, have been published by the Chetham Society. In addition there are the many books dealing nationally with particular aspects: H. M. and J. Taylor for Anglo-Saxon churches (2 vols., 1965), M. Whiffen for Stuart and Georgian churches (1947), Mrs M. Wood for *The English Medieval House* (1965), *Country Life* for country houses, Colvin's *Dictionary* for architects of 1660–1840, Gunnis's *Dictionary* for sculptors of 1650–1850, E. Croft-Murray for Decorative Painting (vol. 1, 1962), A. Gardner for alabaster monuments (1940), Mill Stephenson for brasses (1926), A. Vallance for church screens (1947), Granville Squieres for priest holes (1933), H.-R. Hitchcock for Early Victorian architecture (2 vols. 1954), W. H. Godfrey for almshouses (1955), Barbara Jones for follies (1953), C. C. Oman for church plate (1957), Ll. Jewitt and W. H. St John Hope for corporation plate (1895), and so on.

BUILDING MATERIALS*

BY ALEC CLIFTON-TAYLOR

Industrial Lancashire was largely built of brick, for which there is an abundance of locally available clay and shale. The shales from the Coal Measures were brought into service for brick-making about 1800. They make very hard bricks of screaming redness. It is easy to understand why one of the two principal varieties produced by the brickfields at Accrington (N) is known locally as 'Accrington bloods'. All too familiar in this part of Lancashire

* This account covers both North (N) and South (S) Lancashire.

are these harsh red machine-pressed bricks of uncomfortably large dimensions (a thickness of 3 in. is common), now coated with grime, and anything but enjoyable. In the Victorian period the roofs of these brick buildings were usually of Welsh slate. About the turn of the present century slate began to give place to smooth red or pink tiles which in the hillier parts of the county are even more unwelcome than the brickwork of the walls, for they are wrong in colour, wrong in texture and wrong in scale. Perhaps no English county has suffered more in the past hundred years from the employment of ugly building materials than Lancashire.

Brick was little used, however, before the C17, and then only in the south-western area. Even as late as 1700 brick buildings in Lancashire were by no means common, but during the C18 the situation gradually changed and some very pleasant bricks were produced, partly owing to the growing scarcity of wood. For in the Middle Ages this had been one of the best wooded counties in England, and until the Georgian period even Manchester (s) still remained predominantly half-timbered. As far north as the Ribble, timber-framed buildings prevailed everywhere away from the Pennines until the end of the C17. Originally the infillings were wattle and daub: that is, clay reinforced with willow-sticks. These infillings were heavily whitewashed, while the timber framework was blackened with pitch. These 'black and white' buildings were often elaborately if somewhat naïvely ornamented; a local characteristic which Lancashire shared with Cheshire was a liking for a shaped cove under an overhanging upper storey.

Considering the extent of Lancashire's industrialization it is remarkable how many half-timbered buildings have survived, including a few really major examples such as Speke Hall (Liverpool; s). Some of the cottages were formerly of the cruck-framed type. The usual roof for the timber-framed house in Lancashire, as so often elsewhere, was thatch, which was of rye-straw wherever this was available, because that was the toughest of the varieties of straw, with an average life of about thirty years. Thatch in Lancashire is to-day rare.

Apart from wood, the traditional building material of Lancashire was stone, with which the county is decidedly well endowed. Some of this stone is, it is true, not of the best quality; much of the New Red sandstone is coarse-textured and friable, and in the south-western parts of the county such medieval churches as have survived have suffered a good deal from patching and refacing. It is unfortunate too that so much Lancashire stonework has been blackened with soot. Nevertheless the county can still offer considerable pleasures to the lover of stone.

Sandstone plays a much more important part than limestone in the Lancashire picture. Some of the sandstone is Triassic, some Carboniferous. The Triassic (New Red) sandstone underlies the clays of a considerable part of southern and western Lancashire and reappears at the extremities of the Cartmel and Furness peninsulas (N); but usually it is at too great a depth to be quarried. The principal quarries, Woolton and Rainhill, were on the ridges in and near Liverpool (s). Stone from both these quarries is still being used for the Anglican Cathedral at Liverpool; the colour is a somewhat sombre pink, by no means gay despite its comparatively warm hue. Triassic sandstone was also brought into south-west Lancashire from Runcorn and Storeton on the Cheshire side of the Mersey.

The Carboniferous sandstones come partly from the Coal Measures and, outside the coalfields, from the immediately underlying Millstone Grit. These mostly dull buff or grey sandstones, although they lack charm, are much tougher and more reliable than those from the Triassic formation; moreover, they possess the inestimable property, in Lancashire, of being largely resistant to the disintegrating influence of a smoke-laden atmosphere. The sandstones of the Coal Measures are confined to a region well s of the Ribble, well N of the Mersey and well back from the coast, but they make an important contribution to the appearance of such cotton-spinning towns as Oldham (s), Rochdale (s) and Colne (N). The gritstone, often quarried in enormous blocks, is more characteristic of the rural areas; there is plenty of it in the Pennine villages, and everywhere between Morecambe Bay and the Trough of Bowland, not excluding Lancaster itself, which is largely built of pale yellow gritstone (all N).

Despite inevitable losses every year, Lancashire still preserves many thousands of Carboniferous sandstone roofs. In certain places these sedimentary rocks are sufficiently fissile to be split into 'flagstones' at the tap of a hammer, and although by comparison with the famous oolitic slates of the Cotswolds and Northamptonshire these sandstone slates are larger, thicker, darker in tone, more sombre in colour and much heavier, they have a rugged dignity which never fails to impress. Specially sought after were the Rossendale flags quarried in the Forest of Rossendale, between Rochdale (s) and Burnley (N). Their size and weight rendered even a moderately steep pitch unnecessary, and indeed impossible, and the Lancashire roof-builders were not concerned with elegance: their materials alone ruled out any such thoughts. What they achieved was immense sturdiness combined with complete visual harmony, not only with the stone buildings of which they form a part but also with the moorland landscapes in which some of the best preserved of these stone roofs are still to be seen.

Not until we reach the valley of the Ribble (N) does limestone play any part in the Lancashire scene. Carboniferous limestone is in evidence at Clitheroe and at Whalley, and along the valley of the Hodder which marks the boundary with Yorkshire, and finally displaces the gritstone half-way between Lancaster and Carnforth. In North Lancashire, on both sides of Morecambe Bay, the light grey limestone, usually in rather small, rough pieces, recalls neighbouring Westmorland; and so also at Ulverston and Dalton-in-Furness. One of these limestones, from near Ulverston, will take a polish and so qualifies as a semi-marble, a handsome stone employed in the 1870s at Holker Hall.

Of still more ancient origin is the Silurian stone which characterizes that part of North Lancashire which falls within the Lake District, and which spreads down to the coast at Grange-over-Sands and at Ireleth. This extremely hard, splintery, flaggy material was only normally used as rubble, and its dour colouring, dark greys, blacks and browns for the most part, does not make much aesthetic appeal; but it was a common practice, as can be well seen at Hawkshead, to render with roughcast, and so long as the roughcast is frequently limewashed, this is probably the best method of making use of this intractable stone. There are still a good many whitewashed cottages in the remoter parts of Lancashire, and one is glad of it.

Ordovician and Silurian slate-stone also figures among the building materials of Lake District Lancashire, but the principal role of these slates has been, needless to say, as a roofing material, and in recent years for cladding structures of steel and concrete. Between Kirkby-in-Furness and Little Langdale at least five slate quarries are still working, producing slate varying in colour from lead-pencil grey to the attractive grey-green of the slate from Moss Rigg used for facing parts of Coventry Cathedral. The local slate roofs in this area are a constant pleasure: the best of all this county's roofs. The only trouble is that for most people it requires a real effort to remember that this *is* still Lancashire.

PREHISTORY*

BY DEREK SIMPSON

It was only with the final retreat of the ice at the end of the last glaciation that the region became habitable by man and the earliest penetration by hunting and fishing peoples took place. Scant traces of these settlers have been found at several sites in the vicinity of Bolton (s), on Anglezarke Moor near Rivington (N), and at Radcliffe (s). In these areas have been found microlithic blades and other tools indicating temporary camping sites or flint knapping. Much of the region must have been thickly forested, and an efficient flint axe for forest clearance and wood-working was employed by these Mesolithic groups (an example has come from Radcliffe).

The earliest surviving monuments belong to the succeeding period of the introduction of farming and presumably a more settled mode of life. The chambered tomb beneath the long cairn on Anglezarke Moor (N) is related to a series of such monuments to the N, while the remarkable decorated stones, the Calderstones, now housed in Liverpool Museum (s), but formerly elements in a passage grave, show in their art style-links with Ireland. Throughout the prehistory of the region one finds evidence of such contacts across the Irish Sea. Although these two monuments attest to the elaborate nature of burial during this phase, the evidence for domestic activities is slight. A possible settlement site has been located at Storrs Moss, Yealand Conyers (N) where a timber floor consisting of brushwood surmounted by planks was revealed by excavation. The only artefact was the rim of a wooden bowl, but radiocarbon dates suggest that it is to be ascribed to this period. Other evidence for these Neolithic settlers is again provided by flint-knapping sites (e.g. Clitheroe (N); Grange-over-Sands (N); Chorlton-on-Medlock, Manchester (s)), and stray finds of polished stone axes from the axe factories of Great Langdale (e.g. Walney Island, Barrow-in-Furness (N)).

Although the evidence for Neolithic settlement so far recovered is slight, it is the traditions of this period which are predominant in the Early Bronze Age (from *c.* 1650 B.C.) at a time when adjacent areas were subject to new ideas and new cultural groupings. A cave site, possibly domestic, has been examined at Fairy Holes, near Chipping (N), but the surviving monuments are again

* This account covers both North (N) and South (s) Lancashire.

largely sepulchral. Many of the cairns in moorland areas of the
county must belong to this period, and this supposition is confirmed by the few excavated examples. They have normally
produced cremation burials in collared urns, a pottery form
which has its origins in Neolithic ceramic traditions, as has the
rite of cremation itself. Indigenous too are the platform cairns
and embanked cemeteries also generally associated with collared
urn burials, and the remarkable funerary and ceremonial timber
monument at Bleasdale (N). The group of free-standing stone
circles, again in some cases associated with collared urn burials,
in the N part of the county, could also be considered as part of
this surviving Neolithic tradition, although their immediate
links are with a group of circles in Cumberland and Westmorland
(see The Buildings of England: Cumberland and Westmorland). The
Bronze Age Culture in our region did not develop in complete
isolation from the rest of the country, however. It shared, if only
peripherally, in the trade in Irish metal products as evidenced by
stray finds of flat copper and bronze axes from several localities in
the county (e.g. Risley and Rixton, both s, and a decorated example from Read, N). Links with the metal industry of the flour-
ishing Wessex Culture to the s are suggested by a rare bronze
tanged spearhead. The lack of datable association and especially
metalwork makes it difficult to estimate how long the collared urn
tradition survived in the region. The only material which can
be assigned with confidence to the later phases of the Bronze Age
is stray finds of metal objects, mostly in river valleys, and hoards
of tools and weapons. A number of socketed axes have come
from the Ribble, and hoards from Winmarleigh, Walton-le-Dale,
and Portfield Camp, Whalley (all N). The latter hoard, deposited
in the C7 B.C., consists of two socketed bronze axes of North
English type, a socketed gouge, two knife blades, and a bracelet
and tress ring of gold. The tress ring is an Irish import and shows
the maintenance of Hibernian contacts at this period.

The Portfield Camp hoard was found inside the ramparts of
the hillfort of presumed Iron Age and therefore later date. Its
possible relationship with a hillfort however emphasizes the
problems of conservatism and the survival of earlier traditions in
our area which is such a recurring feature of its prehistory. Portfield Camp is one of five hillforts, all in North Lancashire. With
the exception of the 15 acres of Warton Crag near Carnforth the
forts are small in comparison with the great fortified earthworks
of the South and reflect the broken nature of the countryside and
a smaller and more scattered population. Few contemporary

domestic sites have been excavated. A rectangular embanked enclosure at Urswick containing five round huts produced Iron Age pottery and similar unexcavated sites at Birkrigg Common Urswick, Torver, on Heathwaite Fell near Woodland, and elsewhere probably belong to this or the succeeding Romano-British phase. The native population in Lancashire appears to have been little affected by the Roman occupation, and both the nature and pattern of rural settlement remained unaltered. The only pieces of native Celtic metalwork belong to the latter half of the CI A.D. – the fine scabbard from Pilling Moss (N), the sword and scabbard from Warton near Carnforth (N), and the beaded torc (lost) from Rochdale (S).

ROMAN LANCASHIRE*

BY BARRY CUNLIFFE

Lancashire is not rich in Roman remains. Six forts, a few unimportant civil settlements, a group of kilns and scattered peasant settlements are all the county can boast. The reasons for this dearth are threefold. In the first place the area was always under military control, and the conditions were therefore not conducive to civil development; secondly large areas of the county were not suited to primitive farming methods; and thirdly, until comparatively recently, competent archeological activity within the county has been negligible. With the growing local interest in the subject, however, it cannot be long before our knowledge of the region is considerably extended.

Even though actual sites and visible remains are thin on the ground, the broad picture of the Roman development is clear enough. The area was finally stabilized by the Roman army at the beginning of Agricola's governorship, but the building of the great legionary base at Chester had been initiated a year or two earlier, and we may suppose that even before Agricola's campaigns some attempt had been made to control the region. The principal line of communications and supply, probably constructed under Agricola, was the road running from Manchester (S), past the forts at Ribchester and Burrow-in-Lonsdale (both N), to link with Hadrian's Wall at Carlisle. Like other military roads of the first century, it cut across important river valley routes, such as the Ribble, the Hodder, the Wenning, and the Greta, enabling the troops to deploy rapidly in the event of the Pennine

* This account covers both North (N) and South (S) Lancashire.

tribes showing signs of aggressive activity. The encircling roads, as it were, could be used to bottle up dissidents in the hills. Cross-communications were also essential to the efficiency of the system, and both Manchester and Ribchester were joined by trans-Pennine roads to York. A second N–S road was provided nearer to the coast, running from Wilderspool, through Wigan (s) and Walton-le-Dale (N) to Lancaster (N). In all probability this road, too, originated as a military way.

The history of the individual forts has not been worked out in detail, but most show signs of a more-or-less continuous occupation from the c1 to the c4. They would have been required as bases for the troops whose job it was to police the routes from Chester to the Wall, as well as to control the tribes in the hills. The fort at Lancaster, on the other hand, may have developed as a semi-naval base in the late c3 or early c4 to guard against pirate raids from the Irish Sea in much the same way as the Saxon shore forts protected the North Sea and Channel coasts, but large-scale excavation will be needed before the nature of the site can be fully understood.

Practically nothing is known of the civilian occupation of the region. Some of the forts developed *vici* outside their gates, and scattered finds from the open country and from caves reflect a generally sparsely populated area. The urban development and villa system of the South East is unknown here.

NORTH LANCASHIRE

*

ABBEYSTEAD see OVER WYRESDALE

ACCRINGTON

Accrington was a village of c.3,000 inhabitants in 1801; it had grown to c.18,000 by 1861, to c.45,000 by 1911. The population now is only 41,000 – a Lancashire fate. The town grew up along the Whalley Road. The textile industry first appeared with Robert Peel's calico printing works at Church, near by, c.1760 and Taylor, Fort & Bury's Broad Oak Print Works in 1782. Torrington in his diary in 1792 says that 'they are building rows of houses, as every vale swarms with cotton mills'. Union Street was laid out in 1787, Peel Street and Church Street (to the church) c.1815, Warner Street in 1821–2. Architecturally Accrington has little to offer except the dignity of blackened stone. Accrington brick, the smooth, immutable, obtrusively red brick beloved by the Victorians, is not prominent.

THE CENTRE

St James, Cannon Street. Built in 1763 and enlarged by a w tower in 1806 and otherwise in 1826. A large church. The windows are in two tiers. The tracery is typically North Country, i.e. still with something of the playfulness of c17 Yorkshire windows. Round-arched, one transom, three lights, the first forming a pointed arch with the l. side of the window arch, the second with the r. side. Interior with three galleries on iron columns. – PLATE. Chalice inscribed 1694.

Baptist Church, Cannon Street. Much more like the parish church of a town than St James. It cost £15,671. High spire recessed on a sw tower. Geometrical tracery. Built in 1874 to the design of *George Baines* of London.

Town Hall, Blackburn Road. Built as the Peel Institute in 1857–8 to commemorate the Peels as the biggest employers in the district. The architects were *J. Green* and *T. Birtwhistle*. It served as the Mechanics' Institute, Public Hall, and News Room. It has a rusticated ground floor with a big porte-cochère with large arches from front, l., and r. On this is a deep portico of six columns, the outer two clustered at the corners. It is a remarkably dignified building, and altogether this one corner of Accrington has much dignity.

OLD MARKET, Blackburn Road. 1868–9 by *John F. Doyle*. The market lies next to the town hall. Its front is ornate, with a centre crowned by a heavy attic with sculpture, but its side is monumentally severe, with Doric pilasters and blank arches surrounding lower windows and upper lunettes. Behind is the NEW MARKET, not at all a monument, but successful with its interlocking concrete vaults. 1958–62 by *Bernard Hartley*, the Borough Engineer and Surveyor.

At the corner of Willow Street and St James's Street is the former MECHANICS INSTITUTION, 1878 by *George Baines*, classical, with an upper Venetian window, and next to it the LIBRARY, 1906–8 by *W. J. Newton*, the Borough Engineer, five bays in a quiet Cinquecento style with upper pilasters and arched windows. Round the corner in Cannon Street the CONSERVATIVE CLUB, 1890–1.

Finally, as a forceful contribution to the centre of Accrington, the railway VIADUCT which closes the vista of the centre on the w side. It was built in 1847.

OUTER ACCRINGTON

ST ANDREW, Empress Street (W). 1912–13 by *Grimshaw & Cunliffe*. Nicely detailed sw tower. Perp style with Arts and Crafts touches. The interior less deserving of comment.

(ST AUGUSTINE, Bolton Avenue, Huncoat. Consecrated in 1909. Architects: *Grimshaw & Cunliffe*.)

CHRIST CHURCH, Christ Church Square (SE). 1838–40 by *A. Y. Williams* (GR). Commissioners' type. The nave with pairs of lancets. Transept and a short chancel. Clumsy pinnacles. The w tower has been taken down.

ST JOHN, Higher Baxenden (SE). 1877 by *Varley*. With a polygonal apse and a s tower. The tower turns octagonal at the top and with a spire – all this with odd details.

ST JOHN EVANGELIST, Addison Street (E). 1864–70 by *H. Macauley*. Rock-faced with a sw steeple. Lancets and plate tracery. A robust piece.

ST PETER, Richmond Street (SW). 1886–9 by *H. Ross* of Accrington. Well detailed. No tower, but a bell-turret between nave and chancel.

NEW JERUSALEM CHURCH, Abbey Street (SE). 1849 by *James*

Green of Portsmouth (Swedenborgian). No tower, but two turrets *à la* King's College Chapel flanking the front. Very tall lancets.

POLICE AND FIRE STATION, Manchester Road (SE). 1932–3 by (*Sir*) *Percy Thomas*. Ashlar-faced, in a squared-up Georgian with classicist details. Exactly the same style and details as at Lancaster.

WAR MEMORIAL, Oakhill Park (SE). By *Sir Charles Reilly*. Large and a little pompous, with a statue of Compassion in front of a tall, bold obelisk and the unexpected addition of attached fluted pilasters to the l. and r. sides of the obelisk reaching about halfway up.

The remaining items must be treated singly. There is no coherence among them.

In BLACKBURN ROAD close to the viaduct are a few notable early C19 ashlar houses, especially one of five bays with a three-bay pediment.

In MANCHESTER ROAD the HOWARTH ART GALLERY was the house of the cotton manufacturer William Howarth. It was designed by *W. H. Brierley* of York and built in 1908–9. It is neo-Jacobean, nearly but not quite symmetrical, and has a fine view on to the moors.

In the WHALLEY ROAD is DYKE NOOK, an uncommonly good neo-Jacobean house by *Walter Brierley*, built *c.*1910–11.

NEW HIGH RILEY is a late C18 eye-catcher. It lies on a hill, $1\frac{1}{4}$ m. E of the parish church, beyond the end of Plantation Street. It has a tower in the middle and gabled side-pieces. In the gables quatrefoil windows. The other windows and the doorway are all pointed. What estate did this folly go with? Where was it supposed to be seen from?

HUNCOAT HALL, $1\frac{5}{8}$ m. NE. The house is irregular and has some windows with arched lights. But there is more to it, a pre-Reformation hall and chapel possibly, also possibly some priest-holes, and an investigation ought to be made.

(HUNCOAT POWER STATION. By *McKellar*; opened in 1956.)

ADLINGTON

CHRIST CHURCH. 1839. Ashlar, neo-Norman. W tower with an octagonal top stage crying out for a spire. The church was paid for by the Commissioners (£1,560). The architect was *E. Welch*.

ST PAUL. 1883–4 by *Thomas D. Barry & Son*. The cost, Kelly

says, was £8,000. It is in fact a big church. The s tower is placed outside the s aisle.

HALLSWORTH FOLD FARMHOUSE, 1½ m. NNE of St Paul. The house had a date read as 1606, but an auxiliary building is dated 1681. Mullioned windows, but the room above the porch has a window whose lights have semicircular heads. Here lies the problem.

HALL O' T' HILL, 1 m. N of St Paul. A three-storeyed house with mullioned and mullioned and transomed windows. The house is said to be of 1724. That would be interesting; for it still has two all-glass mullioned and transomed bay windows, five-eighths of an octagon. The doorway however has indeed an C18 moulded surround. Round the corner to the r. are mullioned windows, the top one of three stepped lights, and above it a vertically placed oval.

(EGYPTIAN GATE. On the E side of the A5106, SW of Adlington, halfway between Chorley and Wigan. Noted by Mr Fleetwood-Hesketh.)

AINSDALE see SOUTHPORT, p. 235

ALDINGHAM

2070

ST CUTHBERT. Overlooking Morecambe Bay. Dec w tower. Thin N aisle of 1845–6, the s aisle with new windows of the same date. The chancel is the most valuable piece. It must date from c.1300, see the head-stops of the arch to the nave, the E window of three stepped cusped lancets, the low-side window of two such lights with a transom, and the priest's doorway with a trefoiled (not pointed) head. There is also a C15 window, and one of the C17 with mullions treated as columns. The s arcade is the earliest work in the church. The short round and octagonal piers carry elementary moulded capitals and one waterleaf capital. The arches are round and have one step and one chamfer. All that makes it c.1190. The tower was built into the nave. – COMMUNION RAIL. Later C17. – BOX PEWS.

ALDINGHAM HALL. By Sir Matthew Digby Wyatt, 1846–50. The house was built for the Rev. John Stonard, who left it to his butler. White stone, very Gothic. The front towards the bay is symmetrical. Two angle motifs with canted bays between angle turrets with pinnacles. At the back a big square tower with higher stair-turret and battlements. The staircase runs up in it. The hall is in the centre between the two angle

motifs and has three large windows. All these main windows
are straight-topped. The entrance porch is on one short side,
and a corridor runs right across, with the hall on one, the
staircase on the other side.

ALLITHWAITE

3070

St Mary. 1865 by *E.G.Paley*. Apparently one composition
with school and vicarage. The church has a polygonal bell-
turret and plate tracery. – STAINED GLASS. E window by
Morris & Co., but as late as *c*.1920.

Kirkhead Tower, on the hills s of Allithwaite. Embattled.
Probably late C19.

ALSTON

6030

Our Lady (R.C.). On the Preston road. 1856 by *I. & C.
Hansom*. Rock-faced, with geometrical tracery and a weird bell-
turret, square but set diagonally, partly on a buttress. –
STAINED GLASS. The E window obviously by *Hardman*.

Alston Old Hall, 1¾ m. SE. With mullioned windows.
Picturesquely placed by the river Ribble.

Alston Hall, 1½ m. SE. By *Darbyshire*, 1876, for John
Mercer, a colliery-owner. Ashlar, gabled Tudor, with a square
porch tower, but a Gothic portal under it, and in the spacious
staircase hall with its skylight, a Gothic gallery.

ALTCAR

3000

St Michael. 1879 by *Douglas*. A roomy timber-framed building with bell-turret and tiled roofs. Neatly detailed straight-
topped windows. – PLATE. Chalice and Paten presented in
1747.

Old Gore Farmhouse *see* Lydiate.

ALTHAM

7030

St James. Perp w tower and Late Perp nave and aisles. The low
windows with uncusped lights are at once recognized. The
arcades have standard elements. The chancel was rebuilt in
1881. – FONT. Perp, octagonal, with panels carrying the
Instruments of the Passion and the IHS and the M (for
Mary) signs (cf. Padiham). – Victorian BOX PEWS with
poppyheads, a rarity. – SCULPTURE. Norman tympanum
with rows of small chip-carved St Andrew's crosses. It is not
import, it seems. So a Norman church was here (chancel s).

ANGLEZARKE *see* RIVINGTON

ANSDELL *see* LYTHAM ST ANNES, p. 175

5070

ARKHOLME

CHURCH. The church lies at the end of the village street close to the river Lune. Nave and chancel in one. Perp s arcade of four bays. One capital has some basic ornamental motifs. The bellcote with segmental pediment may be of *c*.1700 – (C14 or early C15 BELL.)

Very pretty street. Among the houses CAWOOD HOUSE is dated 1748. It has been much restored and enlarged in the C20, but the old part is of three bays, symmetrical. A house of 1752 is of course symmetrical too, and has in addition instead of a Yorkshire lintel a pediment over the door.

STORRS HALL. Storrs Hall was built in 1848. It is Tudor Gothic, with a symmetrical façade and an imitation pele tower at the back. It is a sizeable mansion and was built for Francis Pearson, a Kirkby Lonsdale solicitor. Before 1848 Storrs Hall was Elizabethan.

ARLEY HALL *see* HAIGH

ARMOT HOUSE *see* CHATBURN

4030

ASHTON

ASHTON HALL. The house consists of a C14 tower house of red sandstone with diagonally set angle towers and a grey stone range of 1856. The old part is tightly composed, the new part spreads irregularly and picturesquely with battlements and turrets. In the old part the original windows are blocked and have been replaced, in the basement by mullioned windows of *c*.1600, above by simply Gothick windows of *c*.1800. The hall in the new part has a hammerbeam roof, and the main drawing room an ornately coffered ceiling. The designs of 1856 are by *William Le Gendre Starkie*. The back courtyard is approached by a Jacobean GATEWAY with coupled thin Tuscan columns, and at r. angles is a Jacobean STABLE block with mullioned windows. Lord Ashton (*see* Lancaster, p. 163) bought the estate in 1884. The tower was probably built only then.

ASHTON-ON-RIBBLE *see* PRESTON, p. 198

ASPULL

6000

In the centre is an over-large GREEN. Close to it the METHO-
DIST CHAPEL, of 1858, but still entirely Georgian, of brick,
with plain arched windows, three by three.

Along the road sw to New Springs first DUKE'S ROW, a row of
seventeen cottages built by the Earls of Crawford, lords of
the manor, late in the C18. It is a completely even row, each
cottage with one window below, one above, and a chimney
sticking up. Then, by the canal, the scanty remains of the
HAIGH FOUNDRY. Three bays with cupola, the centre of a 60
building of 1839. A pity.

At NEW SPRINGS is ST JOHN BAPTIST, 1897 by *J. M. & H.
Taylor*. Stock brick and very red trim. w tower with the upper
part corbelled out and ending in a pyramid roof on a truncated pyramid. Very odd w windows.

At PENNINGTON GREEN is ST ELIZABETH, 1876, also by
J. M. & H. Taylor. Stock brick and red brick. No tower. w
front with a typical Taylor motif: stepped-up lancet lights for
the aisle w windows to follow the roof-line of the aisles.

ASTLEY HALL *see* CHORLEY

AUGHTON
2 m. sw of Gressingham

5060

ST SAVIOUR. 1864 by *Paley*. Not of importance. Nave with
bellcote and chancel. Lancets and cusped lancets.

AUGHTON
near Ormskirk

3000

ST MICHAEL. An interesting church, very varied externally.
The oldest part is a Norman s doorway, largely blocked. The
Norman wall extended to the w, see a lancet again hardly
visible from outside. Then follows the N tower, and this is
Dec. There was only a narrow N aisle then, as the chamfered
arch and the external elements on the w side show. To the
nave and a chancel aisle also chamfered arches. In the N wall
a cusped tomb recess. The bell-openings C14 too. They
are in a top part of the tower which is octagonal. The octagon
is reached by plain broaches, and on it is a spire. It is almost
exactly like the steeple of Ormskirk next door. The N aisle

arcade is Perp, with octagonal piers and double-chamfered arches. But the N aisle walls are an earliest post-medieval job. It seems to have been built by a rector of 1528–48 and is decidedly post-Perp. The windows are round-headed and have uncusped intersecting tracery. It looks in fact more C17 than C16. The chancel was rebuilt in 1876, but the chancel chapel – see its E window – must again be 1540 or later. Nave and N aisle have splendid roofs with arched braces to collar-beams and with wind-braces. Those of the N aisle form elongated quatrefoils. – CROSS HEAD. Part of an Anglo-Saxon cross head in a recess in the N wall. It has crude interlace. It has been dated C9–10 and compared with crosses at Bolton (South Lancashire) and Whalley.

CHRIST CHURCH, 1¼ m. NE, more part of Ormskirk than of Aughton. 1867–70 by *W. & J. Hay*. Large, rock-faced, Dec, and not attractive.

ST ANNE (R.C.), Prescot Road, 1¾ m. NE, and even more part of Ormskirk. 1850.

ST MARY (R.C.), on its own, 1½ m. SE. 1823. Plain oblong, of brick. A pity it is stuccoed. Arched windows. The short chancel has a pretty saucer dome and an E wall with pairs of giant attached Corinthian columns. – PULPIT. A simple, but magnificent wooden piece.

A good recent house by *Anthony Grimshaw* is *c.*¼ m. SW of the church in Red Fold, at the corner of Long Lane.

BACKBARROW *see* HAVERTHWAITE

8020

BACUP

ST JOHN, Burnley Road. 1882–3 by *Medland Taylor*. The SW tower remained unbuilt. It serves as a porch, and this leads into a kind of nave lobby or narthex separated from the nave by one middle column. The nave is very wide, and the arcade also consists of columns. They all have a fat shaft-ring. Off the lobby to the W is a polygonal baptistery. The arch between chancel and sanctuary stands on detached shafts which come out of the responds like stove-pipes – just one more of Medland Taylor's tricks.

CHRIST CHURCH, Todmorden Road. 1854 by *Sharpe & Paley*. In the Second Pointed, with a SW tower with higher stair-turret.

ST SAVIOUR, New Line. 1864–5 by *Edward Wyndham Tarn*.

Large, with a NE steeple and a polygonal apse. Odd rhythm of the closely set aisle windows. – (FONT. For baptism by immersion.)

HOLY TRINITY, Tunstead, Stacksteads. 1840–1, with a transept of 1873. Norman, with long round-headed windows. The w tower is octagonal at the top and carries a small spire.

(FOREST HOUSE. Probably by *John Foster* of Liverpool, possibly for himself. The date is c.1828. Five bays, two storeys, recessed centre with four giant Ionic columns. Good, domed staircase. MHLG)

(FEARNS HALL. Dated 1696. With rows of long, low, mullioned windows. MHLG)

(ACRE MILL. 1877 and earlier. Acre Mill Lodge has a date 1864. With two tiers of nineteen round-arched windows. MHLG)

BAILRIGG *see* LANCASTER, p. 161

BALDERSTONE
6030

ST LEONARD. 1852–4 by *Rampling* of Preston. Early-C14-style tracery. The interior with its open timber roof better than the exterior. NW steeple of 1906–7.

BAMBER BRIDGE
5020

ST AIDAN. By *R.K.Freeman*, 1894–5. Yellow stone and red stone dressings. Perp, with double transcpts and the bellcote on the nave E end. The w extension is of 1914–15.

(ST SAVIOUR. 1837. Chancel of c.1887.)

BLESSED VIRGIN MARY (R.C.), Brownedge. The steeple of 1867–8. The rest by *Pugin & Pugin*, 1892. Very long, with double transepts and a broad apse. Open timber roof. The interior spreads out without any tension. The exterior somewhat bleak. Long nave of four wide bays, single lancets and some unexpected cross-gablets.

BANK HALL *see* BRETHERTON

BANKS
3020

ST STEPHEN. 1868. Brick; the sw tower of very weird details. The rest is humble, rather as if it were 1830. Aisleless interior.

BANNISHEAD MOOR *see* TORVER

BARCROFT *see* BURNLEY, p. 82

BARDSEA

3070

HOLY TRINITY. 1843–53 by *George Webster* of Kendal. White stone, with a W tower which has a spire, but the broaches below the level of the bell-openings. Polygonal apse, plate tracery. A building without poetry, but beautifully placed above Morecambe Bay.

BARNACRE

5040

ALL SAINTS. 1905 by *Austin & Paley*. Paid for by the Rushton family. Broad W tower, well grouped, with the stair-turret in an unusual position. Well grouped at the E end too. Tiled roofs.

BARNACRE LODGE. Built in 1876–7 by the Earl of Bective. The architect was *T. H. Myres* (GS). Brick, gabled, with a tiled roof and some tile-hanging. Also much pargetting.

KENLIS ARMS HOTEL, by Garstang and Catterall Station. Built in 1871 by the Earl for his friends during the shooting season (Kelly). Does that mean an overflow of friends? Barnacre Lodge seems big enough.

BARROWFORD

8030

ST THOMAS was being pulled down at the time of writing. The new church is by *T. Maldwyn Jones* of Lancaster, and uneventful. On the way to it three CHAPELS: The first is BETHEL, dated 1860, four bays of arched windows; the second is the CONGREGATIONAL of 1880–1 by *John Gibson & Son* of Malton, with a clumsy SE tower and arched windows; the third is simple again.

In CHURCH STREET, at the E end, a house of 1696 with a five-light top window in the gable which is stepped, with the second and fourth light having as their heads convex quadrant curves (cf. Southfield Fold, Nelson, and the former Old Lodge, Burnley).

INGHAMITE CHAPEL, Wheatley Lane. 1749–50, the oldest of that denomination anywhere.

(In GISBURN ROAD Nos. 99–103A are a terrace of weavers' cottages; the WHITE BEAR of 1607 was formerly a private house and has three gables, a three-storeyed porch, and mullioned and mullioned and transomed windows; No. 140 was a toll-house and has a canted front, and Nos. 195–211 is a row of cottages dated 1824. MHLG)

BARROW-IN-FURNESS

2070

INTRODUCTION

The monks of Furness Abbey (p. 123) smelted iron with wood as early as the C13. In the early C18 charcoal was used at Backbarrow, and the first blast-furnaces appeared. About 1840 Ulverston had over 5,000, Barrow about 300 inhabitants. Jetties had been built at Barrowhead to ship out Furness ores from 1790, and in 1839 H. W. Schneider came as a young speculator and dealer in iron; he built a fourth jetty in 1842, and a few years later, in 1846, the railway arrived. With the railway came James Ramsden, locomotive superintendent, aged twenty-three, and a man with a vision of a thriving city of the future. The Furness Railway opened up the area, and when in 1850 Schneider discovered the fabulous Park deposit of iron all the ingredients needed for Barrow's growth were there. In 1849 the Furness ironfield as a whole produced 182,000 tons, in 1856 465,000 tons; so in 1857 Schneider erected blast-furnaces at Barrow and by 1876 they were the largest steelworks in the world. The two chief landowners were the Duke of Devonshire (until 1856 Earl of Burlington) and the Duke of Buccleuch. Ramsden succeeded in interesting them in the development of Barrow. About 1847 he submitted a very elementary plan for a small area SW of the future Duke Street. Still in 1847 ten cottages for railway workers were built in Salthouse Street. St George as the parish church of the future Barrow was built in 1859–61. The planned district reached 3,000 inhabitants in 1861. In 1864 the figure had gone up to over 8,000. A larger area was laid out to Ramsden's plan in 1865. So it was due to Ramsden that Barrow became a planned town. There are few in England, and fewer of the C19. The plan, God knows, is not imaginative, but the wide, tree-lined streets to this day convey a sense of space and ease which even the casual visitor is likely to comment on. Ramsden deserved to become the first Mayor of Barrow. That was in 1867. In the same year the railway built the Devonshire Dock. Buccleuch Dock followed in 1873. The Barrow Shipbuilding Company was conceived in 1869, in terms of the building of iron ships. It was another idea of Ramsden's, and it turned out to be

the best; for the company in 1897 became Vickers', at a time
when the Thomas process of steel producing had made haematite less valuable. In terms of population the greatest jump forward was in 1871–81, from 19,000 to 47,000. In 1891 it was
52,000, in 1901 57,000. It reached its peak (74,000) in 1921, but
is now (1967) only 65,000.

CHURCHES

St GEORGE, St George's Square. The parish church of Barrow,
situated in the centre of Ramsden's new Barrow. Hence
not an old church. It was built at the suggestion of Ramsden
in 1859–61 to the designs of *E. G. Paley*. The N aisle is of 1867,
the S chapel is the Ramsden Chapel. SW tower, geometrical
tracery. The arcade piers have moulded alternating with
foliage capitals. On the N side of the chancel an arch to the
organ, on the S side two to the chapel – a motif which Paley
& Austin were to make much of.

St JAMES, Blake Street. The best church in Barrow. 1867–9 by
E. G. Paley (who, it must be remembered, was joined by
Austin in 1868). Red brick, with dark-blue brick patterns, with
a splendid steeple, the spire keeping close in outline to the
tower, owing to four gables at its foot and very low broaches
in the diagonals. Might these top parts of the steeple be an
Austin improvement? Polygonal apse. The inspiration for the
interior came clearly from Street. The interior has the astonishing feature – astonishing for its date – of brick arches on the
slim red-sandstone C13-style piers. The upper part of the
walls is of grey brick. It has unfortunately been whitewashed.
That debilitates the impression. It is a strong, honest piece of
work.

(St JOHN, Island Road. 1935 by *Seely & Paget*. Concrete,
cruciform, with a strange outline.)

St LUKE, Roose Road. Brick, with a detached concrete bell-
tower. By *Cruickshank & Seward* of Manchester, 1962–4.
(The PULPIT, the LECTERN, and the dove over the FONT
are by *W. Soukop*.)

St MARY (R.C.), Duke Street. 1866–7 by *E. W. Pugin*, the
steeple of 1888. A large and ornate church, especially multi-
form the W front, with the steeple and the polygonal baptistery.
In the middle a low lobby with a large rose over. Polygonal
apse. Arcades alternating between foliage and typical E.W.
Pugin abstract capitals. A very odd feature is the E bay. It

is not a transept. On the contrary, the arcade is suddenly half as wide, and with this crowding of piers and arches corresponds a change in the clerestory, where equally suddenly a little rose appears above the lancets.

St Mary, Walney Island. 1907–8 by *Austin & Paley*. Large; no tower, a tiled roof, and Perp features. Inside, exposed stonework. The arcade arches die into the piers. The chancel has the one arch to the N and two to the S just like St George's. – PLATE. Chalice, Newcastle-made, *c.*1725–30; Paten, London-made, 1723–4.

(St Matthew, Harrogate Street. 1965–7 by *Schomberg Scott* of Edinburgh.)

St Paul. After damage in the Second World War the church now consists of the chancel and two nave bays by *Habershon & Brock* of 1871, and a new, unassuming, white-brick nave with attachment. This new work is by *C. L. Mawson* of Kendal.

Presbyterian Church, School Street. 1874–5 by *Paley & Austin*. An odd façade, where a short tower l. is balanced by a polygonal feature facing S. The church cost £5,000.

Walney Island Presbyterian Church. Small, roughcast, with typical Voysey buttresses. Red terracotta trim and a cupola. All rather too pretty.

Former United Methodist Church, Alison Street. 1894. Fiery red brick with a SW cupola. The features are a mixed C17 to Baroque assembly.

Former Wesleyan Church, Hartington and Nelson Streets. Built in 1907. It is of red brick and yellow terracotta with a prominent corner cupola.

PUBLIC BUILDINGS

Town Hall, Duke Street. By *W. H. Lynn* of Belfast, 1882–7. He had won the competition. Large, a monument to Barrow's prosperity. C13 Gothic, like the Manchester and Rochdale town halls. High tower in the middle with a top one would not have expected. Four steep gables and an octagonal top-stage. L. and r. of the tower the elevation is not quite symmetrical. The Council Chamber is made visible by four extra-large windows. The original main entrance was at the back (to the sea). It has a porte-cochère. The interior is a little disappointing. The only vaulted part is the entrance recess.

Market, Market Street. 1866 by *Paley*. Brick, Gothic, nothing notable.

COLLEGE OF FURTHER EDUCATION, Abbey Road. 1900 by *Woodhouse & Willoughby*. The typical technical-school building of that date. Red brick and yellow terracotta. Asymmetrical with a cupola on a turret. Varied C17 and C18 motifs.

WORKING MEN'S INSTITUTE, Abbey Road. 1870–1 by *H.A.Darbishire*. Low, symmetrical, with a pediment and a cupola. A modest building.

LIBRARY, Ramsden Square. 1915–20 by *J.A.Charles*. It fits the circus by having a centre and two diagonally projecting wings. Beaux-Arts Classical, well handled.

ABBEY HOUSE, Abbey Road. A mansion built in 1913–14 by *Lutyens* as a guest house and a flat for the managing director of Vickers. It is not an inspired work. Red sandstone. The exterior symmetrical Elizabethan, on the H-plan, and no fling of Lutyensian fancy. Inside, the hall has the traditional bay to the garden side and a minstrels' gallery, and the one inspired motif is the main staircase reaching this gallery at a landing so that at that level the two rooms are connected. In one of the garden projections of the H is a room with a saucer dome.

MONUMENTS. It is part of the Barrow plan that at two main intersections squares are made (which have now become welcome roundabouts). In them stand the two main commemorative monuments: Ramsden by *Noble*, 1872, in Ramsden Square, and Schneider by *Percy Wood*, in Schneider Square. Moreover, to complete the triumvirate, opposite the town hall Lord Frederick Cavendish (representing the Dukes of Devonshire) by *Bruce Joy*, 1885.

PERAMBULATION

What makes a perambulation attractive has already been indicated. Few individual private buildings need be looked at. In ABBEY ROAD the CONSERVATIVE CLUB, of 1899, looking down, it seems, on the Mechanics' Institute opposite. It is higher, ashlar-faced and has chastely handled mixed Georgian motifs. Round the corner in Duke Street is the equally restrained, more Italian MARTINS BANK of 1873.

Opposite Vickers, on Barrow Island, in MICHAELSON STREET are two rows of red-sandstone flats with corner turrets where they meet. They look as if they might be in Glasgow. Their date is 1884, and they were not built for executives, but for workers. They have long access balconies at the back.

Vickers also built VICKERSTOWN on Walney Island as a job
for the same purpose, but on the new ideals of Port Sunlight.
The estate was begun in 1901. By 1904 there were 930 houses.
Pebbledash and timber-framed gables.

BARTON

5030

ST LAWRENCE. 1895–6 by *R.Knill Freeman*. Quite large.
Yellow stone and red-stone trim. SW steeple. Dec style.

ST MARY, Newsham or Newhouse. 1905–6 by *Gilbertson* (?).
Nave and chancel under one roof. Bellcote. Polygonal apse.
The transept has two cross-gables.

NEWSHAM HOUSE. Five-bay Late Georgian house of ashlar
with a Tuscan porch and a handsome lodge.

THE KNOLL, Station Lane, 1 m. SW of the parish church. By
Ernest George, late 1890s.

BAXENDEN see ACCRINGTON, p. 46

BEAUMONT GRANGE see HEST BANK

BECCONSALL

4020

NEW ALL SAINTS, Station Road. 1926 by *Austin & Paley*.
The broad W tower with an on-two-sides-recessed pyramid
roof is impressive. Aisleless interior.

OLD ALL SAINTS, ⅜ m. E. Built in 1764. Brick, only two bays
long. The windows are arched, but the E window is of the
Venetian type, treated very elementarily. Small bellcote. –
FONT. C18. – PLATE. Chalice inscribed 1627.

BECKSIDE

2080

3½ m. SE of Broughton-in-Furness

ST CUTHBERT. The church has quite an ambitious Norman S
doorway. It has two orders of columns with decorated scallop,
leaf, and waterleaf capitals and beak-head in one arch order.
The date may be 1170. One chancel N window is Norman too,
and the window opposite was Norman before being blocked.
Otherwise externally all features are the work of restorers.
The W tower was rebuilt in 1829. The N aisle and arcade are
all C19. – FONT. Octagonal, goblet-shaped, with just panels
and one shield on the stem. – STAINED GLASS. Some
fragments, including a C14 seated Christ in chancel side
windows. – PLATE. Small Chalice C17; small Plate inscribed
1698; Chalice and Cover Paten of 1737, by *S.B.*

RING CAIRN, 1¼ m. ENE. The cairn has a diameter of 75 ft
with an inner revetment of large upright slabs to the bank.
The earthen bank is broken by an entrance on the SE. 100
yds NE are three pairs of stones which may represent the
remains of an avenue leading to this site. 350 yds N is a large
round cairn, 90 ft in diameter.

BELMONT

6010

Immediately E and some way up the range of hills which includes
the Rivington Pike. On the highest eminence, 1,498 ft up, unfortunately Television has struck roots. The one highest slender
mast would not matter, but the other pylons etc. are a mess.

ST PETER. 1849–50 by *J. E. Gregan*. Sizeable and conventional,
with a w steeple and plate tracery in most windows.
CONGREGATIONAL CHURCH. 1898 by *Bradshaw & Gass*. A
much jollier proposition, with the roguish outline of its SW
tower and the W front, where the W porch curves up and down
and the six-light window above has quite original and resourceful details.

BESCAR *see* SCARISBRICK

BICKERSTAFFE

4000

HOLY TRINITY. 1843 by *Sydney Smirke* for the Earl of Derby.
The N aisle is probably the enlargement of 1860. The older
part still has pairs of lancets and buttresses between, in the
Commissioners' tradition. But in the w tower is a portal with
quite correct E.E. detail, though the tympanum with the
three angels adds a happy touch of Victorian romanticism.
Wide polygonal apse with shafted lancets.
The substantial PARSONAGE, quite asymmetrical, is probably
by *Smirke* too. It was the enlargement of an existing house.

BIGLAND HALL *see* HAVERTHWAITE

BILLINGTON

7030

OLD ST LEONARD, Old Langho, ¾ m. NW of the new church.
Said to have been built *c.*1557. Low, of nave and chancel under
one roof. Bellcote. In the outer walls fragments from Whalley
Abbey. The E.E. PISCINA inside may come from the same
source. Squat S porch. No aisles, no chancel arch. – STOUP.
Ornately Perp. From the abbey? – COMMUNION RAIL.

Probably of the 1630s. – BENCH ENDS. With shields and dates: 1688 etc. – STAINED GLASS. Ancient fragments in the SE window.

NEW ST LEONARD, on the A road. 1879–80 by *Paley & Austin* (cost £4,600). Nave with nice, simple, well-shaped bell-turret. The style adopted is E.E. to Dec. S arcade with quatrefoil piers. The chancel windows are set high up, and on the N side they are quatrefoiled squares.

ST MARY, 1⅛ m. w. Built in 1836. Disused. It never was anything but depressing. Lancet windows and a w tower octagonal from the bottom. Hat-like spire.

HACKING HALL, 1½ m. N. Dated 1607. A fine symmetrical façade to the river Calder. Hall centre with porch and corresponding hall-bay in the re-entrant angles between the centre and projecting wings. Five gables. The hall window is of six lights, the others of three to five. Irregular s side, dominated by the very large hall chimneybreast.

By the bridge towards Whalley TERRACE ROW, a flat terrace of five early C19 houses with Gothic windows, and in the same style, but more enterprisingly handled, MARJORIE, right by the river, with a castellated porch.

BILSBORROW
5040

ST HILDA. 1926–7 by *Austin & Paley*. Nave and aisles, central tower and chancel. Free Perp, with a crossing tower. Inscription above each bell-opening. The arcade arches die into the piers.

BIRKDALE *see* SOUTHPORT, p. 235

BIRKRIGG COMMON *see* URSWICK

BISPHAM *see* BLACKPOOL, p. 69

BLACKBURN
6020

INTRODUCTION

Blackburn has its quality. It is hilly, and it is not so big that one is not everywhere close to the open country. For the centre on the other hand not much can be said. With its population of 63,000 in 1861 and 106,000 in 1961 it might have done more to introduce civic dignity. As it is, the mills do all the impressing, especially when one looks down from the hills, and it is not architectural impressing. Blackburn is an ancient place. It is named in Domesday, is called a market town by Lambarde in 1570 and 'an opulent and respectable town' by Whitaker in 1801. Weaving was done already in the C16 and C17, but the industry began to develop only after the reduction of the tax on cotton goods in 1774. By 1867 at Blackburn and in the immediate neighbourhood, there were 107 cotton spinning and weaving mills. But the most famous works at Blackburn were those founded in 1764 by Mr Peel (*see* Accrington), Mr Haworth, and Mr Yates, and they were textile printing works. Robert Peel was the grandfather of Sir Robert Peel, the first Prime Minister to come from the manufacturing class (cf. also Accrington and, in South Lancashire, Bury).

INNER BLACKBURN

CHURCHES

CATHEDRAL. The parish church of St Mary was raised to cathedral rank in 1926. *W. A. Forsythe*, the architect selected to do the necessary alterations, kept the W tower and nave and added an E end with transepts in a conventional, if simplified Gothic. Only the *corona* over the crossing with its pinnacles and its long spire brings in a modern element. This is by *Lawrence King*, 1961. The intended octagonal lantern tower proved too costly. The parish church dated from 1820–6 and was designed by *John Palmer*. After a fire in 1831 it was reconstructed in consultation with *Rickman*. High three-light Dec windows with a transom, buttresses between. Clerestory. The W tower looks later but isn't. The nave piers are tall and round with four thin attached shafts. Tierceron-star vaults of plaster. The W wall has a nice composition of three ogee arches, the middle one for the entrance, the others crowning vaulted niches. – (STALLS. Eight, with MISERICORDS, in the underground choir vestry. One has Adam and Eve's Temptation, one the fox preaching to the geese, one a fine angel with a scroll, one an ape, one a bearded monster. – STAINED GLASS. Some *Morris* glass now in various lights in the transepts.) – PLATE. Chalice of 1630; Chalice inscribed 1645; Cup inscribed 1653; Breadholder, 1685–6; undated Chalice; Flagon, 1764–5; Breadholder 1807. – Fine GATE of c.1825 towards Church Street.

The DIOCESAN OFFICES are in the former CHURCH

SCHOOL, a quite sizeable, asymmetrical building of 1870–1 by *Frederick Robinson* of Derby.

ST JOHN EVANGELIST, Victoria Street. Built in 1789. The 57 architect is not known. The church has a bold w tower, square and rusticated on the lowest stage, then with chamfered edges and then octagonal. On that stage there are columns carrying an architrave against the diagonal walls. Top cap. The sides have three tripartite windows, each centre carrying a pediment, and an upper tier of lunette windows. Large Venetian window on the pedimented E wall. Some tactful enlargements, the vestry 1865 by *J. Brindley*, the s addition to the chancel 1891. The interior has three Victorian galleries and a flat ceiling. In the chancel a scheme of giant pilasters of 1891.

ST MARY (R.C.), Freckleton Street. 1860–4 by *J. Cundall*. With a sw turret and an apse. Short granite piers and foliage capitals. Oddly tiny clerestory with detached granite colonnettes.

ST PETER, St Peter's Street. 1819–22 by *John Palmer*. A Commissioners' church. It cost £11,491 – a large sum. Ashlar masonry. w tower, two-light Dec windows with buttresses between. Short chancel with vestries l. and r. Thin compound piers; plaster vault. – STAINED GLASS. E window and one s window with large figures. Is it the glass by *Edmondson*, 1858, mentioned in the TK Index?

CHAPEL STREET CONGREGATIONAL CHURCH, Freckleton Street. 1873–4 by *J. Tarring & Son*. Large. sw steeple, triple w porch. Geometrical tracery.

METHODIST CHURCH, Feilden Street. Rebuilt in 1871. Latest classical, but with segment-headed windows. Five bays with a five-bay pediment. Brick and stone dressings.

ST GEORGE'S PRESBYTERIAN CHURCH, Preston New Road. 1865–8 by *James Patterson* of Blackburn. With a sw steeple.

PUBLIC BUILDINGS

TOWN HALL. 1852–6 by *Patterson*. Big, Italianate, and indifferent. Upper arched windows, and upper columns.

KING GEORGE'S HALL, Blakey Moor. 1913 etc. by *Briggs, Wolstenholme & Thornely*. Conventionally classical, with a giant portico. The side towards Northgate is more personal, with a large amount of sheer wall and the three window aedicules set into it.

Immediately N of this are the POLICE COURT and SESSIONS HOUSE, big stone buildings, also by *Briggs, Wolstenholme & Thornely*, 1912–21.

POST OFFICE, Darwen Street. 1907–8 by *Walter Pott* (Office of Works). A nice composition, almost symmetrical. Brick and much stone. Mildly Baroque, with two semicircular pediments.

TELEPHONE MANAGER'S OFFICE, Duke Street. By *H. G. Swann* of the Ministry of Public Building and Works and the *Building Design Partnership*, 1965–6. Noncommittally modern.

FIRE STATION, Byrom Street. 1921–2 by *Walter Stirrup*. Brick and much stone trim. Beaux Arts to Baroque, with the tower behind, its Baroque top being prominent from afar.

LIBRARY AND MUSEUM, Library Street. 1872–4 by *Woodgate & Collcutt*. Enlarged in 1893. Quite a large block. Mildly Gothic with touches in the direction of the Arts and Crafts. Sculptural panels by *Seale*.

COLLEGE OF TECHNOLOGY AND DESIGN, Blakey Moor. Begun in 1888. Architects *Smith, Woodhouse & Willoughby*. A nine-bay front of brick with lavish decoration in yellow terracotta. The style is a kind of free French Renaissance; or what else is it? Opposite a large, more utilitarian annex by *Willink & Dod*. Behind, in Feilden Street, the new buildings with curtain-walling, entirely indifferent.

MARKET, Ainsworth Street. 1962–4 by *W. H. Sutton* of the Borough Engineer's Department. With a large asymmetrically curved concrete roof and a somewhat frilly front.

PERAMBULATION

The cathedral lies immediately opposite the station square and, viewed from the station, is in competition with the irresponsible curligigs of the PALACE THEATRE of 1899. CHURCH STREET is no longer the street which hides and exposes what was then the parish church. The N side has largely been rebuilt. On the S side, against the churchyard, still e.g. one stuccoed six-bay house, latish classical and dated 1856, and the noble three-by-two-bay ashlar block of 1860 with its giant Doric pilasters.

One should now first go NORTH. In VICTORIA STREET great changes are taking place. An interesting new building with an oddly detailed staircase contraption and windowless upper floors faced in vertically set white tiles is complete. It was built for Messrs Lewis's by the *Building Design Partnership*, as is the building which has been started immediately s of the town hall. But opposite the town hall is the former Ex-CHANGE, 1862–5 by *Brakspear* of Manchester. White, stuc-coed, and ornately Gothic. The entrance lobby is polygonal like a chapter house, and along the side to King William Street are five large bay windows. A little further N, around St John's church, are early C19 survivals, brick houses with columned doorways. They are in VICTORIA STREET and RICHMOND TERRACE, though E of the church is the new office building for the ROYAL EXCHANGE ASSURANCE (1964–5 by the staff of a property company), very acceptable in a neutral way. In Richmond Terrace, near its W end, is a long terrace, completed in 1838. All doorways have heavy lintels instead of pediments.

WEST of the cathedral first at the N end of DARWEN STREET the OLD BANK, one of the best buildings of Blackburn, very individual, and with its block-shape and its amplitude of bare wall very convincing. The doorway is large and arched and set diagonally into the angle, which has an odd, unexpected effect. Set in the wall to Darwen Street a three-bay arcade of windows, to the side street a two-bay arcade. The best Georgian houses of Blackburn are in KING STREET, five-bay brick houses, the best No. 39 of 1779, with a three-bay pediment and a delicately detailed doorway. The group laps over into PRINCES STREET.

OUTER BLACKBURN

NORTH WEST, NORTH, AND NORTH EAST

ST ALBAN, Larkhill. Only the gatepiers are from the church of 1824–6. The successor has a SW tower of 1861 and is other-wise of 1900–1. Geometrical tracery and several unusual features, especially the traceried triforium inside and the high clerestory. Architect: *Edward Goldie*.

ST GABRIEL, Brownhill Drive. By *F. X. Velarde*, 1932–3. One of the milestones in the (late) development of English church architecture towards a C20 style. Brick, and blocky through-out. The W front would be impressive, could it be seen well. It has four high and narrow nave windows and a square cam-panile. The nave windows along the side are pairs of very elongated round-headed lancets. The sanctuary is represented by a raised block. The nave is tunnel-vaulted. The aisles are reduced to low passages. The vault is continued towards the E

3—N.L.

end with a number of closely spaced transverse arches. Only above the altar is a bit of modernistic detail. The low SCREEN with PULPIT and READING DESK on the other hand is perfectly smooth. The material is travertine.

ST JAMES, Shear Brow. 1873–4 by *Frederick I.Robinson* of Derby. High N tower with pyramid roof, mostly lancets, apse. Dull interior.

ST MICHAEL, Whalley New Road. 1866–9 by *Stevens & Robinson*, the SE steeple 1883. C13 style.

FOUR LANE ENDS CONGREGATIONAL CHURCH, Shear Brow. 1925 by *Frank W.Parkinson*. Low, Perp, but with a Jacobean façade, *à la* Edgar Wood.

In BANK HEY LANE SOUTH is BANK HEY, one of a number of Jacobean farmhouses with mullioned windows surviving inside Blackburn.

In ROBINSON STREET, Little Harwood, is another kind of survival: a stuccoed late C18 house (Baines: 1791). Seven bays with a one-bay pediment, and a pedimented doorway.

EAST

ST JOSEPH (R.C.), Cumberland Street. 1875–7 by *Goldie & Child*. This is Blackburn's most bewildering building, large and uncouth – a church on top of a whole ground floor meant for a school. Hence two staircases lead up to the lobby, which is in the big W tower. The church itself has a roof with deep eaves and rectangular windows. As the church had only an upper floor at its disposal, the room is low for its width. There are no aisles, but two-bay-deep transepts. Shallow altar apse.

ST JUDE, Accrington Road. 1912–14 by *Gradwell*. Yellow stone with red-stone trimmings. Square NW tower, its buttresses rising squarely a little above the top. The same motif along the sides. The arcade piers carry blank arches including the clerestory, whereas the arcade arches die against the piers. Low aisles, shallow chancel.

ST OSWALD, Stanhill Road, just outside Blackburn. 1878 by *J.S.M.Aspinall*.

ST THOMAS, Lambeth Street. 1864–5 by *E.G.Paley*. The W front has two identical gables, for nave and S aisle. The N porch is close to the E end, with polygonal cross-gabled apse. Plate and geometrical tracery.

HOLY TRINITY, Mount Pleasant. 1837–46* by *Sharpe* for the

* These are Mr Jolley's dates.

Commissioners. A large church (cost £5,019) with short nave, aisles, transepts, and a straight-ended chancel. The aisles have tall Perp windows, transept end walls and chancel E wall groups of tall two-light, three-light, two-light windows. Inside slim compound piers, and a flat ceiling. An elegant interior.

SOUTH

CHRIST CHURCH, Grimshaw Park. 1857–9 by *Taylor & Foggett*. Dec with a SE steeple. Near by the picturesque SCHOOL with a turret. This is of 1857 too.

WEST AND SOUTH WEST

ST BARNABAS, Addison Street. 1884–6 by *W. S. Varley*.

ST FRANCIS (R.C.), *see* Livesey.

SACRED HEART (R.C.), Preston New Road. 1937–8 by *E. Bower Norris* and *S. M. Reynolds*. Brick, Romanesque, with a NW campanile.

ST LUKE, Bank Top. 1877 by *Robinson*. The NW steeple of 1908. Late C13 style. Wide nave with wooden pointed tunnel-vault. Low round piers and aisle passages. Quatrefoil clerestory windows. Short chancel.

ST MARK, Buncer Lane. One of the most interesting churches of Blackburn, even if internally not an architectural success. The architect is *Sharpe*, and the church was built in 1836–8. The style adopted is Romanesque rather than Norman, i.e. with Lombard friezes. There is also a big tower, but that is placed in a way as un-Victorian as it is un-Romanesque. It stands above the sanctuary, followed only by the low polygonal apse. The effect is a harassing interior – wide, aisleless, with transepts and then suddenly contracting into a narrow chancel. The tower has an octagonal top with gables to all sides and a spire. – STAINED GLASS. The E window is signed by *Thomas Willement* and dated 1838. One large, bad figure.

ST MATTHEW, Cambridge Street. 1886 by *W. G. Habershon*.

ST PHILIP, St Philip's Street. 1880–1 by *John Lowe*.

ST SILAS, Preston New Road. 1894 by *Paley & Austin*. The church has their seriousness and dignity but nothing of their spatial ingenuity. Dec style. High W tower with higher stair-turret, embraced by the aisles. Yellow stone outside, red stone inside. Slim piers, not very high. – STAINED GLASS. Two *Morris* windows, but of 1908, when Morris and Burne-

Jones were both dead. – Adjoining a window by *Holiday*, as late as 1921–3, more restless in the composition.

AUDLEY RANGE CONGREGATIONAL CHURCH. 1889–90 by *Isitt & Verity*. The church has a specially fine E.E. steeple of Pearson derivation. Nave with cross-gables, transept.

OXFORD STREET METHODIST CHURCH. 1873. Latest classical, but with many segment-headed windows. Five-bay front with a five-bay pediment.

BANK HOUSE, Adelaide Terrace. This is another farmhouse left over in mid-C19 houses. Jacobean. Gabled porch; mullioned windows.

8040   BLACKO

BEACON TOWER, N of the village. Little is known of its erection. It has been assumed to be on the site of the Malkin Tower which came into the infamous witchcraft trial of 1612.

3030   BLACKPOOL

INTRODUCTION

The Ministry of Housing and Local Government has issued no list for Blackpool, which means that there are no buildings of architectural or historic interest in the town. It depends of course on what one means by historical and by architectural. The historical interest should certainly not be denied. English social history of the second half of the C19 and the first half of the C20 cannot be written without Blackpool. But *The Buildings of England* are not social historiography. So it is enough here to say this. About 1788 six houses are referred to as 'appropriated for the reception of company'. On engravings of 1840 there seem to be no more houses on the sea front than about twenty. Indeed no development worth following took place until after 1850. The railway had come in 1846, but Central Station was built only in 1863; the first pier was built in the same year. Then things began to happen. The Winter Garden was built in 1875–8 for over £100,000. In 1887 the *Morning Post* wrote: 'Blackpool has discovered the lost art of entertaining . . . [and offers] more fun for less money than anywhere else.'* In 1900 there were about three million visitors; there are now about eight million annually, and the permanent population is up to 150,000, which makes Blackpool the fifth town in size in the whole of Lancashire.

* I owe this passage to Mr John Myerscough of the University of Sussex

As for buildings of architectural interest, the following pages will show what in the eyes of their compiler deserves to be looked at.*

CHURCHES

St John, Church Street. 1878 by *Garlick, Park & Sykes* of Blackpool. Bournemouth would not have gone to local men, which shows at once the lack of aesthetic discrimination which we shall find everywhere at Blackpool. Spacious; of yellow stone, but the interior red ashlar. Lancet and plate tracery; sw tower. Wide nave and wide transepts. Rounded apse. – PULPIT. The tester of wood, openwork filigree, probably of the 1880s.

All Hallows, All Hallows Road, Bispham. This was once the village street of Bispham, but of that one notices nothing any longer except for one minor cottage orné. The church existed in the c12, but now dates from 1883; for, although the s doorway tries hard to be Norman, there are no more than odd stones that are original. The signs of the Zodiac are supposed to go back to what was there. The architect of 1883 was *John Lowe* of Manchester. Rock-faced and terribly mechanical-looking. w tower; aisleless nave. – PLATE. Chalice of 1608.

Christ Church, Abingdon Street. 1865–6. By *J. Medland Taylor*, who proves himself here the brutalist of the 1860s. It is a ruthless building externally, a deliberately confusing one internally. Red brick, with yellow brick, bluish-black brick, and cobble panels. nw tower with pyramid roof, lancets and plate tracery, along the long side with a row of cross-gables. The nave is wide and separated by thin columns from low aisles. Big timber roof, crazily complicated and asymmetrical in the s aisle. The double transepts seem to be filled with timber. Everything is done to avoid beauty.

Sacred Heart (R.C.), Talbot Road, i.e. right in the centre, and hence much larger than the parish church. By *E. W. Pugin*, 1857, enlarged by the amazing e end in 1894. The architects of the enlargement were the successor firm, *Pugin & Pugin*. The nave and aisles are of 1857 and uneventful, but the crossing of 1894 is octagonal, on the principle of Ely Cathedral or rather St Paul's. Transepts and chancel. – STAINED GLASS. The e window by *Wailes*, 1857.

* Perhaps one ought to add to them the first English MONORAIL, 1 m. long. Blackpool also prides itself on having had the first electric TRAMWAY in the world.

ST PAUL, Dickson Road, North Shore. 1898–9 by *Garlick & Sykes*. The tower has not been built.

ST PAUL, Whitegate Drive, Marton. 1909, said to be by *Freeman* of Bolton.

HOLY TRINITY, Dean Street. Built in 1894–5 by *R. K. Freeman*; his *chef d'oeuvre*. Large, yellow stone with red-stone dressings. NW tower with triplets of two-light bell-openings. Dec to Perp features. High nave, triple transept. The aisles are crossed by bridges on arches and have in addition arches high up continued as transverse pointed tunnel-vaults towards the windows. The chancel side walls differ one from the other. The chancel is rib-vaulted in wood. The whole is evidently influenced by Austin & Paley.

ST WILFRID, Mereside Estate. By *Tom Mellor*, 1965–6. A plain brown brick block with a few slim vertical windows from top to bottom. A lower porch at the W end; sacristies to connect the E end with the older vicarage. It is an impressive exterior, but the inside is disappointing.

BAPTIST TABERNACLE, Springfield Road. 1904 by *W. T. Oldrieve & C. A. Hindle* of Manchester. An interesting and dignified design, in a classical, somewhat Italian style, but not at all imitative. Red brick, with a W turret with dome. The long side is along the street. The church is no longer in ecclesiastical use.

RAWCLIFFE STREET METHODIST CHURCH. 1888–9 by *J. H. Burton*. Gothic with NW steeple.

PUBLIC BUILDINGS

TOWN HALL, Talbot Square. 1895–1900 by *Potts, Son & Hennings*. Brick with stone dressings. Jacobean, with a square tower in the middle of a symmetrical façade.

CENTRAL LIBRARY AND ART GALLERY, Queen Street. By *Cullen, Lockhead & Brown*, 1910–11. Brick and yellow stone dressings. Edwardian in style, and with no quirks.

TECHNICAL COLLEGE, Palatine Road. Built in 1936–8 by *Potts, Son & Hennings*. In a free Beaux-Arts classical style. Centre with columns *in antis*, of no known classical details. Big attic.

These are conventional public buildings of a town of the size of Blackpool. The following are Blackpool in its own right.

BLACKPOOL TOWER. 1891–4 by *Maxwell & Tuke*. What a pity its base is wrapped up in a big brick building! Just remember how beautiful are the ascending curves and arches of the Eiffel Tower of 1889, Blackpool's admitted model. However, their tower is 500 ft high, not 984 ft, and has a fussier top with an ogee cap and four little corner domes.

WINTER GARDENS, facing down Victoria Street, and OPERA HOUSE, Church Street. A vast group, all faced in white faience. 1875–8 (Pavilion; £107,000), 1896–7 (Empress Ball Room; £130,000), the opera house rebuilt in 1912 and 1939. The interior is much changed, but the glass dome still exists. It is now over part of the entrance hall.

CASINO, South Shore. The core by *Joseph Emberton*, 1937–8. In the International Modern, but the thin spiral tower adds an appropriate note of gaiety. The rest of the original building has long curved window bands.

DERBY BATHS, Promenade. 1937–9 by the Borough Surveyor (architect *J.C.Robinson*). Large, modernistic. Addition of 1965.

NORTH PIER. Opened in 1863.

CENTRAL PIER. The first pier was built in 1868. The new building at the land end has a flat roof on inverted pyramids. It was put up in 1966–7 (architects: *MacKeith, Dickinson & Partners*).

PERAMBULATION

Blackpool of course is the crowds and the sideshows and the fancy hats and transistors, not the buildings. But if buildings it must be, there are first two HOTELS.

The VICTORIA HOTEL, Promenade, near Chapel Street, with its three storeys and two canted bay windows is still what it was when it was built in 1841. The IMPERIAL HOTEL, Promenade and Derby Street, of 1867–8 cost £50,000 and is the climax of Blackpool *hôtellerie*. It started as the Imperial Hydropathic Establishment. The architects were *Clegg & Jones*. In 1875 followed a new wing (by *Mangnall & Littlewood*). As built it was symmetrical with a tower, but in 1904 a wildly Edwardian part was added by *J.B.Broadbent*.

Between these two much can be filled in. In the very centre close to the Tower is the new store of LEWIS'S, by *Duke & Simpson*, 1962–4, with a closely honeycombed façade to the sea and only one asymmetrical strip of window. It suits its place well. To the S of this group there is then a telling hiatus, mean properties and much loudspeaker stuff. The Victoria

Hotel without this would be quite a dignified little thing. Then from the centre along the front to the N. First, by the town hall and the North Pier the CLIFTON HOTEL of 1865–74, four-storeyed, stuccoed, with segment-headed windows. Then, much larger, of brick and irregular, the METROPOLE HOTEL. Further on, LANSDOWNE CRESCENT, 1864 etc., typically joyless, and the CARLTON HOTEL with two big shaped gables. After that the Imperial. Then the SAVOY HOTEL, brick, symmetrical, decent, by *Lumb & Walton*, *c.* 1913, and CLIFFS, a florid, red brick and yellow terra-cotta pile, by Empress Drive. The CONVALESCENT HOME is much better architecturally than any of these. It is by *Bradshaw, Gass & Hope*, of 1925–7. It lies back so as to present itself more becomingly. Red brick and ample stone dressings, large, monumental, and symmetrical. The style is between late Wren and Vanbrugh. A tower with an ogee cap at the back. Finally the NORBRICK HYDRO HOTEL, rather gloomy with its cemented, embattled walls and its two towers. It is two blocks, not connected physically or visually, and seems to have a complicated story: a house of 1869 plus a large addition of 1915 completing the S wing, plus 1934 the N wing.

Two postscripts. One that there is only one ten-storey block on the front. Apparently there is no demand for flats as there is along the south coast.

The other concerns private building away from the front. Only two qualify. The DISTRICT BANK, former Manchester & County Bank, at the corner of Corporation and Birley Streets has the architecturally best building of Blackpool, one-storeyed with excellent, very large, tripartite and arched windows. It is by *Cooper & Tullis*, of 1881. The second is the WINDMILL at Mereside, a tower mill, still with its four sails.

BLACKROD

ST KATHARINE. 1911 by *R.B.Preston*. Large and conventional. The only distinguishing feature is the NW tower, and that is in its lower part Perp.

SCHOOL (former; now Council Offices), SE of the church. The MHLG says 1799, but this modest gable and these mullioned and transomed windows can hardly be earlier than 1840.

HILTON HOUSE, 1¼ m. SE. Georgian, of five bays and three storeys with two-bay links and two-bay pavilions. Stone surround to the doorway.

BLAWITH

2080

St John Baptist. 1863, according to Mr Fleetwood-Hesketh by *E.G.Paley*. Local rubble and red sandstone dressings. Nave with bellcote and short chancel. Lancets and plate tracery.

Opposite, the ruinous outer wall of the preceding CHAPEL, which was built *c*.1560.

White Borran Cairns, 1½ m. w. Close to the summit of the hill are two round cairns 40 and 20 ft in diameter. Both sites have central depressions, suggesting that they have been opened, but no record of this work survives.

BLEABERRY HAWS *see* TORVER

BLEASDALE

5040

St Eadmor. 1835. Aisleless with lancets under hood-moulds and with a w tower – all cemented. The chancel was built in 1897. The two w windows of the tower look as if they came from the preceding church, which existed in Queen Elizabeth's time.

Bleasdale Tower, 1 m. NW. The house was built about 1840–50 by William Garnett of Lark Hill, Salford and Quernmore near Lancaster. He died in 1863. The house has steep bargeboarded gables. The porch is later.

Blindhurst, 1 m. SE. 1731, and yet still with cross-windows and even three-light mullioned and transomed windows.

Bleasdale Circle, ½ m. NNE. The site consisted of a small barrow beneath which was a grave containing two cremations in collared urns and an incense cup. This structure was surrounded by a ring of eleven posts (now marked by concrete pillars) with outliers forming an entrance on the E, and these in turn were bounded by a ditch. This group was surrounded by a timber palisade (not visible on the ground) 150 ft in diameter, with an entrance on the sw.

BLINDHURST *see* BLEASDALE

BOLTON GREEN FARMHOUSE *see* CHARNOCK RICHARD

BOLTON HALL *see* SALESBURY

BOLTON-LE-SANDS

4060

St Michael. Late Perp, ashlar-faced w tower and arcades. The arcades are of standard elements, and the one oblong pier

marks the place of the ROOD SCREEN. Good hammerbeam
roof in the nave. The rest is 1813 (nave), totally victorianized,
and 1846 (chancel). – SCULPTURE. Two Anglo-Saxon fragments, one with specially fat interlace. – CHANDELIER. Of
brass, with two tiers of arms; C18. – PLATE. Chalice, 1725.

ST MARY (R.C.). 1882–4 by *E. Simpson*. Thin SW porch tower
with quite irresponsible details. High nave and chancel, round
granite piers. Chancel arch with two tiers of responds. The E
window with geometrical tracery high up.

THE NOOK, E of the above. The first house on the l. is of 1665
and has mullioned windows, their hood-moulds connected.
A house on the r. is dated 1701 and has a symmetrical three-
bay façade with a simple Yorkshire lintel and the upper
windows of 3–2–3 lights.

BONDS *see* GARSTANG

BORWICK HALL

5070

Borwick Hall consists of a C14 pele tower with turret on one
corner, but no preserved interior features, and an Elizabethan
house of *c.*1590–5 incorporating the tower. The house was
built for Robert Bindloss, a Kendal clothier. It has a façade
which would be symmetrical if it were not for the pele.
Mullioned and transomed windows, recessions and projections, a porch about in the middle, leading into a one-
storeyed hall, and small gables. The main staircase has as its
top newel post and railing a delightful display of short Tuscan
columns of two gauges, six on the newel and three more as a
railing. The GATEHOUSE is dated 1650 but is still in the
Elizabethan style. So are the STABLES attached to it. The
upper floor was not a barn but sleeping accommodation.

Of a CHAPEL on the Green no more than two or three stones are
left.

AQUEDUCT. Late C18, of stone. One arch; fine proportions
(MHLG). The aqueduct carries the canal over the river.

BRANTWOOD *see* CONISTON

BRATHAY
1 m. SW of Ambleside

3000

HOLY TRINITY. Built in 1836 by Giles Redmayne of Brathay
Hall, a wealthy man who had made his money in the ribbon-
trade in London. A large, rendered building, joyless in its

utilitarian Romanesque. SW tower. Some windows have received Victorian tracery.

BRATHAY HALL. Late C18. Five bays, two and a half storeys, with a pretty semicircular porch with Adamish columns.

BRETHERTON

4020

ST JOHN BAPTIST. 1840 by *Sharpe* for the Commissioners. Cost: £1,058. Four bays, long, square-headed Perp windows and buttresses between. Thin W steeple with porch under, open to N and S as well as W. The chancel was added in 1909, in a correct Perp.

BANK HALL, ⅞ m. W. A large Jacobean brick house, enlarged in 1832–3, but derelict at the time of writing. The Jacobean parts are supposed to date from 1608 (*see* below). They are characterized by bold shaped gables, consisting of two convex quadrants below the semicircular top. The back of the house has a big, square, and very high staircase tower. The stair balustrade has balusters looking rather mid than early C17. The main windows have transoms. The work of 1832–3 comprises the porch on which the date 1608 is recorded, and the whole W wing. Mr J. Haworth assigns it to *Webster*.

CARR HOUSE (Elder Museum of Dolls). Built, according to the inscription over the porch entrance, by 'Thomas Stones of London, haberdasher and Andrewe Stones of Amsterdam merchant' in 1613. Brick, with flat quoins, of two storeys with a three-storeyed porch. Its pediment is the one flaw; mullioned windows, and this, as indeed the whole roof, is a recent remodelling. The composition is absolutely symmetrical. The porch has above the entrance one five-light window per floor, the side parts have one four-light window per floor each, and in addition there are slightly projecting wings, each also with one four-light window per floor. That is all; but it is sufficient to convey a feeling of great clarity and determination.

BRIERCLIFFE

8030

ST JAMES, at Haggate, 1¾ m. SE of Brierfield church. 1840. The architect, according to Mr Robert Jolley, was *Sharpe*. W tower, in its upper part octagonal, and with a spire. Twin lancet windows and thin buttresses. Three galleries inside.

EXTWISTLE HALL, 1 m. SE. A low l. half and a towering r. half. In this, in its recessed part, the hall window, a spectacular affair of five plus five lights and two transoms. Above the doorway a horizontally placed oval, nearly always a sign of the later C17.

BRIERFIELD

Brierfield is not noticeable as an entity. It just leads from Burnley to Nelson, and as for buildings it has hardly any worth talking about. The MHLG lists three, only one of them Grade II and that, the FRIENDS' MEETING HOUSE, appears here under Nelson (p. 181).

ST LUKE. 1871–3 by *J. Green.* C13 style, with a SW tower of fanciful outline and detail. The top has a steep pyramid roof. It is buildings like this that make people refuse to take Victorian architecture seriously.

(ST ANNE, Old Lawn Booth. 1837. With lancet windows. MHLG)

PRIMITIVE METHODIST CHURCH, Burnley Road. Built in 1864. Five bays with a five-bay pediment and subdued Italianate forms. No longer in ecclesiastical use.

(WHEATLEY LANE METHODIST CHURCH. 1867. One composition of church, house, and school, the latter dated 1859. Italianate. MHLG).

BRINDLE

ST JAMES. The W tower is Perp, and so is the N chapel, unless the blank arch above the E window indicates an earlier date. The rest of two C19 dates. The nave was built in 1817, taking in the former N aisle so as to give it the suitable width for galleries. These have been taken out. The chancel was rebuilt in 1869–70. The nave has large three-light windows with intersecting tracery and a transom to indicate the existence of galleries. – FONTS. A small one may be elementary Late Perp or perhaps 1660s. – Another font is of the Georgian baluster type. – CHANDELIER. 1792. The body of the usual Baroque shape. Two tiers of arms. – PLATE. Paten, 1714–15; Chalice inscribed 1729; Chalice by *R. L.*

ST JOSEPH (R.C.), at the S end of the grounds of Brindle Lodge. Built in 1780 and large, if of that date. Four bays of big arched windows. The interior all altered.

BRINDLE LODGE. Built for William Heatley, who died in 1840. The ashlar-faced exterior looks early C19. The front has seven bays and two storeys. The doorway is tripartite with segmental fanlight, and looks not beyond suspicion. The porch of two unfluted Ionic columns looks as if it had been overstretched later. And as for the sumptuous plasterwork inside, the MHLG grades the building I, largely on the strength of this, it seems. But can it be as early as the exterior? Such a date appears highly improbable, and it is actually said that, when a Whitehead bought the house in 1869, he made considerable improvements.

TOWER, in the grounds, a folly. Round, with an archway attached on one side, a piece of crenellated wall on the other. All red sandstone.

BROADLEYS see CARTMEL FELL

BROOKHOUSE see CATON

BROUGHTON
Near Preston

5030

ST JOHN BAPTIST. Ashlar-built Perp w tower, dated 1533. The tower arch dies into the imposts. w respond of a Perp arcade. But the church was rebuilt in 1823, in smoother ashlar, and with lancet windows. The chancel is of 1905–6 and proclaims its architects, *Austin & Paley*, at once. On the N side closely set, narrow, segment-headed arcade arches, on the s one low wide bay and then two slender narrow segment-headed windows with stepped-up sills. – CHANDELIER of brass, dated 1817. Two tiers of arms. – PLATE. Two Chalices, inscribed 1782.

ST MARY (R.C.), Fernyhalgh, 1⅝ m. ESE. 1792–4. Brick, with long and wide arched windows. Two-bay transepts. Only the w bay of the nave has two tiers of windows. This is because of the w gallery. So it is functional, but no one will say that it is aesthetically successful. The façade has a semicircular porch with Tuscan columns. This dates from before 1870. The church was redecorated in 1844–7.

w of the Catholic church is the CATHOLIC SCHOOL, a very dignified little stone building. Two-storeyed, three-bay centre, and one-storey-one-bay wings with pediments on pilaster strips. The building is dated 1836.

BROUGHTON EAST

3080

ST PETER. 1892–4 by *Paley, Austin & Paley*, and eminently characteristic of them. High crossing tower, with stair-turret and recessed spire. Nice unexpected detailing of the bell-openings. Aisleless nave, transepts, chancel, all with tiled roofs. Straight-headed Perp windows with Austin & Paley detailing. Porch attached to the w bay – that also is Austin & Paley.*

59 BROUGHTON LODGE. Late C18 house of five bays and two and a half storeys. Porch with unfluted Ionic columns. Two pavilions with pediments and contained Venetian windows. (Fine drawing room. NMR)

(HAMPSFIELD HALL. C17 with mullioned windows. MHLG)

(On HAMPSFIELD FELL are two ornamental towers; one of them, called the HOSPICE, is dated 1846, and is open in the front so that one can sit inside and enjoy the view.)

2080   BROUGHTON-IN-FURNESS

St MARY MAGDALENE. A consecration 1547. But the s doorway is Late Norman, with waterleaf capitals. The E window is Perp; several of the other windows are of the early C16. In 1874 much of the detail was renewed and the N aisle built in a neo-Norman way. The sw tower is of 1900. – FONT. Octagonal, with a goblet bowl and shields. – PLATE. Chalice by *Joyce Issod.*

The MARKET PLACE with its trees is handsome. On its s side is the TOWN HALL, of seven bays, not detached, with arcading formerly open. It dates from the late C18. In the middle of the Market Place stands an OBELISK erected in 1810. On the N side are the gates of Broughton Tower.

BROUGHTON TOWER. A spacious mansion built round a C14 pele tower. On the N side the tower is visible up to about 60 ft. Its basement is tunnel-vaulted, as usual, and the spiral staircase survives. The Gilpin Sawreys in the mid C18 (one rainwater-head 1744, a bell 1747, two rainwater-heads in the wings 1777) built the house and especially the charming centre of the s front. The porch with clustered shafts is uncommonly pretty. The windows are all ogee-headed. In 1882–3 the wings were added, keeping on the front in harmony with the Georgian work. In the hall is a re-erected French early C16 portal (two angels at the top), in the dining room an Italian Renaissance chimneypiece. Nothing seems to be known of them.

ECCLE RIGGS, ¾ m. s. Dated 1865. Asymmetrical, Tudor, not of special interest.

* I was unable to see the interior.

BROWNEDGE see BAMBER BRIDGE

BURNLEY

8030

Burnley has a sizeable Perp parish church, but Pococke in 1750 still called it only 'a small market-town with some share of the woollen trade'. Market-rights go back to 1293. Population in 1801 was under 5,000. It is now about 78,000. The growth is due to the textile industry, first spinning, after 1880 more weaving. But coal-mining had also been done ever since the C17. Textile prosperity continued into the C20. Between 1900 and 1914 twelve large mills were built. Burnley was favourably placed on the Blackburn–Todmorden or Blackburn–Bacup road, and on the Liverpool–Leeds Canal which reached Burnley from Liverpool in 1796, from Leeds in 1801. The town has little of architectural interest, but the hills come close to its centre, though the mills come yet closer.*

INNER BURNLEY

One can hardly write at the present moment about the town centre. So much is under reconstruction: streets are being obliterated and others made. Of worthwhile architecture this overdue renewal has not yet produced anything. The KEIRBY HOTEL (by *H. Hubbard Ford*, 1959–60) is not promising; it is showy and restless.

ST PETER, Church Street. N of the centre and pleasantly set in trees by the high retaining wall of the river Don. It is a church of substantial size, the successor of one of before 1122. It is basically Late Perp, with a W tower, a long nave with aisles, and a long chancel. However, considering it in terms of Late Perp, one may very soon become suspicious of the height in relation to length, of the very even small crenellation, and decidedly of the windows in two tiers. They have admittedly the uncusped arched lights of the Perp style, but two tiers means galleries, and galleries means nearly always the Georgian age. As one steps in, the impression is at once confirmed by the very tall, very slim octagonal piers. The S aisle dates indeed from 1790, the N aisle from 1803, and the arcade piers from 1854. At that time the clerestory was built too, and the very pretty pierced wooden chancel arch made. The small ogee-headed N doorway is the only purely Georgian

* It would have been interesting to say more about the mills. This I could not do. Much will be found in Walter Bennett's Burnley vol. III.

feature; the rest of the work of *c*.1800 was evidently done
under inspiration from the Late Perp work, for which a
contract of 1533 has been preserved. Genuine C15 work is the
w tower and the tracery of the N chapel (Townley Chapel). –
FONT. Octagonal. 1532; with the Townley arms. Also a
monster and a goat. – COMMUNION RAIL. Elegantly convex
front and elegant balusters. From the private chapel of Townley
Hall; C18. – STAINED GLASS. Several windows by *Kempe*.
– PLATE. Flagon by *W.D.*, 1722. – MONUMENTS. Coffin lid
with a foliated cross, C14? (s chapel). – Charles Townley
† 1805, collector of the Townley Marbles, one of the constituent
parts of the British Museum. Simple sarcophagus tablet with
inscription, partly in Greek. By *Nollekens*. – In the s chapel
three eminently Victorian monuments: Clara Thursby † 1807,
Sir James Yorke Scarlett (with a bust) † 1871, and Mrs
Townley † 1874, by *Saul*, 1881.

ST JAMES, Bethesda Street. 1846–9 by *H.P.Horner*. A Commissioners' church (cost: £2,556). The NW steeple was added
in 1869. Were the tracery and other things altered at that
time too?

ST MARY (R.C.), Yorkshire Street. By *Weightman & Hadfield*,
1846–9. Dec, the w tower, designed on the pattern of Hecking-
ton in Lincolnshire, unfortunately not built. Large church and
an early example of the antiquarian respect established
by Pugin. Nave and aisles, transepts, chancel chapels, and a
straight-ended chancel. The chapel arcades have rich foliate
capitals. All the rest is very subdued. – ALTAR by *E.W.Pugin*,
richly carved. It dates from the 1860s and was paid for by the
steward of the Townley estates whose mare had won The
Oaks and by Col. Townley's shorthorn keeper. The N
chapel is the Townley Chapel and was decorated in 1879.

BETHESDA CONGREGATIONAL CHURCH, Bethesda Street.
1879 by *W.Waddington & Son* of Burnley. Round-arched
windows with Gothic crocket capitals. Symmetrical, but a NW
tower planned. A tolerable façade.

AEMON BAPTIST CHAPEL, Red Lion Street. 1850–2. Italianate.

OLD TOWN HALL, Manchester Road. 1885–8 by *Holtom &
Fox* of Dewsbury. Symmetrical, in an enriched Cinquecento,
with a copper dome. To its r. the former MECHANICS'
INSTITUTION (now Casino Club), 1855 with a wing of 1888,
much better architecturally. In Barry's *palazzo* style. Five
bays, two storeys.

POLICE AND MAGISTRATES' COURT. 1951–5 by *Bradshaw*,

Gass & Hope. Ashlar, with a tetrastyle pedimented portico. Fifteen by seventeen bays.

LIBRARY. Opposite the former. 1929–30 by *Arthur Race*, the Borough Engineer and Surveyor. Beaux-Arts classicism, with an entrance loggia with two giant columns. This has so much more body than the town hall.

MUNICIPAL COLLEGE, Ormerod Road. 1905–9 by *G.H. Pickles*, another engineer. Large, symmetrical, gabled. The details Jacobean to Stuart in a typical mixture of *c*.1900.

CENTRAL STATION. 1964–6 by *R.L.Moorcroft*, architect to the Midland Region.

Some search for private buildings worth singling out has not produced more than the dignified houses in BANK PARADE above the parish church, especially Nos 64–8.

OUTER BURNLEY

WEST

ALL SAINTS, Padiham Road. 1846–9 by *Weightman & Hadfield*. Paid for by the Dugdale family, cotton manufacturers, and by Sir James Kay Shuttleworth. W tower with broach-spire. Correct interior, early for its date, early, that is, for antiquarian accuracy (but cf. St Mary, above). – (PAINTING. Said to be Venetian.)

ST JOHN BAPTIST, Gannow Lane. 1880 by *Waddington & Son*. An excellent tower by these local architects, with lancet bell-openings and blank arcading. Plain parapet on top. Big roof to the nave. The interior is alas an anti-climax. The arcades are perfectly normal, but in order to reduce the aisles to passages, the arcades are pushed close to the walls, a preposterous deformation.

HOLY TRINITY, Accrington Road. 1835–6 by *Vulliamy*. A Commissioners' church (cost £2,918) with the usual features such as paired lancets. They are here used also for the bell-openings of the W tower. Altogether the church has an impressive sheerness. Three galleries and open timber roof.

NORTH

ST ANDREW, Colne Road. 1867 by *J. Medland Taylor*. SW tower with broach-spire. W attachment, aisleless nave; polygonal apse. – Nearly all the STAINED GLASS is by *Kempe* (e.g. W window, date commemorated 1894).

ST CUTHBERT, Townley Street. 1906 by *R.B.Proctor*. Brick,

a material rarely used for churches in this stone area. sw turret. Central buttress in the w wall and tall windows l. and r.

St Margaret, Abel Street. 1897–8 by *Thomas Bell* of Burnley. Red brick (*see* above) and yellow terracotta. No tower.

SOUTH

St Catherine, Todmorden Road. 1897 by *J. Medland Taylor*. Not of special interest.

St Matthew, St Matthew Street. 1879 by *W. Waddington & Son*. c13 style, with only a sw turret.

St Stephen, Oxford Road. 1879 by *Green* of Portsmouth. Geometrical tracery: nw tower with higher stair-turret.

Manchester Road Methodist Church. 1905 by *Waddington, Son & Dunkerley*. One of the most prominent churches of Burnley. Fine, slender sw steeple. Individual façade.

Former Methodist Chapel, Todmorden Road. 1860–1. Grandly Victorian classical. Five bays with a pediment all across. Loggia of giant Corinthian columns.

Barcroft, near the sw corner of Townley Park. This is the only farmhouse worth mentioning within the Burnley boundaries. It has an extremely interesting archway dated 1636. The stepped top suits that date, but can the Norman zigzag frill of the arch be 1636? The house itself has a façade on the E-scheme with a date 1614. A few of the windows still have the uncusped arched lights of the c16. (At the back is a large, transomed hall window.)

And so at last to the one outstanding monument of Burnley, Townley Hall.

Townley Hall. Townley Hall in the Middle Ages was a courtyard house. The great hall was in the w range, chapel and gateway in the E range. The house probably still has the same extent as it had then, but in 1700 the E range was demolished. So what remains is three ranges of about the same length. Only the s range has medieval masonry in evidence. The walls here are 6 ft thick. The later periods of building activity are those of Richard Townley who died in 1628, of another Richard Townley who made changes in 1725–30, and of Peregrine Edward Townley, who employed *Jeffry Wyatt* (Wyatville) in 1817.* Seen from the E, the two fronts of the

* Charles Townley, whose famous collection of antique statuary was in No. 14 Queen Anne's Gate and is now in the British Museum, came in between. He lived from 1737 to 1805.

wings have thin diagonal buttresses dating probably from
c.1725. The recessed W range has a porch by *Wyatt*. The
fenestration all round is mostly Jacobean. A puzzle is the small
parabolic doorway in the S range. Is it simply made up of parts
that were about, or is it a later C17 fancy? That time,
especially in Yorkshire, did odd things like that to doorways.
The date of the battlements all along is not known. The
W side of the W range provides a very different picture. Here
we have a typically Early Georgian façade. Five bays, two
storeys, and all openings with rather clumsy Gibbs surrounds. To the l. of this is Jacobean fenestration, to the r.
a long window with round arch and details looking decidedly
Early Victorian. The same windows go on round the corner
on the S side of the S range. They are in fact much earlier
than they seem. They belong to *Wyatt*'s alterations.

The porch leads straight into a grand and sumptuous
decorated HALL, two storeys high. This is what Richard 51
Townley made his Gibbsian façade for. One can now see that
the façade is not simply windows put into the older wall, but a
doubling of the depth of the former hall range. His *stuccadori*
were *Francesco Vassali* and his assistant *Martino Quadri*. Vassali
is known to have worked for *Gibbs* at Ditchley. He was in
partnership there with Artari,* and Artari, in partnership with
Bagutti, was the stuccoist for Gibbs's churches of St Martin-
in-the-Fields and St Peter, Vere Street. They also did the
chapel at Canons, now at Great Witley (Worcs.), all in the
twenties. The hall has coupled pilasters and two splendid
chimneypieces with big scrolls and two pieces of antique
statuary against a stucco baldacchino. The pilasters carry a
full cornice above which are small windows with penetrations
towards the stucco ceiling. Many medallions with busts. The
DOOR between porch and hall is dated 1530 and comes from
Standish Hall. It has decoration characteristic of that date and
done in thick relief. S of the hall is the Georgian STAIRCASE,
cantilevered, with wrought-iron handrail and a stucco ceiling.
The S range contains two large rooms made by *Wyatt*. They
have stucco decoration of rather heavy Regency forms. The
elegant chimneypiece in one of them must be late C18 and
may not be *in situ*. N of the hall is a Jacobean staircase and then,
in the NW corner, the CHAPEL, transferred here with some of
its furnishings when the E range was pulled down. There is a

* As he was at Sutton Scarsdale (Derbyshire).

fine carved frieze of *c*.1500 and other woodwork including an early C16 door with linenfold panelling and other panelling with the date 1628. In the N range are two rooms of the 1620s, the first with panelling of a very unusual pattern reminiscent of Chippendale Chinese, the second with a small angle chimneypiece of *c*.1725 with an urn in the overmantel.*

6070 ## BURROW HALL

Built for Robert Fenwick after 1732 and about 1739. The Fenwicks were North Country gentry but Robert was a lawyer. It has a fine façade of seven bays with a carved three-bay pediment and an unassuming Ionic porch, and at the back larger, but entirely utilitarian wings. The size of the front would not lead anybody to expect the lavish display of first-class stucco-work inside, in the style of the Italians such as *Vassali* whom Gibbs liked to employ. The ornament is typically 1740, and there are medallions with busts in profile everywhere,‡ deities, allegories, and also Milton and Newton. Some doorways have elegantly detailed pediments. The staircase with its balustrade of slim turned balusters and its carved tread-ends is separated from the entrance hall side by two Roman Doric columns. The stucco-work extends to the principal first-floor room: Flora in the centre.

Handsome STABLES with two projecting wings. In the centre and at the ends of the wings broken pediments with lunette windows.

The Roman fort of GALACUM is sited on the promontory between the Leck Beck and the River Lune. At least four periods of occupation were recorded in recent excavations, but the exact form and history of the site are still vague.

4010 ## BURSCOUGH

ST JOHN, Burscough Bridge. 1829–31 by *D. Stewart*, a Commissioners' church, costing £3,340. Façade with four polygonal buttresses carrying uncouth embattled pinnacles. Also a bell-turret. Two-light windows with incorrect Perp tracery. The three galleries have been preserved.

BURSCOUGH PRIORY, 1½ m. SSW. Founded *c*.1190 for Augustinian canons. In 1296 there were a prior and six canons. The

---

*Several priest holes are mentioned by Squires and Haward.
‡ For such medallions cf. Townley Hall Burnley, the Music Room at Lancaster, and also Lumley Castle (County Durham).

church had transepts, a central tower, and a N aisle. The cloister was on the s side. All that survives above ground is the two piers between N transept and crossing plus the semi-octagonal NE arcade respond and a stump of the chancel N wall. This must date from the late C13.

CALDER VALE

5040

St John Evangelist, Oakenclough, ½ m. NE. Quite large, and yet in a place where there can never have been a congregation. The church was built in 1863* on land given by W. J. Garnett (*see* Quernmore and Bleasdale and also Salford, South Lancashire). w tower with pyramid roof, Perp features, the interior brick-lined. – STAINED GLASS. Three windows by *Morris & Co.*, but all C20.

At Calder Vale is still the mill which two Quakers, Richard and Jonathan Jackson, built in 1835, a building of nine bays and four storeys, and the terraces of workers' cottages, all in a wooded seclusion – a typical settlement of early factory industry.

CANON WINDER *see* FLOOKBURGH

CAPERNWRAY

5070

Capernwray Hall was built in 1844 by *Edmund Sharpe* for 74 George Marton. It is a grand ashlar-faced mansion in the Perp style – not the Dec, as one would expect from Sharpe. The front is symmetrical, with a big porch with angle turrets and an oriel. The only asymmetrical feature is one canted bay window. The staircase hall is open to the top, and has a hammerbeam roof. The dining room has a panelled ceiling and a good Gothic chimneypiece. (The SCREEN of the minstrels' gallery comes from St Mary, Lancaster.) George Marton also built the (former) CHAPEL, ¼ m. NW, with its SW tower and geometrical tracery as well as lancets. The former is most probably a later Victorian alteration. It is known that *Paley* did something at the Hall.

CARK HALL *see* FLOOKBURGH

CARNFORTH

4070

Carnforth is the architecturally most unrewarding Lancashire town. Apart from the church there is nothing one would seek

* The architect, Mr Buttress tells me, was *Corrie*.

out. It is a railway town, and the railway only reached it in 1857. It is also a town of ironworks. The Haematite Iron (i.e. steel) Company was established in 1864 (cf. Barrow).

CHRIST CHURCH. 1875, with a N aisle of 1900. By *Brade & Smales* (P. Fleetwood-Hesketh). Large, and not uninteresting in the management of s aisle and s transept. No tower.

CARR HOUSE *see* BRETHERTON

CARTER PLACE HALL *see* HASLINGDEN

CARTMEL

3070

CARTMEL PRIORY. Cartmel Priory was founded in 1188 by William Marshall, Earl of Pembroke, for Augustinian Canons. It was spared at the Dissolution because it was also the parish church. The decision of the Chancellor of the Duchy was that it should 'stand still'. So we have here a complete priory church, and although, apart from the gatehouse, no buildings for the canons have come down to us, the church can still give us an unparalleled impression of the relation of scale between such a building and the little town at its feet. For the architectural historian moreover Cartmel is of special importance because it can teach what forms were used *c*.1190 and in the following twenty or thirty years. They will come as a surprise to many.

25   EXTERIOR. Of the earliest building phase are the chancel, the transepts, and the N wall of the nave, but little of features has been left unaltered. Looking at the chancel, e.g., what one sees is the s chapel with its splendid display of flowing tracery in windows of four and five lights. It will be shown that this is likely to date from the 1340s. The small clerestory windows look Perp. The E window is decidedly Perp and of enormous size. It has nine lights and much panel tracery. The E window of the N chapel, now of the vestry, is Perp again, and the N chapel windows are the same. So there is nothing of *c*.1190 etc. here except the massive walls and the broad buttresses with very slight set-offs.

The transepts have a little more of the early work to show. In the N transept N wall are two blocked lancets and a round arch, also blocked, and looking earlier than the lancets. It must have been the access doorway to the dormitory, but how can it then be cutting into lancet windows? We shall have an answer later. Perp window high up. In the E wall a broad Perp window, and in the w wall one shafted lancet too, and in the least restored state. The s transept s wall has just such an upper doorway, and this one undoubtedly Norman. The explanation is that the cloister was begun on that side and later shifted to the N. In the E wall is a blocked lancet, in the w wall a blocked Norman window and a recess below which was probably the book cupboard inside the cloister. There is more minor evidence of the existence of a cloister.

The nave was begun at the same time as the E parts, though it was not continued for a long time. Proof of this early start is the gorgeous s doorway which led into the cloister. It has three orders of detached shafts and a highly decorated round arch. The motifs are of simple geometrical types. The hood-mould ends in a snaky turn. The N doorway is E.E., with stiff-leaf capitals and dogtooth. Was this the end of the first build? The interior will indicate an answer.

The nave is remarkably short and has no portal other than the two mentioned. Was it meant to be longer? The windows are Perp, and Perp is the surprising top stage of the tower, surprising in that it is put on the early square walls of the lower stage diagonally, at an angle of 45 degrees, a structurally dubious but visually entertaining motif.

INTERIOR. The E parts belong clearly to the s doorway. The decorative motifs of this re-appear first of all in the two-bay chancel arcade, though the arch mouldings are finer. But zigzag, also combined into lozenges, is present prominently, and the arches are round. But the arch from the N transept into the N chancel aisle has them also, and this is quite sharply pointed, and pointed also are the other arches into the transept, from w as well as E. And as for capitals, the same basic type is applied everywhere, from the chancel arcade to the arches between transepts and nave aisles. Basic type; for it is in many cases left basic, but in others carved into, and where that is done, the motifs are without exception post-Norman, i.e. what nobody would call anything but E.E.: crockets and even early stiff-leaf (small leaves, close to the bell). So the N doorway may well mark the end of this one campaign, a campaign running from c.1190 to c.1220. In favour of such an interpretation is the fact that lancet windows occur, as we have seen, in the transepts. They also occur at the E end of the chancel, N and s. And the chancel triforium, admittedly of necessity later than the arcades below, consists entirely of a long row, originally unbroken, of small pointed arches on

E.E. shafts. The clerestory above is evidently interfered with, and the roof is in fact a restoration of the C17. That is the evidence. Now some supplementary facts. The arcade piers are of eight shafts, quite sturdy. The N chapel is rib-vaulted, and the ribs have the unexpectedly plain profile of just a single chamfer.* The SEDILIA, cut into by the Harrington tomb, are again purely E.E. The clerestory is rough and must be partly due to the C17 reconditioning of which more anon. That leaves the N transept, where it turns out that the Perp E window has E.E. jambs, i.e. replaces lancets, and that the mysterious round-headed doorway which cuts into a N lancet is indeed, in spite of the round arch, in its details of c.1300. The crossing piers are of the same type as the others. So are the nave E responds. A few capitals were carved with leaves, but the rest was left uncarved, as it was obviously decided to do the nave cheaply. The coarse masonry, the piers, etc., are C15. Three bays only, though wide bays, octagonal piers and double-chamfered arches, reasonable features, after the demonstrative display of the E parts. Display also, though of a more sophisticated kind, is the details of the Dec S chapel, the SEDILIA with their nodding ogee arches and the small PISCINA, the two delightful figured corbels for the former roof timbers, and of course the Harrington tomb. Finally the interior of the crossing tower, above the wooden floor of the bell-chamber. One can here see how the diagonally placed upper stage is supported. The square lower stage had its four corners filled by heavy, raw, unmoulded pointed arches set diagonally. They carry the top stage. It seems a hazardous arrangement, as the diagonal arches stand on the apexes of the high crossing arches below. Still – the tower has not given trouble. So to the furnishings.

FURNISHINGS. STALLS and SCREEN. The stalls are of the C15, as they have the initials of a Prior William.‡ They have poppyheads and MISERICORDS Among them are the following representations. S: the *signum triciput*, the Pelican in her piety, an angel with a shield, an ape with a flask, a mermaid, Alexander carried into the sky by eagles, a dragon, a peacock, birds. – N: the unicorn, a green man, a griffin, a face, hounds, the elephant and castle. – The WEST SCREEN and the STALL BACKS are the gift of George Preston of

* Capitals for vaulting also at the W end of the S chapel and the E ends of the aisles.

‡ One was elected in 1418, another in 1441.

Holker Hall, who generously contributed to restoring the church in 1618–23, when it was badly in need of restoration. The roof e.g. is due to him. The elements and the details of stalls and screen are equally interesting. There are slender columns trailed round by vine and decorated by Instruments of the Passion, and very elaborate openwork tracery panels between them, of a type initially French Flamboyant but taken over by the North of England already about 1500. They are proof of a true Gothic Revivial here. In the rood screen the tracery panels are on hinges. – FONT COVER. Simple, dated 1640. – CHANDELIER. Of brass, 1734, with two tiers of arms. – SCULPTURE. Bronze group of the Virgin asleep, St Joseph, and the Child. By *Josephine de Vasconcellos*, 1966. – STAINED GLASS. A certain number of whole figures of the mid C15 is preserved in the E window. More of this Cartmel glass is now at Cartmel Fell and in the church of Bowness in Westmorland. – In the S chapel small but beautiful parts of an early or mid C14 Jesse window. In the N chapel also bits of figures in two windows. – PLATE. Cup, Cover Paten, and Plate, 1667–8, the former two by *Marmaduke Best*, York, the latter by *R.D.*, London; Cup and Paten, 1694, London; two Flagons, 1736 and 1739, London.

MONUMENTS. The Harrington tomb is one of the best of its 15 date in England. It is not quite but almost certain that the effigies are of the first Lord Harrington who died in 1347. He also no doubt provided the S chapel. The architectural setting is disturbed, as the middle part of the two-bay canopy clearly shows. The monument is not in its original place either. One can see that the short sides are meant to be exposed. Sculpturally the monument is of prime importance. The base 16 frieze of bedesmen crouching on the ground and reading is of a poignancy almost like Sluter's *pleureurs*, though of course on so small a scale that deeper emotion can hardly be aroused in the spectator. The monument has in addition *pleureurs* or 17 mourners, and they are not placed in niches but carved without any architectural surround direct out of the same stone as the effigies. This is a unique feature. The posts of the canopy are carved too, with shields, square fleurons, and also figures, the Virgin and the Christ on a foliated cross being especially fine. Both are of types internationally current in the early C14. The canopy has ogee arches and a straight top with leaf motifs and on it Christ showing his wounds on the one side, the Coronation of the Virgin on the other. Inside a ceiling of wooden boards and on three of them remains of important PAINTING: medallions, complete and fragmentary, of the Signs of the Evangelists, and the feet of a large seated Christ. They look c.1300 rather than c.1350. The ceiling ought to be investigated. – Prior William of Walton † 1292. Slab with cross and inscription in Lombard lettering. Now in a C14 recess in the chancel N wall. – Effigy of an Augustinian Canon; C13 (S chapel). – Preston family; 1646. Painting on canvas with coat of arms and inscription recording the Preston family and especially George Preston (see above) and what he did for the church (W wall, centre). – Sir William Lowther † 1705 and Dame Katherine Lowther † 1700 (S chapel). Busts in an oval medallion with putti l. and r. and an urn on top. – Sir Thomas Lowther of Holker Hall † 1745 (S chapel). A putto holds a portrait medallion. An excellent piece. – James Newby † 1834 by *Fawcett* of Liverpool. With a big draped urn. – Lord Frederick Charles Cavendish † 1881 (cf. Barrow-in-Furness). By *Thomas Woolner*, 1885. White marble effigy on an alabaster tomb-chest.

GATEHOUSE. This, as has been said, is the only part of the priory left. It is a simple C14 building with a high archway and two long windows of ogee lights high up. The gable side has a stepped C17 window. The building is now part of the Square and has nothing visually to do with the church. The SQUARE extends to the church, however, and it is visually enjoyable everywhere. A bridge divides it in two. The best house is close to the church, an early C18 house of five bays with arched, keyed-in windows and a doorway with a big segmental pediment. More attractive houses in CAVENDISH STREET (through the gatehouse) and also E of the priory.

(FRIENDS' MEETING HOUSE, Height, ½ m. N of High Newton, 2½ m. SE of Newby Bridge. 1677, but with sashed windows. It is now partly a cottage and partly empty.)

₄₀₈₀   CARTMEL FELL

ST ANTHONY. Far away in the fells. Built about 1505, according to a deposition of Anthony Knipe made in 1561 to the effect that his father and others had built the church about fifty-five years before. Unfinished W tower with an (aesthetically successful) low-pitch saddleback roof. Transepts as shallow as recesses. Chimney on the vestry. Some of the straight-headed windows with arched, uncusped lights, are original. Nave and chancel in one; open timber roof. – COWMIRE PEW. Early

C16, with one-light divisions and canopy. – Small traceried CANOPY in this pew, but not *in situ*.– BURBLETHWAITE PEW. C17, but largely re-done in 1810. The long, sparingly placed balusters are Jacobean, the charming Gothick pierced top frieze of 1810. – PEW of 1698, made up of bench ends. – Three-decker PULPIT of 1698, a rarity. – SCULPTURE. Crucified Christ, torso, C13 ?, about 2 ft 6 in. high. Of wood, which is a very exceptional survival in England. – STAINED GLASS. More of the C15 than in most Lancashire churches. It comes from Cartmel Priory (cf. Bowness, Westmorland). The E window has Christ, St Anthony, another saint, and small groups of the Seven Sacraments. – More in one N window. – PLATE. Cup and Cover Paten, Elizabethan; Cup of 1808.   29

3½ m. WNW of the church, on Windermere and immediately S of the Westmorland boundary, are two of *Voysey*'s best houses, BROADLEYS, now a club, on the lake side of the road, and   90
MOOR CRAG, a little further S, on the other side. They date   89
from 1898–1900, Voysey's years of greatest success and fertility, and there is nothing of the date on the Continent to come up to their standard. The future and the past blend effortlessly indeed. They are C20 pioneer work and yet free Tudor. Their language is unmistakable, and yet they are very different one from the other. Voysey's language means pebbledash, low mullioned windows with completely unmoulded members, iron brackets under the eaves, battered buttresses, and a less analysable sense of comfort and of things falling easily into place. Broadleys has a front to the lake more formal than anything at Moor Crag, and yet not in a set symmetry. The front has three semicircular bow windows, the l. and the middle ones with two transoms, the r. one representing two storeys and expressing them. And there is some bare wall to its r. which is not matched on the l. The entrance side is L-shaped, with a long low service wing under a big roof. The main block has a porch and to its l. a square projection with large windows. This contains the staircase, with typical Voysey slats. The porch leads into the hall, which corresponds in axis with the middle bay window. The hall has a huge inglenook and a wooden gallery to which the staircase leads up. Moor Crag has greater emphasis on big sheltering gables. They appear on both main sides and again without formal correspondences. The three upper cross-windows on the entrance side represent the staircase landings, and the staircase again has Voysey's close vertical slats.

CASTERCLIFF see NELSON

CATON

ST PAUL, Brookhouse. Built into the w wall of the N aisle are the sad remains of a Norman tympanum reduced to an arch order with figures which do not make much sense now but seem to have represented Adam and Eve and the serpent. One order of columns, with scalloped capitals. The w tower is Perp, the rest of 1865–7,* sizeable and acceptable. – MONUMENTS. Many coffin lids with crosses, swords, and shears in the Norman arch. One has a C14 inscription referring to Roger Burgh Senior. – Robert Welch † 1775. By *Regnart*. Good relief with the usual draped woman by an urn. – Elizabeth Hodgson † 1795. With a medallion of a young woman and an urn on a pedestal.

NE of the church and E of the bridge by the Crook o' Lune is the WHITE CROSS MILL of 1838, originally a cotton mill. It is four storeys high and ten bays long. At one end a high staircase tower. The chimney is detached.

GRESGARTH HALL, 1 m. SW. In grounds beautifully and most romantically landscaped about 1805–10, when also the house was given its present appearance, castellated, with a nearly symmetrical façade. In the centre is a porch, but of the two projecting wings one has – for no good reason – a large chapel-like window. The back has a large bow, and that may well be C18. But inside is all the evidence of a pele tower with tunnel-vaulted ground floor.

CATTERALL see CALDER VALE

CHALLERTON see RAMSBOTTOM

CHAPEL ISLAND see ULVERSTON

CHAPELTOWN see TURTON

CHARNOCK RICHARD

CHRIST CHURCH. 1860–9. Largish, Perp, with w tower and polygonal apse. There are no aisles. The interior is distinguished by two cross-arches, a chancel arch and an apse arch. – MONUMENT. Frances Darlington. By *J. Nesfield Forsyth*, 1903.

* The architect most probably was *Paley*. The Paley family, the Rev. R. W. H. Entwistle tells me, lived at Moorgarth, Caton.

Recumbent white effigy. She was the wife of James Darlington who had given the church (cf. also Coppull).

LOWER HOUSE FARMHOUSE, ¾ m. NE. 1654. Brick, with mullioned windows, each three lights under a relieving arch (cf. Rufford Old Hall, 1662). In the porch gable a lozenge made of projecting headers.

(BOLTON GREEN FARMHOUSE, 1¼ m. N. 1612. Three- to six-light mullioned windows. MHLG)

CHATBURN

7040

CHRIST CHURCH. 1838 and 1883, the earlier work by *Sharpe*, the later by *F. Robinson*. But who did what? The tower is known to be by Sharpe. The rest, if by Robinson, would be a remarkably faithful interpretation of an Early Victorian style. One can hardly believe it; all is so entirely of a piece. The style is Romanesque with Lombard friezes, like Sharpe's St Mark, Blackburn. The three cross-gabled transeptal bays and the E apse also look 1838 rather than 1883.

METHODIST CHURCH. 1883. Free Renaissance.

ARMOT HOUSE, ¾ m. NNE. 1677 in the plasterwork of a chimney-piece on the ground floor. Square porch, five-light mullioned windows on the ground floor l. and r. The porch has a Yorkshire lintel which goes well with 1677 and a stepped three-light window over.

CHEETHAM CLOSE STONE CIRCLE *see* TURTON

CHIPPING

6040

A little stone-built market town or village close to the fells.

ST BARTHOLOMEW. The exterior entirely of the Victorian restoration. Just occasionally some tracery is original. Inside, however, the five-bay arcades are both Perp. They are coarse and rustic, that on the N side entertaining by heads in the capitals, some of them making faces. From the headgear of a lady this can be dated late C14 or, maybe, early C14. However, the chancel PISCINA betrays a C13 past (pointed-trefoiled with nailhead decoration). – FONT. Octagonal, with concave sides and very primitively carved motifs. Probably Late Perp. – PLATE Chalice of 1601–2, by *R. B.*

ST MARY (R.C.), Windy Street. 1827. A large building of the usual Catholic type, i.e. oblong with arched windows. The three-bay presbytery is attached. It has a Tuscan doorway. Inside the church, the nave E wall has four giant Corinthian demi-columns and the narrow chancel has pairs of such columns on its E wall. – The adjoining SCHOOL is of exactly the same type as the church, only much smaller.

Many nice stone houses in TALBOT STREET and WINDY STREET. In the latter BRABINS SCHOOL of 1683, with one of the elementarily decorated Yorkshire lintels. Mullioned windows.

HESKETH END, Hesketh Lane, 1⅝ m. SSW. Built in 1582. A farmhouse with mullioned windows, memorable for the fact that Richard Alston who built it provided the façade with inscriptions mostly as a running frieze of two line panels referring to English history from the Romans and the Saxons to their own day. You can read that Brutus built London in 1108 B.C., that Caesar conquered Gaul, and also that the battle of Flodden was in 1513.

ST WILLIAM (R.C.), Lee House, 2⅛ m. SSW. 1827. Small and oblong, only two bays long, and with a bigger three-bay presbytery.

FAIRY HOLES CAVE, 3 m. NE, on New Laund Farm, ½ m. E of Whitewell. The cave has a southward-facing entrance and is 65 ft long, 6 ft wide, and 10 ft high. In front of the cave is a flat platform on which lay occupation debris, including animal bones, and sherds of an Early Bronze Age collared urn.

CHORLEY

Chorley, as industrial Lancashire towns go, is a friendly town. It has the hills, it is hilly in itself, it has much new housing, and the centre is neither confused nor gloomy, and of course it has Astley Hall. Only, as far as the centre goes, the A6 makes it impossible to appreciate anything.

ST LAURENCE, Church Brow. The church is now at the level of the A6, i.e. Park Road. Originally it lay on the brow indeed, with streets to the N steeply below it. Just at the foot in HOLLINSHEAD STREET is in fact the best row of Georgian houses in Chorley, of brick, admittedly very minor, but one at least with a handsome tripartite doorway with a segmented fanlight. The church has an ashlar-faced Perp W tower, though its details are Victorian. The church, i.e. the aisles, arcades, and transepts, dates indeed from 1859–61. The nave E wall and the chancel have again old masonry – but no more. In the S wall of the chancel, low down, is a small recess, formerly protected by bars. It is supposed to have contained relics of St

Laurence brought from Normandy by Sir Rowland Standish in 1442. – STANDISH PEW. Early C17. The back has two niches with special seats and above them strapwork, caryatids, and a pediment. – PARKER PEW. Late C17, with openwork posts of different twists. – PLATE. Cup and Cover Paten, 1770; Cup and Cover Paten, 1793–4. – Several acceptable TABLETS. – Also two funeral HELMETS, probably of Standishes.

ST GEORGE, St George's Street. 1822–5 by *Rickman*, a Commissioners' church, built for £12,387, an exceptionally high sum. It is indeed a stately and attractive building. The w tower faces axially down ST GEORGE'S STREET, which has l. and r. terraces of brick houses also probably of *c.*1825. Some have combined doorways with pilasters and wreaths in the frieze. Rickman's church has a w tower with pinnacles and lancet windows, and also lancets along the sides. The piers inside consist of eight very thin attached shafts. The galleries are kept behind and rest on cast-iron columns and cast-iron arches with pretty tracery. Flat ceiling on equally prettily decorated hammerbeams. Every second of them stands on a wall-shaft.

ST GREGORY (R.C.), Weld Bank. Built in 1814–15, but of that little is recognizable. The aisles were added in 1831, the façade in 1845, and the interior now is evidently a good deal later. It was altered in 1908. The exterior is very fine, of ashlar, with an impressive w tower with four aedicules and an ogee cap. The façade follows the Italian scheme of low sides for the aisles and a higher pedimented centre for the nave. The articulation otherwise, also along the sides, is by pilasters. Three niches for images in the façade. The shallow apse has giant demi-columns, and such evidently also went along the nave before the aisle arcades cruelly cut them off.

SACRED HEART (R.C.), Brook Street. 1894 by *E. Kirby* (P. Fleetwood-Hesketh). Dec, no tower, polygonal apse, granite columns.

ST JAMES, Canterbury Street. 1878 by *Ladds & Powell*, enlarged 1888.

ST MARY (R.C.), Market Street. 1853–4 by *Joseph A. Hansom*. The NE tower with pinnacles and a clumsy higher stair-turret with spire is of 1894 (by *Pugin & Pugin*). Towards Market Street a pretty GATEWAY.

ST PETER, Harpers Lane. 1849–50 by *C. Reed*. A Commissioners' church (price: £1,981), and a very late one. Hence no longer of the type one calls Commissioners' churches, but a straight-

forward Gothic mid-century building. Nave and aisles, transepts, a polygonal NW turret, and mostly lancet windows, but
no longer very long ones. – STAINED GLASS. In 1951 the
church received a gift of pieces of Flemish late medieval glass.

ST GEORGE'S BAPTIST CHURCH, St George's Street. 1836.
Lancets, long and thin, as the thirties still favoured them.

PARK ROAD METHODIST CHURCH. 1842. Five bays. Classical,
with a three-bay pediment.

UNITARIAN CHAPEL, Park Street. 1725, but little of that date
in its original state. The side with two doorways and two
cross-windows between, however, no doubt represents the
original arrangement. No original woodwork.

TOWN HALL. 1875–9 by *Ladds & Powell*. Of no architectural
value. Three-storeyed, with pavilion roof and a campanile-like
central tower with steep pyramid roof.

POLICE STATION, Peter Street. 1966–8 by *Roger Booth*, the
County Architect. High and clean.

TRAINING COLLEGE, Union Street. 1905. By *Cheers & Smith*.
Very red brick and very yellow terracotta. Asymmetrical composition, rather ham.

(GRAMMAR TECHNICAL SCHOOL. Recent. By *Lyons, Israel
& Ellis*.)

EAVES LANE HOSPITAL, the former WORKHOUSE. 1869–72 by
Bradshaw & Leigh Hall. Red brick with blue brick trim. Two
storeys. Turrets with pagoda roofs.

Early C19 houses in Hollinshead Street have already been men-
tioned. There is also of that date a group, ashlar not brick, in
PARK ROAD, and there is the GOLDEN PENNY in FAZA-
KERLEY STREET with a Tuscan porch.

GILLIBRAND HALL, off Grosvenor Road. Good ashlar-faced
three-bay house of 1807–8 with an Adamish porch. Near by a
fine BARN, dated 1669. It has two segment-headed entrances,
two still quite medieval-looking cross-arches inside to correspond with the entrances, but not axial with them, and five
rows of small slits for ventilation purposes.

ASTLEY HALL. As you arrive in front of the house after the long
walk through the park, it hits you hard and squarely. There
are nothing but right angles, and the grid of mullions and
transoms dominates to an extreme degree over the solids of
walls. Few houses of the 1930s would have gone as far as
Astley Hall in the glazing of a façade. What is a little distressing is that this front is not symmetrical. It calls for symmetry,
and nearly, but not quite, achieves it. This is due to the fact

that the range containing the façade was set in front of an existing timber-framed C16 house of two storeys and probably no great pretensions. It survives behind the grand front forming with it the ranges round an inner courtyard, and it does not call for comment, except to say that the E range was refaced, modestly, in 1825.*

Astley Hall had belonged to the Charnock family ever since the C15, but it became their principal house only about 1575. A stone in the garden has the date 1577. On a sill of the w range is the date 1600. The N wing adjoining the dining room dates from 1828. The original access was from the N into the courtyard.

The s façade now needs a closer look. It has a portal of [39] barbaric detail and l. and r. of it a bay window, five-eighths of an octagon in plan and with three transoms. The portal has paired columns with Ionic capitals such as one would not expect even the most isolated backwoods mason to have been capable of, especially at the time when it was done; for that time is not the mid C16 but the mid C17. In all probability the actual date lies shortly after 1653, when the last Charnock died, leaving the house to his daughter married to Richard Brooke. Their arms are on the cornice of the hall. The bay windows run through the storeys, and this represents the medieval arrangement of the one on the r. which is the hall bay, but not of the other, where two storeys hide behind the bay. To the l. of the latter is only a short strip of wall and then the incomplete return towards the old timber part, where – as one must expect – the kitchen for the hall was contrived. Its big brick chimney will at once be recognized. The stacks have a little decoration by cut bricks.

But, to return to the façade, to the r. of the r. bay is a different rhythm – a three-plus-two window and a cross-window, both with only one transom and low mezzanine windows over. That takes you only to the height of the bay windows; but above them is a long gallery the whole length of the house, and that is as completely glazed as a long office in any recent block. Except for a punctuation by strange mullions there is no solid wall left. It starts on the short sides with 2 + 3 and then runs along the façade from r. to l. 4–4–3, the 3–2–2–2–3 of the bay window, the 4 + 4 above the portal and the 3–2–2–2–3 of the other bay window, and the 3–4–4 above the different part of

---

* According to Mr J. Haworth the early C19 work is by *Lewis Wyatt*.

the front, and so round the corner to end with another 3–2. On top of all this, at last, runs a solid parapet all along, with round recesses which once contained busts and a balustrade at the very top. Cemented as it now is, the whole display has something ruthless and even grim; were it still of exposed brick, with stone dressings, as it originally was (like Gawthorpe), it would look more cheerful.

46

The impact of the interior is no less forceful than that of the façade. The great hall has a large fireplace with a big overmantel and a stucco ceiling, exceedingly rich, exceedingly skilfully done, but again barbaric in its very excesses, and badly modelled, as far as the many cherubs go. They are not even all of stucco, but also of lead and leather. The ceiling is divided by beams, and in the panels are wreaths with flowers or cherubs. More cherubs disport themselves along the frieze. The undercutting is breathtaking, even more perhaps in the adjoining low drawing room. The room on the l. of the hall on the other hand (the one with the second bay window) has much simpler plasterwork.

Round the lower part of the walls of the hall runs panelling with pilasters and blank arches on which there are paintings of famous men – the Renaissance theme of the *uomini famosi* – but their choice up here and in the 1660s is very puzzling indeed. They were probably painted for, or brought in by, Thomas Charnock M.P. who died in 1648, and are the following (in chronological order): Tamerlane, Sultan Bajazet I (defeated by Tamerlane), Skanderbeg, Mohamed II (Skanderbeg's adversary), Columbus, Magellan, Philip II, Leicester, Queen Elizabeth I, Drake, Alessandro Farnese (of the Battle of Lepanto), Henry IV of France (Alessandro's adversary), Ambrogio Spinola (victor over the Netherlands), Gabor Bethlen (adversary of Austria and the Emperor), and – added later – William of Orange. What had Charnock read to make him select these men?

47

The staircase starts in the hall and has the kind of pierced leaf-scroll balustrade which became the fashion in the 1660s. It is again done skilfully but somewhat barbarically. In the E wing are rooms with panelling re-used from somewhere else, some of it with inlay patterns. On the first floor in the w wing is a chimneypiece with good Mannerist caryatids and an elaborate crude plaster overmantel, and in another room a coved ribbed ceiling and plaster wall panelling with pilasters and arches.

CHURCH

7020

This is the place where Robert Peel, grandfather of Sir Robert, started his calico printing works. They are by the canal, N of the church.

St James. Nicely a little away from the centre of the little town. Perp w tower; the rest of 1804–5. Three galleries; flat ceiling, two tiers of arched windows. The tracery is of course Victorian; so is the chancel (1895–6). – FONT. Perp, with blank tracery. – REREDOS and surround with mosaic; 1809. – STAINED GLASS. Two excellent *Morris* windows in the s aisle; 1890.

CHURCHTOWN

3010

Churchtown, although part of the County Borough of Southport, is still primarily a village and deserves the benefit of being treated as such. Its GREEN with the trees, the C18 OBELISK, the white houses and cottages around, kept neatly, especially the HESKETH ARMS* and the BOLD ARMS, the gatepiers to Meols Hall, and the SCHOOL of 1826, one-storeyed, with Tudor window overlooking the church, are a picture of great charm and an intimacy one does not expect so near the town.

St Cuthbert. 1730–9. Of stone, with a solid, dependable w tower and spire, and a side of three windows and one more and the chancel to go with it. The s porch carries the date 1909, and that is the time of a radical restoration carried out by *Isaac Taylor* and sweeping away what had been done in 1860. The chancel e.g. is entirely of 1908–9. So are the curious wooden posts and the other wooden motifs inside. The Venetian window in the N wall was the E window of the C18 chancel. – FONT. A strong baluster. – BENCH ENDS. Simple, with double volute tops, probably of c.1740. – The REREDOS and the woodwork surrounding it comes from St Peter in Liver- 48 pool which was demolished in 1922. They are the work of *Richard Prescot* and date from c.1704, and they are gorgeous indeed, in the Gibbons way. The reredos is of course only the pediment of the grand reredos of St Peter's. In its centre is a pelican. Deeply undercut foliage, putto heads, etc. – From the same source the COMMUNION RAIL with its twisted balusters and the balusters of the SCREEN of 1925. – ROYAL ARMS. Carved; c.1835. – PLATE. Two Chalices, London-made of 1579–80 and 1607–8; Paten probably of c.1637; Flagon,

* But the Doric entrance is of 1932.

London, 1757–8. – MONUMENTS. Two good tablets, one to
49 Thomas Fleetwood † 1717, the other, by *Nollekens*, to Roger
Hesketh † 1791. Nautical instruments at the foot of an obelisk.

MEOLS HALL. A comfortable-looking brick house, with a date
1695 (*ex situ*) on a back gable. However, the motif of pilasters
l. and r. of one upper front window is really more 1670 than
1695, and there is minor evidence of *c*.1600. The garden side
is recent, in the style of the early C18. So are two gazebos. But
the garden doorway is genuine early C18 work. It has alternating rustication and comes from *Leoni*'s Lathom House. The
early C19 GATES of the front drive are from the South Lodge
of Bold Hall (*see* below).

BOTANIC GARDENS, Bankfield Lane. The gateposts come from
the West Lodge of Bold Hall; the gates themselves are a copy
of the gates there. They must be early C19.

CHURCHTOWN *see* KIRKLAND

CLAUGHTON
5040
6 m. SSW of Chipping

ST THOMAS (R.C.). 1792, but the façade of 1835. It is an impressive, remarkably original façade, a rectangular block,
rendered white but framed in ashlar and with three lunette
windows. The side windows have been spoiled by hideous
Venetian tracery with nailhead amongst other things.

CLAUGHTON HOUSE. In spite of the date 1573 on a lintel,
the façade must be of the late C17. Three-bay centre and short
two-bay wings. All the windows except the middle one of the
cross-type. The fenestration is indeed completely symmetrical.

MATSHEAD FARM. Dated 1703. All cross-windows, except for
the staircase window, which is two such windows, one on top
of the other.

CLAUGHTON
5060
1½ m. SW of Hornby

ST CHAD. The W side has a panel dated 1602 and a bellcote
which looks *c*.1700, and the VCH indeed gives a date 1702 to
the church. Medieval only the E window, with cusped intersecting tracery, i.e. of *c*.1300. Otherwise 1904. – PLATE.
Chalice of 1709–10. – BELL. The church has a bell dated 1296
which makes it the oldest dated bell in England.

CLAUGHTON HALL FARM, E of the church. With mullioned
windows. The interest of the house is that it is no more than a

wing of CLAUGHTON HALL, the rest of which was shifted in 1932–5 to the top of the moor, N of the village. The job was done for Mr Esmond Morse. There it stands now in a splendid isolation such as it had never enjoyed down below. It was a bold thing to do, and the result looks Lutyens rather than Elizabethan, especially as some of the original features are historically speaking unexpected and other features have been adjusted in shifting. Claughton Hall was built for the Croft family. It is a very high house, and its façade is symmetrical in the centre, with two tower-like eminences and a recessed part between in which two chimneys stand symmetrically on corbels. The middle oriel is earlier than the rest. It proves that part of the house is pre-Reformation (cusped lights), but the oriel was originally in a different place, and the axially placed main doorway below was not there. As for the towers, the surprising feature is that right below their eaves they each have a room with a continuous band of mullioned and transomed windows along the front and round the corners. They are like the look-out places of a standing. At the same time one may well be reminded of the fenestration of Astley Hall, Chorley. To the S the porch is as it initially was, and so is the Music Room window, of six lights, with two transoms and nicely moulded details. Inside, at the time of the removal, a new upper Great Hall was formed making use of huge cruck beams brought from a barn at Eardisley in Herefordshire. On the ground floor is some uncommonly fine linenfold panelling from Grundisburgh in Suffolk.

CLAYTON-LE-MOORS   7030

ALL SAINTS, ¼ m. W of the main N–S road, and by the park. 1838–40 by *John Harper*. Lancets, separated by buttresses, the eternal motif of 1820–40. The W tower has excessively high stepped triple lancets. The galleries, curiously enough, were only inserted in 1852 – more than a decade after the battle against them had been joined. The chancel was rebuilt in 1882. – Of that time also are the sumptuous, still entirely High Victorian marble FONT, REREDOS, and PULPIT, DESK and low SCREEN.

CLAYTON HALL, I m. NE. Alas derelict at the time of writing. A fine house of 1772, five bays with a doorway with fluted pilasters and a pediment. One-bay links with (later ?) doorways to one-bay pavilions with Venetian windows. The body of the house could actually be older than the pavilions.

DUNKENHALGH, ½ m. SSW. Mostly of c.1815–20. Ashlar, castellated, with a shallow, very unconvincing porch tower. The present entrance must be later. Round the corner is another porch, high and shallow, with angle buttresses and pinnacles. It goes with c.1815–20. In one room good, bold, rather heavy plaster ceiling, also in the style of c.1820. Frieze with oak leaves.

CLAYTON-LE-WOODS

5020

ST BEDE, Clayton Green. 1822–3. Three widely spaced bays of arched windows. Broad façade. Nice recent bell-turret with spirelet (1964 by *Weightman & Bullen*).

CLERK HILL see WHALLEY

CLIFTON

4030

ST JOHN EVANGELIST. Chancel 1852, nave and W tower 1873. Minimum Dec.

WINDMILL, SE. A brick tower mill, alas reduced to two sails.

CLIFTON HALL. Built in 1832 (Burke's *Seats*) and yet already Tudor, i.e. gables and mullioned and transomed windows. Brick and stone dressings. A medium-sized house.

CLIFTON HILL see FORTON

CLITHEROE

7040

Clitheroe is a small hill-town of stone houses below the foremost Norman keep of Lancashire – a county admittedly poor in keeps. The castle stands on a natural rock. It belonged to the de Lacy family and then by marriage to the Earls and later Dukes of Lancaster, whence it reached the crown at the time of Henry IV.

CASTLE. The keep is Norman and supposed to be the smallest in the country. It is no more than 35 ft 9 in. square. Entry was by the doorway on the first floor. From that level a spiral staircase rises to the top and ends in a turret. The ground floor was originally lit by slits only. The bailey is recognizable by the walls to the SW and the houses in a Georgian and later medieval dress. Lord Torrington in 1792 wrote of 'a foolishly fancied Gothic house'. How much of genuine medieval survives around these houses and walls has not been sorted out yet.

ST MARY MAGDALENE. Before the present church was built, there existed a Norman chancel arch. Today the only medieval reminders are the five-light Perp E window with good panel tracery and the W tower. The tower arch is double-chamfered.

Tower and chancel wall appear to be C15. But is not the NW angle of an aisleless nave earlier? Otherwise the church is *Rickman*'s work and dates from 1828–9. He gave his aisle arcades long, thin octagonal piers and long, thin two-light windows of a Perp character. He also provided a clerestory and kept his chancel short. The galleries are behind the piers. Nice open roof. The octagonal top stage of the tower and the spire with its flying buttresses were added later, in 1844. – SCULPTURE. C17 panels in the front of the S aisle altar. – STAINED GLASS. The heraldic E window may well be of the 1830s. – PLATE. Chalice of 1681; Chalice and Paten of 1828–9. – MONUMENT. Mutilated couple of *c*.1440.

ST JAMES, ⅝ m. S. Built in 1839. Norman, with W tower and long round-headed windows. Open timber roof; no aisles; short chancel.

ST MICHAEL (R.C.), Lowergate. 1847 by *J. A. Hansom*. C13 style, the façade with two turrets. Short nave, three-bay arcades, broad apse. – PLATE. Recusant Chalice with decoration of cherubs; *c*.1650–70.

ST PAUL, Low Moor. 1867–9 by *Stevens & Robinson*, the spire by *Grayson*. Quite a large church; C13. To its W still stands its predecessor, a small church of *c*.1820, with lancet windows, a short chancel, and a W tower, octagonal in its upper part and with a spire.

A former CATHOLIC CHURCH built in 1799 is in Lowergate. It is of three bays with arched windows and has the presbytery attached in the usual way.

CONGREGATIONAL CHURCH, Castlegate. 1863. Gothic, with details of *c*.1300. No tower.

Former METHODIST CHAPEL, Lowergate. Rather ambitious, in a free Renaissance. Built in 1888.

CEMETERY CHAPEL, ⅝ m. NW of the church, on the Waddington Road. 1879–80 by *Nicholl*.

TOWN HALL AND LIBRARY. On a good site at the fork of two roads. The original town hall by *Rickman* of 1820 made no use of that corner. It has a flat front with lancets. The corner building is by *Briggs & Wolstenholme*, 1900, in their jolly Loire style with Gothic touches. – CORPORATION PLATE. Mace, silver-gilt, *c*.1675–80; Punch Bowl by *F.B.*, London, 1681–2.

HOSPITAL, former WORKHOUSE, 1 m. NE. By *Bradshaw*, 1870. Modest, two-storeyed, in a style one can probably call Italianate.

Clitheroe is a townscape pleasure. It has no putting-off buildings, it has changes of level, and it has streets with bends. The main axis is CASTLE STREET, wide, but not with strictly parallel frontages, and extending from the castle to the town hall. What new buildings were provided are imitation C16 and C17 and quite agreeable. The nicest individual building is the SWAN AND ROYAL HOTEL of c.1840, white, with three-light mullioned windows. Up CHURCH STREET for more agreeable houses, especially one dated 1808, of three bays with a middle pediment and a columned doorway. On the r. of the house a doorway with a C17 Yorkshire lintel.

LOW MOOR, by St Paul's church, is not without interest. The MILL along the Ribble is early C19, and the housing close to it is on a planned, if elementary, layout. The mill was started by Mr Jackson in 1782, and 28 houses were built. It was enlarged by the Garnetts and Horsfalls after 1799, and by 1841 there were 238 houses.* The mill is best seen from the EADSFORTH BRIDGE, a fine five-arch bridge, the middle arch segmental and much wider than the others.

PUBLIC PARK, below the castle. In it a TURRET transferred to Clitheroe in the 1930s from the Houses of Parliament.

Finally two houses in the neighbourhood.

PIMLICO FARM, Pimlico. The interest is that it is dated 1715 and yet still has mullioned and transomed windows and a stepped hood-mould over the door.

STANDEN HALL, 1¼ m. s. A fine Palladian mansion with a seven-bay front, the centre three bays half a storey higher, enriched by attached giant Tuscan columns and a pediment and also by pediments over the principal windows. Round the corner the house is clearly of three parts. There is a handsome Adamish porch here.

CLOUGHFOLD see RAWTENSTALL

4050

COCKERHAM

ST MICHAEL. Ashlar-built Perp w tower. The rest by *Austin & Paley*, 1910. Large, nave and chancel in one, with clerestory. Square-headed Perp windows. Transeptal chapels of two

---

* Mr A. Hanson, the Borough Librarian, tells me that the partners were Jeremiah Garnett and Timothy Horsfall, brothers-in-law. Their parents started the young couples at Low Moor. The partnership lasted until 1858, when Garnett paid the Horsfalls £60,000 for their interest. The mill was for the spinning and weaving of cotton.

bays, the N one of two low bays with a round pier and capital, the s one of two high bays with arches dying into the pier.

SHEPHERD'S FARM, ⅝ m. SW. Dated 1705. Six bays, upright mullioned two-light windows. The doorway not yet in the centre, but a continuous course above doorway and windows instead of separate hood-moulds.

CROOKHEY HALL, ¾ m. SE. By *Waterhouse*, 1874. Medium-sized mansion. Asymmetrical, with a porte-cochère and a tower with steep French hipped top. Central hall with gallery and skylight. The house was built for Col. Bird, son of a Cockerham mother and a Massachusetts father. It is rather a dry job.

COCKERSAND ABBEY. Of the Premonstratensian abbey, founded in 1190, there remain only the chapter house and some inarticulate fragments of walls. Excavations in 1923 have shown that the church had an aisleless nave and aisleless choir and transepts with the pairs of straight-ended chapels which were standard Cistercian and Premonstratensian custom. The cloister was s of the church. Walls indicate the E, s, and W ranges. In the E range is the chapter house. This, if it were better looked after, could be a very beautiful room. It is small (27 ft 6 in.) and octagonal, with a compound mid-pier of four major and four minor shafts and a rib-vault with one pair of tiercerons for each two cells. The pier has one luscious stiff-leaf capital. The doorway is still round-headed. The most likely date is *c*.1230. The crenellation must be of the time when the chapter house was used as a burial chapel of the Dalton family. It looks early C19. Behind the chapter house is the beach, with a small lighthouse not far away.

COCKERSAND ABBEY *see* COCKERHAM

COLNE

Architecturally there is not much to Colne. It has 19,000 inhabitants, and it feels small, mainly one long street, with town hall and parish church, following the course of the valley between the hills.

ST BARTHOLOMEW. The exterior is typically North Country, all Perp and mostly Late Perp, with straight-headed windows, their arched lights uncusped. Inside, the story takes one back much further. The N arcade is early C13, with round piers, moulded capitals, and double-chamfered arches. The s doorway seems Dec, the rest is Late Perp, i.e. also the s arcade and the three-bay chapel arcades – all with standard elements. – FONT. Bought in 1590 by Lawrence Townley, but obviously early C16. Concave-sided-octagonal, with plain shields. – SCREENS. Perp the chapel screens, with simple one-light divisions. – CHANDELIER. Of brass, bought in 1773, with a bell-body and two tiers of arms. – PLATE. Flagon, 1774–5; two Chalices, 1790, by *I.L.* – MONUMENTS. Christopher Emmott † 1745 and John Emmott, a London merchant, † 1746. By *Sir Robert Taylor*. Large tablet with bust above the inscription part and higher up a portrait medallion in front of an obelisk. – Richard Emmott, late of Basinghall Street, London, † 1761. Tablet with a putto standing by an asymmetrical Rococo shield.

CHRIST CHURCH, Keighley Road. 1836. A standard product. W tower, lancet windows between buttresses. Entirely the Commissioners' type, though not a Commissioners' church. – (STAINED GLASS. E window by *Lavers & Barraud*, 1863.)

HOLY TRINITY, Burnley Road. 1912 by *R.B.Preston*. A pity the tower (NE) has never been built; for it is an interesting church, Romanesque, with rather military corbel-friezes instead of Lombard friezes. Round-headed windows, but the clerestory windows circular. Romanesque arcades with an only slightly free variety of block capitals. Apse, very shallowly polygonal.

BETHEL METHODIST CHURCH, Burnley Road. 1872. In the Free Renaissance style.

TRINITY BAPTIST CHURCH, Keighley Road. 1883 by *G. Baines*. Quite large, also Free Renaissance.

INGHAMITE CHAPELS (cf. Barrowford). One is in Midgley Street (1877; formerly the Inghamite Sunday School), a second in Cotton Tree Lane (1900), a third in West Street (1908).

CEMETERY CHAPELS. The chapels are of 1860 by *Pritchett* of Darlington. The two have identical fronts and are linked by a gateway with a tower over.

TOWN HALL, Albert Road. 1894 by *J.W.& R.F.Beaumont* of Manchester. Symmetrical, mildly Domestic Gothic, with a middle tower. Really entirely undistinguished.

MUNICIPAL HALL. 1901–2 by *Woodhouse & Willoughby*. Elizabethan, not high, but quite a long frontage, wholly informal. The skyline includes a cupola.

LIBRARY. In its front garden is the re-erected MARKET CROSS, a C15 cross.

The most interesting building of Colne was allowed to disappear, the CLOTH HALL, of twenty-three bays with a five-bay pediment.

In the neighbourhood of town hall and library are the CO-OPERATIVE shop, the most ambitious commercial building of Colne, 1906–7 by *R. Worcester*, and the offices of the Co-op by *F. E. L. Harris* in LINDEN ROAD, very competently Gothic, an asymmetrical composition.

EMMOTT HALL, 2½ m. E. The house is in ruins. What still stands is the five-bay classical front of 1717. The main windows have pediments, and they are separated by giant pilasters. Porch with two unfluted Ionic columns. This set-piece is flanked by C17 wings, one with a stepped three-light window at the top. Monumental GATEPIERS.

COLTHOUSE *see* HAWKSHEAD

COLTON
3080

HOLY TRINITY. Consecrated in 1578, enlarged in 1721 and 1762, but to the eye that hardly appears. The impression is entirely Victorian and later. Roughcast. w tower and nave and chancel in one. The straight-headed uncusped windows probably represent 1578. – COMMUNION RAIL. C17. – PLATE. Chalice and Cover Paten of 1571–2; London-made.

CONISHEAD PRIORY
2 m. SE of Ulverston
3070

Richard Holden in 1808 found it a 'tolerable Gentleman's House'. It belonged to 'Braddyll Esq'. Less than fifteen years later Col. R. G. Braddyll built for himself a mansion in size the pre-Victorian counterpart to the Victorian Holker Hall. The architect was *Philip Wyatt*, youngest son of James Wyatt, and the cost has been assessed by tradition as £140,000. It is sweepingly Gothic, of the late, i.e. Perp, variety handled with the freedom from antiquarian qualms handed down from the C18. The entrance side is wholly asymmetrical, with a large gatehouse-type centre flanked by turrets with spires. The great hall is behind this and goes through two floors. The recessed wall on the l. with its high three-light window represents the staircase, the five tall two-light windows on the r. the high corridor which runs right through, starting from the porch in the middle of the symmetrical N side. The E (garden) side is symmetrical too. There is a wing projecting to the w,

at the r. end of the entrance side, and STABLES dated 1853.
The lobby of the porch is rib-vaulted (in plaster of course). So
is the corridor, quite a spectacular sight. The hall has a rib-
vault high up as well. At first-floor level it also has a gallery,
and this has a Perp wooden screen of one-light divisions coming
from Samlesbury Hall. The mixed and partly very impressive
woodwork of the Oak Room on the upper floor also comes from
Samlesbury. The chimneypiece has slender termini-caryatids
and a date 1623. The woodwork was brought over in 1834.
There are in addition quite a number of ornate ceilings, Gothic
to Jacobean. The house was begun in 1821 and completed in
1836. – STAINED GLASS. In the hall w window by *Willement*,
on the staircase by *Wailes*.

(A TOWER on a hill to the N, an OCTAGON on the hillside to
the SW.)

3090

CONISTON

1
&
3
Coniston has the Lake District character of, say, Ambleside: a
village, a few old-established white hotels (Black Bull, Crown),
a totally townish shopping street, and a village church.

ST ANDREW. First built in 1586. The church now of 1819 by
J. Matson. w tower with battlements. The chancel and the low
bays l. and r. with battlements were built in 1891. The sides
have arched windows. Are the curious segemental arches
original? – STAINED GLASS. The w window 1893 by *Kempe*.
– PLATE. Chalice and Paten Cover, silver-gilt, 1632–3, York,
by *I.P.* – MONUMENT. In the churchyard (NE corner) a high
Anglo-Saxon-type Cross for John Ruskin † 1900. The sunk
figure carving is by *H. T. Miles* to the designs of *W. G. Colling-
wood*, the great expert on Anglo-Saxon crosses: St George, an
artist drawing, a nude youth playing the lyre, a seven-
branched candlestick, etc.

SACRED HEART (R.C.). A plain rectangle of 1872 by *James
O'Byrne*, including, it is reported, the attractive s tower with a
saddleback roof. – STAINED GLASS. The e window obviously
by *Hardman*.

CONISTON HALL, ⅞ m. SSE. A C16 farmhouse with a display
of mighty chimneys, round and square.

BRANTWOOD, 1½ m. SE, overlooking Coniston Water. Ruskin
bought the house in 1871. The origin was a cottage of *c*.1797,
and the history of the building is complicated.* The cottage is

* The following is a summary of what *A Brief History of Brantwood*
reports.

where the present entrance hall and study are. Probably in the 1830s four ground-floor rooms at the back and the drawing room were added, and in the 1850s the outbuildings near the back door. Then Ruskin added the small turret room c.1871–2, the lodge in 1872, and the dining room probably c.1878–9. In the late 1880s followed the large studio at the back and the whole second floor. The estate also grew, until by 1900 it comprised about 500 acres.

COPP see ECCLESTON, p. 116

COPPULL 5010

CHURCH. 1861. Brick, Norman, with a w tower.

ST JOHN THE DIVINE, ⅝ m. NW. 1911 by *Dudley Newman*. The church was given by James Darlington, an industrialist, residing at Broughton Hall in Warwickshire. Large, with a w tower. Dec details.

(The MHLG reports a brick barn at BOGBURN HALL with cruck trusses. The Hall is dated 1663.)

COPPULL MILLS (Ring Mill and Mavis Mill). 1906. Two vast 93 red-brick ranges, with yellow-brick trim. They each have a tower with a copper cupola, the tower of one with decidedly enterprising detail.

COTTAM see WOOD PLUMPTON

COWAN BRIDGE see LECK

COWHILL FOLD see RISHTON

CRAWSHAW BOOTH see RAWTENSTALL

CROOK FARM see GLASSON

CROOKHEY HALL see COCKERHAM

CROSSENS see SOUTHPORT, p. 236

CROSTON 4010

CROSTON HALL by *Edward W. Pugin* has unfortunately been pulled down. It dated from 1857. Only the avenue leading to it from the N survives, and *Pugin*'s church of HOLY CROSS, of the same year, a building of nave and chancel without architectural interest.

ST MICHAEL. This is a very strange building. It is all Late

Gothic, but nothing seems quite right.* Baines in fact reports rebuilding for 1577 and beautifying for 1682, 1708, 1710, 1715, and 1768; also much was done in 1823. The large aisle windows have intersecting tracery, some with an odd motif in the apex. The bell-openings of the tower also have intersecting tracery. When was this late C13 motif revived? – not before the Reformation surely. The s chapel alone has convincing-looking tracery, and that chapel was rebuilt in 1875. The N doorway (with leaf spandrels) could be C15 or early C16, the window above it early or mid C16 (straight-headed, with uncusped arched lights). The arcades of four bays have octagonal piers and double-chamfered arches. Again, they may be late C15 or C16. The s chapel arcade has the same elements, but may be a little earlier. – FONT. Dated 1663, and very characteristic of the date. Note especially how the quatrefoils have been geometricized. – BENCHES. A few in the N aisle. – PLATE. Two Chalices inscribed 1743.

RECTORY. A fine Baroque front, typical of its date: 1722. Big central bow. The wings l. and r. climb up to its top by curves as complex as the sides of shaped Jacobean gables. Doorway with demi-columns and a broken pediment. The window above it with pilasters. The GATEWAY to the street is a tripartite Gothick piece with ogee arches apparently meant to appear ruinous.

The approach to the church porch is delightful, though not graced by any one specially valuable house, just low varied terraces l. and r. of brick cottages, and at the N entrance a small cross on steps.

CUERDEN

Cuerden is immediately s of Bamber Bridge and indistinguishable from it. The church is close to the motorway access.

ST SAVIOUR. 1836–7 by *E. Sharpe*, the chancel by *T. H. Myres*, 1886. In the Romanesque style, with lesenes and Lombard friezes, and of course lancet-like round-arched windows. w tower turning octagonal and finished by a spire. The work of 1886 is Romanesque too.

CUERDEN HALL. There was a house here built in 1717. This is supposed to be preserved as the middle piece of the large present mansion. To it on the E a new main block was added

* The Rev. F.B.Bruce draws my attention to a C13 DOUBLE PISCINA and a C15 AUMBRY in the chancel.

by *Lewis Wyatt* in 1816–19, and on the w service ranges. All is of brick. Wyatt's block has a façade of five widely spaced bays, two storeys high, and at the four corners are four turrets containing chimney flues. The staircase is a large room rising into a high lantern storey with big arched windows. Rather heavy stucco decoration.

(Two LODGES, also by *Wyatt*. J.Haworth)

DALTON

4000

ST MICHAEL. 1875–7 by *T.H.Wyatt*. How did he get a client up here, one would like to know. The church is a strong job, with a sw tower carrying a saddleback roof. No aisles, but transepts. Lancet windows, and a polygonal apse.

On Ashurst Hill is a low BEACON TOWER with a spire, erected, it is said, in 1798. It is a remarkably austere design – a block below, one step, and then the pyramidal spire – no mouldings, no decoration.

ASHURST HALL, by the church. The house is dated 1649 and not of special interest. But it has in front a detached GATE-HOUSE, with a round arch and low one-bay wings with two-light windows. Also a square DOVECOTE.

STONE HALL, 1 m. SE. A highly rewarding façade with very personal touches. The date must be *c*.1710. Three bays only, but each bay separately flanked by rusticated giant pilasters. Doorway with open curly pediment. The whole central bay is crowned by a one-bay pediment, rather steep, with an oval opening. But the windows are still of the cross-type.

DALTON-IN-FURNESS

2070

ST MARY. In a fine, elevated position behind the castle and the market place and yet looking into trees and fields. The church is of 1882–5 but replaces a pre-Reformation one. *Paley & Austin* are the architects, and this is one of their most spectacular churches, especially externally. It is large, it is in a free Dec,[84] it has a big w tower with a higher stair-turret, and it uses chequer of white and red in several prominent places. The porches are close to the NW and SW ends; they are hexagonal and entered from the E at an angle. They lead into the w bay of the aisles, and these and the w bay of the nave are separated from the rest by big transverse arches forming a kind of narthex. The interior has octagonal piers, a broad chancel arch with five continuous mouldings, and, in the Paley &

Austin way, a different treatment for chancel s and n sides, the former with two high openings into the s chapel, the latter with one wider arch into the organ chamber, and then, E of it, some blank wall. The windows on both sides of the chancel are small and placed high up. They are cusped quatrefoils and have segmental rere-arches. – STAINED GLASS. Some C15 fragments in the N porch. – PLATE. Chalice and Cover Paten of 1570–1; Chalice and Cover Paten by *James Smith*, 1716–17; Paten, 1819–20. – MONUMENT. In the churchyard is the monument to *Romney*, the painter, who was born at Dalton.

ST MARGARET, Ulverston Road. 1902–4 by *Preston*. White and red stone. Big roof with a change of pitch between nave and aisle. No tower, but a big bellcote rising above the N aisle facing N. Grouped small lancets. An indifferent interior.

Nice MARKET PLACE, triangular, with friendly houses, and a funny little Victorian cast-iron DRINKING FOUNTAIN. But like another Gogmagog the castle stands among the houses facing the market place.

DALTON CASTLE. A C14 pele tower, a completely unbroken rectangle with top parapet, 44 by *c*.30 ft. By 1545 it was 'in great ruin'. It had three upper floors, the entrance close to the SE corner and the spiral staircase in the W wall. The large s window is an insertion of 1856; so are the other windows, except for one two-light window in the E wall.

TYTUP HALL, 1½ m. NNE. An Early Georgian five-bay house with a pretty doorway. It has a segmental pediment and a frieze with the typical motif of two concave curves leading up to a truncated middle top.

6020

DARWEN

Darwen is a town of *c*.30,000 inhabitants. It lies in a valley surrounded by hills, and it is a town of stone houses and cottages. Therein lies its attraction. It would be dishonest to claim architectural beauties for it. The staple industries in the prosperous C19 were cotton spinning and weaving, paper making and staining, and cotton printing.

HOLY TRINITY. The church is well placed above the messy centre. It was designed by *Rickman* and built in 1827–9. It was a Commissioners' commission and cost £6,786 to build. It is of course in the Perp style. It has a W tower, long two-light windows, a clerestory, and a shallow polygonal apse. The thin piers have capitals only to the shafts of the arches themselves – a correct Perp motif. The three galleries are preserved. Flat ceiling.

ST CUTHBERT, Blackburn Road. 1875–8 by *Paley & Austin*. A fine, sheer E wall to the street, with the window high up. The transepts differ. Low S aisle with cross-gable. W tower slender and with a tiled saddleback roof. The arch to the nave is so high that it takes in the pair of very long two-light W windows. High single-light clerestory windows. Roofs with wind-braces. Sound and serious, but no more.

SACRED HEART (R.C.), Blackburn Road. 1882 by *E. Simpson*.

ST JAMES, Chapel Brow. 1722. Low, broad façade with pilasters, similar to that of Billinge (South Lancashire). The Gothic windows and the bellcote are of 1850. The sides have pilasters too, and the windows are round-arched. The tracery is again later. The E end was rebuilt in 1937–40 by *Sidney Eaton*. For this also cf. Billinge. Formerly there were three galleries.

ST JOSEPH (R.C.), Bolton Road. 1884. Gothic, with a thin polygonal NW turret with spire.

BAPTIST CHURCH, Bolton Road. 1862. The façade with Roman Doric columns *in antis* is quite lavish, the rest is entirely undecorated. Not a large building.

CONGREGATIONAL CHURCH, Blackburn Road. 1853. The NE steeple has a resourceful bell-stage.

INDEPENDENT MEETING HOUSE, Belgrave Square. 1847 by *E. Walters*. Like a Commissioners' church, with long, paired lancets and buttresses between, if it were not for the enterprising front, the most rewarding bit of ecclesiastical architecture at Darwen. Very high W porch, open to the sides as well, and behind and above it a triple bell-gable, openwork too, and set between two turrets. It creates quite a fantastic skyline.

METHODIST CHURCH, Railway Road, immediately above the centre. 1864–6. It cost £7,700. Three widely spaced bays, giant columns and pilasters. Classical, with a central Venetian window, but also segment-headed windows.

METHODIST CHURCH, Blackburn Road. 1903. Typically Edwardian, with giant columns on excessively high pedestals. Two short turrets with copper domes. French Dixhuitième ovals with garlands.

CEMETERY, Cemetery Road. 1860. The chapels by *J. Stevens* are startling in their architectural naughtiness, even as cemetery chapels go.

TOWN HALL. 1881–2 by *C. Beel*. Two-storeyed, with a middle tower – a feeble effort.

LIBRARY etc. 1893–4 by *Raymond Harrison*, also feeble.

INDIA MILLS. Built in 1859–67 by Eccles Shorrock Brothers & Co., cotton spinners. The chimney will not easily be forgotten. It is a campanile of brick, about 300 ft high, with a diversified head, and a huge base of rockily rusticated stone which connects by an arcaded link with the mill proper, a long five-storeyed range, all rock-faced stone. The firm had other mills at Darwen as well. The earliest was BOWLING GREEN MILL, 1830. Another early mill, but not of Eccles Shorrock, was NEW MILL, no longer extant. The date here was 1835. Eccles Shorrock lived in LOW HILL HOUSE, Bury Fold, on the Bolton Road, ¾ m. S.

JUBILEE TOWER. On a hill SW of the centre – a stumpy, awkwardly proportioned piece.

In BELGRAVE SQUARE just one group of three houses of about 1830, two of them treated as a pair, with a three-column double entrance.

DEEPDALE *see* PRESTON, p. 203

2070
DENDRON

ST MATTHEW. First built in 1642 by a Londoner born here, as a brass inscription inside (nave W wall) records. Rebuilt in 1795. Five bays, arched windows. The W tower is of 1833.

DIGMOOR *see* SKELMERSDALE

DIMPLE *see* TURTON

5050
DOLPHINHOLME

ST MARK. By *Austin & Paley*, 1897–9, for £3,000. The church hugs the ground happily. Squat, broad central tower. The arches across which help to support the tower are visually as successful as they are in other churches of the same architects and period. Fancy Dec tracery in the E window.

WYRESIDE HALL, ½ m. SE. Early C19, of a dark grey stone. The front has giant pilasters and a porch of four fluted Ionic columns. Round the corner an impressive short side with narrow recessed centre and more closely set giant pilasters. Parapets with acroteria. (Good staircase and ceilings. MHLG) The SW LODGE has an Ionic porch, and there is a fine BRIDGE in the park. Rusticated round arch.

DOWNHAM

St Leonard. Stubby Perp w tower; all the rest by *Mervyn Macartney*, 1909–10. Externally nothing special, but inside the s arcade with the arches dying into the piers is handled quite individually. – FONT. Octagonal, Late Perp, with shields, not in panels. – CHANDELIER. Of brass, Baroque shape, one tier of arms. Presented in 1802. – PLATE. Chalice and Cover Paten, 1613–14; Flagon, 1728; Breadholder, 1804. – MONUMENTS. Frances Arabella Assheton † 1835. By *Westmacott*. Fine horizontally oval relief with a seated female figure.

Downham Hall, w of the church. The main front is by *Webster* of Kendal, 1835. Nine bays with a one-storey portico of Tuscan columns. Tripartite doorway. Round the corner the masonry and the window details change, indicating Elizabethan walls and C18 windows.

Downham is an excellently kept village of stone cottages and houses. Old Well Hall, on the road to Worston, has a square porch and mullioned windows.

DUNKENHALGH see CLAYTON-LE-MOORS

DUTTON

Dutton Hall. A C17 house with a splendid later C17 bay added to the hall. Centre and two cross wings, mullioned windows, that of the parlour (l.) of nine lights. The later bay is square and over-mighty. It has seven-light transomed openings on ground floor and upper level. Top balustrade instead of a gable. The fireplace in the hall incidentally is against the former screens passage.

Huntingdon Hall, 1½ m. N. 1619. H-shaped, the façade with mullioned windows of six lights below, five above, and three in the gables. Flat quoins.

ECCLE RIGGS see BROUGHTON-IN-FURNESS

ECCLESTON
4 m. w of Chorley

St Mary. By the river Yarrow. A characteristic North Country church, low, with battlements running along the s side without break and a squat w tower. On the N side on the other hand are rather assertive windows of 1868 with the plate tracery they liked so much in those years. As one looks closely, however, one can see that the Victorians only remodelled what was

Georgian windows of *c.*1720–35. The medieval work is part
Dec, part Perp. The tower and chancel arches with their continuous chamfers may be early C14, and so is probably the
priest's doorway, re-set no doubt, as the rere-arches of the
chancel N windows are Dec too. The arcades of S aisle and S
chapel on the other hand are Late Perp, and that of the chapel
may be datable by the creation of a chantry by a rector of
1493–1511. Perp also, though earlier, the bell-stage of the
tower. – FONT. Late C15, octagonal, with quatrefoils containing among other motifs the eagle's claw of the Stanleys and
the three legs of the Isle of Man. – BENCH ENDS. A few odd
small panels are preserved. – PLATE. Chalice and Paten of 1633
by *H.B.;* Chalice of 1661 by *P.P.;* large C17 Paten, Norwich-
made; Flagon of 1779–80 by *M.B.;* Almsdish of 1781 by the
same. – MONUMENTS. Brass of a Priest, late C15, a 24½ in.
figure, on a tomb-chest. – A number of tablets, especially Rev.
John Douglas † 1766.

ST AGNES (R.C.). The body of the church, with lancet windows,
is supposed to date from 1922–3. The apse by *J. W. Tate* is an
addition of 1958, the tower an addition of 1963 (by the same).

SAGAR HOUSE, S of the above. An impeccably refined office
building of only two storeys with a projecting wing at the r.
end, its windowless front wall faced with slate. By *William
Field*, 1965–6.

ECCLESTON
1 m. N of Elswick

4040

ST ANNE, Copp, ½ m. S. It looks all of a piece, and completely
mechanical, without a spark of creativity. The date is 1884,
but for the lower parts of the tower 1841. And the nave is
supposed to be still that of 1723. Can it be so completely
disguised?

ST MARY (R.C.), Hall Lane, Great Eccleston. 1835. Arched
windows; the altar wall inside with attached unfluted Ionic
columns.

EDENFIELD
7010

CHURCH. 1778, and exceptionally unspoilt. Only the W tower is
older. It carries a date 1614. Windows in two tiers, the lower
ones arched. Even the glazing bars are original. Low, small
chancel with a Venetian window. Three galleries. – BOX
PEWS in the aisles.

EGTON

ST MARY, Penny Bridge. First built before 1786. The present building is of nave, chancel, S aisle, and bell-turret. Plate and geometrical tracery. By *Thompson* of Kendal, 1856. The nave was rebuilt in 1864 at the expense of the Countess Blücher von Wahlstadt. – PAINTING. Christ taken from the Cross; English, *c.*1800.

PLUMPTON HALL, 2½ m. S. A Georgian-looking front with sash windows, but a doorway with lintel and pediment in the C17 Yorkshire tradition. There is indeed a date 1706 inside. The l. portion of the house is older, with big C16 or C17 chimneys.

ELLEL

ST JOHN. 1906–7, without doubt by *Austin & Paley*, see the porch in the W bay, the central tower with its square stair-turret,* the introduction of a clerestory only on the N side, where there is an aisle, the splendidly rounded piers supporting the tower, and the differing treatment of the chancel N and S walls.

The church lies at the far NE end of GALGATE, and in approaching it, one passes the buildings of the oldest SILK SPINNING MILL in England, started in 1792. One building is even older than that time. It was built as a corn mill. The large red-brick building is of 1852, and the building opposite this which is called No. 39 is older than 1852. The C18 building is behind, and attached to, No. 39, closer to the river than the road. There are also terraces of millowner-built cottages.

ELLEL GRANGE. This is probably the finest Italianate villa left in Lancashire, large, with two towers – in this, as in the choice of style altogether, inspired by Osborne. A broad tower is over the entrance. The doorway is flanked by pairs of columns with alternate blocking, the blocks having diamond-cut panels as well. The other tower, slimmer and higher, is behind. The upper windows are segment-headed, which is certainly not an Italian motif. The house was built for William Preston, a merchant, in 1857–9.

ST MARY, in the grounds of Ellel Grange. 1873 by *W. & G. Audsley*. Paid for by William Preston, the sum involved being, it is said, £7,000. A decidedly roguish design, especially in the details of the almost entirely detached N tower. Note e.g. the

* A spire was intended.

way the buttresses merge into broaches to connect the square lower part with the octagonal upper. The church has a round apse and geometrical tracery.*

₄₀₃₀

ELSWICK

CONGREGATIONAL CHURCH. 1873–4 by *H.J.Powell* of Lancaster. It looks exactly as though it were the parish church. N tower turning octagonal higher up. Features *à la* 1300.

ELSWICK MANOR. The house is nothing special, but the STABLES etc. are dated 1819 and have a castellated brick tower and a castellated brick wall.

(HODGKINSON HOUSE. A barn has crucks. NMR)

EMMOTT HALL *see* COLNE

ESTHWAITE LODGE *see* HAWKSHEAD

₅₀₁₀

EUXTON

CHURCH. The date on the W front is 1513, but the lettering is later, and so 1573 has been proposed, and of either date the building could be, except for the C14 (?) N doorway with continuous chamfers. The windows are in the style of the N doorway, but re-done. The chancel was rebuilt in 1837, but the SEDILIA look Perp and may be of 1573 or 1513. The bellcote could be of that time too, or somewhat earlier. The nave roof with wind-braces may be 1513 or 1573, but remains puzzling. – PULPIT. C18; simple. – PLATE. Cup by *P.H.*, 1739–40, London.

ST MARY (R.C.). By *Edward W.Pugin*. Large, without a tower, but with a turret on the attached presbytery. Red stone, rock-faced, with the features of *c.*1300, except for the capitals which Pugin Junior liked to make so elementary that they are no longer period at all. Shallow apse.

CATHOLIC CHAPEL. Aisleless, 1866, attached to the Hall.

EUXTON HALL. What remains after demolitions of some thirty years ago is a one-storeyed house the masonry of which – but neither the cupola nor the design of the portal – belongs to the former Euxton Hall, which was a house of 1849–50 with giant pilasters and altogether much more ornate.

EXTWISTLE HALL *see* BRIERCLIFFE

FACIT *see* WHITWORTH

* It is disused at the time of writing, and I did not see the interior.

FAIRHAVEN *see* LYTHAM ST ANNES, p. 175

FAIRY HOLES CAVE *see* CHIPPING

FARINGTON 5020

ST PAUL. 1839–40 by *Sharpe*. A Commissioners' church (cost: £1,700), i.e., though by Sharpe, still entirely pre-archeological. Brick, with long, lancet-like, round-headed windows and Romanesque stone trim. The odd thing is the vertical bands and Lombard friezes of the tower, all up the three tiers of paired windows. Similar vertical bands for the body of the church as well. Aisleless interior. The chancel is of 1909–10, by *J. A. Seward* of Preston.

COTTON SPINNING MILL, Lostock Hall. Built *c.*1850, for Bashall & Boardman, brick, long and high. Around it the terraces of workers' houses built by the mill-owner. The VCH reports a school with library and museum also built by him.

Lostock Hall is now just part of the industrial landscape of Preston and Leyland.

FAR SAWREY 3090

ST PETER. 1866–72 by *Robert Brass* (P. Fleetwood-Hesketh). Aisleless, with transepts and a NE tower. Lancet windows. A decent, honest piece of work.

STATION COTTAGE, near the ferry. With a castellated wall and pointed archway, and above it on the hillside a castellated TOWER, all probably early C19.

(WATERLOO GARDENS, by the ferry. Of *c.*1810. Square centre with pyramid roof and a rough timber veranda. One wing has an overhanging timber floor with steep roof and carving on the window lintel. MHLG)

GRAYTHWAITE HALL, 2½ m. S. An Elizabethan house, remodelled *c.*1840 and again, by *R. Knill Freeman*, *c.*1887–90. More alterations still *c.*1920. Comfortable Tudor, stucco and red sandstone, with an entrance loggia of four central arches (which existed already by 1855), a straight gable and a shaped gable. Gothic windows. The rear is still the typical Lake District house.

FENCE *see* HIGHAM

FENISCOWLES *see* LIVESEY

FERNYHALGH *see* BROUGHTON

FIELD BROUGHTON *see* BROUGHTON EAST

3080

FINSTHWAITE

St Peter. First built in 1724. Rebuilt in 1873–4 by *Paley &
Austin*. It cost £4,170, and the money was given by Thomas
Newby-Wilson. With a mightily buttressed central tower
crowned by a short spire, and all details Late Norman. Good,
low interior, with the two tower arches. Goodhart-Rendel
calls it, with Flookburgh and St George, Stockport, his favour-
ite Paley & Austin church. – REREDOS. By *Salviati* of Venice.
– STAINED GLASS. The E window possibly by *Powell*.– PLATE.
Chalice, c.1710. – MONUMENT. Margaret Taylor † 1827, by
Webster of Kendal. With an urn and books.

(On the hill is a TOWER to commemorate the English naval
victories over France, Spain, and Holland. Early C19 probably.)

3040

FLEETWOOD

Fleetwood is the brain-child of Sir Peter Hesketh Fleetwood. He
visualized it as a port, promoted the railway from Preston, got
Decimus Burton to design it with streets radiating from a centre
and to design its first fine classical buildings, made a great success
of it for a few years, and then fell victim to circumstances and
died impoverished. The railway was complete in 1840. Fleetwood was the terminus for the N from Euston, and here passen-
gers for Scotland had to embark. This is what Queen Victoria did
(the reverse way) in 1847. But in the same year the railway
reached Carlisle and soon Scotland. That was the end of the
boom. The grand plan was never carried on. Fleetwood still
served Belfast and the Isle of Man, but gradually fishing and
holiday guests became the income.

Of *Burton* as an architect chiefly two buildings tell us, QUEEN'S
TERRACE, a long ashlar range, facing not the sea but the
station, with three pediments, the middle one of seven bays
and with handsome iron balconies, and the NORTH EUSTON
HOTEL, built on a curve, with a three-storey centre and long
two-storey wings. The centre has a big porte-cochère of Roman
Doric columns. The wings are absolutely smooth. The l. wing
is much shorter than the r. wing. There are also fine ashlar
houses SE of the point.

St Peter, Adelaide Street. 1840–1 by *Decimus Burton*. Lancets
along the sides. W tower with lancets too. Short polygonal

pinnacles. It could be by anybody. The E end was remodelled by *Paley & Austin* in 1883. Burton's nave is aisleless.

ST MARY (R. C.), Lord Street. 1867–8 by *E. W. Pugin*. Nave and chancel in one; no tower; polygonal apse. The features are of *c*.1300, except for the capitals of the columns, which are oddly abstract and not at all period. The nave has four normal bays, followed by two excessively narrow ones – an unexpected rhythm.

(ST NICHOLAS, Broadway. 1964 by *Lawrence King*.)

LIBRARY. 1863. Brick, Gothic, of five bays.

NAUTICAL COLLEGE RADAR STATION. 1964–5 by the County Architect, *Roger Booth*. A cute little piece on the sea front.

MINISTRY OF HEALTH COMPUTER CENTRE. By *Leach, Rhodes & Walker*, 1966–7.

FLOOKBURGH

3070

Flookburgh had a charter for holding markets, though it never was more than a village. It therefore possesses REGALIA: a sword of *c*.1600, a staff, and a halberd (in private possession).*

ST JOHN. A large church, the gift of the Cavendishes of Holker Hall. By *Austin & Paley*, 1897–1900, and of excellent design. The general character, with the broad W tower and the powerful apse, is Romanesque, but the windows are widely spaced lancets. The apse stands on an undercroft; the W tower has a low saddleback roof, recessed on two sides. The tower opens towards the nave in a broad, low arch. The chancel arch is followed by an apse arch, all these motifs far from obvious. Equally unexpected but less successful are the chancel side walls, which have one broad arch to the chancel aisle and then a lancet not happily placed. Similarly the nave has one lancet before it begins with its aisles.

In MARKET STREET No. 32 is of considerable interest, as it is dated 1686 and has a completely symmetrical façade of mullioned windows and a Yorkshire lintel.

CARK HALL, ½ m. N. Late C16, with mullioned windows. Worth mentioning because of the grand late C17 doorway with attached Ionic columns and a big segmental, nearly semicircular pediment.

CANON WINDER, 1¼ m. SW. A C16 house with a very large chimney at the back. The façade may be a little later. It has mullioned and transomed windows, and the original doorway

* At the time of writing they are in the parish church.

with four-centred head has been blocked and replaced by a
more conveniently set late C17 doorway.

WRAYSHOLME TOWER. Oblong pele tower of 40 by 28 ft,
attached to a farmhouse. The tower is probably late C15, the
farmhouse has a date 1848. The tower originally had three
storeys. A garderobe projects at the SE corner.

3000

FORMBY

Formby was once a fishing hamlet. It is now 2 miles from the sea,
and the old channel is silted up. So most of Formby is C19 and
after. Pre-C19 Formby is represented by only two buildings.

FORMBY HALL, 1¾ m. NW of the centre. The house is ascribed
by Mr Fleetwood-Hesketh to the later C16, by the MHLG to
1620. But the façade now has all the characteristics of early
C19 Tudor, i.e. big hood-moulds over square-headed heavy
mullioned windows with ogee lights, and in the l. and r.
attachments curious doorways with truncated ogees. There are
battlements too.*

ST PETER, Green Lane. 1746. Brick with stone quoins and arched
windows framed by pilasters. W projection with stone cupola.
The sides of the projection bulge out oddly, in a trefoil way,
between pilasters. W gallery inside. The stone chancel is of
1873.

ST LUKE. In the wood, W of the station. The building dates only
from 1852–3, but stands on the site of an ancient chapel.
Aisleless, with bellcote, i.e. no tower. Geometrical tracery.
Somewhat dreary interior. The architect was *W. Culshaw.* –
FONT. Norman, simple, with a rope moulding.

OUR LADY OF COMPASSION, School Lane. 1863–4 by *Clutton.*
(Estimate £5,693. GS) Brick, red with yellow trim; also stone
trim. Robust and not attractive. No tower. It is an interesting
building in so far as it is inspired in plan by Italian Romanesque
churches with transepts and three parallel apses. This E end is
rib-vaulted solidly. The nave has Clutton's favourite arcades
of two slender columns, paired in depth and provided with
shaft-rings. Naturalistic capitals. The NW view is enlivened
by a round turret and the rounded projection of the baptistery.

HOLY TRINITY, Rosemary Lane. 1889–c.96 by *C. A. Atkinson*
and then *Woolfall & Eccles.*

* The MHLG mentions CRUCKS in two cottages in Formby: WATT'S
COTTAGE, Brewery Lane, and DEAN'S COTTAGE, Ravenmeols Lane.

FORTON

ST JAMES. 1889 by *Adams & Kelly*.

ST PAUL, Shireshead. 1801. Oblong, with quoins and pointed windows, the E window with Y-tracery under a depressed arch. – Two GALLERIES. – BOX PEWS.

CLIFTON HILL, ⅞ m. W. Built by *Richard Gillow* of Lancaster for himself. Grey ashlar. Four-bay centre with a two-bay pediment. The entrance in a porch with two columns coming forward in a shallow ellipse. Links and end pavilions. On the garden side the chief windows and the doorway are tripartite under a blank segmental arch. – The CATHOLIC CHAPEL of 1878 is not of architectural interest, though it ought to be said that it is not Gothic.

HAMILTON ARMS, 1¼ m. S on the A6. Handsome, Late Georgian.

FOULRIDGE

ST MICHAEL. Pleasantly near the reservoir lakes N of Colne. By *R.B.Preston*, 1903–5. An excellent, quite personal composition to the E, taken in as one approaches the church. The chancel has an undercroft, the Lady Chapel a canted bay; N tower near the E end. Uneventful interior.

(BREEZE HOUSE. C17 with two large mullioned and transomed windows. MHLG)

(ACORNLEE HALL. Dated 1613 on an outbuilding. H-plan. Centre porch, large gabled wings. MHLG)

FRECKLETON

HOLY TRINITY. 1837. Norman, of dark brick, with a small W tower, octagonal at the bell-stage and ending in a small spire. Short chancel. The arch responds also Norman. – PULPIT. 1633. With arabesques and the familiar short blank arches. The pulpit came from Kirkham church. – BOX PEWS.

SCHOOL. By the church. 1839. Small and one-storeyed.

FULWOOD see PRESTON, p. 200

FURNESS ABBEY

In 1123 Stephen, Count of Mortain and later King Stephen, gave a site at Tulketh near Preston to monks of the Order of Savigny. In 1127 they moved to Furness and began to build there. In 1147, in connexion with the amalgamation of the Orders of

Savigny and Cîteaux, Furness became Cistercian. By then the E end of the church was built and the monastic part of the premises begun.

Like all Cistercian houses, Furness Abbey was built in a wilderness and by a stream. The site is still in the trees and sheltered from Barrow. Much stands up and, as it happens, in such a fashion that it makes the ruin, in the warm colour of its red sandstone, one of the finest in England. The following description takes the church first, the domestic quarters after, and the church from E to W.

The E end of the CHURCH is of the standard Cistercian plan, with a straight-ended chancel and transepts with an E aisle divided originally into three chapels to each arm. The CHANCEL is of two bays and has blank arches formerly open to the transept aisles. The windows are Perp, their tracery broken. The E window is very wide, the N windows have transoms, the S windows have not, because the sacristy is here. The doorway into it has an ogee gable. Inside are four SEDILIA and a tripartite group of PISCINA and towel recesses. Row of projecting canopies, straight top band with ogee cresting and complicated miniature vaults inside. It is one of the best *ensembles* of sedilia and piscina anywhere in England – Perp, of course.

The NORTH TRANSEPT is separated from its E aisle by piers of eight attached shafts with waterleaf capitals and simply profiled pointed arches. The capitals determine the date, *c.*1175 or so. The vault of the E aisle remains recognizable. Above is a gallery with trefoil arches and again waterleaf capitals. It is the only part of the gallery of the church remaining. The upper windows are Perp. Good N portal of three orders with moulded round arches. Late Norman decorative details. Above the portal is a large window, deprived of its tracery. In the W wall Perp windows, set in the original round-arched surrounds.

The SOUTH TRANSEPT is similar. The N bay of the E aisle was converted into part of the Perp sacristy. The rest has its eight-shaft piers, waterleaf capitals, and pointed arches. Externally there is a frieze above the aisle roof with Norman lozenges, but also bits of arch mouldings, perhaps tampered with. Perp upper windows. In the S wall the night stair to the dormitory remains recognizable. C13 arch at the landing. In the W wall two round-arched windows set sufficiently high to allow for the cloister, and two upper Perp windows.

The CROSSING has only its E piers intact. The others were

strengthened in the C15, perhaps because of an abortive plan to build a tower here. The strengthening of the SW pier is continued by a wall with Flamboyant panelling. There is a small closet behind. Can it have been a chantry? The E piers have multiple shafts, waterleaf capitals, and three thin parallel rolls in the arch.

The NAVE was originally ten bays long. Little remains upright: the S arch of the E respond, the semicircular NE respond, the shape of the piers, alternating between eight-shafted and circular, and what is now the W responds. A C13 stone screen ran across after the seventh, now sixth, bay from the W. The choir stalls filled bays 9–10, now 8–9. The N aisle E arch to the transept remains in its original form, with waterleaf capitals. The S aisle E arch is interfered with. There is now a small doorway in an infill wall, but the latter shows traces of two arches. Both aisles retain signs of vaults at the E and W ends. One round-headed upper doorway from the S aisle into the upper storey W range of the cloister, i.e. the lay brothers' dormitory. What is the purpose of the steps in the N aisle W bay? They probably led into the upper parts of the W tower.

For the plan to build a crossing tower was given up, because it had been decided to build a big WEST TOWER. It was set partly into the W bay of the nave and is a mighty and sheer piece. Niches in the buttresses to hold images. Very high arch to the nave. No W doorway, but a very large W window.

The MONASTIC QUARTERS repay study. The plan of the CLOISTER is laid out on the ground. The NE doorway to the church is round-headed with a continuous moulding. The E range starts from the N with a doorway now leading into the S transept. The Ministry of Public Building and Works makes a good case for the theory that in the 1120s the plan had been for a shorter S transept, so that this doorway would have led into the slype, as was usual. Now the slype is in an anomalous position. There follows immediately S of the transept as built the chapter house. From the cloister what is seen is a fine group of five openings, with many thin shafts and many delicate arch [11] mouldings, all still round. The first and the third belong to tunnel-vaulted library rooms. One vault is round, the other pointed. In between is the entrance to the CHAPTER HOUSE. [12] All this must date from c.1230–40. Vault of the entrance bay of the chapter house with diagonal and ridge ribs and a small boss. Blank pointed-trefoiled arcading along the N and S walls. The chapter house itself is of four by three bays and was rib- [13]

vaulted. The piers still have eight shafts, but now the four to the principal directions have fillets. Large blank arcading of twin arches with splendid paterae in the tympana. The windows in the E half are of the same pattern. So is the doorway. To the outside the windows have detached shafts, and the buttresses are chamfered.

To return to the E walk of the cloister. After the second library room comes the doorway to the walled-off N bay of the dormitory undercroft, then the doorway to the slype, and then the DORMITORY UNDERCROFT itself. This was originally of fourteen bays. Row of octagonal mid-piers. Against the wall corbels with stiff-leaf capitals in the N bays, simpler capitals in the S bays. The DORMITORY projected by seven bays beyond the S range of cloister buildings. Its S wall was open on the undercroft level. The dormitory itself has lancets in a long, even row and plain buttresses.

E of the E range were more rooms. The stream which any monastery needs runs roughly N–S here, and the LAVATORIES or reredorter, late C12, can be recognized. Pair of round arches. Yet further E, and built into the rock, is the building supposed to have been erected in the mid C13 as the infirmary but later converted into the ABBOT'S LODGING. Five-bay hall with mid-piers of octagonal section. Small lancets to N and E. To the E also a fireplace with dogtooth on the corbels. A branch of the stream runs under the building, and there is a sluice.

Of the range SOUTH along the cloister little can be observed. The E room was the warming house. To its N are signs of the day stairs in the rubble, and to the W of the warming house the outline of the REFECTORY, placed, as was Cistercian custom, at r. angles to the cloister walk, not along it. The corner of a smaller, earlier refectory can be seen inside, late C12 as against C13. At the start, in fact, the refectory lay parallel to the cloister, but a smaller cloister. The present N wall of the refectory was the S wall of the earliest refectory.

The WEST RANGE is a little more eloquent. It is long and again two-naved. It sticks out to the S, though not as far as the dormitory. It has a total length of sixteen bays, but is subdivided on the ground floor. The cross-walls creating the outer parlour at the N end (two by two bays) and the entrance passage five bays further S are original. The N respond of the range is eminently interesting. It is semicircular with two completely detached shafts. As the capital still has scallops, i.e. as it will be c.1170–80 at the latest, it is one of the earliest cases of what the French call columns *en délit*, i.e. fully detached. It should be seen in conjunction with the remains of the C12 crypt of York Minster, which is also still entirely Norman.

W of the range are walls of another building, and SW of the W range the traces of the lay brothers' lavatories, again across a stream. This stream turns E then and runs under the most interesting of the monastic buildings, the INFIRMARY, which is placed S of refectory and dormitory. It dates from *c.*1300 and consists of a large hall with a W chamber divided off (lavatories ?), and at the E end a vaulted chapel and a smaller vaulted room which connects by a twice broken passage with the octagonal infirmary kitchen. This is not far from the abbot's lodging further E – on which *see* above. The E wall of the infirmary hall has arcading with higher thin arcading above. The lower arcading is interrupted by the doorways to the chapel and the other vaulted room. The latter is of two bays, the former of three larger bays. The vaults have ridge as well as diagonal ribs. Geometrical tracery in the windows. Both arches and sub-arches are straight-sided, not curved. Wide E window with a depressed arch. – In the chapel are what MONUMENTS survive at Furness Abbey. Two Knights of *c.*1250–60, with crossed legs but still with square early helmets. – Defaced cross-legged later Knight. – Stiff figure of a Deacon with a book. – Very good early C14 Lady. – Another early C14 cross-legged Knight. – Several slabs with foliated crosses. – Also ARCHITECTURAL FRAGMENTS. – The smaller vaulted room goes by the name of BUTTERY. It is entered by two doorways with plain quadrant mouldings.

There now only remain three isolated buildings, all N of the church. An irregular one of several dates has been identified as the GUEST HOUSE. It lies on the NE. The other two are gatehouses. The OUTER GATE is a reconstruction with old materials – a large and a small arch. Close to them is the CAPELLA EXTRA PORTAS, late C13 and well preserved. Geometrical tracery; chamfered buttresses; to the outside only one window; doorways with round arches to N and S (re-used materials ?). The SEDILIA and PISCINA have steep gables.

Of the GREAT GATEHOUSE, S of the chapel, only foundations survive. It was very big and wide and dated from the late C12.

GALGATE *see* ELLEL

4040

GARSTANG

St Helen. St Helen is the parish church, but it is at Kirkland (*see* p. 151).

St Thomas. 1770. w tower, three-bay nave, and a chancel of 1876. Arched, keyed-in windows. Obelisk pinnacles on the tower. The nave windows are interesting, as they are not Gothic, but of the type with arched lights which was fashionable in the Italianate of the 1840s. They are here perhaps meant as a compromise between Georgian and latest Perp. – font. Dated 1770; baluster type.

Opposite three Georgian houses, two of them a pair with doorways under one pediment.

St Mary and St Michael (R.C.), Bonds. Later and larger than the Anglican church. 1857–8 by *E. G. Paley*. There was a church here of 1775. w tower with higher stair-turret. Style of 1300, with rounded piers and moulded capitals. Foliage only at the e end. Roof with wind-braces.

Garstang is a little town, not a village. At the e end is the market cross, a Tuscan column with a ball on top. It was erected in 1754 and restored in 1897. Further w the Town Hall, an attractive and quite ambitious three-bay building of 1755–64, partly rebuilt in 1939. It is of brick with stone quoins and other dressings. The ground floor has a group of three stepped arches, originally open, the upper floor a pediment to the middle window. Balustrade and square cupola.

Aqueduct of the Lancaster–Kendal Canal, across the river Wyre. By *Rennie*, *c.*1793 (mhlg). One segmental arch. Alternating rustication.

Greenhalgh Castle, ½ m. ne of the Catholic church. Remains of the tower, *c.* 25 ft up. Licence to crenellate was given to Thomas Stanley, Earl of Derby, in 1490.

8030

GAWTHORPE

The house lies on the outskirts of Padiham. It was built in 1600–5 for the Rev. Lawrence Shuttleworth and is still Shuttleworth property. The building accounts survive. The house is of a rare but not unique type of plan – compact, without any wings or inner courtyard. Barlborough in Derbyshire of 1584 is the nearest parallel. It was built round a probably preexisting tower, no doubt of the pele type. Its compactness makes Gawthorpe's three storeys – at the back, owing to the fall of the ground, four – appear very high. Kitchen and offices, moreover, are in a basement. The w façade is strictly [37] symmetrical. It has a square porch and two canted bay windows. The doorway has Roman Doric columns carrying obelisks on fancy pedestals. The segmental entrance arch and the window above it date from *Sir Charles Barry*'s drastic restoration of 1849–51. The other sides are less regular. Both s and E have – not in the middle – a square recess. Behind the N recess rises the tower. Barry heightened it and also gave the house its openwork parapet. He also did much to the interior. Of original interiors the best are the following. The drawing room on the ground floor has a stucco ceiling with [38] broad flat bands and in the panels patterns of pomegranates and leaves. A few small grape pendants and a frieze. Original also the chimneypiece and the wall panelling with marquetry. The gallery is on the top floor and explains the external irregularity of a corbelled-out shallow bay window near the s end of the w and E sides. It is a splendid room, with the three bay windows to the s and an overmantel with stucco caryatids. Close frieze and ceiling with a pattern of thin ribs, and a few bigger and a number of very small pendants. Thin ribs also on the ceiling of the room above the porch. In the first-floor room at the NE corner and another first-floor room are awkwardly carved overmantels (one with Prudentia and Justicia) and again friezes and ribbed ceilings. The original hall of the house was the large NE room on the ground floor. Its ceiling is by *Barry*, but its screen and gallery are original. The dais was at the N end, and there is behind it, in the N wall, a seven-light window.

GLASSON   4050

The Glasson Dock was built in 1787 to serve Lancaster. Later (in 1825) a branch of the Lancaster–Kendal Canal was built as far s as Glasson. The dock took the place of Sunderland Point and prevented this from further development. But Glasson itself never significantly grew.

CHRIST CHURCH. 1840. Nave with groups of three stepped lancets, bellcote, and a later Victorian chancel.

CROOK FARM, $1\frac{1}{2}$ m. SW, to be reached from the road to Cockersand Abbey. The house has two heads of Perp two-light windows, and the shippon one complete such window and two doorways with a continuous hollow chamfer. They come most probably from Cockersand.

2070
GLEASTON CASTLE
1¼ m. w of Aldingham

Gleaston Castle is assigned to the C14, probably its first half. It is an irregular oblong with angle towers of different shapes and sizes. The N side may never have been completed, and the castle was given up in the later C15. The principal tower, 92 by 53 ft, is in the NW corner. It stands in one corner up to *c.* 30 ft. The staircase is not a vice. Immediately s of this tower is a narrow gateway. Midway down the W wall is a projection, once probably a mid-tower. The sw tower is less than half the size of the NW tower. It stands up almost to the top and also has a straight staircase. The se tower again has a straight staircase. On the first floor is a fireplace. Of the NE tower less is preserved.

GOLDSHAW BOOTH see NEWCHURCH

5030
GOOSNARGH

The centre would be a handsome group, if it were not for one spec builder's red house and the SCHOOL of 1839. The two white pubs, the hospital, and the church are what make up the group.

ST MARY. Not a small church, but rustic throughout. Nothing is earlier than probably the early C16.* Massive W tower with stair projection and a round-arched doorway. Nave with low aisles and pretty dormers of 1869. (The work of that date is *Paley*'s.) Uncusped lights to the E and s windows. Six-bay arcade of standard elements. No chancel arch. The chancel is said by Glynne to have been rebuilt in 1553. – SCREEN to the N chapel. With a date 1622 and another 1721. – TOWER SCREEN dated 1678. – CHANDELIER of brass with two tiers of arms. C18. – PLATE. Chalice of 1746. – MONUMENT. Enormous slab with tracery panels and shields; barbaric. It is probably of the C14 and was appropriated in the early C17 by A. Rigby.

BUSHELL HOSPITAL. Founded in 1735.‡ A remarkably large and especially high stone block. The façade of thirteen bays, completely flat and three storeys high. The curious thing is the

---

* However, Canon A. Hodgson suggests that the N chancel wall, being 4 ft thick, might be C12 or C13 and refers also to the three small lancet windows in the E wall. For the N aisle he proposes the C14 and refers to the tomb recess.

‡ But are there not rainwater-heads dated 1722?

centre. It has a doorway with broken segmental pediment on attached columns, but instead of one pediment above it on top of the façade, two of two bays l. and r. of the doorway bay. Round the corner a three-bay side façade with a pedimented doorway and attached to it a wing of 1844–5. In front of that side an obelisk of 1844.

HILL CHAPEL (ST FRANCIS, R.C.). 1802, with a façade of 1835. Arched windows and an open bell-turret. The E wall inside has four pilasters and a blank arch behind the altar.

GRANGE-OVER-SANDS

4070

Grange-over-Sands began to develop as a resort when the Furness Railway arrived in 1857. The STATION is low and symmetrical, with half-hipped gables. The earlier houses are mostly of the gabled Tudor kind.

ST PAUL. 1853–4 by *J. Murray*, the N aisle 1861, the S aisle 1867, the chancel 1932. W bell-turret of 1853 between the gables of nave and S aisle. Arcades of low black marble columns set in pairs in depth. Polygonal apse.

(ST CHARLES (R.C.). 1883 by *E. Simpson.*)

The best building in Grange is the CLOCK TOWER by the parish church. It was put up in 1912, and is inspired by Edgar Wood, with its battered diagonal buttresses, its small band of bell-openings, and its short octagonal spire.

GRANGE HOTEL. 1866. Stone, large, nearly but not quite symmetrical. The window shapes still Early Victorian. The top parts more undisciplined.

NETHERWOOD HOTEL, originally called Blawith. Built as a private house in 1893 to the design of *Willink & Thicknesse.* Conservative for its date, with its gables, its Tudor wings, and its asymmetrical composition.

CONVALESCENT HOME, Risedale. 1914–16 by *W. Wadman.* Large, symmetrical, of brick, with white wooden trim and Edwardian motifs.

GRAYTHWAITE HALL *see* FAR SAWREY

GREAT ALTCAR *see* ALTCAR

GREAT ECCLESTON *see* ECCLESTON, p. 116

GREAT HARWOOD

7030

ST BARTHOLOMEW. At the N end, on the bend of the A road. A typical North Country church, Perp, with a squat W tower and a low nave. The W tower is probably C15, but the rest with the straight-headed windows with arched, uncusped lights will be Henry VIII. The chancel was rebuilt in 1886. The interior is as typical with its arcades of standard elements and its unsophisticated capitals. Very nice C17 nave roof, not *in situ*. – FONTS. In the S porch the panelled shaft of the Perp font. – Under the tower a font of 1663. Octagonal, with square panels, mostly with basic blank cusped arches in pairs. – BENCH ENDS. One, with a poppyhead, Perp, the other with a characteristic C17 top. – PLATE. Chalice by *Langland & Robertson*, 1809.

ST JOHN, St Hubert's Road. 1911–12. The plans by *Austin & Paley*, subsequently simplified.

OUR LADY AND ST HUBERT (R.C.), opposite the E end of St Hubert's Road. 1858–9 by *E.W.Pugin & Murray*. N porch steeple, cross-gabled double transepts; apse. The style is that of *c.*1300. – STAINED GLASS. Most of it evidently by *Hardman*.

TOWN HALL. 1900 by *Briggs & Wolstenholme*. Five bays, with the heavy Gibbs surrounds revived in the late C19 with so much gusto. To the l. of the building is BARCLAYS BANK, with a corner turret and forming a group with the town hall. Also part of the group is the CLOCK TOWER, 1903 by *A.H. Dunkin*. It commemorated a local man, John Mercer, who in 1850 invented the process of mercerizing textiles.

PUBLIC BATHS, formerly Mercer Hall, a hall for concerts etc. Hence so grand, and in the classical way, with giant columns on the façade. (Completed 1921; the interior remodelled by *W. Stirrup*, 1966.)

MARHOLME. Easily the most interesting house in the whole area. It dates from three periods, pre-Reformation, 1561, and 1607. 1607 is the date on the outer archway, and the mullioned and transomed windows go with it, 1561 is the date of the most spectacular work, the big, blocky inner gatehouse and most of the fenestration of the house. The windows are straight-headed and the lights have uncusped arches. In the gatehouse the main windows to outside and inside also have a transom. The arches into the gatehouse are round. But in addition the front of the house has a doorway next to the l. end of the front which has a two-centred arch, and recently it has been found that this led into a screens passage with exit (now inside the house) and two service doors. So the medieval hall was l. of this, and nothing remains of it. What we have is merely the service wing, and it has indeed two very large fireplaces, one now blocked up. Finally on the upper floor to the back, and a little to the r. of the screens passage, is a two-light window with pointed trefoiled lights – a form one would like to connect with c.1300.

GREAT PLUMPTON 3030

ST ANNE (R.C.). 1860–1 by *Edward W. Pugin*. Brick, nave and chancel in one. Not even a bellcote. The side windows are large foiled oculi or roses. Idiosyncratic interior with iron columns not carrying arches but wooden braces helping to support an elaborate timber roof.

GREAT URSWICK see URSWICK

GREENGORE see HURST GREEN

GREENHALGH CASTLE see GARSTANG

GREENMOUNT see TOTTINGTON

GRESGARTH HALL see CATON

GRESSINGHAM 5060

ST JOHN EVANGELIST. Rebuilt in 1734. Of that date the w tower with its vertical and horizontal bands and its still mullioned w window. The body of the church is of that date too, though the window details were made medieval by *Paley* in 1862. But the church is in fact much older. The s doorway is Norman. The three orders of the jambs have odd mouldings, the arches zigzags placed horizontally one on top of the other and also a rope moulding. And the N arcade is Perp. The N chapel arches look Perp too. – PULPIT. Of nice plain panels, one dated 1714. – BOX PEWS. – SCULPTURE. Two bits from a Saxon cross, a piece of scrollwork and a cross head with seven blobs in the centre. Also a stone with a trail built into the nave w wall at the s corner. – STAINED GLASS. Two windows with late and bad *Morris & Co.* glass. – MONUMENT. In the chapel oversized Gothic tomb-chest to George Marton of Capernwray House, † 1867.

GRESSINGHAM HALL, E of the church. L-shaped, with mullioned windows and one front of the early C18, still with two-light mullioned windows and still with a Yorkshire lintel, but already a standard five-bay composition.

5030

GRIMSARGH

St Michael. 1868–9 by *Paley & Austin*. Not specially good, except for the w tower with its tiled pyramid roof. Curious the way in which the N respond arch dies into the tower wall. The rest is dull. Low N arcade, tracery *c.*1300.

GRIMSHAW PARK *see* BLACKBURN, p. 67

GRIZEDALE HALL *see* SATTERTHWAITE

HACKING HALL *see* BILLINGTON

HAGGATE *see* BRIERCLIFFE

6000

HAIGH

St David. By *Rickman*, 1831–3. A Commissioners' church (price: £3,433). Nave with bellcote and chancel. Long lancet windows, shafted inside with shaft-rings, which shows Rickman's antiquarian leanings. Wide interior, originally probably with galleries. The ceiling panelled with large spiked quatrefoils. The E end was extended in 1886 by *Medland Taylor*. It is tripartite and has a hammerbeam roof. Medland Taylor probably also did the w gallery.

School. Symmetrical, brick, with three gables – quite handsome.

Our Lady of the Immaculate Conception (R.C.). 1857–8 by *J. Goodwin*. Small, with the presbytery next door.

Haigh Hall. Built 1827–40 for the *24th Earl of Crawford and Balcarres* and, it is said, to his own design.* The house is of two and a half storeys, all in beautiful ashlar-work. The s front is of eleven bays with two two-bay bay windows and a porch of 2–1–1–2 Tuscan columns. An urn crowns the parapet. There is no other decoration. Round the corner is a front with three canted bay windows. Inside, the entrance hall has a coffered ceiling. The staircase hall, oddly not in axis with the entrance hall, is magnificently spacious and has a glorious sail-vault with segmental lunettes and a glazed centre dome. The stucco-work is somewhat heavy-handed, but all the more impressive. The rich stucco decoration continues in the main rooms on the first floor. One smaller room has a shallowly apsed end. The subsidiary staircase comes from an earlier

* I owe the date 1827 to Mr J. Haworth.

house. It is clearly early C18. Three balusters to the tread, and carved tread-ends.

The STABLES must be of about 1850 or 1860. They are of red brick, with yellow-brick trim, and have a picturesquely placed tower, They are decidedly common, in comparison with the house.

Towards WIGAN LANE is the main GATEWAY, large, arched, with pairs of Doric pilasters. The two lodges have set-back Tuscan columns, two to the outside, two to the inside.

The PARK is spacious and in parts wild and romantic. It is a boon for Wigan.

ARLEY HALL (Wigan Golf Club), 1¾ m. NW. A delightful picture, with the moat and the odd and various gothicisms. The front with shaped gables and large straight-topped windows must be C19, but the side has little quatrefoils and mullioned windows with concave-sided triangles as tops and must be still C18. At the back two projections connected by a low link with a stepped gable and a cupola.

HALL BARNS see HURST GREEN

HALL FOLD see WHITWORTH

HALL O' T' HILL see ADLINGTON

HALLSWORTH FOLD FARMHOUSE see ADLINGTON

HALSALL

3010

ST CUTHBERT. Much of the exterior of the church is of 1886. The earliest medieval feature is the four-bay arcades with octagonal piers and arches with sunk quadrants. They are Dec. The inner surround of the S aisle E window goes with the arcade. The W tower of the type of Ormskirk, i.e. square, continuing by broaches into an octagon, and finished with a spire, is later C14 or early C15 – see the straight-headed two-light bell-openings. Perp S porch entrance and S doorway (re-set?) and large Perp chancel with two rood-turrets and tall three-light windows. The E window is of five lights. SEDILIA and PISCINA are Perp too, but the masonry of at least part of the chancel must be older, see the N recess (below) and the wide typically Dec doorway to the vestry. The rood window on the S side must be post-Reformation and hence rather a pulpit window. – STALLS. Late C15, with excellent

MISERICORDS. – BENCH ENDS. In the chancel, with poppy-heads and tracery. – DOOR to the vestry, with reticulated, i.e. Dec, tracery. – STAINED GLASS. Dec fragments in the S aisle E window, with much ruby-red. – PLATE. Chalice and Paten, 1609; Chalice and Paten, 1641; Paten and Flagon, 1730; two small Chalices, 1740. – MONUMENTS. Alabaster effigy of a priest, early C14. But the recess in which he lies is likely to be somewhat earlier. – Thomas Blundell † 1816. By *Crake* of London. Mourning woman by an urn with weeping willow.

S of the church tower is the former GRAMMAR SCHOOL, founded in 1593. It originally had two storeys. The windows are, it seems, early C19 Gothic.

N of the church is some WALLING with an arch. It has three doorways and three two-light windows. The VCH assigns it to the medieval priest's house.

RECTORY. By *S. Smirke*, 1844–5. Dignified, with a symmetrical entrance side with a Gothic loggia of four-centred arches.

HALTON

ST WILFRID. By *Paley & Austin*, 1876–7, except for the W tower, which (says Kelly) has a date 1597.* Paley & Austin are easily recognizable by their tiled roofs and the subtly composed variety of the Dec S windows. The church has a N aisle only. The chancel E window is placed high up, and the chancel N and S sides differ. On the N side is one arch opening to the organ chamber. – PLATE. Chalice and Paten, 1697–8; Flagon and Breadholder by *Edward York*, inscribed 1715; Chalice by *I.L.* of Newcastle, 1740–1. – MONUMENT. In the churchyard the fine two-tier façade of the family vault of the Bradshaw family. It is built against the hillside. The first burial was in 1760. Urns in niches l. and r. of the plain doorway. Top pediment. – Also in the churchyard is the HALTON CROSS, or what is left of it and has been well assembled into a whole cross. It dates from the C11. At the top of the shaft are the Signs of the Evangelists.‡ The figures below are too fragmentary for any identification. The scenes at the bottom of the shaft have been connected with the Sigurd saga. Higher up the Crucifixion (?) and the Resurrec-

* The Rev. G.O. Clayton tells me of Saxon and Norman stonework in the tower and much rebuilding in the C14.

‡ The Rev. G.O. Clayton thinks that they do not belong to the Halton Cross but rather to the Saxon cross – *see* below.

tion. Of the head only one arm remains, with close interlace. Interlace also on the sides and back of the cross, and on one side Sigurd's riderless horse Grain. – (In the church parts of several other crosses with figures and scrollwork.)

TOWER HOUSE, s of the church. To the street a fine classical three-bay façade with the main windows pedimented. If it were not for the battlements one would not expect that this façade belongs to a tower which ends a long stable range, at whose other end is another, smaller tower. It must be pre-1800 and may be as early as *c.*1760. Nothing precise seems to be known about it. Next to it CLOCK HOUSE, originally the coach house. Three bays with keyed-in arched windows and the large, now blank arch of the former gateway.

HAMBLETON 3040

ST MARY. The VCH says rebuilt 1749, Baines enlarged 1768. Neither date can apply to what we now see. This is clearly in the character of the early C19. Pointed windows with Y-tracery and buttresses between, E window of four lights with intersecting tracery. The w tower with its awkwardly corbelled-out pinnacles carries a date 1877.

HAMILTON ARMS see FORTON

HAMPSFIELD see BROUGHTON EAST

HAPTON 7030

ST MARGARET. By *R. Martin*, 1926–7. Small; Perp. Pretty façade, canted backward on both sides.

SHUTTLEWORTH HALL, ¾ m. NW. A substantial C17 house with a front with two projecting, cross-gabled wings and the porch attached to the r. hand one. Mullioned windows except for that of the recessed hall, which is of eight lights with a transom. In the gables odd three-light windows of a Yorkshire type. The head is a truncated ogee arch.

HARE CRAGS see TORVER

HARROCK HALL see WRIGHTINGTON

HASLINGDEN 7020

The westernmost of the string of overgrown industrial villages along the river Irwell. They have the hills N and s, but are

singularly poor in architectural rewards. Haslingden, says Dr
Aikin in 1795, 'has greatly improved within the last 20 years,
chiefly from increase of woollen manufacture, tho' much of cotton
trade has likewise been introduced within a few years'. It is the
same story everywhere around.

St James. 1780, enlarged 1827. In the same year the w tower
was built. The church has seven bays of arched windows in
two tiers. The galleries inside are Victorian in their details.
– Font. Early c16. Octagonal, with shields.

St John Evangelist, Stonefold, 1½ m. NNW. By *Basil
Champneys*, 1885–6. Nave with bellcote and chancel. Dec
style. A substantial and well detailed job.

St Stephen, Haslingden Grane, ¼ m. SW. With a NW tower
with broach-spire and a polygonal apse. Plate tracery. The
church was built in 1868 and transferred to its present site in
1927.

St Peter, Laneside, ½ m. SE. Also by *Champneys*. Built in
1890. Also Dec, but with a small E turret. The nave has
never been built.

St Thomas, Musbury, 1½ m. S. 1850–1 by *Shellard*. Slender
broach-spire. Reticulated tracery. Conventional interior. It is
a Commissioners' church (cost £2,500).

Trinity Baptist Chapel, Blackburn Road. 1872. With an
attached Tuscan giant portico. The windows, as usual, round-
as well as segment-arched.

Helmshore Station. Single-storeyed, with the windows of
two or three round-arched lights characteristic of the 1840s.
The Illustrated London News in 1848 wrote indeed that the
building was 'not yet completed but promised to be a very
tasteful little structure'.

Carter Place Hall, 1 m. N. An ashlar-faced late c18 house
of five bays with a three-bay pediment. The porch with its
surround is of course Victorian. The rest has delicate Adamish
decoration.

3080   HAVERTHWAITE

St Anne. 1824–5. Goodhart-Rendel writes of it: 'The architect
is uncertain, and no one would want to claim it.' w tower.
Nave and chancel with pointed windows with Y-tracery.

(Bigland Hall, 1¼ m. SE. Mainly of 1809, with a Roman Doric
portico *in antis*. MHLG)

Backbarrow, ¾ m. NE. Isaac Wilkinson settled here about

1738. He developed ironworks at Backbarrow and built himself in the 1740s BREWER SYKE HOUSE. The house has an C18 back garden for which the rock had to be cut away. For the Wilkinson story *see* Lindale, p. 168.

HAWKSHAW LANE *see* HOLCOMBE

HAWKSHEAD

3090

ST MICHAEL. In an elevated position. A church of the C16 to 27 mid C17, long and low, with a low W tower. On the S aisle a date 1578. This refers to work by Archbishop Sandys and suits the odd rounded mouldings of the lights of the straight-headed windows. On the N the clerestory is dated 1633, again convincingly. The interior is baffling. Shapeless piers and shapeless arches. It has been called Norman, but is more likely debased C16, however engaging it may be. The walls are white with INSCRIPTIONS of 1711. Earlier than the C16 only one C15 S aisle window and the jambs of the N doorway, which could be C13. – STAINED GLASS. The E window must be by *Hardman*. – PLATE. Chalice by *T.F.*, 1720–1; Paten by *R.B.*, 1736; Chalice by *W*. (or *W.C.*), 1759–60. – MONUMENTS. William Sandys and wife, formerly dated 1578. They were the Archbishop's parents. Tomb-chest with two rustically carved recumbent effigies, he a Knight in early C16 armour. – Col. Thomas Myles Sandys, M.P., † 1911. White marble effigy by *Wade*. – WAR MEMORIAL in the churchyard, *c*.1919. An Anglo-Saxon cross designed by *W.G.Collingwood*.

Hawkshead is a delightful village. The centre is the MARKET PLACE, with the TOWN HALL on the N side and on the S side houses liberated from all building lines. The town hall was built in 1790, with open arcades below and windows in blank arches above. The lengthening is of 1887.

GRAMMAR SCHOOL, S of, and below, the church. Endowed in 1575 by Archbishop Sandys. The windows which could be of his time were made in 1891 to replace sashes. The doorway is of 1675, with its bold lintel moulding and its curly pediment. Wordsworth attended the school from 1777 to 1783.

HAWKSHEAD HALL. The GATEHOUSE is now a detached building, but was originally part of a courtyard house. It dates from the C15 and has stepped gables. The hall and solar lay on the S side, SW of the gatehouse, and of the C16 W range part now forms a house of no special interest. In the gatehouse on the upper floor is a fireplace with a dogtooth moulding. This may have come from Furness Abbey. The manor was the abbey's.

BELMOUNT, ¼ m. N of the Hall. Later C18. Five bays, two and a half storeys. Doorway with Tuscan columns and pediment. L. and r. two one-bay pavilions.

(ESTHWAITE LODGE, I m. S. Three bays with a Greek Doric porch. MHLG)

FRIENDS' MEETING HOUSE, Colthouse, ½ m. NE. Built in 1688. The façade has Georgian windows, but on one short side are two cross-windows, and at the back is one of three lights with a transom. Above the lobby was the separate women's meeting room. The furnishings are C18.

HEAPEY

6020

ST BARNABAS. Transepts and chancel of 1865. But what is the date of the nave? It has large arched windows with mullions and transoms. That looks mid to later C17. The VCH indeed calls it late C17. Kelly says enlarged 1740, enlarged 1829; D. S. Rennard's *History of Heapey Church* (1915) rebuilt 1752, enlarged 1829. The W front with three stepped arched windows could be either. Fine, wide view to the W.

HEATHWAITE FELL see WOODLAND

HEIGHT see CARTMEL

HELMSHORE see HASLINGDEN

HESKETH END see CHIPPING

HESKIN

5010

HESKIN HALL. A mid C17 brick house* with an asymmetrical gabled S front. Two storeys and a third behind the gables. Three canted bay windows and a three-storeyed porch. The kitchen at the back has three equal small gables and a very thick back wall with the fireplace and a slightly projecting stair-turret. The W part of the back looks early C19. (The room W of the hall has panelling with Ionic pilasters and elaborate strapwork. VCH, vol. VI)

HOWE BROOK HOUSE. An C18 brick front of three bays, but behind it timber-framing of *c.*1600 including a gable with herringbone struts.

* One rainwater-head has the date 1670.

HEST BANK

The seaside development is essentially C20.

In the Lancaster Road is SLYNE MANOR HOUSE, dated 1681,
and already with a symmetrical five-bay front. The windows
are of the cross type, and the doorway has a Yorkshire lintel
of a pattern found in North Lancashire. (Nice Chippendale
staircase. NMR)

(BEAUMONT GRANGE, ½ m. SE of the former, is early C19
castellated. Three bays, two storeys, with a three-storey
centre. Screen walls l. and r. and pavilions with splayed walls
and battlements. MHLG)

HEY HOUSE see HOLCOMBE

HEYSHAM

Heysham is now simply part of Morecambe, but the village and
its early C19 surroundings survive to a far greater extent than
anywhere at Morecambe: the venerable village church, cottages
close by, and two of the seats of rich people also close by.

ST PETER. Low and of modest size. The W doorway is Anglo-
Saxon; so is the S aisle W window, which cannot be *in situ*, and
the N doorway now displayed separately by the path up to St
Patrick's Chapel. How early they are is anybody's guess. The
chancel arch has responds with coarse Early Norman capitals
with rope mouldings. The chancel E window with intersecting
tracery is of *c.*1300, the S window (of a time before there was
a S chapel) is Dec. The S side has mixed Dec to Perp windows
and an elementary Perp two-bay arcade. The N aisle of 1864.
The double bellcote must be C17. – SCREEN. Perp, of one-
light divisions. – FONT COVER. C17; openwork. – SCULPTURE.
In the churchyard is the lower part of an exceedingly interesting Anglo-Saxon Cross. The ornament is foliage scrolls,
but there is also a gabled building with arched niches or 7
windows. In the top three of them are busts, between the
others stands a swathed figure (Lazarus ?). On the opposite
side is a seated figure with a halo. – Inside the church two
fragments with scrolls. – PLATE. Two Chalices, C17 (York) and
1788. – MONUMENTS. Hogback tombstone, the type with
two bears biting into the ends. – Coffin lid with a richly
foliated cross; C13.

ST PATRICK'S CHAPEL, N of and above the church. A plain
rectangle, 27½ by 9 ft. The S doorway has an arch made of one

stone with concentric grooves. Dating varies between the C8 and C9. Rock-cut graves near the chapel.

N of the village the MIDDLETON ARMS. This was Heysham Old Hall. It has a recessed centre and two slightly projecting wings with low-pitched gables. The porch is attached to the l. wing. Mullioned and transomed windows. A stately house, probably of 1598 – only the 9 and the 8 are recognizable in the r. hand gable.

HEYSHAM TOWER, now in the holiday camp, built *c.*1830–40 for J. T. Knowlys. The date-stone 1839 is *ex situ.* Castellated and machicolated, with asymmetrical front with a porch and a canted tower on the r. Also castellated walls.

Another castellated house, now in the entertainment centre, dates probably from the late C18. It is just a three-bay block, with a small porch. Gothic only the glazing bars of the windows. The LODGE in the centre of the village belongs to this house. It is also a castellated block and has an archway.

HIGHAM

8030

ST JOHN EVANGELIST. 1874. E.E., with a SW turret.

ST ANNE, Fence, ½ m. E. Built in 1836–7. W tower, very long lancets, short chancel. – (STAINED GLASS. The E window is by *Kempe, c.*1890.)

METHODIST CHURCH. Stone front of four bays. Italianate style. Built in 1872.

(LOWER WHITE LEE. C18, three storeys. At the back a circular window with radiating tracery bars. MHLG)

FENCE HOUSE. The big arch seems to be made up of stones not originally belonging. The MHLG dates it C14.

HIGHER WALTON *see* WALTON-LE-DALE

HILTON HOUSE *see* BLACKROD

HODDER BRIDGE *see* HURST GREEN

HODDLESDEN

7020

ST PAUL. 1862–3 by *E. G. Paley.* W tower with higher stair-turret. Nave, N aisle, and chancel. Late C13 form. Not an attractive church.

MILL and mill housing belong to the village, especially one terrace with a pedimental centre.

(HOLKER HOUSE FARMHOUSE. 1691. For details *see* MHLG.)

HOGHTON

HOLY TRINITY. 1824. With the usual lancets. The W tower of 1887. The chancel also must be Victorian.

HOGHTON TOWER. The Hoghton family has resided at Hoghton ever since the early C14. However, the large and spectacular mansion which one sees now apparently holds no certain medieval evidence. It belongs mainly to the second half of the C16 and to the C17, with a date 1565 over the archway between the lower and upper court, and a date 1700 on the W range of building along the S side of the lower court. The position of the house with the steep fall to the N and E makes one think of a medieval predecessor placed here for defensive reasons. Thomas Hoghton in 1561–2 said that 'hee hath enterprysed and begun to bylde a Howse'. This must from the beginning have had the two courtyards; for the outer and the inner archways have the same elements (semi-octagonal responds, chamfered arches), which for the 1560s were conservative.

The lower court is reached at the end of a long, straight drive by the first of the gateways. This is a three-storeyed embattled tower. L. and r. are embattled walls leading to two square pavilions. As a composition all this strikes one as late C18 or early C19, though the gatehouse and the pavilions have C16 masonry. The N side of the lower court has one part whose masonry is again C16, but most of that side is of 1901. The S side has the date 1700, but still two-light mullioned windows, though they are set fairly regularly. The range was originally detached at its E end. In the centre of the lower court are gate piers with fine C18 iron gates. They lead to a front garden, as if there were no outer court. The E range, i.e. the one between lower and upper court, originally had in the middle a high tower, the tower from which the mansion takes its name.

The upper court had in its centre until not so long ago a STATUE of William III cast in lead. This however has been sold. The great hall is in the N range, the chapel was originally 34 in the NE corner. The porch to the outside at the E end of the smallest room is recent, but includes a doorway of *c*.1300 which must be *ex situ*. Does it tell of a previous chapel on the site? All four ranges are assigned by the VCH to the C16, but since there are several straight joints indicating breaks in the building process, it is possible that work went on into the C17.

James I visited Hoghton Tower in 1617. Perhaps one may assume that alterations or completions were made against that visit.

The great hall has a doorway with leaf spandrels, three windows of four lights with two transoms, and canted bay windows to court and outside. They have three transoms. The gable of the bay stands on corbels coming from the canted sides. To the doorway from the courtyard corresponded an exit to the outside, but this is now hidden by a mysterious attachment. It has pilasters on corbels and on the E side a blocked doorway, to the N two arches, Was it a porch? If so, what for? Also the pilasters look Early Elizabethan, i.e. c.1560–5, but the hall details are more likely to be Late Elizabethan or Jacobean. The general character of this upper court resembles on a smaller scale that of Stonyhurst, i.e. work of c.1600. All windows have mullions and transoms. Inside the hall is a big fireplace with monsters in the spandrels. Screen and minstrels' gallery have C17 balusters. The state rooms are on the first floor of the E range. Panelling etc. seems to be of c.1700. To the same date belongs the main staircase with its twisted balusters.

A high BARN NW of the lower court is dated 1692. It is 120 ft long.

RAILWAY VIADUCT. Mid C19. With three very high rusticated piers carrying arches.

7010 ## HOLCOMBE

EMMANUEL. 1852–3. Large, with a W steeple with broach-spire. Aisles and transepts.

ST MARY, Hawkshaw Lane, 2 m. SW. 1890–2 by *Maxwell & Tuke*. The tower was never completed.

PEEL MONUMENT. 1851–2, in memory of Sir Robert Peel. By *Grant, Ashton, Knowles & Gorton*. An obelisk, 120 ft high.

HEY HOUSE, ⅝ m. SW. The old part is C17, a centre with two projecting wings. Mullioned and transomed windows below, mullioned only above.

3070 ## HOLKER HALL

Pronounced Hooker. The architectural interest of the house is almost entirely Victorian. There is however in addition the so-called Old Wing extending at r. angles to the Victorian building, and this contains work of the early C17 built for George Preston (cf. Cartmel) and a sweeping rebuilding by

Webster of Kendal *c.*1840, for the Cavendish family. The Old Wing with its Tudor windows and hood-moulds represents that build. Behind is much utilitarian Georgian work. The Victorian building, a replacement after a fire of 1871, is the grandest of its date in Lancashire, and it is moreover by the best architects then living in the county: *Paley & Austin.* It is their outstanding domestic work, red sandstone, in the Elizabethan style. The three sides – the fourth has the older left-overs – are all calculatedly asymmetrical, the entrance side with a porch and a four-storeyed tower which contains 85 the staircase, the short side with a triangular oriel and a stately round angle bay, and the garden side that angle bay and then a flat front with asymmetrically placed dormers. It is a pleasure to follow the compositional *finesse.* Nor does it interfere with the unabashed display which was obviously expected. The motifs are all Elizabethan – mullioned and transomed windows, gables, etc. – yet the house is like no Elizabethan house and to that extent a pattern of Victorian originality.* – In one room in the Old Wing is a chimneypiece made up of C17 woodwork – a relief of Adam and Eve in Paradise and statuettes of the four Evangelists.

(ICE HOUSE, in the park, on a knoll. Rectangular entrance room and domed storage room. MHLG)

ESTATE HOUSING of more than one period around the estate.

HOLME
8020

ST JOHN. Built in 1788–94, but the chancel and vestry, tactfully done, of 1897. Ashlar-faced, with a handsome bell-turret, square with an octagonal cupola. The façade is rather bitty. Three bays l. and r., two tiers of windows, in the middle a pedimented doorway and a lunette window seat in a blind arch. The side windows are treated in the same way. The interior is entirely of 1897 and decidedly disappointing. – PULPIT. Early C16 panels of elaborate flamboyant tracery. 22 But can they originally have been pierced? St Mary, Lancaster permits an affirmative answer (*see* p. 154). – BENCH ENDS. A few of the early C16. – PANELLING. Some, of the linenfold variety. – MONUMENT. Bust of T.D. Whitaker, † 1876, the historian of Whalley. By *C.R. Smith.*

* Mr J. Haworth tells me that for the library ceiling the RIBA has drawings by *J.G. Crace.*

Whitaker lived at THE HOLME. It is an attractive, low, two-storeyed stone house with centre and two wings with low-pitched gables. The windows are mullioned, but all the detail looks mid C19, especially the tall mullioned windows of the wings. (Inside, a date 1603, some fine ceilings, and interesting C19 fretwork panelling. MHLG)

STONE CIRCLE, 1 m. NE, on Moseley Height, 1000 ft above sea level. It consists of a circular embankment 42 ft in diameter enclosed by eighteen large boulders. Within the circle were four stone cists containing cremations, three within Early Bronze Age collared urns.

4020

HOOLE

ST MICHAEL. Small, but uncommonly interesting. The church represents worthily two periods: 1628 and 1722. The body is of 1628, brick, with mullioned windows, their lights arched. The S porch with segmental entrance arch and leaf spandrels (still!) is also of 1628. But the W tower was added in 1722. It is stone-faced and projects only slightly. Hence its E angles rest inside on two big detached columns. The motif is taken up outside by two Tuscan demi-columns and a blank arch embracing the doorway and a big oculus window. The upper openings are altered. – FONT. Polygonal, massive, and completely undecorated. How would one date it, if it did not have an inscription with the date 1663? – PULPIT. With a fine sounding board dated 1695. – DESK. C17 woodwork, not *in situ*. – BENCH ENDS. A few, minor, C17. – WEST and SOUTH GALLERIES. – BOX PEWS. – PLATE. Two Chalices inscribed 1629; Breadholder, early C17.

5060

HORNBY

ST MARGARET. The church is of 1817 and 1889 except for two important parts, W and E. W is a tower starting octagonal from the ground and, on its second stage, remaining octagonal, but, by means of broaches, with a twist of half a side. The E end is a polygonal apse, a great rarity in England. Both parts are connected with the building erected by Sir Edward Stanley, Lord Mounteagle. He built the tower in 1514 and died in 1524, leaving the church unfinished. The architect of 1817 is responsible for the aisle walls with windows, altered in 1889. The architect of 1889 did a remarkably refined job. The arcades have slim piers, and the arches die into them. – SCULPTURE. Part of an Anglo-Saxon cross shaft with two fishes and loaves of bread and above two figures separated by a tree. On one other side a demi-figure; otherwise all interlace. – Also a cross fragment with zigzag, and, in the churchyard, a stone with tapering sides and on every side an arch on shafts. – PLATE. Two silver-gilt Cups and two Patens by *G.S.*, 1761. – MONUMENTS. (Dr Lingard † 1851. Tablet by *Hardman*. A tablet to a Catholic priest in an Anglican church – *see* below.) – W.H.Forster † 1908. An angel on a cloud. Still signed *Gaffin* of Regent Street.

ST MARY (R.C.). 1820. Built by the then priest, Dr Lingard, the historian. An amorphous building enriched with parts of the Catholic chapel at Claughton. The doorway has a Venetian shape, identical with that of the Venetian windows of the presbytery. Here there are two on the ground floor, and the windows above it are tripartite.

HORNBY CASTLE. At the back is a spectacular pele tower of the C13 below, the early C16 above. The oriel was discovered only recently. The original windows are pairs in the early C16 style. 'At the back' means at the back of an even more spectacular castle of 1849–52 and later. The work of 1849–52 was done for Pudsey Dawson, a financier, by *Sharpe & Paley*. It includes the façade, which is not quite symmetrical in so far as the gatehouse-like centre has a higher turret on one side. In the middle of this frontispiece is an oriel. (Vaulted porch and panelled entrance hall.) About 1889 a good deal more was done, this time for the Forsters of Bradford and by *Paley & Austin*, and in the last thirty years much has been demolished and remodelled. The castle looks from the bridge as if seen in a picture book.

HORWICH

HOLY TRINITY, at the upper, i.e. E, end of the little town. 1830–1 by *F.Bedford*. A large and dignified Commissioners' church which cost £5,999 to build. Ashlar, with a tall, slender W tower. The side windows of two lights, cusped. The chancel added in 1903 by *R.Knill Freeman*, short but solid, a real addition to the value of the church. The interior has slender arcade piers of canted lozenge shape and ribbed plaster vaults. – MONUMENT. Joseph Ridgway † 1842. By *R.Westmacott Jun*. Free-standing, white marble, with a kneeling female figure.

E of the church a SCHOOL of 1793 with two Venetian windows, W of the church another, of 1832, with Tudor details.

LEE LANE CONGREGATIONAL CHURCH. 1855–6 by *Woodhouse* of Bolton. Gothic, with Commissioners' lancets. No tower.

PUBLIC HALL, Lee Lane. 1878, brick; no interest.

COLLEGE OF FURTHER EDUCATION, Victoria Road. 1959–61 by *C. H. Simmons*, the then County Architect. Neatly grouped and neatly detailed. More materials perhaps than is good for the group.

MECHANICS INSTITUTE, Chorley New Road. 1887–8. Red brick. Remarkably large. The side to the street is of thirteen bays, the seven middle ones with large round-headed windows. It is a solid block, with no nonsense about it.

LOSTOCK HALL. Only the gatehouse survives. It is supposed to date from *c.*1563. The building is remarkably broad. The gateway itself is round-arched, and the room above has a transomed window of four plus four lights on the first and another on the second floor. To the l. and r. are paired columns, but very widely spaced, incorrect Doric, incorrect Ionic, incorrect Corinthian. Outside them are the small rooms with small windows. The whole is crenellated with semicircles.

LOWER HOUSE, Lostock, Junction Lane and Chorley New Road. Built for W. H. Lever by *Jonathan Simpson* early in their careers and architecturally nothing special.

(WALSUCHES MILL, 1 m. E. Built in 1777 and later for John and Thomas Ridgway's bleaching works. A Walls engine was installed as early as 1798. How the existing buildings compare with these dates has not yet been investigated. The main building is of thirty bays and three storeys. Smaller buildings adjoin, and they are probably earlier. The Ridgways' house is of ashlar, five bays, and has a segmental centre bay with tripartite window and porch. It looks early C19.)

HUNCOAT *see* ACCRINGTON, pp. 46, 47

HUNTINGDON HALL *see* DUTTON

HUNTROYDE *see* SIMONSTONE

6030   HURST GREEN

ST JOHN EVANGELIST. 1838. Lancets and a short castellated tower. No aisles.

Former SCHOOL. The front has a raised canted centre with battlements. There is a date 1686, but the house was enlarged and virtually rebuilt in 1859.

GUILDHALL, at the junction with the Stonyhurst road. A private house, but cross-shaped, with a raised square centre. The arms are two bays long.

SHIREBURNE ALMSHOUSES. Transferred in 1936 to the site near Stonyhurst from Kemple End on Longridge Fell. They were built in 1706. The top storey is not original. Centre of seven bays with three-bay pediment and two-bay projecting wings, also with pediments. The windows are all of the cross-type. Fine balustrade connecting the wings.

GREENGORE, ¾ m. NW. A strange house, said to be of the C15. The buttresses seem at first to confirm that, but they are obviously an addition. The windows are not older than Elizabethan. That leaves the odd garderobe-like or chimney-like corbelled projection on the first floor.

HALL BARNS, ⅞ m. NE, close to Stonyhurst. Large stone barn with enormous cruck-trusses inside.

HODDER BRIDGE, on the Yorkshire border. Medieval, and in picturesque ruin. Three segmental arches.

CEMETERY CHAPEL. Ashlar, with Ionic columns *in antis*. The land was given in 1825. The chapel looks not much later, but Father Clark of Stonyhurst favours a date *c*.1865.

HURSTWOOD
¾ m. SE of Worsthorne

8030

(HURSTWOOD HALL. 1579, perhaps with an older core. With gables and mullioned windows. The house is the centre of an architecturally rewarding hamlet. The best house is SPENSER HOUSE, also with gables and mullioned windows. In addition a barn and five buildings are graded II. MHLG)

INGLEWHITE

5040

CONGREGATIONAL CHAPEL. 1826. With arched windows.

ST JAMES, Whitechapel, 1¼ m. NE. 1738, enlarged 1818, restored 1889. It is the latter date which is insensitively written all over the walls.

INSKIP

4030

ST PETER. 1848 by *J. E. Gregan*. N tower with broach-spire. Nave with a bellcote as well. Lancet windows, but geometrical tracery in the chancel.

IRELETH

2070

ST MARY. 1865 on the site of an Episcopal chapel of 1612.
White and red stone. Small N tower. The church lies high up
with a view across to Millom.

MARSH GRANGE, 1⅜ m. N. A late C17 five-bay house with
wooden cross windows and a pair of gatepiers too grand for it.
They are heavily moulded and have up their middles thin
pilasters with sunk panels – all very English Baroque.

KIRKHAM

4030

Kirkham is an attractive little town, quite a relief between
Preston and Blackpool. It has hardly any houses one would note
specially, but two churches of interest.

ST MICHAEL. 1822, with an excellent steeple of 1843–4 and a
chancel of 1853. The work of 1822 cost £5,000 and has the
usual lancets and thin buttresses. The steeple is 150 ft high,
with a recessed spire. Crockets run up the edges and flying
buttresses support the spire. All this is Dec and perhaps the
finest work of *Edmund Sharpe*, scholar in the field of the Dec
style. The interior is determined by three galleries on iron
columns. – The few BOX PEWS with poppyheads must be
Victorian. The plate with the date 1770 cannot apply. –
CHANDELIER of brass, 1725, by *Brown* of Wigan. – PLATE.
Set of 1845. – MONUMENT. In the S aisle a Dec tomb recess
with big pierced tracery.

Opposite the church is the former NATIONAL SCHOOL, brick,
of 1814, five bays, with a three-bay pediment and the ground-
floor windows set in blank arcading.

ST JOHN EVANGELIST (R.C.), The Willows. By *Pugin*, who,
according to Mrs Stanton's unpublished research, received
the commission in 1842. The building was paid for by the
Gillow family. The church was opened in 1845. It is a modest
building and, like so much of Pugin's, really very impersonal.
He was unquestionably greater as a publicist than as an architect, although he could rise to occasions. Early Dec style. W
tower with broach-spire. The clerestory windows pointed
quatrefoils. Round piers and double-chamfered arches. The
E end must be altered. – ALTAR. The altar in the N chapel was
formerly the high altar. It is by *Pugin*, but has been altered. –
SCREEN. Also by *Pugin*; now at the W end. – The GATEWAY
is very characteristic of *Pugin*.

(ST ANNE (R.C.), Westby. 1860 by *E. W. Pugin*.)

CONGREGATIONAL CHURCH, Poulton Street. 1896–7 by *Briggs & Wolstenholme*. Also Gothic, and also with a spire, but next to Pugin, let alone Sharpe, barren and rather coarse.

GRAMMAR SCHOOL, W of the Catholic church. 1909–11 by *Greenaway & Newberry*. A delightful design, simplified Tudor in the Voysey sense and entirely free in composition. Small fancy lantern on top in the centre, but no strict symmetry otherwise.

Of houses only two must be singled out. One is No. 2 CHURCH STREET, later C18, of five bays and two and a half storeys, with a rather heavy door surround. Fine staircase. The other good house is HILLSIDE, Preston Street, built, it is said, after 1825. Outer staircase of two arms with nice iron railing.

The site of a ROMAN FORT or fortlet lies to the N of the main road. It was first occupied in the late C1.

KIRKLAND

ST HELEN, Churchtown, the parish church of Garstang. The story begins with the arcade between chancel and N chapel. The pier and the E respond have stiff-leaf capitals, the section being similar to that of the pier in the chapter house of Cockersand Abbey. The W respond is clearly contemporary but much shorter. What is the explanation? All this work will be of c.1220–30. Then follows the N arcade, also entirely E.E. Of about 1300 the S aisle W window (cusped intersected tracery) and probably also the S arcade. The N aisle W window is a typically Dec version of intersecting, with all arches straightened (cf. infirmary, Furness Abbey). Dec chancel arch. The W tower is Perp (stair-turret with little spire), and most of the windows of the church are Perp too. The two-storeyed vestry is Latest Perp and probably post-Reformation. The clerestory windows date from 1811. The S chapel ceiling is inscribed 1529, the chancel roof 1620. The PISCINA in the chapel must be of c. 1300, i.e. *ex situ*. – PULPIT. 1646, yet still entirely Elizabethan in its carved arabesque panels. – SCREEN. The dado at least of the screen to the S chapel is ancient, i.e. C17. – CHANDELIER. In the nave, of brass, undated, but no doubt C18. – PLATE. Chalice of 1658, by *T.C.*; Chalice inscribed 1690, by *R.M.*; Paten of 1719; two Flagons of 1795. – MONUMENTS. Defaced effigy, praying. – Alexander Butler of Kirkland Hall † 1811. By *T.Franceys & Spence* of Liverpool. Tablet with a seated figure, with sword and *fasces*.

Close to the entrance of the churchyard a five-bay house with a porch of fluted columns. Some small distance to the E the OLD VICARAGE, with a semicircular porch of Composite columns.

In the middle of Churchtown the MARKET CROSS, a column with a ball on top, put up by Alexander Butler (*see* above).

KIRKLAND HALL. The front is of brick, dated 1760. It is of seven bays and two and a half storeys, with a three-bay pediment. The doorway has a porch of two columns and also two pilasters l. and r. Behind are two wings forming an L and, according to the brickwork, C17. There are indeed date-stones
41   1668 and 1695, but the windows and the gables look remodelled about 1840 or so.

KNOTT END *see* PREESALL

4060

LANCASTER

INTRODUCTION*

One may be fascinated by many a North Lancashire town, but it is not aesthetic qualities one would remember. Lancaster remains in one's memory for many visual beauties, the view from
4 the N to the river and the castle and the church on their rock, the view from the castle and the church towards the bay and the fells, and the streets still in a number of cases almost purely Georgian. Lancaster is a Georgian town, despite its great medieval past. There is apart from castle and parish church nothing early – no monastic ruin, no remains of the Blackfriars, who came about 1260 and settled round Sulyard Street. And yet the town received its first charter from John, Count of Mortain, brother of King Richard I, in 1193 and its first royal charter in 1199. When in 1351 the county of Lancashire was made into a County Palatine, the then Earl became Duke of Lancaster. His son-in-law, John of Gaunt, succeeded to the title. With Henry IV the Duchy became royal, and has remained so to this day. The importance of Lancaster went down in the C16, but the town enjoyed a certain prosperity again in the C18. It was a port trading mostly with the West Indies. Arthur Young in 1770 reports more than a hundred ships trading from Lancaster. 'It is a

* Lancaster was the site of a ROMAN FORT. Limited excavations some years ago produced evidence of a C1(?) rampart, C2 timber buildings, C3 military stone buildings, and a stone defensive wall of a late C3–early C4 fort which may have been built to counter the threat of pirates raiding the west coasts.

town increasing in buildings,' he writes, 'having many new piles, much superior to the old.' The warehouses along St George's Quay and the Custom House still tell of that phase. However, competition arose already in the early C18, when Robert Lawson, a Quaker, developed Sunderland at the mouth of the Lune into a harbour. The attempt failed in the end, but from 1787 Glasson Docks were built by Lancaster and took over sea trade. Now Lancaster is a comfortably busy county town, nicely balanced in its functions and of a size to be able to do justice to them and offer the citizens amenities. The university has recently added a new function, new amenities, and new possibilities. A pity it is not nearer the town.

INNER LANCASTER

CHURCHES

St MARY. The church originated in the foundation of a priory church on the castle by Roger of Poitou in 1094. It was Benedictine, a cell of Séez in Normandy. It was not built on a virgin site; for excavations in 1912 exposed a wall beneath the chancel area which may be Roman, and also an apse just E of the present chancel arch. This is in all probability Early Norman. Moreover, in the w wall of the present nave a small Saxon doorway is exposed. The present nave and chancel are essentially Perp, but there is an E.E. s doorway with one order of columns and some continuous mouldings. The Perp work is connected with the transfer of the church from Séez to Syon outside London in 1431, but there is no certainty, and the E parts look late C14 rather than of the 1430s. In examining the church the w tower will at once be recognized as a good deal later than Perp. It was in fact rebuilt in 1754 by an architect called *Sephton*. The bell-openings are a typical pre-Strawberry-Hill Gothic, with Y-tracery, but rather clumsily handled and with C17-looking cherubs' heads in the spandrels. The nave, before a tower was built, had a doorway to the w. This sur-vives and is without doubt C14. The s side of the church is of seven bays, with windows with the plainest stepped and cusped lights under four-centred arches. The buttresses come to a front edge in plan. Battlements, and an embattled clerestory also with three-light windows, and with pinnacles. The s porch, two-storeyed and ornate with a stair-turret, dates from 1903 and is by *Austin & Paley*. The E window is of five lights with the Perp panel tracery one would expect.

The N side has an outer N aisle with polygonal apse, and this was added in 1903 too. It has handsome piers, their capitals with black-letter inscriptions. The church is 145 ft long and the tower 96 ft high.

The interior is as impressive as the exterior. The nave has four bays, and the arcades are standard, but the chancel arch, the arches into the chancel chapels, and the four-bay chancel arcades are finely moulded and decidedly later C14 in character. The piers have the familiar four-shafts-and-four-hollows section.

The furnishings are plentiful and rewarding. One will start of course with the STALLS. They are said to come from Cockersand or Furness Abbey. They were certainly the inspiration for the stalls of the C17 at Cartmel. But at Lancaster they are Dec, and they have about the most luxuriant canopies in the country. The tracery is very much like French or North Country Flamboyant of 1500, and the gables are encrusted with thick foliage. The arms between the seats have heads, and there are MISERICORDS. – PULPIT. Dated 1619 and closely carved. – SCREEN. See Capernwray. – STAIRS to the W gallery. C18. – CHANDELIERS. Three, of brass, large, with round bodies and two tiers of arms. Dated 1717. – SCULPTURE. Many Anglo-Saxon fragments in the N chapel. They are two fragments from the upper part of a cross with vine and scroll patterns on all sides, two fragments of a shaft, one with an Orate inscription, one fragment of the same age and character, one fragment with Adam, Eve, and the Serpent and the Crucifixion, one irregular fragment of a cross head with Christ in a circle, one fragment with two birds and two human figures, one fragment with hart and hounds and snakes, and one recently found fragment with an Orate inscription to one Cynibad. – STAINED GLASS. The E window was designed by *Paley* and made by *Wailes*. – In the N chapel glass of 1857. – (Four BRASS CROSSES, brought from Abyssinia about 1870. With naive engravings of Gospel stories.)* – PLATE. Four Flagons by *W. S.*, 1678–9; Chalice by the same; two Breadholders by *F. A.*, 1697–8; Small Chalice presented in 1728; Cup, Newcastle, by *R. M.*, 1757. – MONUMENTS. Not one is medieval. Sir Samuel Eyre † 1698. Large tablet with a small bust above a big curly open pediment. – William

* My attention was drawn to these by Mrs Mason, who also kindly checked the list of cross fragments for me.

Stratford † 1753. By *Roubiliac*. At the foot a medallion with a tender group of Charity. – Sibyl Wilson † 1773, aged six. Signed *Fishers* York. Relief group with the child on a couch, the mother sitting by it, and the father in Roman dress standing by the child's feet. The decoration is elegant, the figure carving provincial. – Frances Atkinson † 1779. Urn and lettering as good as that of the previous monument. – In the churchyard monument to the Rawlinson family, *c.* 1790, with a white semi-reclining female figure.

St Peter, the Catholic cathedral, St Peter's Road. A fine, aspiring building, with a high, excellently detailed NW steeple, 240 ft high, and a high nave and chancel. The style imitated is that of 1300. The baptistery on the N side like a polygonal chapter house, stone-vaulted. Five-bay nave with slender round piers. Two-light clerestory windows with detached shafts. Transepts, two-bay chancel chapels, and a polygonal apse. By *Paley*, 1857–9. – The STAINED GLASS in the apse clearly by *Hardman*.

The BISHOP'S HOUSE, in a domestic Gothic, is by *Paley* and *Paley & Austin*, 1859 and 1895.

St Anne, Moor Lane. No longer a church. Built in 1796. The side had lunette windows above oblong windows.

St John, North Road. 1754–5, the W tower 1784 by *Harrison*. 56 Five bays of arched windows, the side entries into the first and last. Apse with two windows. The tower has bell-openings with pilasters and pediments, and then a rotunda of attached Tuscan columns and a spire – a design robust and of distinctive character. The nave has a coved ceiling and three galleries with unfluted Ionic columns on them. – COMMUNION RAIL and BOX PEWS are original. – The openwork iron PULPIT is, need one say, Victorian (1875).

St Thomas, Penny Street. 1840–1 by *Sharpe*. Lancets in stepped triplets along the sides, a stepped group of five between two starved turrets on the front. The NE steeple was added in 1852–3 by *Sharpe & Paley*. It shows what ten years had done in making architects aware of the duties of antiquarian accuracy.

Congregational Church, High Street. 1772–3. Five bays, with arched windows. The SCHOOL of 1865 has the grouped round-arched window lights which were a fashion of the forties.

Centenary Congregational Church, Stonewell (now a university building). 1879–81 by *J.C. Hetherington* and *G.D.*

Oliver of Carlisle. It cost £7,500. With a NW steeple, 120 ft high. Crude in the details; mixed Early Gothic.

INDEPENDENT METHODIST CHAPEL, Nelson Street. 1829. Humble, with arched windows.

METHODIST CHURCH, Sulyard Street. 1874; attributed to *Paley & Austin*, but that can't be correct. Large and grim, the front with a gawky NW turret and a rose window. The side appears three-storeyed. There is a big round apse at the E end. A new porch is under construction at the time of writing.

FRIENDS' MEETING HOUSE, Meeting House Lane. 1708, with sashed windows, quite sizeable.

PUBLIC BUILDINGS

CASTLE. Lancaster Castle rises in a splendid position above the river Lune, even if much of the splendour is due to remodelling of the C18 and restoration of the C19. Indeed the medieval remains are not extensive. The castle stands half inside and half outside the Roman castrum. The Normans probably first put up a motte and bailey. Then, before 1102, Roger of Poitou built the KEEP. It is *c.*80 ft square and *c.*70 ft high, though the top is an Elizabethan rebuilding. The keep is divided into two by a cross-wall all through its three storeys. (No internal features are said to survive.) About 1210 further stone defences were erected, i.e. Adrian's Tower (the round SW tower), the range between it and the keep in which was once the great hall, walling running E from Adrian's Tower to the square Dungeon Tower, and the great gatehouse and the Well Tower somewhat N of the gatehouse. Of the hall nothing exists, but the VCH reports one small tunnel-vaulted undercroft. In the Well Tower are two vaults, one above the other. (The lower vault, supposed to be Norman, is slightly pointed, the upper is of the date of the gatehouse.) The GATEHOUSE is very large and imposing. It is mostly of *c.*1400 (see the arms of Henry IV and Henry V as Prince of Wales). But the inner arch is C13. The responds are hollow-chamfered with small nail-head. The arch is depressed pointed and single-chamfered. It stands on short shafts with fillets, placed on stiff-leaf corbels. The façade of *c.*1400 has large canted side-projections to the outside. The arch between them dies into the imposts. There is a pointed tunnel-vault between it and the C13 arch. Above the entrance arch is a niche with a statue of John of Gaunt. Machicolation and a parapet are the crowning features. Behind are square turrets with higher stair-turrets.

In 1788 *Thomas Harrison* made designs for alterations à propos the adaptation of the castle to be shire hall and gaol. They were however superseded in 1802 by designs commissioned from *J.M.Gandy*, and it is Gandy's style we see in the present buildings. He built first and foremost the w side with the wide semicircle – or rather seven-sided half of a polygon – of the SHIRE HALL. In the process of this work a round tower close to the SW corner of the keep was demolished. The Shire Hall is in the Gothic taste, with a frieze of small pointed arches and battlements with pointed and cusped panels. The windows have Perp tracery. The whole N side is of *c.*1800 as well, with its towers high up.

The INTERIOR of the Shire Hall has slim quatrefoil shafts 70 separating a rib-vaulted ambulatory from the centre. Against the back (E) wall are rich stone canopies. The dais has a panelled arch over, and the apsidal vault has pierced panels of stone. All the FURNITURE is Gothick. (Most of the other parts of the castle are C19, especially the Governor's Residence N of the gatehouse.*)

TOWN HALL. 1906–9 by *E.W.Mountford*, the gift of the first 9 Lord Ashton (*see* p. 163). Grand neo-Georgian, eleven bays, with a tetrastyle giant portico. The staircase hall is tunnel-vaulted and has a dome in the centre. The state suite on the first floor consists of three rooms all with segmental stucco tunnel-vaults. – CORPORATION PLATE. Elizabethan Measures. – Mayor's Wand of 1613. – Bowls of 1615 and 1618. – Salt Cellar of 1632. – Tankard by *I.C.*, London, 1676–7. – Silver-gilt Mace, 4 ft 6 in. long, by *William Henry*, given in 1702. – Salver by *J.C.*, 1740–1. – Salver by *Hester Bateman*, 1783–4. – Punch Bowl by *I.A.*, London, 1803–4. – Salver by *I.L.T.H.*, London, 1827–8.

VICTORIA MONUMENT, Dalton Square, in front of the town hall. By *Herbert Hampton*, 1907. Presented by Lord Ashton. Stone, with bronze statue and very interesting bronze reliefs of groups of Victorian worthies, e.g. round Prince Albert artists including Watts, Millais, Thornycroft, Luke Fildes, Alfred Stevens, Barry, and Ruskin. Also writers, scientists (Darwin), politicians, reformers (Shaftesbury), explorers, etc.

MUSEUM, Market Street, the OLD TOWN HALL. 1781–3 by 58 *Major Jarrat*. Five by three bays. Giant tetrastyle Tuscan portico. Pediment to the S, one-storeyed porch of paired

* The castle being a prison, no more of the interior could be inspected than what is shown to the public.

columns to the w. The ground floor has smooth rustication. The windows are all arched. The cupola with a rotunda of unfluted Ionic columns is not by Jarrat but by *Harrison*.*

STOREY INSTITUTE, Meeting House Lane (Art Gallery, School of Art). Built in 1887 by *Paley & Austin* at the expense of Sir Thomas Storey. Large, free Jacobean, with a corner turret. Extension 1906.

GIRLS' GRAMMAR SCHOOL, Regent Street. 1914 by the County Architect, *Littler*. Symmetrical, free C17–18, good.

FIRE STATION, George Street. 1909 by *E.W.Mountford & F.D.Clapham*. Part of the town hall. Small, with a nice tower with a hemispherical copper cupola at the back.

CASTLE STATION AND GREEN AYRE STATION date from 1846 and 1848 and are both Gothic, Green Ayre low and symmetrical, Castle with an appropriate keep display.

POLICE STATION, Thornham Street. 1966–7 by the County Architect's Department (*Roger Booth*). Concrete, with a detached outer staircase on a post. A strong and convinced job.

SKERTON BRIDGE. 1783–8. Designed by *Harrison* of Chester. Five elliptical arches and aedicules between them. Balustrade. The roadway is kept level. The bridge cost £14,000.

PERAMBULATION

It is difficult to recommend a route – the street net is so intricate. One may start on CASTLE HILL and CASTLE PARK, where there is at once a fine display of stately Georgian houses. One faces the castle gateway and has a three-bay pediment. The date 1845 in the cartouche cannot apply. On the S side an entry into the Storey Institute. It originally led to the house of John Fenton Cawthorne, M.P. for Lancaster. The house was built in 1806. The entry has Tuscan columns and a pediment placed too high up. Then follows a specially fine five-bay house, dated 1720. The doorway has detached fluted Ionic columns and a broken segmental pediment. Next to it its stables, with keyed-in circular windows. Castle Hill bends towards CHURCH STREET and is nearly all Georgian. At the top of Church Street stands four-square the JUDGE'S LODGING, with a date 1675 recorded by Rigbye. Seven bays and three storeys, with windows in moulded surrounds. The doorway has a big broken segmental pediment painfully detached

* Peter Howell drew my attention to this, referring to an article by K.H. Docton in the *Lancashire and Cheshire Historian* for August 1965.

from the thin Tuscan columns. Terrace, gatepiers, and an open staircase.

E of the Judge's Lodging a three-bay house with a good doorway and then a house with a big bow in its middle. The columned doorway is in this. The CONSERVATIVE CLUB is of five bays, again with a columned doorway. No. 74 is the former MA-SONIC HALL, imitation C17; built in 1884–5. The DISTRICT BANK is of 1870 and looks earlier: classical, with upper pilasters and two oblong relief panels, a dignified front. Then, rather unfortunate, though in itself irreproachable, the new MASONIC HALL by *C. B. Pearson & Son*, sheer walls and only some well-placed windows at ground floor level. Opposite the COOPERATIVE, 1901, high, Jacobean, with shaped gables.

Meanwhile BRIDGE LANE has branched off N. In it a fragment of the ROMAN WALL* of Lancaster and the CARPENTER'S ARMS, with some mullioned windows. At the end of the street turn N along Downside Street to ST GEORGE'S QUAY for a number of Late Georgian WAREHOUSES, high and gabled with hoist doors, and for the CUSTOM HOUSE, a fine Palladian job of 1764, designed by *Richard Gillow*. Five bays, rusticated basement, upper three-bay portico with slender unfluted Ionic columns.

Back to Bridge Lane and along CABLE STREET, which also has its Georgian houses, e.g. one pair with three columns and a pediment to the doorways, and one with a Venetian doorway with broken pediment. The continuation of Cable Street is PARLIAMENT STREET, where, facing the bridge and no doubt meant as an eye-catcher, a composition of three houses was built, connected by screen walls with niches alternatingly oblong and arched. The middle house has coupled columns on the upper floor, in the Cinquecento tradition, the side houses are lower and have pediments. The group has been attributed to *Harrison*.

Back by North Road and Rosemary Lane. Close to the corner of ST LEONARD'S GATE, in the latter, r. of the Centenary Chapel, again a Georgian group, once again a pair with three columns and a pediment for the two doorways, the other two with normal columns and pediments, much as in Cable Street. From the w end of St Leonard's Gate s to the corner of GREAT JOHN STREET and Moor Lane for a Georgian house with a pedimented doorway and Venetian windows l. and r. From there w, down St Nicholas Street to MARKET STREET,

* Cf. footnote on p. 152

sampling at r. angles to the museum the WESTMINSTER
BANK, a dignified *palazzo*, and at the corner of King Street
the KING'S ARMS HOTEL, 1879 by *Holtom & Connor*,
symmetrical, neo-C17, and quite large.

In a back passage off Market Street to the N, between China and
New Streets, is the Music Room. The MUSIC ROOM is said
to have been built by Dr Marton, Vicar of Lancaster. He became vicar in 1767, and that is a date later than architecture
and decoration could ever make one expect. They point to
1730–40. The building is of three storeys and only three bays
– a glorified pavilion indeed – and has fluted pilasters on the
ground floor and the first floor and sunk pilasters above the
main cornice. The centre on the ground floor is a large arch,
on the first floor a window with a bold open curly pediment.
The main room inside was on the first floor – was, because it is
now so decayed that there can be no hope of saving it. It is a
disgrace for a town like Lancaster. Where were the successors
of the Williamsons and Storeys when it came to preserving the
52 finest interior in the town ? The stucco of walls and ceilings,
with medallions of the muses and Apollo in the overmantel, is
of the kind which such Italians as *Vassali* practised. It is no
good saying more. In a few years it will all have disappeared.

Now into KING STREET. The former ASSEMBLY ROOMS have
five bays and a semicircular porch with thin Tuscan columns.
PENNY'S HOSPITAL is dated 1720 and still looks late C17.
The gateway and the chapel both have big, rather low shaped
gables. The almshouses are one-storeyed and face each other.
They still have stone cross-windows. A good group, earlier
Georgian than most, is Nos 40 etc., with one doorway with a
pediment on brackets, one with a straight hood on brackets,
and the RING O' BELLS, with a particularly good doorway
with Roman Doric columns, a triglyph frieze, and a segmental
pediment. QUEEN SQUARE is a triangle with trees. On its S side
one more good Georgian house with a four-bay pediment with
a tripartite lunette window. In QUEEN STREET Nos 5–7 is of
six bays and has the two doorways under one outsize curly
pediment, although the façades cannot be earlier than Late
Georgian. From King Street W one can reach HIGH STREET,
with one five-bay house and a group of altogether thirteen bays.
The centre has a three-bay pediment. Finally from King
Street E by Common Garden Street into PENNY STREET for
THE LANCASTRIAN, a new pub by *Mackeith, Dickinson &
Partners*, 1967, and the end – the pair of hotels, ALEXANDRA

1 (top) *Scenery:* Coniston, Coppermines Valley
2 (above) *Scenery:* Tarn Hows

3 (above) *Scenery:* Coniston, High Arnside Farm
4 (top right) *Townscape:* Lancaster (*Copyright Country Life*)
5 (right) *Industrial Townscape:* Preston

6 (top left) Whalley church, cross, Anglo-Saxon
7 (left) Heysham church, cross shaft, Anglo-Saxon
8 (above) Cartmel Priory, south doorway, c. 1190

9 (left) Cartmel Priory, begun *c.* 1190
10 (below left) Furness Abbey, waterleaf capitals, *c.* 1175
11 (above) Furness Abbey, cloister, *c.* 1230–40, with chapter house entrance and dormitory

12 (left) Furness
Abbey, entrance to
chapter house,
c. 1230–40

13 (below left)
Furness Abbey,
chapter house,
c. 1230–40

14 (right)
Cockerham,
Cockersand Abbey,
chapter house,
c. 1230

15 (below right)
Cartmel Priory,
Harrington tomb,
c. 1347

16 (top) Cartmel Priory, detail from Harrington tomb, c. 1347
17 (above) Cartmel Priory, mourners from Harrington tomb, c. 1347
18 (right) Whalley Abbey, outer gateway, early fourteenth century

19 (left) Lancaster, St Mary, stall canopies, fourteenth century

20 (below left) Whalley church, stalls, c. 1420–30

21 (right) Furness Abbey, sedilia

22 (below right) Holme church, pulpit, early sixteenth century

23 (left) Lancaster, St Mary, chancel, probably late fourteenth century
24 (above) Ormskirk church, nave, probably *c.* 1540, restored by Paley
& Austin, 1877–91; screen seventeenth century

25 (above left) Cartmel Priory, begun *c.* 1190, south chapel *c.* 1340, the rest later

26 (left) St Michael's-on-Wyre church, tower *c.* 1549

27 (above) Hawkshead church, sixteenth to mid seventeenth century

28 (top) Blackburn Cathedral, misericord, fifteenth century
29 (above) Cartmel Fell church, stained glass, *c.* 1500
30 (right) Rufford Old Hall, late fifteenth century

31 Rufford Old Hall, late fifteenth century, screens passage

32 (above)
Samlesbury Hall,
c. 1545 and fifteenth
century

33 (left) Standish
church, north
arcade, 1580s

34 (top) Hoghton Tower, great hall, sixteenth to seventeenth century
35 (above) Stonyhurst, west range, begun 1592 (*Copyright Country Life*)
36 (right) Stonyhurst, gatehouse, 1592–*c*.95

37 Gawthorpe, 1600–5

38 Gawthorpe, 1600–5, drawing room (*Copyright Country Life*)

39 (left) Chorley, Astley Hall, south front, probably after 1653 (*Copyright Country Life*)

40 (right) Nelson, Southfield Fold Farmhouse, late seventeenth century

41 (below right) Kirkland Hall, doorway, 1695

42 (top) Cartmel Priory, screen, c. 1620
43 (above) Standish church, monument to Edward Wrightinton †1658
44 (right) Ormskirk church, font, 1661

45 (above left) Scarisbrick church, pulpit, probably Belgian, mid to later seventeenth century

46 (left) Chorley, Astley Hall, ceiling, 1660s (*Copyright Country Life*)

47 (above) Chorley, Astley Hall, staircase, 1660s (*Copyright Country Life*)

48 (left) Churchtown, St Cuthbert, woodwork, by Richard Prescot, *c.* 1704

49 (below left) Churchtown, St Cuthbert, monument to Thomas Fleetwood †1717

50 (right) Stonyhurst, garden pavilion, *c.* 1712 (*Copyright Country Life*)

51 (above left) Burnley, Townley Hall, hall, *c.*1725, the stucco-work by Francesco Vassali and Martino Quadri
52 (left) Lancaster, Music Room, ceiling, *c.*1730–40
53 (top) Burrow Hall, ceiling, *c.*1740 (*Copyright Country Life*)
54 (above) Lytham St Annes, Lytham Hall, 1757–64, staircase ceiling

55 (above) Lytham St Annes, Lytham Hall, by John Carr, 1757–64
(*Copyright Country Life*)
56 (right) Lancaster, St John, tower by Thomas Harrison, 1784
57 (below right) Blackburn, St John Evangelist, 1789

58 (above) Lancaster, Old Town Hall, by Major Jarrat, 1781–3 (*Copyright Country Life*)
59 (above right) Broughton East, Broughton Lodge, late eighteenth century
60 (right) Aspull, Haigh Foundry, 1839

61 (above) Preston, Winckley Square
62 (above right) Poulton-le-Fylde church, chandelier,
eighteenth century
63 (right) Whalley church, monument to Elizabeth Whalley
†1785, by Fisher of York

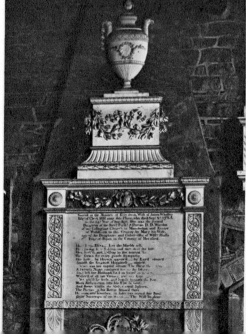

64 (left) Standish church, monument to Richard Watt, by John Bacon the younger, 1806

65 (below left) Lindale, cast-iron monument to John Wilkinson †1808

66 (right) Quernmore Park Hall, by Thomas Harrison, 1793, central hall

67 (above left) Read Hall, by George Webster, 1818–25
68 (left) Lancaster, aqueduct, engineer John Rennie, architect
Alexander Stevens, 1797
69 (above) Haigh Hall, probably designed by the 24th Earl of Crawford and Balcarres, 1827–40, staircase hall

70 (above) Lancaster Castle, Shire Hall, by J. M. Gandy, designed 1802 (*Copyright Country Life*)

71 (above right) Yealand Conyers, Leighton Hall, *c.* 1810 (*Copyright Country Life*)

72 (right) Yealand Conyers, Leighton Hall, *c.* 1810, entrance hall (*Copyright Country Life*)

73 (above left) Conishead Priory, by Philip Wyatt, 1821–36
74 (left) Capernwray Hall, by Edmund Sharpe, 1844
75 (above) Wray Castle (near Hawkshead), by H.P. Horner, 1840–7

76 (left) Pleasington church, by John Palmer, 1816–19

77 (below left) Preston, St Augustine, by A. Tuach, 1838–40, and Sinnott, Sinnott & Powell, 1890

78 (right) Scarisbrick Hall, by A.W.N. Pugin, designed 1837, bay windows in the south front

79 (left) Scarisbrick
Hall, by A.W.N.
Pugin, designed
1837, King's Room
(*Copyright Country
Life*)

80 (right)
Scarisbrick Hall,
by A.W.N. Pugin,
designed 1837,
great hall, fireplace,
shield and figures
by E.W. Pugin

81 (below right)
Scarisbrick Hall,
designed by
A.W.N. Pugin,
1837, door handle
in the smoking room

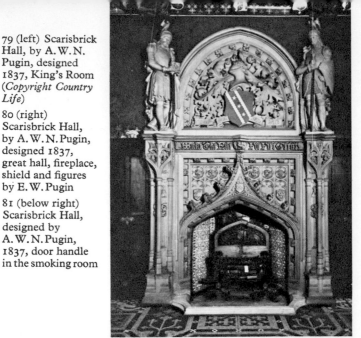

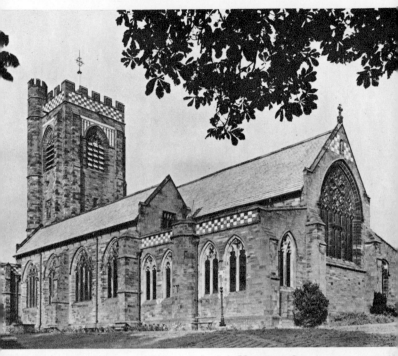

82 (above left) Preston, St Walburge, by J. A. Hansom, 1850–4
83 (left) Preston, St Walburge, by J. A. Hansom, 1850–4
84 (above) Dalton-in-Furness, St Mary, by Paley & Austin, 1882–5

85 (above) Holker Hall, by Paley & Austin, after 1871
86 (above right) Preston, Harris Library and Museum, by James Hibbert, 1882–93
87 (right) Stonyhurst, south block, by Dunn & Hansom, 1877–89

88 (above) Kirkham, Grammar School, by Greenaway & Newberry, 1909–11

89 (above right) Cartmel Fell (Windermere), Moor Crag, by C.F.A. Voysey, 1898–1900

90 (right) Cartmel Fell (Windermere), Broadleys, by C.F.A. Voysey, 1898–1900

91 (left) Lancaster, Ashton Memorial, by Sir John Belcher, 1906–9
92 (above) Lancaster Town Hall, by E. W. Mountford, 1906–9

93 (above left) Coppull Mills, 1906
94 (left) Morecambe, Midland Hotel, by Oliver Hill, 1932–3
95 (above) Lancaster, Castle Secondary School, by Roger Booth, 1965–6

96 Preston, William Temple School, by N. Keith Scott (Building Design Partnership), 1964–6

HOTEL and WHITE CROSS HOTEL, built in the early c20, and both free Jacobean. Opposite are Storey's works and offices and the infirmary, and they belong to Outer Lancaster.

OUTER LANCASTER

ST BERNADETTE, Bowerham Road (SE). 1957–9 by *Tom Mellor*. Well planned. Entry is under the campanile. The baptistery is straight on. One turns r. into the church. The progression is convincing. The church is of stone, except for the campanile, which is of concrete. – REREDOS by *John Piper*. Christ and two angels. Attractive, but a little too easy. – The STATIONS OF THE CROSS carved by *Peter Watts*.

CHRIST CHURCH, Wyresdale Road (E). 1855–7 by *Henry Martin* of London. The w baptistery by *Austin & Paley*, 1895. With two w turrets with long, lean spires. Geometrical tracery. – STAINED GLASS. Much by *Casolani*, made by *Powell*, 1865. – Also *Powell* glass of 1857.

ST LUKE, off Owen Road, Skerton (N). 1833. w tower, lancets, barn roof. – MONUMENT. Joseph Whalley. By *E. Davis* of London, 1851. A woman drops a flower on the coffin.

ST JOSEPH (R.C.), Slyne Road (N). Perp, with a NW tower. 1900 by *Pugin & Pugin*.

METHODIST CHURCH, Owen Road, Skerton (N). 1910 by *S. Wright*.* One of the best ecclesiastical buildings of Lancaster, resourceful and yet controlled. Art Nouveau Dec tracery, a lively outline and skyline, and a slim NW tower with an aubergine cupola.

UNIVERSITY OF LANCASTER, Bailrigg (S). By *Bridgwater, Shepheard & Epstein* (partner in charge *G. Epstein*). Designed in 1963–4. The assumption underlying the plan is that neither final size nor detailed future requirements can be known. What will however be needed in any case is a centre which can grow and should be without any wheeled traffic. Also the university must at all stages appear a complete entity. Finally cars should be able to get close to their destination. Hence the plan provides for a linear pedestrian centre acting as a spine, rib-like buildings stretching E and W from the spine, and two parallel vehicular roads to its E and W framing the 200-acre site on these sides. The W road is met in its middle by the access road from the A6, which runs a short distance W of the site. This

* So the City Librarian tells me on the strength of local papers. But the Scotforth Methodist Church of 1908–9 is by *A. G. Chant* and strikingly similar.

road is continued beyond the w road by an underpass which crosses the centre and emerges midway along the e road. This underpass will be used by the buses bringing the students. There will be a bus stop below the centre. From the e and w roads feeder lanes run between the buildings which form the ribs. Car parking is along these lanes. But what has so far been described is only the diagram of the plan. In fact the spine walk is not at all straight or regular; nor are the rib buildings. The total impression will be one of quite randomly grouped courtyards with buildings of three and four floors around. The buildings are partly for teaching, partly for living. Living accommodation is in so-called colleges each for about 500 students. Teaching buildings are between them. All buildings can be reached by covered ways. Along the spine there will also be shops. The first phase is the central square and the teaching and college buildings closest to it. Construction is concrete-framed with brick facing. The skyline has the variety, partly by erections with monopitch roofs, which pleases more today than an unbroken skyline.*

St Martin's Training College, Bowerham Road (se). The beginnings were the Barracks of 1876–80. But recently many new buildings have been added by the County Architect, *R. Booth*, and his department. One high block, a number of identical lower blocks with the end walls of stone, a chapel with a high funnel-like light source for the altar, and a dining hall with a folded roof.

Grammar School, East Road (e). 1851–5 by *Sharpe & Paley*. Symmetrical, gabled Gothic. On the site in Quernmore Road a good recent extension by *C. B. Pearson & Son*.

Ripley School, Ashton Road (s). Built in 1856–64 by *J. Cunningham* as an orphanage. A grim Gothic building with a gaunt tower, not at all endearing. The beautiful Chapel is by *Paley & Austin*, 1886–8. Dec, with a flèche.

* At the time of going to press the following buildings are complete: Central Hall, Administration Building, Lonsdale College, Bowland College, Bowland Residence, Drama Centre, Fine Arts Studios, and Boiler House, all by *Shepheard & Epstein*, and Chemistry and Physics, both by *Tom Mellor & Partners*.

Half-finished: Library, by *Tom Mellor & Partners*.

In course of construction: Lonsdale Residence, Furness College, and Furness Residence, by *Shepheard & Epstein*; County College, by *Roger Booth* the County Architect; Biology, by *Tom Mellor & Partners*; Cartmel College, Cartmel Residence, and Workshops, by *Taylor Young & Partners*; Religious Centre, by *Cassidy & Ashton*.

CASTLE SECONDARY SCHOOL, Crag Road (NE). 1965–6 by 95 *Roger Booth*, the County Architect. Mainly of load-bearing pre-cast concrete panels with a ribbed finish. The site slopes steeply, and the skyline stresses differences of levels too. Mono-pitch roofs of course. The conception behind the building as well as the execution are interesting and repay study.

ROYAL LANCASTER INFIRMARY, South Road (s). 1894–6 by *Austin & Paley*. Free later C17.

ROYAL ALBERT HOSPITAL, Ashton Road (s). By *Paley & Austin*, 1867–73. Large, Gothic, monumental, essentially sym-metrical. Mid-tower high, with a steep French hipped top rising between pinnacles and accompanied to most of its height by a chimney. Statues of Victoria and Albert. A separate gatehouse.

LANCASTER MOOR HOSPITAL, Quernmore Road (E). The oldest building is of 1811–16. It was built as the County Lunatic Asylum and was designed by one *Standen*. Centre with a Tuscan giant portico and pediment. The ground floor has smooth rustication and arched windows. Later additions. Across the road the huge extension of 1882 by *A. W. Kershaw*. It cost £125,000. It is entirely symmetrical, with a Gothic centre block and tower (lancet windows) and porch and high pavilions along a spine N and S. A serious, matter-of-fact piece of work.

WILLIAMSON PARK. Donated by James Williamson, linoleum manufacturer of Lancaster and later Lord Ashton. The park was laid out by *McClean* and finished in 1881, after the donor had died. In the park is the Ashton Memorial.

ASHTON MEMORIAL. This domed pile, dominating Lancaster 91 from its hill site, was built by Lord Ashton in memory of his wife. It cost £87,000 and is 150 ft high, as against the 175 ft of the Albert Memorial. The design is by *Sir John Belcher*, and building took from 1906 to 1909. Should one look at it as a venture on a level with Sigismondo Malatesta's church at Rimini to commemorate his Isotta, or as the folly to end all follies? Or should one simply envy Belcher for having been put into the position of designing the most sumptuous building in all his career for no utilitarian purpose whatever? It must have been the dream of all Beaux-Arts students ever since the C18 to find themselves with such an opportunity. The Ashton Memorial is the grandest monument in England. The style Belcher and Lord Ashton chose is the highest Italian-cum-English-High-Baroque, but the handling alas lacks discipline.

The main dome is *à la* St Peter's, surrounded by four small subsidiary domes. There are two porticos, one to the E, the other to the W, the latter with an enormous staircase in front, reminiscent of that of the Sacré Cœur. The interior is largely one vast octagonal hall, white, with MOSAICS by *George Murray*. But it is in the details principally that discipline breaks down. The subsidiary domes have pairs of columns in the diagonals like the domes of Greenwich. The main dome has a high drum like St Paul's, but then got another tier of windows (circular), and the drum has not just pairs of columns, but in three places broken segmental pediments rising above its top and in the fourth place instead an awkward piece serving evidently as a staircase. The view from the monument is superb.

Also in Williamson Park, and close to the Memorial, is an ORANGERY. Seven bays, brick and white rendering, with a convex hipped glass roof and a semicircular porch of Tuscan columns. Otherwise the style is that of the ending C17.

RYELANDS PARK, Skerton (N). In it the house of Jonathan Dunn, twice mayor of Lancaster. It was built in 1836 etc. Porch of paired columns carrying a pediment. Also a broad later Victorian tower.

68 AQUEDUCT, Caton Road (NE). It carries the Preston to Kendal Canal across the Lune and was built in 1797. The engineer was *John Rennie*, the architect *Alexander Stevens*. Five arches, decidedly monumental.

PRIVATE BUILDINGS. Nothing to be said.

STOREY'S WORKS have a big building in South Road which was built for the Lancashire Militia in 1854 etc. It is now Storey's Social Centre. Symmetrical Scottish Baronial front with tourelles. Mullioned and transomed windows.

SCALE HALL, Morecambe Road (N), is earlier than 1737. It is of five bays, with a pedimented doorway, and has a front garden with two pairs of gatepiers.

ALDCLIFFE HALL (SW) has been demolished. Only the Tudor LODGE survives.

LANE SIDE see PENDLETON

LANESIDE see HASLINGDEN

LANGHO see BILLINGTON

LATHOM

ST JAMES. 1851 by *Sydney Smirke* for the Earl of Derby. SW
steeple and S aisle, the windows in the early C14 style; yet
in the general impression not yet free of the Commissioners'
past.

LATHOM HOUSE. Lathom House was built for Sir Thomas
Bootle to the designs of *Giacomo Leoni*. It was begun *c*.1725
and finished *c*.1730 and consisted of a centre and two service
wings connected with the centre by quadrant links of unfluted
Ionic columns. The centre was a Palladian block of thirteen
bays and two and a half storeys. The centre three bays were
raised and had an attic with circular windows and a pediment.
The windows of the *piano nobile* were also pedimented. Outer
stairs in two arms reached up to the main entrance, which was
also on the *piano nobile*. That splendid mansion has completely
gone. Only one very large SERVICE WING of two storeys survives. What has happened to the other? It was still there
fifteen years ago (MHLG). The wing is a reminder of the
monumentality of the house. It is of stone, one and a half
storeys high, seven by four bays in size, with a three-bay pediment and an octagonal cupola with ogee cap. The main windows have Gibbs surrounds. Arched entrance.

CHAPEL, W of the former. This was built by the second
Earl of Derby and consecrated in 1500. It is a plain oblong,
and has no Perp features left except for one doorway recently
found. The window tracery is of very pretty (and uninformed)
early C19 Gothic forms. Early C19 also are the prevalently
yellow heraldic STAINED GLASS and the pretty ribbed ceiling.
Behind the chapel is a set of modest ALMSHOUSES. They look
Tudor in details, but have blank arches. Their history is not
visible, but the Earl founded a hospital at the same time as the
chapel. – LECTERN. A wooden eagle; C17, if ancient at all. –
SCREEN. A few parts are indeed Perp.

GATEPIER and LODGES, W of the chapel. The lodges are
plain octagonal structures. The one remaining gatepier is a
sumptuous piece with a niche and stalactite rustication.

PILKINGTON'S RESEARCH LABORATORIES, S of the service
wing. A large building, sound and uneventful. By *Courtauld's
Technical Services Ltd.*

LEA

ST MARY (R.C.). 1801–2. Brick, three bays and an apse. Arched
windows. The presbytery is attached.

WESTLEIGH. 1864 by *Hibbert*, a large Italianate villa, not picturesque. Brick and ample stone dressings, all motifs fussy.

6070

LECK

ST PETER. 1878–9 by *Paley & Austin*, burnt in 1912 and rebuilt, it is said accurately, in 1915. Square, unbuttressed w tower with spire. Nothing special.

LECK HALL. About 1800. Five bays, the mid-window tripartite. Ionic porch of two pairs of columns. A canted bay window round the corner. Close by an ORANGERY of four arches by one. Fine grounds.

At COWAN BRIDGE just by the bridge is the plain house which R. W. Carus Wilson, vicar of Tunstall, in 1824 founded as a school for clergymen's daughters and to which the Bronte sisters went. Cf. also Casterton in Westmorland, a few miles away, where he founded a bigger school.

LEE HOUSE *see* CHIPPING

LEIGHTON HALL *see* YEALAND CONYERS

LEVEN VIADUCT *see* ULVERSTON

5020

LEYLAND

ST ANDREW. In the original centre of the village. Now the town has grown towards the N, and at the N end are the Leyland Motor Works. The church has a high Perp w tower and a low chancel of *c*.1300 with windows with intersecting tracery and SEDILIA and PISCINA, Perp rather than Dec. Of a yet older church fragments were found in 1852, including a Norman respond stone with a block capital now outside the chancel on the s side. Between tower and chancel is a church of 1816–17. The roof-line of its medieval predecessor is visible above the high tower arch. The early C19 nave has three galleries on very thin iron columns. – PLATE. Two Patens inscribed 1716; two Chalices and Flagon by *C.B.*, 1758; Flagon inscribed 1759; two Patens inscribed 1773. – MONUMENT. Sir William Farrington † 1781. Tablet with a bust on top. – Big GATEWAY w of the church, probably also of 1817.

In the churchyard the old GRAMMAR SCHOOL, early C17, with mullioned windows.

Close to the church the VILLAGE CROSS. The shaft is preserved to a certain height. Near the cross the BAY HORSE, with a rustic Greek Doric porch. Along FOX LANE the long row of the OSBALDESTONE ALMSHOUSES, the most noteworthy the one of 1870, with porches, dormers, and bargeboards.

ST AMBROSE, Moss Lane. 1884–5 by *Aldridge & Deacon*. Large, with a fine w tower with two tall lancets as bell-openings and a pyramid roof lower than the pinnacles. Good porch from the N into the tower. The entrance has unexpected rounded mouldings. High interior. Tower arch and chancel arch both have four continuous chamfers. The windows are either lancets or have geometrical tracery.

ST JAMES, Lostock Stream, 1½ m. w. 1855 by *Ewan Christian*, the s aisle 1872. w tower with excellently outlined broach-spire. Otherwise indifferent outside and inside. One odd feature is the absence of a chancel arch. – MONUMENT. Mrs Farrington † 1863, foundress of the church. By *John Hutchinson* of Edinburgh. Recumbent marble figure, asleep. Uncommonly tender and not too gushing.

ST MARY (R.C.), Broadfield Drive. By *Weightman & Bullen*, 1959–64, and one of their best churches. Round, with a radially folded roof so as to allow the altar to stand in the centre.* The roof is concrete with rough shuttering. The inner walls are of small relief tiles. There is an ambulatory all round, and the piers are forked. In the forks are small free-standing bronze groups of the STATIONS OF THE CROSS, by *Arthur Dooley*, realistic enough to be recognized by anyone, yet modern enough in the Giacometti way to pass the critics. – STAINED GLASS. Abstract, by *Patrick Reyntiens*, very beautiful in colours and shapes. But it remains a pity that the concrete setting results in such unattractive and rather confused shapes outside. The rotunda is preceded by a porch, which appears not fully integrated. It might also be said by way of criticism that the detached campanile of open concrete framing is heavier and more massive than suits the church.

Leyland has a few early C19 houses left, e.g. one in SCHOOL LANE with a nice doorway and two canted bay windows and one in WORDEN LANE, of brick, five bays long, also with a nice doorway.

WORDEN PARK. The house has been demolished, and the OBELISK which stood in front of it has migrated. There remains the ARCHWAY, with attached Tuscan columns and vermiculated rustication. Heavy top. Also one LODGE.

---

* But a second altar is at the E end.

2070

LINDAL-IN-FURNESS

ST PETER. 1885–6 by *Ewan Christian*. Bell-turret on the E end of the nave. Plate tracery.

A pleasant GREEN with a fringe of trees.

4080

LINDALE

ST PAUL. 1828 by *Webster* of Kendal, but nothing of interest. W tower, lancets, Victorian chancel, N aisle of 1912. – In the churchyard the severe but massive MONUMENT to Webster † 1861. In a late classical style, and at the top an inscription slab surrounded by a cast-iron railing.

65 Cast iron comes in appropriately; for at Lindale is the OBELISK of cast iron to John Wilkinson, who died in 1808. It was transferred here from Castlehead (*see* below). It has inscriptions in beautiful Trajan lettering and the head of John Wilkinson in profile in a medallion. At the foot you read Labore et Honore. The iron has gone all red, and the obelisk is held together by bands.

Wilkinson's father Isaac was a Cumberland farmer, and also foreman of an iron furnace. He moved to Backbarrow, Haverthwaite (*see* p. 138), where he developed his iron furnaces. John, who was born in 1728, about 1748 started a furnace at Bilston. Father and son together built and managed iron works in Denbighshire. The main works in the end were at Broseley near Coalbrookdale, where among other things cannon and barges were cast. Wilkinson also cast the parts for the Coalbrookdale Bridge, the earliest of all iron bridges. That was in 1779. In the same year he was High Sheriff of Denbighshire. His brother stayed in the business too, and had ordnance factories in France.

(WILKINSON HOUSE. Built *c*.1748 by Isaac and John Wilkinson in conjunction with a furnace. Two storeys; nothing architecturally special.)

CASTLEHEAD (St Mary's College). The Wilkinsons later moved to this house. It is quite stately and remains more or less in its original state. *The Beauties of England and Wales* in 1807 called Castlehead a beautiful modern seat.

LINDETH TOWER *see* SILVERDALE

LISIEUX HALL *see* WHITTLE-LE-WOODS

LITTLEDALE

ST ANNE. Built in 1752–5 by Miss Welch (cf. Caton). Only three
bays and with very curious, entirely incorrect two-light windows, the two arched lights held together by a segmental or
rather a basket arch. – PEWS. Are they Jacobean, or of c.1755,
or a more recent pastiche?

LITTLE HARWOOD see BLACKBURN, p. 66

LITTLE MEARLEY HALL see PENDLETON

LITTLE MITTON

LITTLE MITTON HALL. A stone house of c.1500, built for the
Shireburnes. It is built on an H-plan, with the entrance from
the w, and the chief object of interest is the great hall. The
rest is mostly of c.1844 and c.1875–80. The hall has an open
timber roof of six bays with wall-posts, tiebeams, and arched
braces decorated by blank tracery. The first tiebeam is
above the speres, the last marks off the dais. This was originally set in an oblong recess, as at Samlesbury, and there were
doorways to the l. and r. of the recess. The screen, as it now is,
with its gallery, is of the later C16. It is sumptuously carved,
with the typical Early Renaissance motif of heads in medallions.
The gallery over the E side of the hall is a later addition. The
end wall of the hall on the screens-passage side is timber-
framed and has the motif of quatrefoils, as it characterizes
other Lancashire houses of the C15 as well. The only ancient
windows are the two upper mullioned three-light windows in
the hall bay.

LITTLE URSWICK see URSWICK

LIVESEY

IMMANUEL, Feniscowles, ⅜ m. S of Pleasington station. 1835–6,
designed by the Rev. J. W. Whitaker. But can the large
straight-headed Perp windows be so early, even if one makes
allowance for the possible boldness of an amateur? The church
is small, with a W tower with spire. Nave and chancel are in
one.

ST ANDREW. The church lies on the outskirts of Blackburn.
1866–7 by E. G. Paley. Aisleless, with transepts and a polygonal apse. Incomplete SE tower grouped with the S transept.

The side windows are pairs of lancets; the transepts have rose windows.

St Francis, St Francis Road, Feniscliffe, just within the boundary of Blackburn. 1889–93 by *C.E.Deacon*. Perp. Two-bay nave (incomplete), chancel and s chapel. The distinguishing feature is the clerestory, which has only a group of two three-light windows in the middle, under a gable. The façade is an addition of 1963.

Livesey Hall, off Preston Old Road. A major farmhouse of hall centre, porch, and two wings, on the E-plan. The house has three dates. 1605 refers to most of the building. Mullioned windows, except for the hall window, which has a transom. The porch on its upper floor is mullioned entirely: three lights to the sides, five lights to the front. The r. wing fits into the composition, but is of 1666 – see the running string-courses and the different proportions and details of the mullioned windows. In the gable of this wing is moreover an oval – typical of the later C17 – and also a stepped mullioned window. The date 1689 can have little to do with the exterior.

Mill Hill Mills. Built *c.*1844 by Joseph Eccles (cf. Darwen)

LONGRIDGE
6030

St Lawrence, Chapel Hill. 1822. The two galleries are preserved, but the two tiers of small two-light windows are an alteration of 1899–1906. The w tower was added in 1841, the Perp chancel in 1899–1906.

St Paul, off Berry Lane. 1886–8 by *Ewan Christian*, but the w tower of 1936–7 by *A.C.M.Lillie*. A large five-bay nave, all rather conventional. – STAINED GLASS. The e window is by *Kempe*, pre-1899.

St Wilfrid (R.C.), Derby Road. 1883 (or 86 ?) by *Withnell* of Preston. The sw steeple is the most prominent feature of Longridge. Lancets, plate and geometrical tracery. Polygonal apse. A poor interior.

Old Rib, Halfpenny Lane, ¼ m. wnw of the Catholic church. 1616. With mullioned windows and a little oriel round the r. corner.

LONGTON
4020

St Andrew. 1887 by *J.E.K.Cutts*. Large and quiet. Brown stone with red stone dressings. nw porch meant to carry a tower. Lancets and plate tracery. Goodhart-Rendel praises the church for proportions and details and adds: 'The arcades are most elegantly high and light with quatrefoil columns and good mouldings.' He ends: 'The best Cutts I know – better than any Blomfield.'

ALL SAINTS, New Longton. By *Tom Mellor & Partners*, 1963–5. A good design, especially externally. Square body with low-pitch hipped roof and central pointed lantern. A porch nearly detached on the l., the Lady Chapel with a prominent pyramid roof on the r. The wall of this is windowless brick, and so is the wall of the main body, except for the large broad glazed openings at the angles.

LOSTOCK HALL *see* FARINGTON *and* HORWICH

LOSTOCK STREAM *see* LEYLAND

LOWER HOUSE FARMHOUSE *see* CHARNOCK RICHARD

LOWICK
2080

ST LUKE. 1885. Local rubble and red sandstone dressings. W tower. Lancets.

RING CAIRN, 1½ m. SW, ¼ m. N of Knapperthaw. The cairn is 100 ft in diameter and has a bank 9 ft wide. Stones were set up on its inner face, but only five of those on the NW survive *in situ*. There is an entrance on the SW.

LOW MOOR *see* CLITHEROE

LUMB *see* RAWTENSTALL

LUNECLIFFE *see* SCOTFORTH

LYDIATE
3000

ST THOMAS. 1841, probably by *S. Holmes & Sons*. Nave with lancets and W tower. The chancel etc. of 1912, and of course more varied.

OUR LADY (R.C.). 1854–5 by *J. J. Scoles*. In the Dec style, with a short NW tower and a rich REREDOS, erected in 1878. Aisles with arcades of octagonal piers. – SCULPTURE. Attached to the pulpit a series of uncommonly fine Nottingham alabaster reliefs from the life of St Catherine. In addition a Visitation and a St Cuthbert. They are all of the C15. The iconography of course standard. The panels came from the old chapel of St Catherine. – PLATE. Chalice, considered pre-Reformation.

St Catherine, sw of the Catholic church, and in ruins. Perp, and probably once the chapel of Lydiate Hall, when it belonged to Lawrence and Catherine Ireland, i.e. *c.*1470–80. Their arms and initials are over the s porch arch. The chapel was aisleless and had no n windows at all. Perp s windows. Perp chancel arch. The w tower had a giant arch for w doorway and w window.

(Scotch Piper Inn, s of the chapel. There are 'at least two pairs of cruck timbers'. mhlg)

Lydiate Hall. Much could still be written on Lydiate Hall when the vch published in 1907. Now there are only collapsing fragments closely hemmed in by trees.

Seaford Close. Housing of 1965 between the canal and the A road, n of Bell's Lane. By *Harding & Horsman.* A close of small houses, bright and up-to-the-minute with the zigzag of monopitch roofs and the timber trim.

Old Gore Farmhouse, at the w end of Bell's Lane. The house is of brick and has a plaque with the date 1596. It has low mullioned windows, but the roof is all new, and the whole fails to form into a picture.

LYTHAM ST ANNES

3020

INTRODUCTION

Lytham and St Annes are two different organisms, St Annes a holiday place which developed from 1875 and managed to keep quiet in spite of its immediate proximity to Blackpool, Lytham a pleasant little town with a tree-planted main street, a friendly market place, and a mansion in its grounds within a stone's throw from the market place. One might well forget that it also has a sea front. Lytham began to develop as a resort at the end of the c18. About 1820 elegant villas are mentioned, but today's Lytham owes its appearance mostly to the coming of the railway in 1846 and the local Improvement Act of 1847. Thus, although Lytham and St Annes form one municipal borough, they must here be taken separately.

LYTHAM

St Cuthbert. 1834, but enlarged in 1872 (chancel), 1882 (n aisle), 1909. Long, of dark brick, with a w tower and embattled aisle, clerestory and chancel. The piers inside canted and without any capitals can hardly be of 1834. Open timber roof.

– STAINED GLASS. An uncommonly representative display. In the s aisle a *Hardman* window of 1860, next to it on the l. an outstanding, though badly preserved *Morris* window of 1874 (Mount of Olives, three figures and three sleeping figures below), on its r. an early *Kempe* window. In the N aisle another *Hardman*, then a *Capronnier* dated 1868, two typical *Clayton & Bell*, 1871, and another *Capronnier*, 1874. – PLATE. Set of 1844–5.

ST JOHN, East Beach. 1848–9 by *E. H. Shellard*, already entirely on the side of the Ecclesiologists. SW tower with well proportioned broach-spire. Lancets, a pair in the W, a stepped triplet in the E wall. Low pairs in the aisles, low triplets in the clerestory. Round piers. Transepts and chancel extension 1856–7, also by Shellard.

ST PETER (R.C.), Clifton Street. 1838–9, the W tower an addition of 1878 by *J. O'Byrne*. The chancel and the small polygonal baptistery also additions. Dark brick, without embellishments. Lancets; no aisles.

CONGREGATIONAL CHURCH, Bannister Street. 1861–2 by *W. F. Poulton* of Reading. Gothic, with a lean corner turret with spirelet. Cost: £2,093.

METHODIST CHURCH, Park Street. 1868. A sumptuous façade with two giant Corinthian columns *in antis* and massive details.

TOWN HALL. 1927. Neo-Georgian.

POLICE, Bannister Street. Nice Edwardian Baroque, brick with stone dressings. Asymmetrical tower, big segmental pediment.

LIBRARY, Clifton Street. 1872. Dark red and yellow brick. Steep gables and lancets. Far from ingratiating.

FIRE STATION, Station Road. Pretty, with grey brick, and the necessary tower.

PERAMBULATION. Development began between the market place and the sea. DICONSON TERRACE was started in 1824–5, BATH STREET in 1834, and Queen Street at about the same time. The CLIFTON HOTEL in Bath Street facing the beach dates from 1839–40. It is of five bays and three storeys with two later canted bay windows. Also in Bath Street is a row of original three-bay brick cottages and a former CHAPEL dated 1846.

Round the MARKET SQUARE is estate housing. Round the corner, in Westby Street, a few are perhaps of the 1840s. HASTINGS PLACE, a whole row, is a little later. The MARKET, HOUSE is of 1847–8, by Mr *Reed* of Liverpool, but the tower with its pretty lantern was added in 1872. Typical of c.1850 are the pilasters with rocky bands to make them less classical. Typical of Lytham altogether are the dark brick and the gables with bargeboards, all a little sombre and much as at, say, Bournemouth.

Only one individual building stands out – visually, not architecturally – the WINDMILL, standing right on the sea front. The sails ought to be repaired.*

LYTHAM HALL. Lytham Hall started as a farming cell of Durham. After the Reformation the estate changed hands several times, until in 1606 it came to Sir Cuthbert Clifton. An old drawing of the gabled C17 manor house exists. However, it was entirely rebuilt in 1757–64 by *John Carr* for Thomas Clifton.

The house is of brick with rendered features. It is nine by five bays long and two and a half storeys high. On the N side is an entrance with a porch of Tuscan columns and pilasters
55   l. and r.; the E side however has the main entrance, and above the ground floor a tetrastyle portico of attached unfluted Ionic columns with a pediment. The ground-floor windows have Gibbs surrounds, the upper windows hoods and other minor enrichments according to stress. The chief internal ornament
54   of the house is the plaster ceilings, the richest that over the staircase. This and the entrance hall are decorated in the fanciful style of the fifties, still inspired by Gibbs-Italian, but the dining room with its beautiful apse and another room have already undergone the revolutionary change to the Adam style. The 1760s are indeed the time when one can expect such a change. The entrance hall has a fine, florid chimneypiece, the staircase, which is cantilevered, three fluted balusters to the tread, a roundel of Jupiter in the centre of the ceiling, and a large Venetian window. There are good chimneypieces even on the upper floor.

The GATEWAY, which must date from *c*.1850, i.e. the time of the Market Square, stood in fact originally at its N end. The iron gates are rich and massive. The INNER GATES, however, in the grounds, belong to the time of the house.

ST ANNES

ST ANNE. 1873 by *Paley & Austin*, enlarged in 1887 by *R.K. Freeman*, who built the monumental W tower. The church is

* Written in 1967.

large, with a big tiled roof. It is of brick, with some cobble flushwork. The interior is nothing special.

ST JOSEPH (R.C.), Woodlands Road, Ansdell. 1909–14, said to be by *Pugin & Pugin*. Yellow stone with red-stone dressings. Dec style, with a NW tower. The interior still has the thin columns and abstract capitals of E. W. Pugin, fifty years earlier.

OUR LADY STAR OF THE SEA (R.C.), St Annes Road East. 1890–1 by *Pugin & Pugin*. Aisleless and towerless. Lancet windows.

ST PAUL, Clifton Drive, Fairhaven. 1902–4 by *Medland Taylor*. Hot-red brick, even for window details. A mannered building in such general matters as the placing of the w tower diagonally and in such small matters as the bits of ashlar dressings and the small rock-faced panels. The N aisle was never built. It was intended to differ in its rhythm from the s aisle.

ST THOMAS, St Thomas's Road. 1899–1905 by *Austin & Paley*. Red brick with much stone enrichment. Nave and aisles and a big N tower outside the N aisle. The nave façade is canted. The tracery Dec and Perp. Brick-faced interior, not of as much interest as many other Austin & Paley churches.

The BAPTIST CHURCH, St Thomas's Road, of 1884–8, the South Drive METHODIST CHURCH of 1892, the CONGREGATIONAL CHURCH, North Drive, of 1894–6, and the METHODIST CHURCH, Church Road, of 1905 are all churchy Gothic; only the FAIRHAVEN CONGREGATIONAL CHURCH, South Clifton Drive, of 1907–12 stands out, by size, by colour, by style, only not alas by quality. It is by *Briggs, Wolstenholme & Thornely*, all white faience slabs, and it is in a sort of Byzantine or South West French Romanesque, though the details are rather in the Edwardian Baroque. It needed some courage to put up such a building. – STAINED GLASS designed by *Charles Elliott* and made by *Abbott & Co*. You can see stories of Wyclif, Luther, Latimer, Ridley, and the Pilgrim Fathers, and many single figures.

TECHNICAL SCHOOL, North Clifton Drive. 1907. Mildly Norman Shaw in style. Brick with Dutch gables.

KING EDWARD VII SCHOOL, Inner Promenade, Fairhaven, and QUEEN MARY SCHOOL, South Clifton Drive, Fairhaven are both typical of their date. They are both of brick, symmetrical, with a cupola, but the one, of 1908, is Edwardian, the other, of 1930 etc., is in the between-the-wars scholastic Georgian. The boys were served by *Briggs, Thornely & MacLaughlan*, the girls by *Rees & Holt*.

PERAMBULATION. None is needed. It is patent that St Annes began to flourish when they liked steep gables and bargeboards, and N of the centre much of this type was built to uniform designs. The original layout and some of the early buildings are by *Maxwell & Tuke*. The two large hotels on the front, the GRAND and the MAJESTIC, are both obviously early C20. The Grand is by *F.W.Catterall*, 1906, the Majestic of 1910 etc. Older is the ST ANNES HOTEL in St George's Road, with its Tudor gables, bay windows, and mullioned and transomed windows. This was built in 1875–6.

MARHOLME *see* GREAT HARWOOD

MARSH GRANGE *see* IRELETH

MARTON *see* BLACKPOOL, p. 70

4010   MAWDESLEY

ST PETER. 1840 by *E. Sharpe*. Thin w tower with spire. Straight-headed two-light windows and buttresses between them.

ST PETER AND ST PAUL (R.C.). 1830–1. Oblong, with widely spaced windows of two lights, their detail Gothic, and thin buttresses. The altar recess is shallow and formed quite resourcefully as a Gothic portal, with all the thinness of members of romantic Gothicism. Attached to the altar end is the PRESBYTERY, a four-bay house, quite plain.

MAWDESLEY HALL. Timber-framed hall-space of the late C16 or early C17 with a long, low, twelve-light hall window and a doorway with pointed arch. In the hall a fireplace of 1625 with an overmantel with modest stucco decoration dated 1655. The l. wing is C18, the r. C19.

5070   MELLING

ST WILFRID. The w responds of the arcades must be pre-Perp, and the s aisle w window is of *c.*1300. The rest, w tower and all, is Perp, except that the clerestory was added in 1763 and given today's shape in 1866. – SCREENS. Part of a Perp dado in the porch. – In the tower arch a C17 baluster screen. – BENCHES. Very sensible C17 benches in the N aisle. Square-topped ends with two knobs. – SCULPTURE. Parts of an Anglo-Saxon slab with a circular plait (cf. St Mary Lancaster). – Also a short length of a cross shaft with basket-like interlace. – (In the vestry the lower half of a body, perhaps from a C13

Crucifix; *c.* 20 in.) – STAINED GLASS. The E window by *Holiday*, made by *Heaton, Butler & Bayne.* – PLATE. Chalice (Newcastle) inscribed 1759; Chalice and Breadholder, 1767. – MONUMENTS. John Marshall † 1802. Good, unsigned tablet with a female by an urn. – Thomas Smith † 1831. By *Webster*, with a sarcophagus. – Mrs Hoskins † 1838. By *W. Spence* of Liverpool. – CURIOSUM. A serpent, i.e. a wind instrument, purchased in 1834.

MELLING HALL, now a hotel. Good Late Georgian centre of three bays with a porch of paired Ionic columns.

OLD MALTHOUSE. 1684, and interesting in so far as this is a completely symmetrical façade and, while the upper windows have individual hood-moulds, the lower have one course running through and climbing round the door lintel.

MELLOR   6030

ST MARY. 1825–7 by *Rickman*. A Commissioners' church (cost £5,496). Nave and aisles. Paired lancets flanked by buttresses. W tower with lancets and determinedly recessed spire. W porches l. and r. of it. The E lancets apparently from the restoration by *Paley & Austin*, 1899. W gallery.

METHODIST CHURCH, ¼ m. NE. Very bitty, and with an ignorant S steeple. 1893 and 1900.

STANLEY HOUSE, ¾ m. SW. Formerly dated 1640. Flat front with asymmetrical square porch. Windows of three to six lights. The top window of the porch is of three lights, stepped. The porch leads straight on to the big central chimney opening to hall and kitchen.

(SACCARY HOUSE, Saccary Lane, 1 m. from the church. The same chimney arrangement. The porch here is central, and the date the later C17. MHLG)

WOODFOLD HALL, 1½ m. SW. By *James Wyatt*, 1798. Gutted. But it still has its beautifully smoothly ashlared façade of nine bays with portico of four giant unfluted columns with Adamish capitals. The sides have five bays, and the middle window is tripartite under a blank segmental arch. Good, large STABLES with tripartite lunette windows.

MEOLS HALL *see* CHURCHTOWN

MERESIDE *see* BLACKPOOL, pp. 70, 72

MOOR CRAG *see* CARTMEL FELL

_4060_

MORECAMBE

Morecambe owes its entity to the holiday-makers. Before the railway came in 1848 and the seaside development started, there were just villages. A very little of them can still be discovered, round POULTON SQUARE, with a house dated 1685 on its lintel in the adjoining RABY STREET, and round TORRISHOLME SQUARE, where one lintel bears the date 1663. A few more houses in BARE LANE represent Bare. (No. 20 has a pedimented doorway and gatepiers.)

HOLY TRINITY, the parish church, was first built in 1745 and rebuilt in 1840–1 by _E. Sharpe_.* It has paired lancets along the sides, a W tower with quite an original managing of the bell-openings and the crenellation, and a barn roof inside.
The other churches came later.

ST BARNABAS, Regent Road. By _Austin & Paley_, 1898. Left incomplete and completed in 1961 by a parish hall across the W end which is modern but insignificant. Austin & Paley, as one would expect, did their church in a free Perp. The nave arcades are of three bays. In the chapels the arcades have arches dying into the piers. It is a satisfying piece, but not as moving as St Lawrence.

ST CHRISTOPHER, Marine Road. By _Austin & Paley_. Free Perp and pleasant to look at, but very conservative for its date: 1934 – the end of a distinguished C19 firm.

ST JOHN, St John's Road. 1899–1901 by _Austin & Paley_. With a central tower, as some of their best small churches have. Five-bay arcades, the arches dying into the piers. A sixth, W, bay is narrower and lower. In the chancel there are windows only on E and S, the latter segment-headed. – STAINED GLASS. The W window by _Hugh Easton_, 1956.

ST LAWRENCE, Victoria Street. By _Paley & Austin_, 1876–8, their best church at Morecambe. Big, Dec, the NW steeple never built. Octagonal piers, double-chamfered arches, high chancel arch, two-bay S chapel with more richly moulded arches. The five-light E window is placed high up.

OUR LADY (R.C.), Townley Street. 1895 by _Pugin & Pugin_.

ST PATRICK (R.C.), St John's Road. Brick. 1965–6 by _Reynolds & Scott_ of Manchester.

SION BAPTIST CHURCH, Victoria Street. 1901–2 by _A. Gorton_. Gothic, with a nice canted façade.

---

* I owe the attribution to Mr Jolley.

CLARK STREET CONGREGATIONAL CHURCH (former). 1863 by *E. G. Paley*. Gothic, with a NW tower.

GREEN STREET METHODIST CHURCH. 1875. In typical Nonconformist Italianate, with a big pediment and an open porch with granite columns carrying Early Gothic capitals.

WEST END METHODIST CHURCH, West Street, at the corner of the sea front. 1897 by *Samuel Wright*. E.E., with lancets and a SW tower.

TOWN HALL. 1931–2 by *Cecil Sutton* (*Cross & Sutton*). Very neutral, a brick block, of thirteen bays to the sea side with a one-storeyed portico.

LIBRARY, Moss Lane. 1965–7 by *Roger Booth*, the County Architect. An ingenious design with folded walls and roofs and sloping tops of the walls to meet the lowest point of the roof. The roof is of the hyperbolic paraboloid type, and the three main areas – lending, reference, and children – are hexagonal and have diamond-shaped top lights. The reference room is on the first floor, the other two are placed on the ground floor so that the entrance hall separates them. The *ensemble* is lively and an asset to the town.

PROMENADE STATION. 1873. One-storeyed, symmetrical, Gothic.

WINTER GARDEN, Marine Road Central. 1878 the E part with the two copper domes, 1896 by *Mangnall & Littlewood* the bigger, gabled, symmetrical extension. The original name of the establishment was the People's Palace. Morecambe never in the C19 wanted to be posh. The part of 1878 originally had the big arch between the domes glazed, as if it were the trainshed of a monumental railway station.

ALHAMBRA, Marine Road West. 1910. At a distance like a capital Dutch town church of the C17. It is the lantern on the roof that does it, but there is also a big gabled façade.

MIDLAND HOTEL, SE of the Winter Garden. By *Oliver Hill*, [94] 1932–3. It has aged well. The building is long and only three storeys high. It has a concave front to the sea and is convex towards the entrance. The sea front has a seven-bay solid centre and one-bay solid end-pieces. The rest is long, sweeping balconies on first and second floors. In the middle of the entrance side a convex staircase projection with high window. The l. angle is rounded too. On the r. side is a projecting circular tearoom, glazed to the sea, solid, with boxed-out window surrounds, to the land side.

According to the dates of its growing prosperity, Morecambe's seaside housing is mostly gabled, Tudoresque. A survival from an earlier stage is the QUEEN'S HOTEL, Queen Street and sea front, which cannot be later than 1850 and represents the modest Georgian past.

MORETON HALL see WHALLEY

MUCH HOOLE see HOOLE

MUSBURY see HASLINGDEN

NELSON

8030

Nelson has no past and no architectural shape. The town grew up around a pub called the Lord Nelson (which dates it) and received its name from that. It lies along the valley of the Pendle Water and the Leeds–Liverpool Canal, i.e. also along the main Blackburn–West Riding road. Its industry is cotton. The first spinning mill dated from 1780. The centre of Nelson is entirely inarticulate. Only the parish church keeps up a civic dignity. However, the moors are near, and that makes up for much.

ST MARY, Manchester Road. By *Waddington & Dunkerley*. Four bays of the nave are of 1879, the fifth and the w tower followed in 1905–8. A large town-church, serious and dignified. High tower with a well grouped spire. The chancel has its side windows high up, and they have inner arcading. – STAINED GLASS. Fine *Morris* E window, as late as 1919.

ST JOHN, Barkerhouse Road. 1846–8. W tower with five high buttresses without set-offs. Top with a short spire. The sides have tall two-light windows between buttresses. Aisleless interior. Transepts and chancel are of 1896.

ST JOSEPH (R.C.), Macleod Street. By *Peter B. Nuttall*, 1962–4. Oblong body with square piers to separate aisle passages. Roof of zigzag skyline. Good lobby, with the font slightly sunk and encased in a glass cylinder along which curved staircases rise to the gallery.

ST PAUL, Halifax Road. 1809, with a few unfortunate alterations of 1864 such as the tower top. The church has a good deal of charm, with its two tiers of pointed S windows with Y-tracery and its porch tower. Low chancel. The blank arcading of the altar surround seems *c.*1810 too. The galleries in today's form must be of 1864. – (STOCKS in the churchyard. MHLG)

ST PHILIP, Leeds Road. 1900–2 by *R. B. Preston*. Still entirely Victorian, without a touch of the fresh wind of the Arts and

Crafts. sw tower with higher stair-turret. Windows with plate tracery.

CONGREGATIONAL CHURCH, Manchester Road. The façade is of the type of King's College Chapel, i.e. with two turrets. Geometrical tracery. 1884–5 by *Fell* of Manchester.

CENTRAL METHODIST CHURCH, Carr Road. Four bays with a four-bay pediment. Still in the classical tradition.

WESLEY CHURCH, Carr Road, next to the former. 1864. Also four bays, also a four-bay pediment, but segment-headed windows.

FRIENDS' MEETING HOUSE, Walverden Road, just outside the town boundary. Built *c.*1760, but still with mullioned and mullioned and transomed windows, though the members are now simply square in section.

TOWN HALL, Market Street. 1881 etc. The façade to Market Square – and what a depressing square it is – has features of the Victorian version of Italian Renaissance, but also Gothic features. The façade is symmetrical, except for the corner, where a pavilion roof adds a bit of prominence.

LIBRARY, Carr Road. By *J. R. Poyser* and *W. B. Savidge*. Completed in 1908. Ashlar-faced Edwardian Baroque, but not too frolicsome.

The centre is just a road crossing. BARCLAYS BANK, 1910–11 by *J. W. & S. J. Mould* of Bury and London, with its angle turret gives it a little point. The ARNDALE SHOPPING PRECINCT of 1966–8 on the other hand contributes nothing of civic value (architect *Percy Gray*).

If one un-public building were to be singled out, it ought perhaps to be the STATION HOTEL, of 1893, in the Elizabethan to Stuart style.

Two farmhouses worth notice survive within the boundaries of Nelson.

CHAPEL FARMHOUSE lies immediately SE of St Paul. It has mullioned windows, three of the largest of them (6, 6, 5 lights) still with arched lights.

SOUTHFIELD FOLD FARMHOUSE, Southfield, has a very[40] curious gable window, decidedly of a Yorkshire type. Five stepped lights, but two and four with tops as rising convex quadrant curves (cf. Old Lodge Burnley, which is demolished, and a house at Barrowford). S of this is another house, with a former barn dated 1737. This has all Venetian windows.

(In addition the MHLG lists – October 1967 – some houses which may be worth referring to here. They are COLD WEATHER

HOUSE FARM, C17; LOWER TOWN HOUSE, Barker House Road, probably C16 (with one seven-light and one five-light window), and SCHOLEFIELD HOUSE, Scholefield Lane (with a date 1617 and an eight-light window).)

CASTERCLIFF HILLFORT, ¼ m. NE of Marsden Hall. The defences enclose an oval area with a maximum diameter of 550 ft. The site is unexcavated, but surface fieldwork suggests that the earliest fortification was a univallate structure represented by the inner bank and ditch. This was later replaced by a second rampart and ditch with counterscarp bank enclosing the earlier earthwork. The interrupted nature of the latter defences suggests that this phase was never completed. Additional outworks on the E and W were probably intended to provide defensive approaches to the entrances, but which of the numerous gaps are contemporary with the building of the hillfort can only be demonstrated by excavation.

STONE CIRCLE. ¾ m. E of Catlow, on Ring Stone Hill, was a large stone circle which gave its name to the hill. The structure was broken up in the mid C19.

NETHER KELLET

5060

(ST MARK. 1879.)

NEWBY BRIDGE

3080

The BRIDGE is ascribed to the C17. It is of slate – five segmental arches and cutwaters. With the SWAN HOTEL (C18, with a columned doorway), including its attractive new wing, it makes a satisfying picture. Behind it in the wood the PENNINGTON TOWER, a folly tower.

NEWCHURCH

8030

Most of the villages around here have one factory.

ST MARY. Short Perp W tower (Whitaker 1544). The rest 1740. But Baines says nave and N aisle rebuilt 1788. The round-arched windows with their lugs look 1740 rather than 1788. Odd rhythm of three, then a doorway and a tablet over, then one more large one. On the N side all windows are in two tiers. Small Venetian E window. N arcade of very urbane Roman Doric columns. Well-panelled wooden W and N galleries. – CHANDELIER of brass, 1756. Two tiers of arms. – PLATE. Cup and Cover Paten of 1633; Chalice by *R.C.* of York, 1643.

NEWGATE FARM *see* UPHOLLAND

NEW HIGH RILEY *see* ACCRINGTON, p. 47

NEW LONGTON *see* LONGTON

NEWSHAM *see* BARTON

NEW SPRINGS *see* ASPULL

NEWTON GATE *see* WHITTINGTON

NORTH MEOLS *see* CHURCHTOWN

NUTTALL LANE *see* RAMSBOTTOM

OAKENCLOUGH *see* CALDER VALE

ORMSKIRK

4000

ST PETER AND ST PAUL. From a distance the church is more
odd than attractive, owing to the immediate proximity of a
broad w tower and a thin s steeple a little higher than the
tower. There are of course historical reasons for this oddity,
and they take some deciphering. The story clearly begins with
the one Norman chancel N window, whose surround, however,
is not genuine. The s chapel comes next. The responds of its
two-bay arcade (octagonal pier) belong to the late C13. The
irregularity in the walling of the E bays of the s aisle indicates
that they were once a transept. By then the nave probably had
a s aisle, or at least the curious s tower indicates that a s aisle
existed when it was built. The date of the tower is controver-
sial: about 1435 is given by the VCH, but the forms are almost
identical with those of the tower of Aughton church, and that
is assigned to the C14. Anyway, the bell-openings are Dec,
even if minimum. The tower is square, but the bell-stage by
means of broaches octagonal. A spire finishes it. The arches to
the church are boldly chamfered. Against the nave w wall is the
former lower roof-line. The present nave with its five-bay 24
arcades which take no notice of the s tower belongs to the
restoration by *Paley & Austin* which took place in 1877–91.
Before that time, we are told, the arcades consisted of classical
columns; for the body of the church had been rebuilt in 1729.
But the arcades differ, and the s arcade is not likely as an in-
vention of Paley & Austin. They may have had evidence
for what they did. In any case the arcade appears as one job
with the broad, massive w tower for the building of which

money was bequeathed in 1542. It has pairs of three-light bell-openings with uncusped intersecting tracery – the revival of a late C13 motif typical of post-Reformation Gothic (cf. Aughton). The features of the exterior of Ormskirk church are almost entirely Paley & Austin's. The exception is the Derby Chapel (s), whose simplified Perp windows go well with the date 1572 which is given by Glynne. – FONT. 1661. With the small simple motifs typical of Restoration fonts, in this case a pelican, a cross, an hourglass, and also CR and a crown. – SCREEN to the Derby Chapel, C17, with high balusters. – STAINED GLASS. In the tower windows by *Holiday*, 1880 (w) and 1892 (N). – SCULPTURE. Small panel with two men, quite possibly Anglo-Saxon (E wall outside). – Also a Saint with a book; Flemish(?), C18(?). – Also kneeling marble statue of a maiden with a pitcher. Nothing seems to be known about it: no date, no sculptor, no function. – PLATE. Two Chalices and Patens, 1633; Chalice and Paten, 1674; Patens, 1708 and 1717; Flagons, 1743 and 1759; two Flagons, 1773; Almsdish, 1781. – MONUMENTS. In the Derby Chapel two couples of alabaster, recumbent. Three are late C15 and supposedly the first Earl of Derby with his two wives (the second is the Lady Margaret, mother of Henry VII). They are said to come from Burscough Priory. The fourth is later C16 and probably the third Earl † 1572. Also in the chapel two tomb-chests without effigies. They have shields in quatrefoils. – In the s aisle on the wall brass to Sir Henry de Scarisbrick † 1420, a 5 ft 5 in. figure. – In the churchyard a fat C18 SUNDIAL.

EMMANUEL METHODIST CHURCH, Derby Street. 1878 by *Peter Balmer*. Large, with sw tower and geometrical tracery.

Apart from its church, Ormskirk has little to offer. In the centre at the main crossing is the sorry CLOCK TOWER of 1876.

The HOSPITAL in the Wigan Road incorporates the former WORKHOUSE of 1853. Brick, with the usual octagonal centre and three arms.

The biggest building is EDGE HILL COLLEGE OF EDUCATION, neo-Georgian, 1931–3 by the then County Architect *Stephen Wilkinson*, the finest the WATER TOWER, SE of it, brick, with, round the central core, very tall arches to support the tank.

(The WHEATSHEAF HOTEL in Burscough Street has an entrance passage with an ogee arch and good stucco. Also a capital with L-square and dividers. NMR)*

* Now demolished.

OSBALDESTON

ST MARY (R.C.). 1837–8. Visually rewarding as a group with the presbytery and the SCHOOL (of 1845). Architecturally interesting because no longer Georgian with arched windows, as was the Catholic tradition, but Perp for the church windows (of two lights) and Tudor for the presbytery. The church has a crenellated bell-turret.

(OSBALDESTON HALL. Crucks inside. The rest partly of c.1600, see the two square bay windows and a chimneypiece similar to those at Gawthorpe. J.Haworth)

OXENDALE HALL, 1 m. N. 1656. Most windows alas new, but a nicely varied gabled façade.

OSMOTHERLEY

ST JOHN EVANGELIST. 1874 by *Paley & Austin*. Slate and red sandstone. Lancet windows, a slate-hung bell-turret with a little spire, and an apse. Not as good as some of their village churches.

OSWALDTWISTLE

ST PAUL, Lord Street. 1882–4 by *Habershon & Fawckner*. E.E., without a tower. Short granite piers; apse.

TOWN HALL, Lord Street. 1891 by *R. N. Hunter*. Not detached, yet quite dignified. Eight bays, the first and last with a Venetian window. Money must have run out before any capitals were carved.

OUTHWAITE see WRAY

OUT RAWCLIFFE

ST JOHN. 1837–8 by *John Dewhurst*. This is a very individual building, Prussian rather than English, and of a puritanical cast. Red brick with two tiers of small round-arched windows and four corner turrets – that is all. The Norman W doorway is obviously a recent recutting or remodelling. The interior no doubt initially had three galleries.

OVER KELLET

ST CUTHBERT. The W bay of the S arcade is of c.1200, with an unmoulded round arch. The NW respond seems to be of the same date. Otherwise Late Perp, including the W tower. Much Victorian work of 1863–4.

A number of rewarding houses in the village, the best HALL-
GARTH of c.1820–5, five bays, with a one-storey portico of
paired Greek Doric columns and a pediment – not at all
provincial.

4050   OVERTON

ST HELEN. A Norman church basically. S doorway, badly preserved, with two arch orders with incised zigzag. Excavations
have proved that the church had an apse. The present E window is of 1771. The long N transept, a family pew probably, is
of 1830. – PULPIT. C18. With tester, oddly sunk into the S wall.
– PLATE. Chalice of 1708–9.

Overton has a pleasant main street. The best house is MANOR
FARM HOUSE, Georgian, of five bays.

1½ m. SW is SUNDERLAND POINT. This was in the early C18
the port for Lancaster, especially for the import of cotton. Its
importance was taken over late in the C18 by Glasson. What
remains of this short-lived minor prosperity is disappointing.
The only worth-while piece of architecture is one gatepier.

5050   OVER WYRESDALE

CHURCH. The W tower is of 1733, though it looks C17. The
church is of the same date, and its quoins and the two S doorways look Georgian indeed. The windows must belong to the
Victorian restoration of 1894.* – PULPIT. Dated 1684. The
carving, so far as it is original, looks in its character still Jacobean, though the motifs are later.

ABBEYSTEAD, 1¼ m. ENE. Built in 1886 by the Earl of Sefton.
The architects were *Douglas & Fordham*. Finely placed above
the stream. The house is Elizabethan in style, with mullioned
and transomed windows and gables, and quite extensive. The
main front has three canted bay windows but is kept carefully
asymmetrical. In the courtyard a tower.

A little below, by the gate lodge, another good neo-Elizabethan
house, dated 1891. The whole setting is highly romantic.

OXENDALE HALL *see* OSBALDESTON

7030   PADIHAM

ST LEONARD. 1866–9 by *William Waddington*. A large town-
church in the middle of the little town. Perp style with a S

* The architect of the restoration was *Douglas*. He added a spire and built
a new chancel.

tower. The estimate was £6,000 (GS). – FONT. Octagonal, Late Perp, with panels containing elementary carvings of the Instruments of the Passion, the M for Mary, the IHS for Jesus, and a shield (cf. Altham). – STAINED GLASS. The E window of 1865 (date commemorated) is still in the mid C19 tradition of single large figures in strong colours. – PLATE. Set inscribed 1803. – MONUMENTS. Le Gendre Starkie † 1822. By *Gibson*, made in Rome. Tablet with a seated woman and a standing angel pointing upward. – Mrs Starkie † 1888. She is lying on her side, an angel hovering over her.

METHODIST CHURCH, Cross Bank. 1847. Five bays, of stone, with arched windows. One-storeyed portico of unfluted Ionic columns. No pediment. A good, still classical façade.

NAZARETH UNITARIAN CHURCH, on the road to Blackburn. With NW steeple and geometrical tracery. 1872–4 by *Virgil Anderton*.

TOWN HALL. 1938 by *Bradshaw, Gass & Hope*. Brick with a stone portico and a little open square cupola.

Of the streets and houses there is nothing to report.

POWER STATION. 1927 and considerable enlargement by *Cruickshank & Seward* in 1961–2.

BURNLEY ROAD SCHOOL, by the drive to Gawthorpe. 1963–6 by *Roger Booth*, the County Architect. Good.

GAWTHORPE *see* p. 128.

PARBOLD

4010

OUR LADY (R.C.), Lancaster Lane, in the village. 1884 by *E. Kirby*, for £12,000, according to Kelly. The church has a fine tall steeple with complicated buttress and pinnacle arrangement below and around the spire. The windows are mostly lancets. Large rose window in the E wall. Complex group of SE attachments. Short round piers inside.

CHRIST CHURCH, on Parbold Hill, with its exciting view down into the plain. 1875 by *Myres, Veevers & Myres*. NE steeple not up to its Catholic successor. But the church is also large. The details are late C13. Wide nave; the N arcade piers are short, of granite, and paired in depth. – PULPIT. 1648, with panels of shallow carving and much sunk relief. The church replaces the so-called Douglas Chapel, i.e. the chapel by the river which had been rebuilt in 1621.

PARBOLD HALL, E of Christ Church. A very fine Mid Georgian stone house, seven bays wide, with a broad ashlar centre in which doorway and upper window are of the Venetian type.

L. and r. of the centre the three bays differ oddly. The l. side obviously represents an earlier house – rubble masonry and two and a half storeys. The r. side is what corresponds to the centre – two storeys only and ashlar masonry. As one inspects the s side one finds the whole house of two and a half storeys and with details such as window surrounds of the early C18. Recessed five-bay centre and projecting two-bay wings.

N of the Catholic church is a cul-de-sac with recent HOUSES by *Anthony Grimshaw*, well grouped. Pale grey brick, the walling carried up above the roof-line in the sixties fashion.

7030
PENDLETON
Near Clitheroe

A pretty village with a brook runing along its main street. White railings to prevent accidents which could not be but harmless. TOWN HEAD is a three-bay Georgian house with a pedimented doorway.

ALL SAINTS. 1847, with a s aisle of 1894. Small, nave and chancel in one. Bell-turret. Dec features.

LANE SIDE, 1½ m. NE. Remarkable for its date, 1751, in that the house still has mullioned windows. They are higher now, though not very high, and they have square, unmoulded mullions, but that is all.

LITTLE MEARLEY HALL, ½ m. further NE. The house has a gorgeous early C16 bay-window five sides of a dodecagon. On the ground floor buttresses as mullions, on the upper floor panelled shafts. Blank panel tracery also as a frieze below the upper windows. At the back of the house one window with uncusped arched lights, i.e. also early C16. Otherwise later mullioned windows. There is a date 1590. The early C16 parts are said to come from Sawtrey Abbey across the Yorkshire border, but that need not be so.

2070
PENNINGTON

ST MICHAEL. Built in 1826; extensive additions and alterations in 1926. Straight-headed Dec two-light windows. Polygonal apse. – In the s aisle re-set Norman TYMPANUM with a demi-figure of Christ with raised hands. Runic inscription referring to Gamel, who founded the church, and *Hubert*, the mason, who worked it. In the s porch also a Norman scallop capital. – PLATE. Chalice by *R. S.* 1617–18; Cup by *R.M.R.G.* of 1777–8; Paten by *H.B.*, 1784–5.

(DEVIL'S BRIDGE. A packhorse bridge. MHLG)

PENNINGTON GREEN see ASPULL

PENNY BRIDGE see EGTON

PENWORTHAM   *5020*

Penwortham is Outer Preston. Castle Hill and the church face across the Ribble towards where the docks now are. The old bridge is higher up than the new.

CASTLE HILL is the site of a Norman motte and bailey castle. Its purpose was the defence of the mouth of the river Ribble. No stonework has been found on the site. The parish church is just s of the castle, and yet a little further s, or rather sw, was a small Benedictine PRIORY, founded *c.*1140. There were apparently never more than the prior and two monks.

ST MARY. Perp w tower and early C14 chancel with renewed but credible small windows and a single-framed roof. What is between tower and chancel is by *E.G.Paley*, 1855 and in-different. – FONT (s aisle w). 1667, of characteristic plainness. – STAINED GLASS. A few ancient fragments in the chancel N and s windows. – MONUMENT. Laurence Rawstorne of The Priory † 1850, with an urn and books. Signed by *F. Webster* of Kendal. – Two HELMETS which, according to Mr Fleetwood-Hesketh, belonged to John Fleetwood † 1590.

BRIDGE. Built *c.*1760. Yellow and red stone. Five segmental arches with triangular passing-places.

TOWER. At the corner of Liverpool Road and Cop Lane. Built by L.Rawstorne in 1890 to supply water. Brick, with an odd skyline. It looks 1860s rather than 1890.

PENWORTHAM LODGE, New Lane. Ashlar-built early C19 house of five bays and two storeys with a porch of two pairs of unfluted Ionic columns.

PIEL CASTLE   *2060*

(On an island s of Barrow, reached by a ferry from Roa Island. The date of the licence to crenellate, i.e. in this case to build the castle, is 1327, and the architectural details suit that date. The castle is ruinous, but the remains are substantial. It was a plain tower, like a keep, and only the E wall and the E ends of the N and s walls are missing. There are diagonal and mid-buttresses and a long porch ending in two diagonal turrets on the N side. This led into a corridor with a room l. and a room r. In the SE corner is an oblong projection containing one room

on each floor, their levels not the same as those of the keep
proper. In the NW corner of the keep is a spiral stair. Another
is just E of the entry from porch to keep. This entry bay is
vaulted, as is the small room above it. The W rooms have
fireplaces, one of them a good example of its date. The upper
windows are pointed, of two lights, with quatrefoil tracery. The
inner bailey has remains of three towers. The NW tower is
five-sided. In the S tower are three doorways and a fragment
of the corbelled-out parapet. The gateway is on the W and has
a room with a fireplace over. The outer bailey survives only
on the N and W. It still has three recognizable two-storeyed
towers. Close to the NE tower are the remains of the chapel, 31
ft long. VCH, vol. VIII)

4040

PILLING

ST JOHN BAPTIST. 1886–7 by *Paley & Austin* (cost: £7,000).
Large, with a W tower with recessed spire. Paley & Austin
here make much play with the flushwork motif, usual in flint
and stone in East Anglia, but here transferred to mauve and
beige stone. The fertility of Paley & Austin remains astonishing. Very high tower arch. Arcades of octagonal piers with
concave sides. The chancel chapels, as Paley & Austin liked it,
differing in size and details. The chancel arch dies into the responds, as do the S chapel arches.

OLD CHURCH, 100 yds S. 1717. Five bays long, with a double
bellcote with segmental pediment. The S side windows are
arched, with one mullion running harshly into the apex.
The E window has two mullions. On the N side two tiers of
windows, the upper lunettes. This may date from 1812–13,
when we hear of a new gallery. There are in fact inside a W
and a N gallery. – BOX PEWS, one dated 1719. – PULPIT. A
three-decker.

(A COTTAGE opposite the Methodist church has crucks visible
outside. MHLG)

PIMLICO *see* CLITHEROE

6020

PLEASINGTON

ST MARY AND ST JOHN BAPTIST (R.C.). Built in 1816–19 as a
thank-offering of John Francis Butler (later Butler-Bowden) of
Pleasington Hall. It is an astonishing church, especially
considering the position of Catholicism in England about

1820. It is large and, though without a tower, very prominent on its site. The aisles have large three-light windows and battlements and pinnacles, there is a clerestory with an open-work parapet and a tall polygonal apse, and the w front has a large rose window and a portal of three orders with square 76 fleurons set in a giant arch with dogtooth and small carved figures – badly carved, it must be admitted. Above the portal are three statues, carried on figure brackets, the middle one being the bust of Mr Butler in military uniform. In a side niche is the inscription Johannes Palmer Architectus. So *John Palmer* of Manchester invented this remarkable display. The interior is of five bays, with Perp piers – the whole church is Perp in conception and features – but the arches have dog-tooth. The nave and aisles are rib-vaulted, not in stone of course, and in the nave are large flat bosses with scenes. To the l. and r. of the altar are reliefs of the Beheading of St John and the Magdalen.

PLEASINGTON OLD HALL, NE of the church. Dated 1587. Centre with the hall, two wings, and the porch and a counter-piece to it in the re-entrant angles. The hall window is of three plus three lights, the parlour window of seven with a transom. On the service side there is no window to go with this.

TONGUE HILL, ¼ m. SE. Dated 1735 and yet still with an asym-metrical façade on the pattern of the medieval hall and hall doorway arrangement.

PLUMPTON HALL see EGTON

PORTFIELD CAMP see WHALLEY

POULTON-LE-FYLDE   3030

ST CHAD. The tower seems to be of the C17 – see the bell-openings. But the s doorway is Georgian, and so is the rest of the church. It was rebuilt in 1752–3. The two s doorways are typical of that date, with their Tuscan columns, triglyphs, and pediments. They are in a characteristic Georgian manner, set in with an attempt at counteracting medieval asymmetry. The windows are large and arched; their Y-tracery seems to be later. Above the doorways are horizontally placed ovals, keyed-in as window arches. What looks like the priest's doorway is the entry to the Fleetwood family vault. It is older than the church. The date in the inscription is 1699, and that goes well with the big carved corbels carrying a

broken pediment. The interior has preserved its three galleries. – Nice C18 STAIRCASE to the w gallery. – SCREEN (s
aisle w). Dated 1636 and in a jolly Jacobean. – PULPIT. Of
about the same time, with arabesques and the familiar low
62   blank arches. – CHANDELIER. Brass; C18. – PLATE. Large
Paten by *Hugh Roberts*, London, 1698–9; six-inch Chalice,
inscribed 1735. – MONUMENT. Rev. Richard Buck † 1845. By
C. Lewis of Cheltenham. Rupert Gunnis noted that the two
figures are copied from Flaxman.

MARKET CROSS. A Tuscan column, with a ball on top. Probably C17.

METHODIST CHURCH, Chester Avenue. By *Keith Ingham*
(*Building Design Partnership*), 1965–6. Severely blocky, with
a folded roof and windowless slab walls, white rendering, and
engineering bricks. The church itself is octagonal, but shows
only above the ancillary parts.

3040   PREESALL

ST OSWALD, Knott End. 1896–8 by *Austin & Paley*. This is a
brick church, which is rare in the *œuvre* of the Austin & Paley
firm. s aisle, transepts, shingled bell-turret. The interior is
also brick, except for the chancel and the arcade. The arcade
piers are octagonal with concave sides. It is hard to put one's
finger on what makes such an Austin & Paley church so satisfying. Is it the comfortable proportions ? Is it the crispness of
the detail ?

PARROX HALL. Evidently an Elizabethan house with mullioned
windows, although most of them are now sashed. Centre and
projecting wings. The centre now has a curious loggia, with
Tudor arches standing on Tuscan columns.

5020   PRESTON

INTRODUCTION

Preston has a Roman and a medieval past, although nothing of
it is visible. The town received its first charter in 1179. The
Greyfriars settled about 1260. Prosperity is evident in the C14
and the following centuries. The town profited from being the
lowest crossing point of the Ribble by means of a bridge, and
hence a route centre. It also was a social centre, which it is not
now. Industry has however not wholly wiped out Preston's
amenities. The spinning and weaving industries are docu-

mented already for the C16, but the boom and the ruination of most of the visual attractions came only with the steam engine and the factories. Arkwright was born at Preston in 1732. The first cotton mill was started in 1777. Samuel Horrocks started his first mill in 1791 and with his partners built five mills between 1796 and 1802. The population in 1801 was about 12,000, in 1831 33,000, in 1851 69,000. Now it is 106,000. In 1835 there were forty factories, in 1869 seventy-seven (21 for spinning, 30 for weaving, 26 for both). Now cotton has receded, and many of the mills serve other industries.

From the townscape angle Preston benefits from a pleasant site with the well planted rise above the river Ribble. The town's greatest visual asset is the area s of Fishergate with its large square and its Late Georgian streets. This is a quarter any Lancashire town would have reason to be proud of. The other asset is the C19 churches, some of them, especially *Hansom*'s St Walburge, of great national interest. It is enlightening to follow the building of churches in order to watch the growth of the town: St Paul Park Road, i.e. NE, 1823–5 and St Peter Fylde Road, i.e. NW, 1822–4, St Ignatius, Catholic in Meadow Street, i.e. N, 1833–6, Christ Church, Jordan Street, i.e. W, in 1835–6, St Thomas Lancaster Road, i.e. N, in 1837–9, and so on, to the climax of building the whole parish church afresh in 1853–5.

For today an interesting fact is that Preston has managed to retain a local architectural firm, *Building Design Partnership*, originally *Grenfell Baines*, in spite of a large national practice.

INNER PRESTON*

CHURCHES

ST JOHN THE DIVINE, Church Street. 1853–5 by *E. H. Shellard* and no doubt his *magnum opus*. Large, Dec, with a fine NW steeple the very lowest part of which goes back to the C16 predecessor of the church. Ornate porch into the tower, three-light aisle windows, two two-light clerestory windows per bay, slender cluster piers with nobbly leaf capitals – and still galleries tucked into the aisles. Three-bay chancel aisles, of course without galleries. Both nave and chancel have hammerbeam roofs, that in the nave much higher. – PAINTING. On the W wall large painting of the Sermon on the Mount. Done in 1956 by *Hans Feibusch*, whose gentle Expressionism

* I.e. W to the railway, N to Walker Street, E to Stanley Street and London Road, s to the river.

had a vogue among progressive clergymen in the recent past. – STAINED GLASS. The E and the S chapel windows by *Wailes*, c.1855. – PLATE. Paten and Flagon, 1705; two Patens and a Flagon, 1708; three Flagons, 1719, 1725, 1725; two Chalices, 1729; two Chalices, 1785; Wine Strainer inscribed 1819. – MONUMENTS. A number of Gothic tablets and, under the tower, a Gothic tomb recess to Thomas Starkie Shuttleworth † 1819. – The best of the tablets is that to the Rev. Roger Carus Wilson † 1839. By *J. Theakstone* of London, with a relief of the five churches of Preston erected mainly on his initiative. – Also Gothic William St Clare † 1822 by *Webster*. – Much earlier two tablets in the chancel: Mrs Boughton † 1715 and Dame Mary Hoghton † 1720. Both with small busts on the top.

ST GEORGE, George's Road, off Lune Street. Built in 1724, encased in stone in 1845, almost entirely rebuilt in 1884–5 (by *Garlick, Park & Sykes*). Dark ashlar, Romanesque, with a S porch tower. High, basilican interior with columns and a clerestory. The capitals are Early Gothic in type. The apse looks thinner and could well be of 1845.

ST JAMES, Avenham Lane, right in the area of new development. 1870–81 by *Hibbert*. SW tower with sculpture on top. Geometrical tracery. Apse. Short granite columns inside.

ST MARY (R.C.), Friargate. Reached through an archway. 1856; the smallest of the major Catholic churches of Preston. Arched windows, flat ceiling with two glazed domes. Arched altar-screen. Of nothing like the architectural interest of St Wilfrid and St Augustine.

ST PAUL, Park Road. 1823–5 by *Rickman & Hutchinson*, a Commissioners' church (price £6,214). The chancel rebuilt in 1882. Ashlar, with W turrets. Pairs of lancets along the sides and thin buttresses between. A perfectly preserved interior except for the baptistery and the chancel. Thin cluster piers and three galleries on iron columns. Flat ceiling. – BOX PEWS. – Several Gothic MONUMENTS, especially the tablet to Joseph Rigg † 1847, with the statuettes of Faith and Charity.

ST WILFRID (R.C.), Chapel Street. First built in 1793, rebuilt in 1879–80 by *Ignatius Scoles* and *S.J. Nicholl*. The estimate was for £10,000. Red brick with much brown terracotta, in an exuberant North Italian Quattrocento or early Cinquecento. Six bays in length, but no tower. Marble columns inside, tunnel-vault with penetrations. In the apse giant pilasters. It is a proud and sumptuous building, inspired by St Augustine (*see* p. 202).

FISHERGATE BAPTIST CHURCH. 1857–8 by *Hibbert & Rainford*. Romanesque, with a rather starved s w tower with pyramid roof. Well detailed otherwise, with touches of the Italian c14 and c15 and more than touches of Gothic (the side windows).

CANNON STREET CONGREGATIONAL CHURCH (former). Built in 1825–6 and enlarged in 1852. Ashlar, five bays, with a tetrastyle portico of giant Corinthian columns and pediment.

LANCASTER ROAD CONGREGATIONAL CHURCH. 1862–5. Five bays, a quiet classical design with giant pilasters carrying blank arches.

CENTRAL METHODIST CHURCH, Lune Street. 1817. Remodelled in 1862–3 by *Poulton & Woodman*. White ashlar. A giant arch on paired columns under a pedimental gable. Heavy details.

UNITARIAN CHAPEL, Church Street. 1717. Humble, with arched windows.

PUBLIC BUILDINGS

COUNTY OFFICES, *see* Outer Preston, p. 200.

COUNTY OFFICES, former Park Hotel, *see* p. 198.

COUNTY SESSIONS HALL, Market Place. By *Henry Littler*, 1900–3. A broad front with a middle tower, 170 ft high. Thirteen bays, with giant columns to mark the main accents. English Baroque with a good dose of Italian Baroque.

MUNICIPAL BUILDINGS, N of the former. 1933–4 by *Sir Arnold Thornely* (of *Briggs & Thornely*). – CORPORATION PLATE. Silver-gilt Mace, London, 1702–3, by *P. Y.* – Two Georgian Maces. – Sword, mid c18 and 1845. – Badge and two Chains. By *Alfred Gilbert*, 1888–92. – Two Wands of Office, one inscribed 1644. – Two Halberds, bought in 1703. – Hanap, by *A. B.*, London, 1615–16. – Loving Cup inscribed 1761. – Punch Bowl by *E. G.*, London, 1741–2. – Tankard by *Fi*, London, 1711–12. – Ewer by *N. A.*, London, 1711–12. – Cut-glass Cup with silver-gilt Stand, early c18. – Salver, 1802–3. – Snuff Box, inscribed 1814. – Candlesticks, Birmingham 1788–9.

MAGISTRATES COURT AND POLICE, Lancaster Road. 1857–8 by *J. H. Pack*; enlarged 1901. The row of civic buildings along Lancaster Road is quite impressive. Behind the police, in Earl Street, the PRISON, heavily rusticated and with lunette windows below, arched windows above.

CORN EXCHANGE AND PUBLIC HALL, Lime Street. 1822–4; enlarged 1882. Brick, nine-bay façade with three-bay pediment and cupola. Very long along Fleet Street.

86 HARRIS LIBRARY AND MUSEUM, Market Place. Built by the trustees of E.R.Harris, who had died in 1877, leaving £300,000 to the town for specified cultural and charitable purposes, including a free library. The resulting edifice is one of the most remarkable Victorian public buildings of Northern England. It cost £80,000. The architect was the widely unknown *James Hibbert*, and the date, 1882–93, is almost unbelievably late for the style. For this is a monumental entirely classical building. It ought to be contemporary with St George's Hall in Liverpool, but has quite near parallels of similar dates in Glasgow. It comes off entirely and is an ornament to the town as well as a powerful demonstration of the arts it wishes to serve.

There is a storey-high base first of all to elevate the building, and then a giant portico of six fluted Ionic columns carrying a pediment.* L. and r. are three slightly recessed bays, and they have giant pilasters, but, just as in Elmes's masterpiece, only the lower floor keeps its windows in line with the pilasters. The upper floor recedes, and the pilasters become square pillars. The same effect at the back, where the centre is recessed and there are two projections with the pillar-pilasters. The sides have a different rhythm again, but are managed just as skilfully. The centre of the whole building is a yet higher lantern-lit extra storey, looking from a distance like the stage house of a theatre. Many inscriptions explain the programme of the building. The inscription at the top is in Greek. Inside, the *clou* is the central rotunda of unfluted Ionic columns. It is a monumental motif, especially as a ring opens to the whole great height of the building, but it is architecturally not well managed in that above the ring it turns square and goes on square to the very top. The square on the first floor has as its supports four big Greek Doric columns, and they are placed very awkwardly above four additional Ionic columns below, which in terms of the rotunda are senseless. The upper regions are decorated by parts of the Elgin marbles and the frieze of Bassae. A bad point in the planning is that a processional entry to the ceremonial upper floor is impossible. The staircase is squeezed in behind the base, and the entrance on the ground floor is in semi-darkness.

* The sculpture is by *E.R.Mullins.*

WAR MEMORIAL, Market Place. By *Sir Giles Gilbert Scott*, 1925.

HARRIS COLLEGE OF ARTS, Avenham Lane. 1846–7 by *John Welch*. Ashlar-built, of three bays, classical like the library. Entry with two giant columns *in antis* and a pediment. L. and r. on the ground floor tripartite windows, the upper floor blank. A wide staircase leads up to the entrance. The building started life as the Preston Institution for the Diffusion of Knowledge.

POST OFFICE, Market Place. 1903.

MARKET, N of the Market Place. Simple open iron sheds.

CATHOLIC SCHOOL, Fox Street. 1814. Brick, seven bays with a three-bay pediment.

TECHNICAL SCHOOL, Corporation Street. 1897 by *Cheers, Aspinell & Smith*. Brick. Symmetrical Tudor, nice cross-windows and big dormers. Behind to the NW extensive new buildings for the HARRIS COLLEGE OF FURTHER EDUCATION, by the Development Group of the *Department of Science and Education* and the *Architects' Co-partnership*, 1963–5. An intelligently planned group of buildings with the communal block as its centre. Ungimmicky details.

H.M. PRISON, Stanley Street. The big castellated structure was the Governor's House. It dates from 1834 and was probably designed by *John Dewhurst*.

COURT HOUSE (former), Stanley Street. By *Rickman*, 1825. It originally had a dome, i.e. looked rather like an American state capitol. Ashlar, severely classical and deliberately sparing in adornment. Close to it the DRILL HALL, W of St Mary. Brick, with four angle turrets. It was built as Militia Stores in 1854.

PERAMBULATION

At Preston a really enjoyable perambulation of half an hour can be made immediately s of Fishergate, the chief shopping street. It is to explore the streets round WINCKLEY SQUARE. 61 Preston is lucky to have a square, not only so large, but also on such attractively undulating terrain. And to have this quarter so near the centre is the rarest of advantages. The streets involved are e.g. RIBBLESDALE PLACE, EAST CLIFF, and tailing off into CAMDEN PLACE, CHADDOCK STREET, CROSS STREET, etc. The houses are without exception of brick, and their sole enrichment is the door surrounds. In Winckley Square one house, No. 5, has a big High Victorian portal, another, No. 34, a C17 to Baroque façade dated 1898.

They do no harm. The s side is the least changed, the E side is in the process of a pretty complete change. The MONUMENT to Sir Robert Peel is by *Duckett*. At the end of East Cliff is the former PARK HOTEL (now County Offices), the railway hotel built in 1882 to *Arnold Mitchell*'s design. Red brick with a tower with pyramid roof and a splendid view over the Ribble valley.

There are minor remains of about the same date, again with doorways with columns e.g. in CHAPEL STREET (No. 1) and also in FISHERGATE (No. 89). Otherwise in Fishergate, or rather off Fishergate, in THEATRE STREET, the former ST JOSEPH'S ORPHANAGE, grim brick Gothic of 1877. Nothing else of note in Fishergate.

Off to the N is the new ST GEORGE'S SHOPPING PRECINCT (by *J. Seymour Harris & Partners*), with shops on two levels, the upper being that of Fishergate, a circular centre, and an arcade on top of which is a multi-storey garage. The details are a bit garish, but the concept is good. In the MARKET PLACE the composition of Harris Library and Post Office is carried on by a new office block on the s side. It is called Crystal House and is by *Ardin & Brook*. In LANCASTER ROAD opposite some of the public buildings a row of private buildings (Nos 12–24) joining into a display more monumental than in other streets. The STANLEY ARMS is the best of these buildings, sedately classical. The others have giant pilasters.

That leaves one more area of interest, that of the AVENHAM REDEVELOPMENT. Building went on in two phases. The first was in 1959–61 between Russell Street and Oxford Street, with three- to four-storey terraces by *Stirling & Gowan* in their tough and wilful way, and two eleven-storey blocks by *Lyons, Israel & Ellis*. The second phase, E of Oxford Street, was done in 1964–7 by the *Building Design Partnership*, with two nineteen-storey blocks and more three- to four-storey terraces. The terraces with their Accrington bricks and their heavy arched lintels are evidently an attempt at reverting to the mood of the Victorian vernacular. It is curious that some people should have moved on recently to a nostalgia for the grimmer aspects of Victorian architecture.

OUTER PRESTON
WEST

ST ANDREW, Blackpool Road, the parish church of Ashton-on-Ribble. 1836. The date refers to the mediocre W tower with

Norman details and the masonry of the nave. In 1876 *Ewan Christian* added the wide N aisle and altered the window details. – STAINED GLASS. The E window obviously by *Hardman.*

CHRIST CHURCH, Bow Lane. 1835–6 by *John Latham* in the Norman style. Transepts and chancel by *Shellard*, 1851–2. He just continued Latham's style, but without Latham's extraordinary conceits. One is introduced to them at once by the madly fat Norman gatepiers. So one is prepared for the W façade with two octagonal towers – octagonal from the ground – with two doorways. The nave has two tiers of windows. There is only a W gallery.

EMMANUEL, Brook Street. 1869–70 by *Myres, Veevers & Myres.* Brick with a SW tower, lancets and geometrical tracery. Aisleless interior, the nave with a big hammerbeam roof.

ST MARK, St Mark's Road. 1863–6 by *E. G. Paley.* High, impressive NE tower with long, slender bell-openings. It tries to compete with the steeple of St Walburge in prominence and to defeat it by solidity and sensibleness. The tower adjoins the high polygonal apse. The style is E.E. The only impure feature is the W porch with its three entries. – (STAINED GLASS. One window by *Holiday*, 1868.)

ST MICHAEL, Egerton Road. 1908, evidently by *Austin & Paley*, with all their characteristics. A large church in a well-to-do street. The S tower unfortunately was never built. The features are free Perp. The E end groups excellently. The chancel has Austin & Paley's difference between N and S walls – N two very high arches, S less high, but an outer as well as an inner chapel. There is no chancel arch, only wide panelled responds up to the roof, but there is an arch immediately W of the altar.

ST PETER, St Peter's Square. 1822–5 by *Rickman & Hutchinson.* A Commissioners' church (cost £6,765). The SE steeple an addition of 1851–2 (by *Mitchell*). Rickman has an odd façade with two projecting bays at the aisle W ends and a bellcote. Three-light Dec aisle windows, two-light clerestory windows. The steeple is the best thing – with crockets up the spire and little flying buttresses.

ST STEPHEN, Bird Street. 1888 by *Joseph Harding.*

ST WALBURGE (R.C.), Weston Street. Built in 1850–4. This is *Joseph Aloysius Hansom*'s most personal building, nothing like as accomplished as his Manchester and Arundel churches, but alarmingly individual. It is a building driven to extremes

82　outside and inside. Outside it is the steeple which one does
not forget, of white stone, whereas the rest is brown, and
excessively slender, almost ghost-like. The spire is very
high (the total height is over 300 ft), and the pinnacles are
pushed close to it. The bell-openings are of the slimmest too.
The W front is in contrast broad and spreading, though pulled
together by a very large rose window. As you enter nothing
83　has prepared you for the shock of this interior – a secular hall
rather than a church, or at least like no other church. It is a
66 ft wide room without aisles and with three-light windows
with geometrical tracery and with stained glass entirely patterned and without figures, and it is covered with a hammerbeam roof, much steeper than any of the Middle Ages. The
members are connected by tracery too to secure the dominance
over all the rest of this bad dream of a roof. And finally, the E
end splits itself into a high, almost entirely glazed polygonal
apse and two short pieces of straight wall also with tall windows.
The sudden division into apse and side pieces following after
an aisleless nave is familiar from Gerona. But did Hansom
know it from there? – WEST GALLERY. On iron columns,
with heavy, very 'rogue' details. The organ is attached a good
deal higher up than the gallery parapet. – STAINED GLASS.
In the apse apparently by *Hardman*.

COUNTY OFFICES, Fishergate Hill. 1878 by *H.Littler*, the
County Architect. E extension (to Pitt Street) 1882. N of that
a block of 1934. Brick, large, and of no interest. A better
extension of 1903 into Jordan Street. It is by the same architect and served the County Police. N of it the Computer Block
of 1965.

PERAMBULATION. The well-to-do brick houses with columns
l. and r. of the doorways continue from the centre down
FISHERGATE HILL and into WEST CLIFF. In Fishergate
Hill the best is a pair with proper porches supported by Greek
Doric columns.

NORTH*

ALL SAINTS, Lancaster Road. 1846–7 by *John Latham*.
Classical, not Gothic (nor Norman). Portico of unfluted Ionic
giant columns and pediment. The columns are grouped
1–2–2–1. The sides are brick and have high, round-arched
windows.

* Including Fulwood.

CHRIST CHURCH, Victoria Road. 1864–5 by *Myres & Veevers*. N porch tower turning naughtily octagonal halfway up. Much play is made with roofs. Aisleless interior with hammerbeam roof. The tracery represents *c*.1300.

ST CUTHBERT, Lytham Road. 1913–16 by *Temple Moore*, unfinished to W and S, but with an impressively flat N front with even three-light Perp windows and a doorway further E than usual.

ST IGNATIUS (R.C.), Meadow Street. By *Scoles*, yet Gothic. Built in 1833–6, but the chancel and the outer chapels by *J. A. Hansom*, 1858. W tower with a spire supported by flying buttresses. Entry bays l. and r. of it. High clerestory with pinnacles. The nave interior very thin. That comes out forcibly in a comparison with the chancel, where everything is more convincingly proportioned. – STAINED GLASS. In one S aisle window typical glass of *c*.1830; badly done.

ST JUDE, St Paul's Road. 1893 by *R. Knill Freeman*. The estimated cost was £6,600. Yellow stone and red-stone dressings. Dec features. No tower. The aisles have W angle turrets. The porch leads from the W into the N aisle. The arcade piers inside continue into the arches without capitals.

ST LUKE, Fletcher Road. 1858–9 by *Shellard*. Estimated cost £4,733. It is interesting to see how Shellard reacted to the antiquarian revolution. The exterior is conventional Middle Pointed, including the SW steeple. But the sides still have the paired lancets of the Commissioners' time, even if they are no longer so slender. Also the transept and the short chancel are relics of the pre-ecclesiological past. – (STAINED GLASS. The E window and another by *Holiday*, 1864–5.)

ST THOMAS, Lancaster Road. Built 1837–9 by *John Latham*. Cost £4,500. Norman, with an impressive tower over the chancel and a polygonal apse. The tower carries a broach-spire, which is not a Norman feature. A very odd interior, with the smallest and narrowest sanctuary bay. The sanctuary arch has absurdly short semicircular responds on the most elementary corbels. Along the side walls round piers, meant for aisle arcades.

ST THOMAS AND ENGLISH MARTYRS (R.C.), Garstang Road. 1863–7 by *E. W. Pugin*, enlarged by the *Pugin* firm in 1888. The SW tower has never been built. Extremely high nave, the façade steep with a crowning pinnacle. Geometrical tracery. The interior is disappointing. Eight narrowly spaced bays, taking in the two-bay transepts. Polygonal apse. This and the transepts (and a CLOISTER corridor from the presbytery to the sacristies N of the church and round the apse) are of 1888.

MOOR PARK METHODIST CHURCH, Garstang Road. 1861. Brick, with a pedimental gable and a giant curved porch of fancy Ionic pillars.

CIVIC HOSTEL HOSPITAL, Watling Street. Built as the WORKHOUSE in 1866. Very long brick front with a middle tower with pavilion roof. A large recent extension at the back with a brutalist skyline (by *C.B.Pearson, Son & Partners*).

HARRIS ORPHANAGE, Garstang Road. 1885–8. The interesting fact is that instead of one vast institutional pile the establishment is divided into houses of human size. The only monumental feature is the tower by the chapel.

BISHOP O'REILLY'S CATHOLIC POOR LAW MEMORIAL, St Vincent's Road, off Garstang Road. 1893–7, of brick.

96 WILLIAM TEMPLE SCHOOL, St Vincent Road. By the *Building Design Partnership* (*N. Keith Scott*), 1964–6, gay and up-to-the-minute, with its engineering bricks and white, painted asymmetrical butterfly roofs.

BARRACKS, Watling Street Road. 1842–8. It cost £138,921. It is indeed a fine stone-built job. The entrance is by a tripartite gateway with blocks instead of capitals and a middle arch of basket type. To the inside this feature is crowned by a pediment. The ranges of the quad are of two storeys, even, solid, and honest. It is a pity one side has been demolished.

New HOUSING N of St Thomas in NORTH ROAD. Lively. By *E.H.Stazicker*, the Borough Engineer (architect *J.E. Smith*).

EAST

ST AUGUSTINE (R.C.), St Austin's Place. 1838–40 by a pupil of Scoles called *A.Tuach*, but greatly enlarged since. The apse is of 1878, but most of the enlargement was due to a campaign in 1890 by *Sinnott, Sinnott & Powell*. Until then the façade had just the four-column portico with pediment. Now the two
77 towers with their cupolas were built. They are Italian Renaissance as against the original classical features. The aisleless interior with giant pilasters and the fine, boldly coffered, segmental tunnel-vault are all of 1890.

ST GREGORY (R.C.), Blackpool Road. 1935–6 by *W.C.Mangan*. Brick, with a bold octagonal w tower with pronounced batter. Aisleless interior with concrete arches.

ST JOSEPH (R.C.), Skeffington Road. 1873–4 by *J. O'Byrne*.

Brick; no tower, hall interior with high, slender granite columns provided with shaft-rings. Short chancel, the nave roof boarded tunnel-wise, the aisles half-tunnel-wise. It is an impressive interior.

ST MARY, St Mary's Street. 1836–8 by *John Latham*, that Earliest Victorian 'rogue' (in Goodhart-Rendel's sense). Very large, Norman, with a weirdly built-up high tower. It is stepped back twice and has two tiers of bell-openings and on top a battery of cylindrical shapes and a short spire. Moreover, the w front is widened by side pieces, their turreted façades facing N and s. The nave has long round-headed windows set in blank arches. Aisleless, with a barn roof. The transepts and chancel are by *Shellard*, 1852–3.

ST MARY MAGDALEN, Ribbleton Avenue, Ribbleton. 1889–91 by *R. Knill Freeman*. No tower. Dec features. The arcade arches die into the piers. The transepts have large rose windows.

ST MATTHEW, New Hall Lane. 1881–3 by *James Hibbert*.

ST OSWALD, Harewood Street, Deepdale. 1934 by *W. Tapper* of London.

ST SAVIOUR, Queen Street. 1868 by *Hibbert*. sw tower with a small attachment to the E built as a day school. Geometrical tracery.

GRIMSHAW STREET CONGREGATIONAL CHURCH. 1859 by *Bellamy & Hardy*. Gothic, meant to have two towers.

CEMETERY, New Hall Lane. The three chapels are by *T. D. Barry*, 1854–5.

ROYAL CROSS SCHOOL FOR THE DEAF, New Hall Lane. The buildings (1892–4 by *Soames & Green*) are of no significance. Extensive new additions by the *Building Design Partnership*.

SAMLESBURY BRIDGE. It carries the M6 over the Ribble and the A59 (Preston Bypass). A handsome structure of welded steel in box-girder construction. Three spans of shallow arches, 120, 180, 120 ft.

QUERNMORE

5060

ST PETER. 1860 by *Paley* at the expense of William Garnett of Salford and Bleasdale. Stone outside, but brick-lined inside. The w tower has a higher stair-turret. The features are late C13. Inside naturalistic foliage capitals. Good roof with wind-braces.

QUERNMORE PARK HALL. 1793 for Charles Gibson by *Thomas Harrison*. The Gibsons were a Preston family. In

beautifully landscaped grounds. The house is of five by five bays, ashlar-faced, with two and a half storeys and a porch of two pairs of unfluted Ionic columns. Recessed to the far end of the five side bays are links and pavilions with tripartite windows (with columns as mullions) and with pediments. The entrance hall with pilasters leads to the central hall, which
66 goes through two storeys, a splendid apartment, even if decorated with some heaviness. Coved ceiling, the walls with pilasters below, columns and pilasters above. The doorways in the corners play tricks with the pilasters. The room on the l. of the entrance hall has painted mid C19 decoration in a Pompeian taste. William Garnett (*see* above) bought the estate in 1842 after Gibson had died.

(NARR LODGE has complete mill machinery to be driven by horses. MHLG)

2060   RAMPSIDE
                3 m. SE of Barrow

ST MICHAEL. On its own. 1840, in replacement of a chapel of 1621. The chancel is an addition of 1892. Otherwise w tower and lancet windows, not even with buttresses between.

RAMPSIDE HALL. Late, not early, C17. A symmetrical three-bay façade with cross-windows, and with a Yorkshire door-lintel. On the roof the famous Twelve Apostles, a row of twelve diagonally set chimneys.

7010   RAMSBOTTOM

ST PAUL, Crow Lane. 1844–50, the N aisle of 1866. By *I. & J. P. Holden*. The church was built by the Commissioners and cost £3,270. Large, with lancet windows. w tower with recessed spire.

At the junction of Bridge Lane with the main N–S road is the GRANT ARMS HOTEL, five bays, two and a half storeys, and a columned doorway.

Close to this the METHODIST CHURCH, 1878 by *John Garnett*. Four bays with pediments over the first and fourth and two entrances in the other bays.

ST ANDREW, Bolton Street. 1832–4. Built at the expense of William Grant for the Scottish Presbyterian Church and transferred to the Church of England later. William Grant (1769–1842) was a calico printer at Ramsbottom. The mill was started in 1806. Lancets between thin buttresses. w tower with clumsily projecting square pinnacles on polygonal buttresses.

ST JOSEPH (R.C.), Bolton Street. 1879 by *G.F.Whittenbury*. Lancets and plate tracery. No tower.

CONGREGATIONAL CHURCH, Challerton, 1 m. N. 1866–7. Gothic, with a sw steeple.

BAPTIST CHURCH. 1861–2. Broken segmental pediments below the main pediment.

NUTTALL HALL FARMHOUSE, Nuttall Lane. Towards the approach a Gothic screen wall with a big entrance arch.*

RAWTENSTALL
8020

Rawtenstall has *c.*24,000 inhabitants. Yet it is not a town; it is a chain of villagey or sub-urban (not suburban) centres strung along the Rossendale valley and the side valleys of contributory streams. The churches tend to be placed in elevated positions. The centre is Rawtenstall, though the original parish church was at Newchurch. Rawtenstall grew on the textile trade and has recently suffered with it. In 1867 there were 145 cotton mills, 11 woollen mills, 9 wool printing works, and 5 felt and carpet works.

ST NICHOLAS, Newchurch. First built about 1511 and rebuilt about 1560. The present church dates from 1825–6. It is a large building, seven bays long. The windows are in two tiers, their details Victorian. Only the windows of the w tower look 1825. The chancel is entirely of 1898.

ST PETER (R.C.), next to St Nicholas. Lancets and a later w front. By *Richard Byrom*, begun in 1928.

ST MARY, Rawtenstall. 1829. The nave has coupled lancets, no aisles, and three galleries. The sw end with its porch open to the w and E is an addition. It has a higher stair-turret.

(ST JAMES THE LESS, Rawtenstall. 1844. Said to be by *A.W.N. Pugin*.)

Close to the church is the LIBRARY of 1906 by *Crouch, Butler & Savage* of Birmingham, with a dome on a drum. It was part of a more ambitious town-centre scheme. Near the library the new trunk road from Manchester will run, and there will be a new shopping centre and also a new TOWN HALL extension (begun in 1967. Architects *Peter Nuttall* and the borough architect *N.C.Clarke*).

METHODIST CHURCH, Rawtenstall (Longholme Chapel),

* Mr Jeffrey Haworth kindly told me about this.

opposite St Mary. Built in 1841–2, to the design of *James Simpson* of Leeds. Beautifully classical, with a tetrastyle portico of unfluted Ionic columns. The Whiteheads contributed £1,000.

(No. 3 BACUP ROAD is probably C18 and built for handloom weaving. The two upper floors have six regular three-light windows each. MHLG)

UNITED METHODIST CHURCH (former, now O.A.P. Association), Oakley Road. 1855–7 by *Noble*. The scheme was promoted by the Whiteheads, who had had disagreements with the Longholme Chapel. The Oakley Road chapel has a tetrastyle portico, but, according to the later date, now with Corinthian columns and segment-headed windows.

HOLLY MOUNT, Rawtenstall. Built in 1835. Three houses in one. The residence of the Whitehead brothers, and as such interesting beyond its architectural value. Yet it is quite a fine, long, ashlar-built house with giant pilasters and doorways with set-in unfluted Ionic columns. Access used to be by gates in Bank Street, but is now, quite appropriately, through the mill. The house must indeed be seen as part of a group comprising the mill and the two Methodist chapels largely paid for by the Whiteheads. (The MILL is of 1862. Stone, of four floors, twenty bays long. MHLG)

ST JOHN, Crawshaw Booth. 1890–2 by *Austin & Paley*. Large, thanks to the generosity of the Brooks family. Aisles, a very substantial N tower with prominent pinnacles, and transept. The style is Perp, but already turning to the curvaceous details of *c.*1900. The chancel N differs from the S side in a typical Paley & Austin way.

Next to the church is the MANCHESTER DIOCESAN CONFERENCE CENTRE, an Elizabethan or Jacobean house with much by way of addition and even more by way of restoration. The old part is symmetrical, on the E-plan, although the porch must be an addition of the early C19. The corner pieces are canted bay windows. Inside are two rooms with very sumptuous plaster ceilings, said to come from Whalley Abbey. But how can that be meant? And are they original anyway? The more convincing one, with thin ribs and small pendants, is in the less convincing position. The one in the l. hand front room had broad decorated bands and bigger pendants. In the house also a Perp SCREEN, no doubt from a church. It has one-light divisions. (In the garden STOCKS for three malefactors. MHLG)

s of this house is CRAWSHAW HALL, built by the Brooks family
in 1832–3. Ashlar, two-storeyed, symmetrical, with angle
turrets. The porch on the entrance side is more explicitly
Gothic. So is the LODGE.

FRIENDS' MEETING HOUSE, Co-operation Street, Crawshaw
Booth. Built in 1716 and enlarged in 1736. The arrangement
of the front is that usual in Quaker meeting houses. Two large
cross-windows on the r., and on the l. the doorway and two
small two-light windows one above the other.

ST JOHN, Cloughfold. 1890 by *Austin & Paley*. Perp, not large.
The NW tower not yet built.

ST JAMES, Waterfoot. 1863–5 by *Robinson & Stephens* (cost
£6,000). C13 style. NW steeple.

ST MICHAEL, Lumb. 1847–8 by *J. Clarke*. A Commissioners'
church; it cost £2,060. Norman with transepts and a solid
crossing tower. The round stair-turret rises almost independent
of it, which is the salient feature of the church.

ROSSENDALE GENERAL HOSPITAL, the former WORKHOUSE.
Built in 1869. Thirty bays in length, the centre flanked by two
turrets with cupolas. Round-arched windows.

READ 7030

ST JOHN EVANGELIST. By *Ross* of Accrington, 1884. The only
interest can be the W steeple, and that dates from 1911. The
management of the diagonal buttresses deserves notice. Who
was the architect?

READ HALL. By *Webster* of Kendal, 1818–25. Perfect externally, 67
a little heavy internally. Beautiful ashlar work. The front
of nine bays with a three-bay bow in front of which stand six
unfluted Ionic columns. Above a semicircular balcony with
iron railing. Round the corner portico of two pairs of Ionic
columns, only one storey high. Ingenious entrance hall in
three parts, the middle one singled out by four columns in
the corners. Rich, juicy ceiling decoration. It is this decoration which tends to be ponderous. The anteroom has shallow
apsed ends, the staircase rises in one flight and returns in two
curved ones. Circular skylight.

RIBBLETON see PRESTON, p. 203

RIBBY 4030

ST NICHOLAS, Wrea Green. 1848–9. S tower with broach-spire,
well proportioned. No aisles. Plate tracery and geometrical
tracery.

RIBBY HALL. Built *c.*1830 (*see* Baines). Ashlar, five bays and two storeys. Porch of paired Tuscan columns. The staircase has a screen of two Roman Doric columns at its start and a broad Venetian window at its intermediate landing.

6030

RIBCHESTER

Ribchester was the Roman BREMETENNACUM, and the site of the Roman fort lies partly below the church and churchyard. Other parts have been eroded by the river Ribble. Several phases of occupation are apparent, beginning with a late C1 timber phase which was replaced, possibly in the early C2, by a rebuilding in masonry. Subsequent rebuilding occurred.

ST WILFRID. Essentially a C13 church, see the chancel with its fine group of three stepped lancets and the one smaller S lancet, and the S doorway. The lancet in the N chapel is probably re-used. Additions and alterations are first of all the Dec N chapel with good quatrefoil piers, the foils more than semicircles in plan, and the W and E windows, the former with reticulated tracery, the latter with flowing. Is the straight-headed N window with ogee-headed lights also Dec? Dec anyway is the S doorway. Perp are the straight-headed S windows. The windows in chancel and S aisle with the demonstrative geometrical tracery are Victorian. The W tower is Perp, but was begun before or in the middle of the C14. The mouldings of the doorway are just like those of the S doorway. Perp S arcade of standard elements. – FONT. An octagonal piece of the same width bottom to top. No decoration; only buttresses. Is it C14? – PULPIT. Ornately Elizabethan in style with the usual short blank arches, but actually dated 1636. – BOX PEWS. With dates 1735 and 1761. – SCREEN. Perp, but very little original. – WEST GALLERY. On Tuscan columns. Two of them are supposed to be original Roman pieces from Bremetennacum. – STAINED GLASS. Bits in the N aisle E window. – PLATE. Chalice, 1777; Chalice, 1815. – MONUMENT. In the S porch plain Perp tomb-chest with primitively carved shields.

A house SE of the church has one of the decorated Yorkshire door-lintels.

Nice village centre with the WHITE BULL, dated 1707. Its square middle projection is carried by pairs of Tuscan columns.

RIBCHESTER BRIDGE. 1774. Three segmental arches carry an elegantly curved roadway.

STIDD. *See* p. 238.

RING STONE HILL *see* NELSON

RISHTON

ST PETER AND ST PAUL. 1873–4 by *Maycock & Bell*. Quite
large.

PARKER'S FARMHOUSE, Cowhill Fold, $\frac{7}{8}$ m. s. C17, with
porch and mullioned windows. Only the seven-light hall window has a transom as well.

RIVINGTON

The view of the long reservoir lake, Lever Park, and the hills
behind with their two towers is of great beauty, grand but not
forbidding.

The RIVINGTON RESERVOIR for the Liverpool Water
Supply was built in 1852–7, a little later than the Anglezarke
Reservoir (1847–57). In 1904 Mr Lever, later Lord Leverhulme,
bought Rivington Hall and the land E of the reservoir and had it
laid out as a PUBLIC PARK. He meant it for Bolton, his home
town, which, after all, is only a few miles away, but it became
Liverpool's.

At the SE end of the reservoir lake, closer to Horwich than
to Rivington, he had a life-size replica built of LIVERPOOL
CASTLE, the C13 castle that once stood where Derby Square
now is (*see The Buildings of England: South Lancashire*, p. 173).
It is a splendid sight and ought to be accessible to the public. It
has besides its visual value unquestionably an educational value,
and Lord Leverhulme believed fervently in education and
respect for buildings. His architect was *Mawson*.

The village of Rivington lies at the N end of the park.

CHURCH. Small, aisleless, and with a bell-turret. The windows
are straight-headed, mostly with arched uncusped lights, but
some of the Elizabethan and C17 kind. As we have two dates
for the church, c.1540 and a rebuilding of c.1666, might that not
date the two types of windows? – PULPIT. With linenfold
panels. It could be c.1540. – SCREEN. Only some parts are
Perp. – CHANDELIER. Of brass, C18, and magnificent, with a
big fluted body and two tiers of arms. – PLATE. Chalice of
1799. – MONUMENT. John Shawe † 1627. Large brass plate
with, at the bottom, a skeleton on a mattress. – In the churchyard by the lychgate a collection of decorated LINTELS from
houses. (By the W gate to the churchyard is a BELL HOUSE,
first mentioned in 1611.)

UNITARIAN CHURCH. Founded 1662. Built 1703. Plain oblong plan, windows with stone crosses. On the s side two entrances and two windows between. – BOX PEWS. – The PULPIT is in the middle of the N side.

RIVINGTON HALL. The house in the park. The façade is of 1744, brick, of five bays and two storeys, with a pedimented one-bay projection. Tripartite doorway. But behind is older stonework. One lintel is dated 1694, a plaque 1700. There is a low six-light window which might just be 1694, but must not the small two-light windows with arched lights be yet older ?

BARN behind the house. A most impressive cruck structure of six trusses, and most impressively restored for Lord Leverhulme by *Jonathan Simpson*. He added the aisles, the rather fussy timber-framed porch, and the excellent fenestration of the stone end walls. It is a pattern of how to do such a job. The barn is 105 ft long.

At the car park W of the Hall is another cruck BARN, much smaller, of only two trusses and said to be older than the other. Its exterior is *Simpson*'s again.

On the hill stands a short folly TOWER, square, one-storeyed, with battlements. It dates from 1733.

A good deal further N is Lord Leverhulme's own MOORLAND GARDEN, on the steep hillside, laid out in 1905 by *T. H. Mawson* with drives, terraces, lawns, and water gardens. It is now overgrown and in a state of complete decay. The BUNGA-LOW, rebuilt after being burnt by Suffragettes, has, like the LODGES, been demolished by the Liverpool Corporation, but there remain numerous garden buildings, e.g. the DOVE-COTE, a prominent tower with two-light windows and a pic-turesque skyline. Also the ruins of several sets of LOGGIAS and TERRACES, and the BRIDGE carrying a path over one of the drives. This was designed by *Lord Leverhulme* himself and is a sort of rising viaduct with its arcade interrupted by a single broad arch.

CAIRN, on Noon Hill, Anglezarke, 2 m. N. This is a damaged round cairn with possible traces of a central cist. Excavation revealed several secondary cremation burials with barb-and-tang flint arrowheads. One of the burials was contained in an Early Bronze Age Food Vessel.

PIKESTONES CHAMBERED CAIRN, ½ m. E of Manor House, at a height of 900 ft on Anglezarke Moor. The chamber is now represented by five large gritstone slabs. These lie at the broader, N end of a trapezoid cairn 150 ft long and 60 ft broad. Traces of a double drystone revetment to the cairn are visible at the N end. A further, circular drystone structure lies behind the chamber. The surviving slabs delineate a chamber 15 ft long and 3 ft wide.

ROSSALL

3040

ROSSALL SCHOOL. The school has submerged and destroyed the house of the Fleetwoods on this site. All that remains is some fragments in the Headmaster's House. They are the balusters of a C17 (mid C17?) staircase, the panelling of a room with two pilasters, one big fireplace with open pediment, one smaller, pretty late C18 fireplace, and some door pediments.

Otherwise, of pre-school days, there is only the GAZEBO, small and square, with battlements. It has a staircase inside and three apsidal recesses outside.

The school was founded in 1844. The idea, it is said, was suggested to Sir Peter Fleetwood (*see* Fleetwood) by his chef, the Corsican Vantini. The buildings date of course from various periods. They are mostly of brick.

The school is entered from the E through a big GATEHOUSE feature with four angle turrets and an oriel. This is by *E. G. Paley*, 1867. The ranges l. and r. are of different design. The quad has a range of *c.*1885–90 by *Paley, Austin & Paley* opposite the gatehouse (i.e. w) and a range of 1853 altered in 1897 to the N. 1853 means *Paley*, 1897 *Austin & Paley*.

In the middle stands the original chapel, now LIBRARY, with the usual lancets and bellcote. Nave and chancel are in one and have a hammerbeam roof. It is all of 1850 and rather conservative for that date. The architect of this was *J. E. Gregan* of Manchester.

The second CHAPEL is to the S. It is of stone and consists of nave and chancel, a polygonal NW turret with attached porch, and a s transept. Big open roof. Geometrical tracery. The architect was *E. G. Paley*, the date is 1861, but alterations were made later.

Finally the DINING HALL and adjoining range, by *Hubert Worthington*, 1931, weakly classical, in pale mauvy brick. Inside detached unfluted Ionic columns, also as a screen to separate high table from the boys' tables. Carvings by *Alan Durst*.

8040

ROUGHLEE

ROUGHLEE OLD HALL. Is the date inscribed 1536 or 1586? The house is long and has a front with slight projections. The principal windows are mullioned, and the lights have arched heads without cusps. It could be either date – 1536 being of course the more thrilling. The hall-window had nine lights, the windows to the r. of the doorway eight on either floor.

4010

RUFFORD

30 OLD HALL. As you approach Rufford Old Hall, you see in front of you the cheerful quatrefoiled façade of the hall itself, and you will recognize at once the usual doorway which must lead to a screens passage and the usual bay window which must give light and extra space to the high table. Consequently, you will say, if you have any experience of English medieval domestic customs, that the parlour and chamber wing must have been shaved off at some time – the two doors once leading into it now indeed lead into the garden – and that the service wing has been replaced by the present brick wing. The doorway has a four-centred head, the bay window is of five sides of an octagon and has large mullioned and transomed openings, and in the wall between are two large mullioned windows. The wall has closely set uprights below, and above nothing but quatrefoils to fill all the space between the structural timbers, e.g. squares of four of them l. and r. of the windows. At the back are two windows too and a big stone chimneybreast. The quatrefoils may originally have been there on that side as well.

Rufford Old Hall was built by the Heskeths, but that it was Robert who held the manor in 1463–90 is guesswork. The late C15 anyway is, however, the most likely date, also by comparison with Smithills Hall, Bolton (South Lancs), Ordsall Hall, Salford (South Lancs), and Samlesbury (*see* p. 216), all of that time.

And now the interior. It is the most overpowering of them all, of an exuberance of decoration matched nowhere else in England. Structurally you have five hammerbeam trusses of which two correspond to the bay window, and then the spere truss characteristic of the English North. The hammerbeams have angel figures, and the arched braces lead up to collar-beams with thick bosses in their middles. In addition there are three tiers of wind-braces forming quatrefoils, and in

their middles curious concave-sided square paterae. The
speres are tree-trunks shaped into octagons and covered
with shallowly carved small Perp panels. Quatrefoils again
fill in the space between speres and side walls. And in the
wide space between the speres is the only originally preserved movable screen, a monster of a screen, and movable 31
only if you accept a very optimistic meaning of the term.
The framing is by moulded posts and horizontals of great
size, the infilling consists of eight traceried panels, the posts
are buttressed by diagonal projections coming far forward on
both sides, and on top are three enormous supporters or pinnacles of barbaric shapes, the middle one so big that it has its
own angel corbels on both sides. The component parts of the
supporters look like ropes or scalaria shells. You will be
reminded more of Indonesia than of Lancashire. The beams
of the bay window are thickly moulded too, and in the two end
walls you are back at quatrefoils. Those of the high table side
belong to the restoration of 1949, the other side, i.e. the
screens passage side, has them original. Original also are the
five doorways with four-centred heads and decorated lintels
which led into kitchen, buttery, and pantry. These rooms have
gone, though in the later brick wing the present entrance
room must, according to its huge fireplace, have been used as a
kitchen. The high table was protected by a coved canopy (cf.
Smithills, Ordsall, Samlesbury) and above the canopy the
recent restorers found a well hidden priest hole.

As one looks at the hall from the garden, i.e. the s side,
it is continued by another bay window and then brick walls,
turning round the corner and leading to a picturesque group
of walling with two towers. All this, except for the second
tower, belongs to additions made by Sir Thomas Henry
Hesketh, fourth baronet, in 1821. The second tower, however,
is part of the brick wing mentioned at the beginning.

This wing is dated 1662 and is noteworthy for having a
symmetrical façade at a time when Lancashire still went in
for asymmetrically disposed low mullioned windows. There are
five bays, the doorway has a (later) segmental hood, and the
windows have wooden crosses and segmental relieving arches
with a little brick decoration in their tympana. There are
five bays, but, curiously enough, only four dormer windows.
The tower at the back was for the staircase. At the far end of
the quad is a piece of SCULPTURE, a lead group of two
cherubic bacchantes.

RUFFORD NEW HALL. The house was built by the first baronet in 1760 and given its present shape by the third in 1798. It is a simple oblong block with a one-storey portico of two pairs of unfluted Ionic columns, and round the corner is a veranda of six such columns, grouped 2-1 – 1-2. Spacious entrance hall with domed oval skylight, ample staircase with wrought-iron handrail. (In the grounds is an ICE HOUSE. MHLG)

ST MARY. In the village. Built in 1869 to replace a chapel recorded in 1346 and rebuilt in 1746. The architects hardly deserve recording. They are *Dawson & Davies* (Collins' Guide), and the best that can be said for them is that they did something very typical of the sixties, i.e. something aggressively unattractive. Brick, with a NW steeple with extremely steep pyramid roof and the gables of the bell-openings sticking up into it. Three big grouped w windows. Plate and bar tracery. Arcades with ugly floral capitals. – The PULPIT, REREDOS, and FONT, all with various marbles, the font presented in 1875, are fully High Victorian too. – CHANDELIER. Of brass, with two tiers of arms, 1763. – PLATE. Set of 1842. – MONUMENTS. Brass of a Knight, 18 in. figure. – Incised slab of *c*.1460, Knight and Lady. – Mrs Sophia Hesketh † 1817. By *Flaxman*, but might be by any of dozens of English sculptors. Tablet with the figure of Hope. – Sir Thomas G. Fermor-Hesketh † 1872. By *Noble*. Kelly says it cost £1,000. Recumbent marble effigy on a tomb-chest. His hand is on his heart.

3080   RUSLAND

ST PAUL. First built in 1745. All but rebuilt, except for the tower, in 1868. Aisleless nave, w tower, and chancel. – STAINED GLASS. The E window evidently by *Hardman*.

RUSLAND HALL. Late C17. Of five bays and two and a half storeys with later two-bay additions. Elegant doorway with Tuscan columns and a triglyph frieze.

030   SABDEN

ST NICHOLAS. 1846. Norman, with a thin w tower, its top octagonal and continued in a spire. Along the sides thin round-headed lancets and thin buttresses. A relatively long chancel.

BAPTIST CHURCH. 1910, in a lively Edwardian. A low copper dome on the SW corner, the majority of the windows with mullions running up into a segmental head.

SABDEN HALL, 2 m. E. With two cross gables; under one mullioned, under the other mullioned and transomed windows.

SACCARY HOUSE *see* MELLOR

ST ANNES *see* LYTHAM ST ANNES

ST MICHAEL'S-ON-WYRE   4040

ST MICHAEL. A typical late medieval North Country church.26 Broad, low W tower, W window with uncusped lights, low embattled S aisle, the windows also uncusped, two-bay slightly earlier N aisle, also embattled but with windows of cusped lights. The arcades are again Late Perp. There are, however, also earlier features. The W respond of the S aisle is C13, and so is the small blocked lancet in the W wall of the aisle, token of a former much narrower aisle. The chancel E window is more likely to be later C14 than C16 (VCH). For the W tower we have an approximate date, and that is very late. Money was left for 'the buylding of the steple' in 1549. – PAINTING. On the chancel N wall Ascension, early C14, discovered in 1956. Some heads are fairly clear. – STAINED GLASS. Fragments in the N chapel, including a fine early C14 shield. – PLATE. Two Chalices, 1792.

SALESBURY   6030

ST PETER. With a sweeping view to the N. 1887 by *Stoner & Grodwell*. An unknown firm, but an attractive job. Big roof to the outside, with exposed timbers inside. Timber-framed bell-turret on the roof. The W windows are E.E., the E window is Dec, the side windows are Perp – yet that does not strike one as a mannerism.

METHODIST CHURCH, ½ m. SE, really Wilpshire Methodist Church. With a NW steeple and geometrical tracery. Built in 1903 by one *Morley*, probably of *Walker & Collinson* of Bradford.

CLAYTON MANOR. Next to the former. Victorian, with a weird tower.*

BOLTON HALL, 1 m. NW. 1655. Flat front, with square porch, not in the middle. Five- and seven-light windows, the latter in the hall position. The porch does not lead straight into the

* I was told the date is *c.*1915. Can that apply?

hall. On entering one is faced with the massive chimney opening to the hall l. and the kitchen r.

SAMLESBURY

5030

ST LEONARD. Built in the C14 – the only evidence is the gable-walls – and enlarged in 1558. Nave and chancel in one, i.e. long clerestory and aisle roof-lines. All the windows straight-headed with uncusped lights. But the w window has inter-secting tracery; however, it is not old. Four-bay arcades of standard elements. – PULPIT. A two-decker, originally against a middle s pier. – COMMUNION RAIL. C17. – BOX PEWS, wonderfully complete. Dates 1678 etc. to 1756. But many of the pews are of before 1678. – HELM etc. of a member of the South-worth family. – STAINED GLASS. Fragments (an angel) in the nave w window. – PLATE. Two Chalices of 1819. – MONU-MENTS. Alabaster slab, incised, to Sir William Atherton and his wife who died in 1441. – Geoffrey Hornby † 1801. By *Kendrick*. Hope stands by an urn. Tablet with obelisk background.

ST MARY (R.C.), Preston New Road, ¼ m. E. 1818. Church and presbytery under one roof. The church has excessively short round-arched windows – almost lunettes. Altar wall with two attached unfluted Ionic columns and an over-wide blank arch between them.

SAMLESBURY (UPPER) HALL, 2 m. E. Samlesbury Hall is one of the outstanding Lancashire Halls of the timber-framed variety. It belonged to the Southworth family from c.1330 till 1679. Originally it was larger than it is now. What remains is a s range and at r. angles to it, running N from E of its w end, the hall. The hall range originally carried on, and, at r. angles to its end, the kitchen range ran E again, thus forming a courtyard with buildings on three sides. The hall is C15, the long s range c.1545, except for the w end, which was added in 1862. Much was altered and restored in 1835.*

The hall has a polygonal bay window, C19 externally, but original internally. The upper part is oblong, not polygonal, and gabled. Originally it had the high table in a recess in the s wall with doorways l. and r. (cf. Little Mitton Hall) and a moveable screen as fantastic with its scalaria-like supporters as that of Rufford Old Hall. This screen has a date 1532. Its parts are now used together with some C17 bits and pieces. The screen was originally at the N end of the hall, which was,

32

---

* Taylor, plates 3, 18, 24, shows the state before 1835.

it seems, demolished in 1835. The screen was then incon-
gruously moved to the dais end of the hall. The two dais-end
doorways however survive. The C19 stone chimneypiece is of
enormous size and stands in the original fireplace position,
which appears very prominent outside. The w wall in which
the projection lies is of stone and belongs to the C16. The roof
has arched braces, two collar-beams, and three tiers of cusped
wind-braces. (Two of the trusses are of cruck construction.
VCH)

The s range is of brick to the s (with Sir Thomas South-
worth's initials), timber-framed to the N and inside. The
view from the courtyard is extremely picturesque, but alas
nearly all a re-evocation of the C19, based, with its quatrefoil panels, on such halls as Ordsall. The lower windows are
C19, the upper oriels with their carved sills original. One
has the sign I H S, and this marks the place where the chapel
originally was. This went through both floors; the rest had
two-storeyed accommodation. The chapel E window is of four
lights with panel tracery, the chapel s window of three lights.
The w part was probably of two storeys, the lower having
moulded beams, the upper serving as the family pew. The
room to the r. of the porch has moulded beams and two
straight-headed three-light windows to the s. The chimneypiece has the original date 1545 but is otherwise in an ornate
C19 Gothic. The roof of the s range has arched braces with
blank tracery.*

SATTERTHWAITE

3090

CHURCH. The one detail to be remembered is the diagonally
placed sw porch close to the tower. – PLATE. Salver, London,
1713–14, by *W. A.*; Chalice, later than 1739, by *J. B.*; Chalice
and Flagon, London, 1843–4.
GRIZEDALE HALL, 1 m. NW, has been demolished.

SAWREY *see* FAR SAWREY

SCALE HALL *see* LANCASTER, p. 164

SCARISBRICK

3010

ST ELIZABETH (R.C.), Bescar, ½ m. N of the Hall. 1888–9 by
Pugin & Pugin. Built by the Marquis de Castéja. Big, red,

---

* In the angle between the dais end of the hall and the s wing is a priest
hole (Haward).

rock-faced, and Dec, with a NW tower with pyramid roof. SW baptistery. Wide, polygonal apse; N aisle. – PULPIT. An extremely sumptuous piece, probably Belgian, and consisting of two parts, the body and foot, and the stairs. The latter have openwork acanthus, the former the Signs of the Evangelists, some gristly cartouches, and other ornament a little earlier than the acanthus, i.e. mid or later C17 as against late C17 or early C18.

ST MARK, I m. NW. Nave and bellcote and chancel. Style of c.1300. 1848–9, by *George Shaw* of Saddleworth.

SCARISBRICK HALL.* As it existed at the beginning of the C19, the home of the Scarisbricks (an ancient Catholic family resident here from at least the C13) was a timber-framed Elizabethan house. In 1803 *Humphry* and *John Adey Repton* produced a scheme for improving the park and rebuilding the mansion, in a castellated style, on a new site. Nothing came of this proposal, and in 1815 Thomas Scarisbrick encased the house with stone, and apparently added the W wing, in flat and uninspired Regency Tudor. The architect was either *Thomas Rickman* or, more probably, the younger *John Foster*. Thomas was succeeded by his brother, Charles Scarisbrick, whose reputation as an eccentric recluse attracted the attention of Nathaniel Hawthorne, and whose fortune was increased by interests in the developing town of Southport. In 1836 he employed *Augustus Welby Northmore Pugin* to design a garden seat and a fireplace, and the following year Pugin prepared proposals for remodelling and gothicizing the house. The execution of this lasted well on into the next decade – of the surviving drawings, the latest is dated 1845. Pugin's extensive internal remodelling and decoration included the creation of the great hall (completed in 1842) and the incorporation of numerous items from Charles Scarisbrick's collection of (mainly Continental) wood carvings. Externally, the centre of the S front is entirely Pugin's, but only minor embellishments were added to the 1815 W wing and N front. Ferrey stated that Pugin was hampered by Charles Scarisbrick's insistence that building should be on the foundations of old work, but an examination of the structure and of the drawings proves that, at any rate in the central and western parts, there was no new building, and Pugin's contributions are only skindeep. His proposals for the E wing included an octagonal

* Written by Edward Hubbard.

kitchen, based on the Abbot's Kitchen at Glastonbury, and a modest clock tower which, with the clock stage oversailing the shaft, seems to have formed the model for the 'Big Ben' tower at Westminster. The E wing was almost certainly built as intended, but the alterations of a generation later (*see* below) changed beyond recognition all but the kitchen. In 1836, when first employed at Scarisbrick, and when he published *Contrasts*, Pugin was in his mid twenties. Though a youth of legendary precocity, Scarisbrick was his first major commission. The S front is superb, but when compared with his work at the Houses of Parliament and his later domestic interiors, the inside appears inconsistent and immature. At the outset of the work his characteristic style had not been evolved, and his favourite team of executants – Myers, Hardman, Crace, and Minton – had not been assembled. Charles Scarisbrick died in 1860, and was succeeded by his sister Anne, Lady Hunloke, a septuagenarian widow, who adopted the name Lady Scarisbrick. For reasons which remain obscure, she undertook an ambitious building programme, employing *Edward Welby Pugin*, son of A.W.N.Pugin, who had died in 1852. The E wing was spectacularly transformed, with the tower being raised to an enormous height. The wing is dated 1862, but E.W.Pugin's work is not likely all to have been completed so early. Alterations were carried out elsewhere in the house, and are usually recognizable by reason of E.W. Pugin's unmistakably heavy hand and the frequent appearance of Anne's name and initials. She died in 1872, and Scarisbrick passed to her son-in-law, the Marquis de Castéja.

From 1946 until 1963, Scarisbrick belonged to the Church of England, and was used as St Katharine's College. It did not escape this period of ownership unscathed, but the black year in its history was 1963, when a company (not the present owners) offered for sale the garden sculpture and numerous internal fittings. Despite a preservation order being confirmed (following a public inquiry) and an appeal being dismissed in the High Court, items either designed or incorporated by the Pugins have been removed. The removal turned out to be not against the law.

EXTERIOR. The recessed centre of the SOUTH FRONT owes its appearance entirely to *A.W.N.Pugin*, and his great hall is readily discernible by its high roof, lantern, and huge finials. With its rich Perp ornament, twin bay windows, porch, [78] and traceried gallery window, the hall is more lavishly treated

than the adjoining parts. The generous porch has a stone roof
and sturdy buttresses, the main parapet is particularly elaborate, and the whole eloquently evokes Pugin's passionate
love of the Middle Ages and the sheer joy of his inspiration.
'I have raised up the ruins', reads one of the inscriptions, 'and
I have builded it as in the days of old.' *Edward Pugin* was not
the most brilliant of architects, but with the EAST WING he
produced a splendid *tour de force* of Frenchified High
Victorian Gothic, very exuberantly ornamented, and in strong
contrast with his father's more sober work. From it rises the
slender tower and spire, dominating the house, and visible for
miles around. The spire is not square on plan, and the ridge
has regrettably been deprived of its cresting. At the inner
corner of the E wing fluttering birds surmount an octagon
tower. On the left of the S front projects the gable end return
of the WEST WING of 1815, with a bay window added by
A.W.N.Pugin. On the W front itself, his additions, made
with the intention of producing a more authentically Gothic
effect, include the oriel, buttresses, drip-mould stops, and
grotesques below the parapet. The meeting, near the SW
corner, of his plinth moulding with that of 1815 is instructive.
The NW turret formerly had an ogee roof. Pugin's enlivening
of earlier work continues on the NORTH FRONT, though the
porch with its diagonal turrets is, rather surprisingly, entirely his. Then begins the long N extension of *E.W.Pugin*'s
EAST WING, which in the E side wanders *ad lib* round a
kitchen court. *A.W.N.Pugin*'s octagonal kitchen is best seen
from the S.

INTERIOR. The plan of the central block is ranged round
two intersecting corridors. The shorter of these axes links the
N and S porches, and its S end was used by *A.W.N.Pugin* as
the screens passage of his GREAT HALL. For although there is
no dais or upper end window, he created a hall in true medieval
manner, rising through two storeys within the heart of the
plan, and with screen and open timber roof. The dragons of
the roof trusses are not very Gothic, but the colouring of the
timbers, and the ribbed and decorated ceilings of bay windows and lantern, are more in character with his mature work,
as is the elaborately carved screen (see e.g. the characteristic
roll mouldings and parchemin panels, used here and elsewhere in the house). Open screen work at gallery level. Balconies in the upper floors of the bay windows. Glazed screens
pierce the upper wall on the inner side. Corbels on the screen

and niches around the walls were for statues and busts from Charles Scarisbrick's collection. These were deplorably removed in 1963, but the enormous panel of the 'Crowning with Thorns', framed in an arrangement of Baroque wood-work, remains. It seems to date from the C16. The tradition that this came from Antwerp Cathedral is, it seems, incorrect. The floor, as in the ground-floor corridors, is mosaic, pre-dating Pugin's universal use of Minton tile. *E. W. Pugin* added the shield and figures above the fireplace, and the panelling is 80 his. W of the hall is the OAK ROOM, lined with illustrative panels ranging from the early C16 to the C18. The effect is one of overpowering richness in a confined space, and in the detailed ornament it is difficult to differentiate the ancient from that actually designed by *A. W. N. Pugin*. His stall-like fireplace is curious.

The KINGS' ROOM, in the W wing, i.e. the wing of 1815, 79 in the discipline, consistency, and quality of its treatment anticipates more than anything else at Scarisbrick Pugin's mature manner. The room is panelled throughout, and has gilding and a richly coloured and decorated ribbed ceiling. Narrow wall divisions become miniature vaults at the cove. There is also a frieze of painted panels depicting Tudor and Stuart kings, queens, and other notables. These subjects, which include Henry VIII, cannot have been approved, let alone chosen, by Pugin. Anne Scarisbrick's name on the ceiling must, of course, date from the 1860s. Some whimsical carving on the massive doors, e.g. the faces of figures on one side of a door and the backs of their heads on the other. The cast-iron cusping of reveal panels must date from 1815, and shows how superficial was Pugin's transformation. The RED DRAWING ROOM has a very heavy doorcase and ceiling pat-tern. The chimneypiece, with its Baroque tendencies, has almost got out of (Gothic) hand. The niches in it were for antique statuettes. Over the fireplace two painted panels, by the same hand as those in the Kings' Room, one of them illustrating the house as remodelled by Pugin, and showing his design for the E wing. The DINING ROOM, on the opposite side of the Kings' Room to the Red Drawing Room, was reconstructed after a fire in 1924. Earlier this century, when its door to the staircase hall was cut through, the wall was found to be timber-framed – presumably the W wall of the Elizabethan house.

In the CENTRAL CORRIDOR the screenwork behind the

great hall is by *A.W.N.Pugin*, and opposite it the SMOKING
81 ROOM and the LIBRARY are decorated by *E.W.Pugin*.
A.W.N.Pugin's STAIRCASE, contained within a small area,
is of complicated plan and construction, and is carried on a set
of slender timber columns. It has solid panels for balustrades,
two of which are carved with representations of Pugin's designs for the house and stables respectively. Lanterns with
decorated ceilings over stairs and crossing of the corridors.
On the first floor the roof-light over the central corridor has
been hideously reconstructed and no record of Pugin's treatment of it seems to exist. The corridor is half the width of that
below, forming an open gallery and providing light for the
ground floor. Some spatial complexity where a bridge crosses
to the hall gallery. Near the top of the stairs wooden STATUES
of St Martin and St George. At the end of the corridor an enormous door and case, apparently an amalgam of Pugin designs
and antique carving. On the first floor, the W wing and the N
range of the central block contain a series of weak Tudor-style
chimneypieces and doors with iron cusping – obviously dating
from 1815, as does the staircase towards the NE corner. Some of
these doors have actually been refaced and heavily gothicized
by Pugin on their outer sides. Back on the ground floor two
rooms E of the great hall, across the screens passage, display
all three phases of Scarisbrick's C19 history – 1815 doors,
A.W.N.Pugin fireplaces, and *E.W.Pugin* shutters.

In *E.W.Pugin*'s E wing is the High Victorian BLUE
DRAWING ROOM, with beautifully inlaid woodwork, marble
Gothic fireplace, and stained glass by *Hardman*. Interesting
sliding doors across the bay window. The ceiling is very
elaborate – a dense pattern of panels and colourful stencilling
and gilding. Although Mid Victorian in its heaviness, the
ceiling is derived from A.W.N.Pugin's style, and the door
and now vanished pier tables are reminiscent of his mature
work. This is doubtless due to the presence of *J.G.Crace*,
who did do work here, as Mrs Elfrida Mostyn has shown.
Next is the CHAPEL, a simple ashlar interior with a small
transept. The altar is placed below the great tower of Scarisbrick, and above it angel corbels carry a vault, and higher
still is a ribbed and decorated ceiling, all very delicate and on a
miniature scale. The chapel gates, consisting of ancient
carved work arranged by *E.W.Pugin*, were removed following
1963. Above the Blue Drawing Room, and a simpler version
of it (with stained glass, heavy fireplace, sliding doors across

bay, etc.), is ANNE SCARISBRICK'S BEDROOM. Adjoining is a tiny ashlar-lined room, below the tower, and hence above the altar of the chapel. It is too small for a dressing room. Could it have been Anne's prayer chamber? The EAST STAIRCASE, with a stone tunnel-vault, is remarkable for its stained-glass window with portraits of Anne Scarisbrick and Edward Pugin, who holds a plan for this end of the house (not as executed) – a strange monument to the partnership which so transformed Scarisbrick.

There remains to mention the interior of *A.W.N.Pugin*'s octagonal KITCHEN, with its characteristically meagre roof timbers, and the SERVANTS' HALL (in the E wing but N of the central corridor), with an enormous fireplace by *E.W.Pugin*.

STABLES, immediately E of the house. Brick. The fairy-tale castle frontage (the gatehouse tourelles of which have lost their conical roofs) is undoubtedly by *E.W.Pugin*. Further back the gatehouse with stepped gables is earlier and probably by *A.W.N.Pugin*. The post-war block which intrudes into the stable court was built for St Katharine's College. *A.W.N.Pugin*'s GARDEN SEAT of 1836 is w of the house: a small, square, gabled structure with seats in niches. – GATES. Where the drive crosses a ha-ha S of the house. Brought by the Marquis de Castéja and replacing gates by A.W.N.Pugin which were moved to the Bescar Lodge. Said to have been made for the Marquise de Pompadour. – DAIRY. On the N of the Bescar drive. Late Victorian with a glazed lantern turret. Later used as a mausoleum. A series of Gothic LODGES dates from the time of the 1815 work, but of these, the really important one, CASTLE LODGE, has been destroyed. At BESCAR LODGE, *A.W.N.Pugin*'s gates, brought from the S approach to the house.

SCORTON

5040

ST PETER. By *Paley & Austin*, 1878–9, for James Ormrod of Bolton (*see* South Lancashire). Brown stone, tiled roof, w tower with a shingled broach-spire. Dec features. The church is quite large and cost £14,000.

ST MARY AND ST JAMES (R.C.). 1861–2 by *Joseph Hansom & Son*. Nave with bellcote and chancel; N aisle. A nice group with the presbytery when approached from the E. – STAINED GLASS. N aisle E by *Hardman*.

METHODIST CHAPEL. Dated on the porch 1842, but by Baines 1829–30, which latter seems more likely. Two by three bays, the windows arched and tripartite below a transom at the springing of the arch.

SCOTFORTH

4050

ST PAUL. This is an anachronism, almost beyond belief. *Edmund Sharpe,* expert on flowing tracery and senior partner of Paley in the 1850s, designed this church in 1874, as an old man of sixty-eight, and designed it exactly as if it were thirty years older and as if the antiquarian revolution towards Second Pointed, the Pugin–Scott revolution, had never taken place. The forties were the time of the Norman fashion, and here is a neo-Norman church, large and yet only most summarily Norman. Large E apse, tower over the chancel, low aisles. The arches are of course round, but the tower, the one really impressive piece, has geometrical tracery and moreover a saddleback roof. The clerestory has circular windows. Inside, the tower has a quadripartite rib-vault and blank arcading on its N and W walls. The arcade piers are round. Now it will be remembered that about 1840 Sharpe experimented on a sweeping scale with stone-coloured terracotta as a building material (cf. *South Lancashire,* pp. 90 and 321). Here he is returning to it. The piers are of terracotta, and the decorative trim inside and out is of terracotta too. But the bell-storey of the tower is of yellow brick. It is a strange building.

METHODIST CHURCH, N of the church. 1908–9 by *A. G. Chant.* Almost as excellent as the Methodist church at Skerton, Lancaster (which looks as if it must be designed by him), and with the same freedom in the treatment of tracery and parapets. NW tower with a copper spire. The SCHOOL is to the S. The style is most probably inspired by Edgar Wood.

LUNECLIFFE, 1 m. SW. A Late Georgian three-bay house in its own grounds. Ashlar-faced, with a one-bay pediment and a semicircular porch with attenuated Tuscan columns.

SEATHWAITE

2090

(HOLY TRINITY. 1874 in place of an older chapel. The money was given by H. W. Schneider of Barrow. Aiseless with a bellcote. MHLG)

SHEPHERD'S FARM see COCKERHAM

SHEPHERD STREET see TOTTINGTON

SHEVINGTON

ST ANN. 1887.
GATHURST FOLD see Orrell: *South Lancashire*, p. 362.

SHIRESHEAD see FORTON

SHUTTLEWORTH

ST JOHN. 1847 by *Shellard* and, though paid for by the Commissioners (£1,912), no longer of the Commissioners' type. Small; nave with bellcote, aisles, and chancel. Big slate roof and small aisle windows. Octagonal piers.

SHUTTLEWORTH HALL see HAPTON

SILVERDALE

ST JOHN. 1885–6 by *Ball & Elce*. Big w tower. Mildly Dec features. Quatrefoil piers with carved angels and other figures. A successful design by a hardly known firm.

OLD CHURCH, opposite the cemetery. 1829 by *T. Garrett*. The masonry looks older. Doorway and windows with four-centred arches.

TRINITY METHODIST CHURCH. Built after 1878. It has a sumptuous Dec rose window in the façade.

Silverdale is the most pleasant, i.e. the least crowded, the least urban seaside resort in this area.

LINDETH TOWER, ¾ m. s. A date 1816 on the house. In the garden an embattled square tower of three storeys, not at all demonstratively Gothic. (A little further s, at SENOVY BROWN'S POINT, another tower, this one round and tapering. NMR)

SIMONSTONE

HUNTROYDE. There is a date 1576 over the doorway in the courtyard, and the part of the house to which it belongs confirms such a date. But there are no external features of that date worth mentioning. The rest seems all Victorian, extensive and informal. Dates of building recorded are 1850, 1879, and 1885. What each of these dates represents in the existing building would deserve some study.* A Georgian wing of 1777 has recently been demolished.

* Which the owners did not enable me to do. The MHLG is noticeably vague on the house.

8—N.L.

(The NMR has photographs of a hall with columns and niches with broken segmental pediments, and of a good later C18 chimneypiece in the library.)

SINGLETON

3030

SINGLETON HALL. Built by Thomas Horrocks Miller, cotton spinner, in 1871. Brick and stone trim with an entrance tower. The style is domestic Gothic.

The Millers also built some ESTATE HOUSING, and they largely paid for the church.

ST ANNE. 1861. by *E. G. Paley*. A typical estate church, by position and somehow even by style. E.E., with a NE steeple, and plate tracery. Transepts, but no aisles. — STAINED GLASS. The E window designed in 1859 by *Frederick Preedy*.

SKELMERSDALE

4000

Skelmersdale until recently was a large mining village of no interest. Then, in 1961, it was designated as a New Town for Liverpool and Merseyside overspill. The master plan was made in 1963 by *Sir Hugh Wilson* (of Cumbernauld fame), and it is typical of the most recent thought on new towns. No longer spreading out by means of small single or semi-detached or short-terrace houses with plenty of garden and plenty of road width. No longer a pretty town-centre. All must now be compact, long terraces, a close centre, and architecturally speaking instead of smooth rectangular shapes, single-pitch roofs, a dramatic skyline, and much of cubic projection and recession.

The town is to accommodate about 80,000, of which some 8,500 already lived in the area at the time of designation, mainly in the existing Skelmersdale. The new town is to be self-contained with its own shopping and its own educational, employment, and recreational facilities. The site of just over 4,000 acres is situated on the E edge of the fertile Ormskirk Plain and on the w edge of the extensive South Lancashire coalfield where the shallow seams outcrop. The town lies within the catchment area of the river Tawd, which rises to the s and flows N to join the river Douglas. The Tawd is fed by a number of small streams flowing in a westerly direction down steepish slopes; these form gullies which, with their mature trees, are a prominent feature of the main area of the site. The river runs through a steep-sided valley; to the w

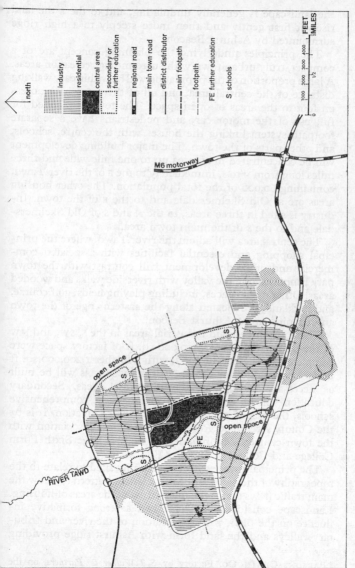

Skelmersdale New Town: basic plan

industry

residential

central area

secondary or
further education

regional road

main town road

district distributor

main footpath

footpath

FE further education

S schools

north

M6 motorway

RIVER TAWD

open space

open space

FE

S

S

S

S

S

FEET
1000   2000   3000   4000

½
MILES

the landscape is generally undulating, and to the E the land rises at first gently and then more steeply to a high ridge surmounted by Ashurst Beacon.

The principles underlying the planning concept are of a compact, truly urban town with surrounding recreation areas. A large proportion of the population will be within easy walking distance of the central area, and all of them can have access on foot to the areas of open space. The town is planned for full use of the motor car, and pedestrians have a separate footpath system linking the houses with the centre, schools, and other parts of the town. The major building development will be concentrated in an area up to one mile wide and three miles long from N to S, immediately to the E of the river Tawd, containing 60,000 of the total population. The other housing areas are at Old Skelmersdale and to the E of the town. Industry is sited in three areas, to the N and S of Old Skelmersdale and to the S of the main town area.

The central area will adjoin the river Tawd, where the principal shopping and essential facilities with associated commercial and office development will contrast with the town park running along the valley with riverside walks and wooded areas. Other open spaces, including playing fields, golf course, and parkland, are located along the eastern edge of the town and running up to Ashurst Beacon.

There are three main industrial areas in the S, SW, and NW of the designated area. 1,400,000 sq. ft of factory space were completed by the end of 1967, with a further 1,200,000 sq. ft under construction or design.* Primary schools will be built as necessary throughout the residential areas. Secondary education will be concentrated in four large comprehensive schools, the first of which is now nearing completion. It is by the County Architect, *Roger Booth.* In close association with the town centre, it is intended to build a large Sixth Form College and College of Further Education.

The principal town roads are carefully sited to relate to the topography of the town and form a ladder pattern to allow the main traffic flows about the town to avoid the areas of housing. Landscape considerations have had a strong formative influence on the plan, with exploitation of the river and tributary valleys and the land form with Ashurst ridge providing

---

*PARSONS CHAIN CO. Factory by *S. T. Walker & Partners,* on the Gillibrands Estate; good.

the backcloth. Shelter planting is designed to give protection to groups of buildings and pedestrian paths on the exposed site.

The first area of new housing (designed by the Development Corporation architects) lies to the E of Old Skelmersdale at NEW CHURCH FARM. The houses, with red-brick walls and dark tiled roofs, are grouped around interrelated pedestrian courts. They range from one to three storeys and provide a variety of accommodation. Minor footpaths link these courts to the main footpath system leading to the town park and central area.

A second major housing development, of 3,000 houses, is at DIGMOOR, where dwellings are being built by industrialized as well as traditional methods. As a typical residential area of the town, Digmoor incorporates local shopping, primary schools, public houses, churches, meeting rooms, and areas for outdoor recreation. Such buildings of a community nature are mainly distributed along the spiral pedestrian way leading to the town centre.*

In connexion with the levelling for the new town, DIGMOOR HALL and DIAL HALL have been pulled down. Was it necessary? Perhaps, though a few old buildings are such an asset to a new neighbourhood.

ST PAUL, in the old village. 1903–4 by *Austin & Paley*. In the free Gothic, Perp, but with many rounded forms in the tracery, as Austin & Paley did in those years. A dignified ensemble. W baptistery. No tower.

SKELMORE HEADS HILLFORT *see* URSWICK

SKERTON *see* LANCASTER, pp. 158, 161, 164

SLYNE *see* HEST BANK

SMALLBRIDGE
1¼ m. S of Wardle

9010

ST JOHN BAPTIST. 1834 by *Lewis Vulliamy* (P. Fleetwood-Hesketh). Lancets and a small, incorrect bell-turret. The E window is Victorian. Three galleries. Very similar to Vulliamy's St Clement, Spotland Bridge, Rochdale (South Lancashire), which is only a few miles away.

---

* The facts incorporated in this description were kindly provided by Sir Hugh Wilson's office.

GREAT HAWORTH HOUSE, 300 yards NW. A fine five-bay late
C18 house, ashlar-faced, with a doorway with broken pediment on columns.

SOUTHFIELD *see* NELSON

3010

SOUTHPORT

INTRODUCTION

Southport before the late C18 was just some scattered fisher-
men's huts. Even the name was invented only early in the C19.
The first villas and the first hotel dated from *c.*1798. By 1808
someone called Southport 'a famous bathing place'. There
were two hotels now. The estates were owned by Henry Bold-
Hoghton and Peter Hesketh-Fleetwood, and about 1850 by
Charles Scarisbrick of Scarisbrick Hall and the Rev. Charles
Hesketh. Population grew rapidly then. In 1801 there had been
100, in 1861 there were nearly 10,000.* For *c.*1870 one hears of
8–10,000 annual visitors. They were not fashionable people.
Hawthorne in 1856–7 writes that the visitors are 'middling
people from Manchester' and that the place has 'a tradesmen-
like air'. Even so, Southport has a decidedly genteel character.
There are no slums, and there are plenty of churches, and chapels,
starting with Christ Church in 1820 and culminating in 1870–
*c.*1914. Consequently the Nonconformist buildings, all but one,
are of the churchy type. The development of the centre of
Southport in terms of the dates of streets will be found under
these streets. Birkdale was developed in the 1860s by Thomas
Weld Blundell of Ince Blundell Hall. The present population of
Southport is *c.*80,000.

INNER SOUTHPORT

CHURCHES

ALL SAINTS, Park Road. 1871–6 by *J. Sidebotham*. Built at the
expense of the Rev. C. Hesketh, who also gave the land for
Hesketh Park. It is a large church of yellow stone, with a
rather astringent façade. The SW turret e.g. starts twice on its
spire. The plan of the church is evangelical with spacious
canted transepts and a canted chancel – a centralizing idea.
The crossing is marked by short granite columns in the

* To the 100 ought to be added North Meols 2,100, and the figure for 1851
including North Meols is 13,000.

corners. The tracery details are of *c*.1300, and after the busy façade the rest of the exterior quietens down.

ST ANDREW, Eastbank Street. 1871–2 by *T.D.Barry & Sons*. Big, Dec, with a NE steeple and transepts. Large W porch arrangement.

CHRIST CHURCH, Lord Street. 1820–1 by *Thomas Mawdsley*. That church still stands, but it has been enlarged later in all directions: first in 1847, then in 1850–1 (transepts and chancel), then in 1860 (aisles), and finally in 1862, when a new W front with SW steeple (the spire does not survive) was given by William Atkinson, a Preston cotton manufacturer. The façade is wide, the tower has big twin bell-openings. All the details are Perp.

EMMANUEL, Cambridge Road. 1895–8 by *Preston & Vaughan*. A large, very ambitious church with a big crossing tower, all 'in a sort of conventional much traceried Gothic'. Ruabon brick and red sandstone. The only distinguishing feature is the double gable of the transept.

ST LUKE, St Luke's Road. 1878–80 by *Mellor & Sutton*, but GR says *H.A.Matear* (who worked for them). Severe and disdainful of enrichment. Lancet windows. Red brick with a little blue brick trim. No tower. The W front with the porches and baptistery is specially exacting. Brick is exposed inside. The columns are of granite with big shaft-rings and quite untraditional capitals. Half-arches across the aisles. Large round apse.

ST MARIE (R.C.), Seabank Road. By *A.W.N.Pugin*, 1841, but unhappily little of his work can be traced in all the additions and alteration. Pugin illustrated it in 1843. It was then small, aisleless, just with a bellcote, single-light windows, and a Dec E window. The rebuilding and enlarging took place in 1874–5. Quatrefoil piers, a wide polygonal apse, and a broad façade with geometrical tracery and a twin porch. The present façade is a replica in Portland stone of that of 1875. The rebuilding was done in 1924.

ST PAUL, St Paul's Square. 1862–4 by *Speckman & Charlesworth*. In the style of 1300, with a NW steeple.

ST PHILIP, Scarisbrick New Road.* 1885–7 by *R.F.Tolson*. Large and competent, in the style of the late C13. Brown stone, with a big SW porch tower.

HOLY TRINITY, Manchester Road. An amazing tour-de-force of Edwardian patronage. By *Huon Matear*, 1903–13. The nave

* SCARISBRICK NEW ROAD was made in 1855.

was given by the Elders of the Elder shipping line; so were tower and w front. The cost of the chancel was met by Joseph Mallineaux and Joseph Dewhurst (cotton manufacturers). The church is built of the finest red brick and the finest white stone. The tower is bold and original, with a top octagon and buttresses detached at that stage and crowned with pinnacles. Large three-light bell-openings with balconies below. The chancel has flying buttresses. The transepts are two bays deep with cross gables. Inside, thrillingly high octagonal piers of red sandstone with the arches dying into them. Fine vista into the N transept with its own round pier. The chancel is rib-vaulted.

HAWKSHEAD STREET CONGREGATIONAL CHURCH. 1887–90 by *William Waddington & Son.* Red brick and stone dressings, with a sw turret and a polygonal sw baptistery. Fancy tracery.

LORD STREET CONGREGATIONAL CHURCH, Duke Street. 1861–2 by *Walker* of Manchester. With a NW steeple. Gutted in 1964. Good church hall behind the altar end by *David Jones* of *Ormerod & Partners* of Liverpool, 1965.

MASONIC HALL, Duke Street. Formerly Free Methodist. 1878–9 by *Maxwell & Tuke.* Large façade, dignified, and not at all run-of-the-mill. Italianate details.

PORTLAND STREET CONGREGATIONAL CHURCH, Portland Street. Rock-faced, with a NW steeple.

SOUTH ROAD METHODIST CHURCH. 1887–8. Brick with stone dressings. Ornate façade with round-arched portal over NW turret. All windows round-arched. Quite an elegant composition.

TRINITY METHODIST CHURCH, Duke Street. 1863–4 by *Starkey & Cuffley.* E.E., with a NW steeple. The church was paid for by John Fernley, a Manchester cotton spinner.

ST GEORGE'S PRESBYTERIAN CHURCH, Lord Street. 1873–4. Style of *c.*1300; w steeple.

CEMETERY, Duke Street. 1865. The two chapels are joined in one composition by a tower over an archway in the middle. The chapels are nearly but not quite symmetrical.

PUBLIC BUILDINGS

TOWN HALL, Lord Street. 1852–3 by *Thomas Withnell.* Quite modest, as Southport then still was. Two-storeyed, stuccoed façade articulated by pilasters, and with columns in two orders in the centre. The porch columns are Greek Doric *in antis.*

CAMBRIDGE HALL, Lord Street. Next to the town hall, and as

it is of 1873–4 (by *Maxwell & Tuke*), it is much more ambitious. It is of ashlar stone with a high tower (132 ft). The enrichments are shockingly mixed: Italian Gothic, French Renaissance, and the favourite Victorian incised ornament. It is all unanalysable. The hall is all along the first floor. Architecturally it has nothing, whereas the spacious staircase goes with the façade.

LIBRARY AND ART GALLERY, Lord Street. This stands next to Cambridge Hall. It was built in 1876–8 as a £15,000 gift of William Atkinson.* The architects are *Waddington & Sons* of Burnley. The façade is more classical than that of the Hall, as befits its purpose. However, the motifs are all very free all the same. The upper floor has instead of windows a series of relief panels.

PROMENADE HOSPITAL, Promenade. The red brick range of 1882–3 by *Paull & Bonella* is a prominent feature of the sea front. Brick with stone all along the top storey. Two symmetrical turrets. North German stepped gables. Dormer windows. The style is a kind of free Waterhouse Gothic, which includes segment-headed windows.

PIER PAVILION. 1901, as such pavilions are. The pier is one of the longest in England.

VICTORIA BATHS, Promenade. 1871–2 by *Horton & Bridgford* of Manchester. Of stone. One-storeyed, with a two-storeyed centre and a pavilion roof. The Victoria Baths replace a predecessor of 1838–9.

RIBBLE BUS STATION, Lord Street. This was the station of the Cheshire Lines. It was built in 1884 and is of brick. It has a high tower in the middle.

WAR MEMORIAL, Lord Street, at the crossing with Nevill Street, i.e. the main crossing of Southport. 1923 by *Grayson & Barnish* (adjudicator of the competition Sir Reginald Blomfield). Obelisk in the centre and two chaste colonnades l. and r.

HESKETH PARK. 1864–8. Laid out by *Edward Kemp*, but perhaps after consultation with Paxton. The park is only 30 acres in size but has a lake, a conservatory, and two pretty bargeboarded lodges.

PERAMBULATION

Nothing of the sort. After the building dates of the main streets have been indicated, one need only walk along the

* *See* Christ Church, above.

two main streets, Lord Street and the Promenade, and otherwise try to pick out a few of the earlier and the most characteristic individual buildings. There is e.g. a Gothic group in MANCHESTER ROAD, opposite Holy Trinity. Nos 23 and 23a have nice porches. This may be of c.1840. Of c.1840 or 1845 is probably the Jacobean terrace in HOGHTON STREET. And so one could pick out others. But Lord Street and the Promenade tell the story most effectively.

LORD STREET. Started in 1825. Lord Street West followed in 1854 etc. Now there are the chief public buildings on the E side, and on the W side a rewarding variety of late C19 office buildings, the shops below sheltered by iron verandas. Otherwise there are the following bits and pieces. At the N end the BOLD HOTEL with a porch of Greek Doric columns. This is by *Thomas Mawdsley* and dates from 1832. At the S end WELLINGTON TERRACE of 1818, of humble white cottages with canted bay windows, and more in the middle, e.g. the MIDLAND BANK, former Preston Bank, 1888–9 by *E.W. Johnson*, one-storeyed, with attached portico of giant granite columns and pediment. Lavish decoration. Interior with a dome on ten polished granite columns. On the l. of this incidentally is a Moorish office building for a change. There are also some of the principal hotels in Lord Street, especially the PRINCE OF WALES HOTEL, large, of brick, in a domestic Gothic, probably built about 1880. The original Assembly Rooms of Southport were at the corner of London Street. They were built in 1829–31.

The PROMENADE is on the whole earlier in its architectural interest. It was laid out in 1834 by Peter Hesketh Fleetwood. Starting from the N there is first the Convalescent Home (*see* above), then the QUEEN'S HOTEL of 1866, of stone, and higher than the terrace houses l. and r. Italianate features. Then the junction with Nevill Street. On the l. the Victoria Baths (*see* above), on the r. the former VICTORIA HOTEL of 1842, fifteen bays long, stuccoed, with a four-storeyed five-bay centre. There is here a curious rhythm of Venetian windows. Italianate features. Towards Nevill Street a gorgeous iron porte-cochère. In NEVILL STREET, begun in the 1840s, first a coarser extension of the hotel, probably of the sixties, and then NEVILL BUILDINGS, a large, symmetrical Gothic building of brick and stone with steep gables. It is probably of c.1885. On along the Promenade to the CLAREMONT HOTEL of 1840–1, a little more classical than the Victoria and very attractive with its three widely spaced bays and its Ionic porch. Cottages such as Nos 29 and 28 are also still Late Classical, but Nos 24–23 are gabled Tudor. Then later and bigger buildings such as the ROYAL HOTEL, a former terrace of 1854 (by *Thomas Withnell*), three storeys, with dormers and a round turret with conical top.

SOUTHPORT SUBURBS

AINSDALE

ST JOHN, Liverpool Road. 1886–7 by *C. A. Atkinson*. Plumcoloured brick and red terracotta, an early use of this combination in church architecture. Bell-turret on the low N vestry. Perp details. Aisleless nave with an open timber roof. The collar-beams carry Jacobean-style balusters. Altogether an individual and an attractive church.

Large GREEN with some surviving early cottages.

BIRKDALE

ST JAMES, Lulworth Road. 1856 7 by *A. Rimmer*. Rock-faced red stone; w tower with broach-spire. Transepts with cross gables. Style of *c.*1300.

ST JOHN, St John's Road. Built in 1890 by *Paley & Austin*, but enlarged in 1903–9 and now apparently entirely of that time. Red brick and red terracotta. High aisle windows under cross gables. Timber-framed gables. The brick is exposed inside too. Perp piers.

ST JOSEPH (R.C.), York Road. 1865–7 by *E. W. Pugin*. Nave and chancel. Brick, with very thin lancets. The E end has a rose window. No interest inside.

ST PETER, Crosby Road. 1870–1 by *T. D. Barry & Sons*. Dec. The s porch tower was built in 1886–7.

ST TERESA (R.C.), Everton Road. 1897–8 by *Sinnott, Sinnott & Powell*. Smooth brick walls and lancets. Bell-turret on the E part of the nave. The aisles start only half-way down, and there are transepts.

TOWN HALL, Weld Road. 1872. Of five bays, symmetrical, with a middle tower and a steep Frenchy hipped roof.

LIBRARY, next door. 1905 by *George Brown & L. H. Dutch* of Manchester.

OUR LADY OF LOURDES SCHOOL, Grantham Street. By *Velarde*, 1935–6, and very modern for its date. Brick and much glass, e.g. the characteristic wholly glazed semicircular stair-case. To its r. the equally characteristic long bands of win-dows. The pattern was probably the de la Warr Pavilion at Bexhill by Mendelsohn & Chermayeff.

Of secular buildings other than public two deserve a mention, one tiny, one very large: a cottage in LIVERPOOL ROAD, white and thatched from the time when there was no Birkdale; and the PALACE HOTEL on the sea front by *Mangnall & Littlewood* of Manchester, 1866, of brick, seventeen bays long, symmetrical, with pavilion roofs. The unstressed parts have iron verandas on two floors.

CHURCHTOWN *see* p. 99

CROSSENS

ST JOHN. 1883–5 by *J. W. Connon* of Leeds. Yellow stone with red-stone dressings. High NW tower with a bold polygonal staircase projection halfway up. Geometrical tracery. – In the churchyard the neo-Norman SCARISBRICK MAUSOLEUM, very ornate. It is of 1899–1901 and was designed by *E. W. Johnson*.

STACKSTEADS *see* BACUP

3040

STALMINE

ST JAMES. 1806. Double bellcote with a segmental pediment, more 1706- than 1806-looking. The side windows of two, also more, arched lights. Short chancel. No aisles; open roof.

STANDEN HALL *see* CLITHEROE

5010

STANDISH

ST WILFRID. This is one of the most interesting churches of Lancashire. It is large and as a general impression entirely Perp – except for the rather illiterate W steeple with its octagonal top stage, which dates from 1867. Perp are the aisle windows and the large clerestory windows (Victorian renewals), Perp the two-storeyed S porch, Perp the crenellation and the short chancel. But what of all this is really Perp – in the chronological sense ? In 1544 the church was 'in grete ruyne', and, according to the documents, in 1582–4 it was rebuilt. The contract dated 1582 exists. It is between Richard Moodie, the rector, and *Robert Charnock*. On the other hand it is known that money was spent on rebuilding in 1539, 1557, and 1558. Also, there are e.g. two rood-stair turrets. If they are 1582–4, they prove the rector's faith in the return of the Catholic faith. Are they not more likely old parts kept? However that may be, the work of the 1580s must be considered Gothic Survival, not Revival. But after all that tenacious adherence to the old style, the interior comes as a new surprise; for the arcades of five bays and those of two bays for 33 the chancel chapels have Tuscan columns on high pedestals. That one expects in the early C17 (Salisbury Chapel Hatfield, St Catherine Cree London, etc.) but not in the 1580s. Yet a plaque with the date 1584 is right above the N chapel arcade. Further, the arches of the nave arcades are pure Dec and too correct for Elizabethan work. Those of the chancel arcades are more complex but look equally un-Elizabethan. Were they re-used? Nave, aisles, and chancel aisles have excellent panelled roofs, again devoid of any specifically Elizabethan motifs. The low E vestries are of 1913–14, by *Austin & Paley*. The elaborate GATEHOUSE is by the same and was completed in 1926. – PULPIT. Typical Elizabethan in style, but presented in 1616. – BENCH ENDS. A few, very humble, dated 1625 and 1626, with simple curves at the top (cf. Upholland). – COMMUNION RAIL. It looks later C17.* – STAINED GLASS. E *H. Stammers*, mildly Expressionist. – N aisle w by *Capronnier*, 1877. – PLATE. Uncommonly fine and rich Chalice and Cover Paten, 1607; two Flagons by *I. W.*, 1656; Chalice and two Patens by *I. H.*, 1677; Almsdish by *John Harvey*, 1768. – MONUMENTS. Purbeck marble effigy of a Priest, C14. Appropriated by an inscription along the rim and by a primitive tomb-chest to Richard Moodie who died in 1586. The tomb-chest has in the middle a motif of short, coarse pilasters, two angels, and a garland. All this has nothing of the accomplishments of the church building. – Edward Wrightinton 43 † 1658. Recumbent effigy of alabaster; very good. On a tomb-chest. – Edward Chisnall † 1653. The tablet with its trophies and, at the foot, its putto heads, looks late, not mid C17. – Richard Watt. By *John Bacon Jun.*, 1806, entirely in the style 64 of his father. Two amply draped women by an urn on a pedestal. On the urn portrait medallion. – Rev. Richard Perryn † 1825. A tablet, wholly Adamish, i.e. very conservative.

* It comes from the staircase of a house at Wigan.

school, by the church. With pretty pointed windows with Y-glazing bars. 1829.

OUR LADY OF THE ANNUNCIATION. 1884 by *J. O'Byrne*. Brick, with lancets. – (CHASUBLE of pre-Reformation date. – CHALICE, 'ancient'. VCH)

STANDISH HALL, 1 m. SW. About forty years ago the house was drastically cut down in size. In the process the chapel e.g. went. What remains has a handsome three-bay Georgian front, with a new pediment and a porch brought from elsewhere. Inside is a staircase with a Venetian window and a very pretty Chippendale-Chinese handrail. In one room is a heavy stucco ceiling. The beams are showing, and among the motifs in the panels are medallions with busts. This part of the house is said to date from 1748.

WORTHINGTON HALL, 1¼ m. NE. Timber-framed with timber decoration in the centre part. On the door-head the date 1577.

(MILEPOST, 4 m. from Wigan, 4½ m. from Chorley. Of cast iron, with a date 1837. Fluted base, ornamental inscription. MHLG)

STANLEY HOUSE see MELLOR

3080
STAVELEY

ST MARY. The church is supposed to have been built in 1793. That one certainly cannot recognize. The masonry looks earlier, the interior later. There was in fact a church in existence in 1618, and there was a restoration in 1897. The windows have arched lights, uncusped, and one of them at least is ancient. The interior has a handsome open timber roof with wind-braces, and the S arcade is of timber posts. – PLATE. Set of 1792–3.

6030
STIDD
½ m. NE of Ribchester

ST SAVIOUR. A small, chapel-like medieval church belonging to a Preceptory of Knights Hospitallers. The N side has two Norman windows and a small doorway with single-chamfered arch. The S doorway is excellent E.E., the arch with deep mouldings, the capitals still including waterleaf. To this doorway belongs the slit lancet further E, but the E and W windows (intersecting and Y-tracery) must be late C13. The blocked doorway in the W wall probably connected the preceptory with a wooden balcony in the church. In the S wall also two

straight-headed Perp windows. – FONT. Late Perp, very
rough, with shields with elementary motifs. – PULPIT. C17,
simply panelled. – SCREEN. C17, with high balusters.
ST PETER AND ST PAUL (R.C.). 1789. Five bays of windows
with keyed-in round heads. Doorway with plain rustication of
alternating sizes. Plain interior.
ALMSHOUSES. 1728. Very curious and very engaging. Five
bays. The three middle bays have on the first floor a three-bay
arcade of rustic Tuscan columns. This loggia gives access to
three dwellings. The loggia is reached by an open staircase
with curved sides. Truncated shaped gable on the top.

STONEFOLD see HASLINGDEN

STONE HALL see DALTON

STONYHURST 6030

What will be foremost remembered of Stonyhurst after an
absence of years, depends on him who remembers. For some it
will be the festive s front of the school buildings in end-of-the-
school-year sunshine, for others it will be the quad, formid-
able and dour on a grey day, and for yet others it will be the
towering gatehouse at the end of the vista of lawn and sheets
of water.

It is all there and part of Stonyhurst and its varied history.
A house was on the site late in the C14. It stood near the NE
corner of the quad and remained into the C19. A late C14
window was found in the kitchen court too. Moreover
Hugh Shireburns built something in 1523 which again survived till after 1800. The Shireburns had been lords of the
manor of Stonyhurst since the late C14. Sir Richard began
the new house in 1592. He started with the gatehouse and
moved s, and his son then moved E. Sir Richard died in
1594. In a SE room was a fireplace with the date 1596, in
the great hall in the E range possibly a date-stone 1597. In
addition there is in the hall a plaster roundel with the date
1606. Additions and alterations especially in the gardens were
made by Sir Nicholas, who inherited in 1690, started to live at
Stonyhurst in 1695, lost his only son in 1702, and died in 1717,
and a few alterations by the Duchess of Norfolk, his daughter.
Then followed neglect and a change of ownership, and in 1794
Thomas Weld offered the house to the Society of Jesus. Their
English College at St Omer had been dissolved in 1762 and

had moved first to Bruges and then to Liège. The small group with pupils fled to England in 1794.

In 1799 they built a range S of the quad S range, known as Shirk. Next, in 1832–5, they built the tremendous church, a proud response to the Act of Catholic Emancipation of 1829. Then, in the mid C19, when the great public school boom started all over England, the school began to extend at a new rate. From 1843 to 1856 the W front was completed and the N range of the quad built, and in 1877–89 the whole enormous S block with the Boys' Chapel behind.

This is the framework. Now for the description. One approaches from the W along Sir Nicholas's avenue between his two sheets of water or canals, through his two GATEPIERS with their securing support by big double-scrolls, and there is the GATEHOUSE of c.1592–5. With its frontispiece of four orders of paired columns it is one of the proudest in England. The orders are correctly arranged – Roman Doric, Ionic, and two Corinthian. The archway is not quite round-headed, and in the spandrels are busts in medallions. The Doric order carries a triglyph frieze, as it should. Inside is a coffered tunnel-vault, the coffering being in terms of ribs rather than the classical frames. The upper windows are of four lights with one transom, and the top of the whole was just battlements, until Sir Nicholas in 1712 provided the two big cupolas whose details are typical English Baroque. N and S of the gatehouse the WEST RANGE has fenestration of three storeys, a mullioned basement, a main floor with two transoms, and a mullioned attic floor. On the N side all is even, because it is of 1843–56 (designer probably Father *Richard Vaughan*), on the S side it is uneven, because it is of 1592–c.95. The main irregularity is the last r. hand window of three plus three lights which corresponds to the W end of the long gallery in the S range, and the churchy window on the ground floor to the r. of the former which was brought from Bayley Hall by the Duchess of Norfolk c.1740–50 and belongs to the chapel of the house. It is of c.1300, with cusped intersecting tracery and the top of the intersections deliberately left out – a typical motif of the revolt of c.1300 against the perfection of the E.E. style. S of this a lower wing projects yet further. It is the back of Shirk, i.e. of 1799 etc., and is characterized by a Venetian window continued downward in a tripartite window, the two seeming to be one. The architect of Shirk is unknown.

Then, to the w after the s, runs the low cloister towards St Peter, the public Catholic church built to *J. J. Scoles*'s design in 1832–5. To see it to advantage one has to move round to the public entrance on the s side and the sw view altogether. The building is large, with the four corner turrets of King's College Chapel, and with three-light aisle and two-light clerestory windows. From the n side of the w range projects an uninspired Tudor range of seven bays and two storeys. This is the INFIRMARY, and was built as such in 1842–4. Behind appears the NEW QUAD, designed in a traditional, neutral, indifferent way by *J. O. Armes* of Darlington.

From the cloister between w range and church one can get a glance at the rather neglected-looking court into which the façade of SHIRK looks. It is a proper façade here and was of course originally exposed. It has three storeys and eight bays with a two-bay pediment. Bays two and seven have again the odd Venetian windows met at the back. It is a poor façade, without fire or indeed coherence.

When *Dunn & Hansom* of Newcastle built the s block and the BOYS' CHAPEL, they intended to pull down Shirk. Hence the w side of the chapel is so ornate in its Perp accoutrements. Large four-light Perp windows. The range facing Shirk with the big canted bay is the back of the s block. The SOUTH BLOCK must be one of the largest single scholastic blocks 87 in England. It is all done in a free and exuberant English Renaissance – the T.G. Jackson way.* The block is three to four storeys in height, but with an even skyline, and consists of a fifteen-bay centre and long projecting wings framing a forecourt. The wings at their ends stretch away from the forecourt to w and E. The five-bay centre of the centre is distinguished by two turrets with cupolas and a balustrade between them, and also by a row of very large upper windows of a highly original design. They are of five lights with three transoms but also – and not at the top but at the bottom – a variant of Norman Shaw's favourite Ipswich motif, i.e. an arch rising above and instead of a transom. Behind these five bays is the library. Right and left all along are mullioned and transomed windows, on the main floor again with three transoms, and punctuated by bay windows. The only exceptions, and special accents, are the s front of the extension to the E wing. This repeats the window motif of the library,

* But, having been designed in 1877, quite possibly independent of him.

but now six times. Here the theatre is located. The other exception is the E side of the projecting w wing; for there suddenly the design turns Gothic. One knows what that means – the Boys' Chapel whose other side had already been seen. Also, quite a bold touch, one more turret with cap emphasizes this crucial part of the building, the most striking break of symmetry.

Sir Nicholas's GARDEN stretches out s of this s front. It contains a pair of PAVILIONS, with concave-sided pyramid roofs, and two of the narrow Queen Anne windows flanking a doorway whose keystone is a Chinaman's face. This is very early for *chinoiserie*. Between them runs a balustrade whose tall twisted balusters are of wood. Also in this south garden is the re-erected outer stone staircase from the quad (on which anon) and the OBSERVATORY, a completely classical building by *Scoles*, begun in 1838, as competent as his Gothic had been in the church. It has an octagonal centre and in the diagonals four lower one-bay arms with pediments. Circular, glazed top.

So much for the external exterior. Now for the internal exteriors, i.e. the quad and the kitchen court. The QUAD is without doubt the most powerful part of the buildings, quite large, but with three-storeyed ranges all around enclosing you irresistibly. The pressure of the buildings can feel sinister at times; it can never have felt specially welcoming. As one enters, one faces the hall range. The hall, now refectory, is again elevated above the ground floor. Originally the open stone staircase was here, to a doorway no longer existing. The broad and big hood-moulding on angel stops which is now where the staircase was comes from Whalley Abbey. What the staircase may have done to this front – and the quad – can be seen at Chillingham Castle in Northumberland, where it still exists. All round the quad the ground-floor and the second-floor windows are just mullioned. The main windows are large, with one (hall), but mostly two transoms. The top is a plain, blunt parapet, not battlements or balustrade. The hall, in the traditional way, has a big bay window at the former high-table end. It ended originally more or less where the down pipe now runs. The DOWN PIPES incidentally have decoration with shields, dating them to 1694. N of the down pipe the Victorian work of 1843–56 begins and runs all round the N range and into the N half of the w range. The designer of 1843–56 was Father *Richard Vaughan*. Until then a gushing gap had existed here, so that

no-one before the mid C19 can have felt the full impact of the
quad. The main room of the N range is the LIBRARY. The S
side has a little more enrichment than the others. The main
floor here contains the LONG GALLERY. Its canted bay window has shafts at the angles, curiously with what can only be
described as shaft-rings. The massive doorway is Sir Nicholas's, with a big broken pediment on big corbels. Before Sir
Nicholas's time there had been four small doorways, obviously played down. They must have led into the dwellings
of higher staff. At the E end of this façade, where it disap-
pears behind the hall bay, incidentally, there is rough masonry
instead of the ashlar-work universal otherwise.

The KITCHEN COURT lies E of the quad. In it you see the
companion piece to the hall bay window, and on its E side a
strangely traditional building of Sir Nicholas's. It is dated
1699, yet has nothing of the classical details of e.g. his quad
doorway. It consists of three widely spaced bays and two
storeys with dormers at the top. The windows are still mullioned, of three lights.

As for the INTERIOR, only the principal rooms need mention. First the GREAT HALL, now REFECTORY. It is 90 ft
long and was 70 ft before the Victorian extension to the N. It
can never have been a showpiece. The fireplace is extremely
simple, and the stucco-work is confined to a rather coarse
frieze and the usual geometrical pattern of thin ribs on the
ceiling, not done with any great zest. To the N of the refectory
is the SODALITY CHAPEL, by *C. A. Buckler*, 1856. It is long,
narrow, and aisleless and has an apse. It was actually lengthened
in 1888. The figure SCULPTURE is by *Earp*, the STAINED
GLASS by *Hardman*. S of the hall and filling the first floor of the
S range is the LONG GALLERY, again with frieze and ribbed
ceiling, the rib-work here in panels between the beams. This
is also true of the rooms in the W range between the gallery
and the gatehouse. In the long gallery incidentally is a PRIEST
HOLE. It is between the ceiling of the small bay looking into
the quad and the room above it.

The Long Gallery was deprived of its S windows when
Shirk was built against it. It is likely that the W bay was
originally divided from the rest and used as the family pew
or tribune for the domestic CHAPEL. This chapel was in the
outer SW angle, and the window transferred by the Duchess of
Norfolk from Bayley Hall belongs to it. It faces W, the altar end
seems to have faced S. There is here, now internal, a five-

light window with Perp panel tracery, all lights being un-cusped. There is also, again internal now, a three-light E window. The N wall is now blank, but it contains an arch c.35 ft high. This must have been the division between chapel and family pew.

In *Dunn & Hansom*'s S block the centre, as has already been said, is the LIBRARY and the yet larger room in the E wing is the THEATRE. There are also a very roomy staircase, the BOYS' CHAPEL, of six bays, aisleless, and with four wooden oriels for the use of the community, and that remarkable room, the AMBULACRUM which was provided in 1851–2 and is simply a glazed-over space, 130 ft long, for sports in bad weather.

That now leaves only *Scoles*'s CHURCH, a room archeologi-cally convincing in spite of its early date (1832–5) and what-ever Pugin wrote against Scoles. It is of seven bays, with slim Perp piers carrying four-centred arches. – The HIGH ALTAR is of 1893, disturbing as part of Scoles's ensemble and not good of its own kind. – The STAINED GLASS in the E window could be of shortly after 1835. There is otherwise much that is signed and dated by *Capronnier*. – STALLS in the cloister, Continental Baroque, with putto heads. – Also in the cloister many TABLETS. – VESTMENTS. Henry VII's Cope. Left by that monarch in his Will of 1509 to Westminster Abbey, and later used by Henry VIII at the Field of the Cloth of Gold: Florentine, red and gold tissue, raised on crimson velvet, with red and white roses and crowned portcullises – 11 ft wide, entirely without seam. – Queen Catherine of Aragon's Chasuble and Dalmatics. Said to have been made by her and her maids 'during her sorrow' – c.1535. Red velvet embroidered with vine branches and grapes. – The Lucca Chasuble. Of c.1460. Cloth of gold, embroidered with the Annunciation and the *Volto Santo* of Lucca – i.e. Our Lord on the cross, clothed and crowned as a King. Inscribed 'Orate pro anima Ludovico Bonvisi', whose arms appear on the vestment. (The Bonvisi were a family of Lucca merchants established in London – a subsequent member of which – Anthony – is described as St Thomas More's 'entire friend'.) – The St Dunstan Chasuble. Pieced together from very beautiful and ancient English orphreys – the older ones thought to have originally been on a Cope worked by the monks at Canterbury Cathedral, and to date from the middle of the C15. – Louis XV Cope. White silk, profusely decorated with floral em-broidery, and with the Lilies of France on the hood: made by the order of that King for a member of his family – possibly his daughter, Louise-Marie, who became a Carmelite.*

STORRS HALL see ARKHOLME

STORRS MOSS see YEALAND CONYERS

SUNDERLAND POINT see OVERTON

SWARTHMOOR
1¼ m. ssw of Ulverston

2070

FRIENDS' MEETING HOUSE. 1688. The porch and the cross-windows in two storeys on the r. are of that date. The l. side, the meeting house proper, has large sash windows.

TARLETON

4020

HOLY TRINITY. By *Basset Smith*, 1886. Style of 1300, treated conventionally. w tower with broach-spire. – PLATE. Chalice inscribed 1744; Chalice, 1836.

ST MARY, ⅜ m. SE. 1719, but the tower of 1824. Simple oblong of brick, four bays long, with a canted apse. Thin oblong tower, its top of stone and crowned by an open rotunda with cap. The bell-openings small and of a curious Chinesey shape. w of the tower a w porch of doorway and two windows. – WEST and half SOUTH GALLERY, on fluted pillars. – (FONT. C18.) – STOVE. Cast iron, with wreaths. – PLATE. London-made Chalice of 1743–4; London-made Chalice of 1836.

OUR LADY HELP OF CHRISTIANS (R.C.), ⅞ m. N. 1951–2 by *Weightman & Bullen*. Brick, the nave front white with a pattern of blue crosses. Campanile with arched bell-openings to the NW.

BRIDGES. The river bridge is of three arches, probably late C17. It has two breakwaters and was widened in 1821. The canal bridge is of one arch and dates from the time of the Leeds and Liverpool Canal.

TATHAM

6060

ST JAMES. Perp, but with a w tower of 1722, much restoration of 1885–7, and a few older features. Thus the s doorway is Norman, with one order of colonnettes with multi-scalloped capitals and with the most extreme form of geometrization (or making-abstract) of the beakhead motif. The SEDILIA and

* This selection of vestments was kindly made for me by Father Clark.

PISCINA are C13 and the E window (intersecting tracery) is late C13. The N arcade, however, has nothing older than Late Perp. The chancel is of 1885–7. The saddleback roof of the tower, recessed on two sides, shows at once that *Paley & Austin* did the restoration.

THE GOOD SHEPHERD, Tatham Fells, 4 m. SW, is their work entirely. It was built in 1888 and has one of their successful central towers. The style is Late Perp. Inside, the two arches of the tower create a dignity beyond the scale of the building. The roofs with their wind-braces are a pleasure too.

(LANE END FARMHOUSE. As late as 1746, and yet the window to the r. of the doorway is given three lights as against the two-light window to the l. That still marks the r. hand window as the hall window. NMR)

3040

THORNTON

CHRIST CHURCH. The chancel 1914 by *Austin & Paley*, the rest 1963 by *Leach, Rhodes & Walker*.

SACRED HEART (R.C.). 1899 by *Pugin & Pugin*. Yellow stone with red-stone dressings. W tower. Dec features.

WINDMILL. This is the best preserved Lancashire windmill, complete with four sails and the fan-tail. It is a brick tower-mill, stuccoed white, and was built in 1794.

COUNTY LIBRARY. 1937–8 by the County Architect, *Stephen Wilkinson*. Light brick, quite large. The details tentatively modern, as was typical of the moderately progressive between the wars.

THURLAND CASTLE *see* TUNSTALL

4050

THURNHAM

(ST JOHN. 1907 by *R. B. Preston*. GR)

ST THOMAS AND ST ELIZABETH (R.C.). Built in 1847–8 by *Charles Hansom* for Miss Elizabeth Dalton of Thurnham Hall. The cost was £5,000. W tower with broach-spire and stair-turret with its own spirelet. Plate tracery, round piers, double-chamfered arches, i.e. certainly an effort to be archeologically convincing. – PAINTING. Last Judgement, over the chancel arch. It looks *c*.1850.– GILLOW MAUSOLEUM. Of red sandstone and unmistakably Egyptian.

THURNHAM HALL. At the back are irregular mullioned windows, but the front is Gothic of 1823. It has angle turrets and a one-storeyed centre projection. The CHAPEL was added in 1854–5.*

TOCKHOLES

6020

ST STEPHEN. Of *Rickman & Hussey*'s church of 1831–3 only the front of the S porch has been preserved. It now leads into a new church (1965–6 by *Houston & Forbes*) of no architectural ambition. Rickman's was a Commissioners' church (£2,804).

SCHOOL. With an outdoor pulpit of c.1900–10, replacing an earlier wooden one from Mellor church.

TORVER

2090

ST LUKE. 1884 by *Paley & Austin*. Very low, with a broad, strongly buttressed central tower. The features all Norman. Goodhart-Rendel calls it 'a capital little building'. He rightly compares it with Finsthwaite.

RING CAIRN, ¾ m. NE, on the summit of Hare Crags. The cairn is 100 ft in diameter and the bank some 6 ft in width. There is a narrow gap in the bank on the SE.

ENCLOSURE, on Bannishead Moor. This is a trapezoid enclosure defined on three sides by a stone bank and on the fourth naturally defended by the Torver Brook on the SW. Part of a hut circle is visible immediately adjacent to the stream. There are entrance gaps on the NW and SE.

100 yds SW is a RING CAIRN, 54 ft in diameter, and in the vicinity of the enclosure are numerous small round CAIRNS which may represent field clearance rather than graves.

STONE CIRCLE, 1¼ m. W, on Bleaberry Haws. This a small circle of seven stones having a diameter of 17 ft.

TOTTINGTON

7010

ST ANNE. 1799. Two by four bays, with arched windows and a bellcote. Galleries inside. – MONUMENT. Ellen Sandiford † 1836. By *Miller & Derks* of Manchester. With a small figure of a pensive woman at the top.

CONGREGATIONAL CHURCH, Greenmount. 1866. Gothic, with a NW steeple with broach-spire.

TOWER FARM, Shepherd Street, ½ m. SE of the above. A folly built in 1840 by the owner of the former Tottington Mill,

* The VCH reports an inscription 1674 in a window at the N end of the house: Catholicae virgines sumus: mutare vel tempore speramus. It comes from Aldcliffe Hall not far away.

demolished in 1927. The building has to the E a dramatically medievalizing façade, all embattled. It is placed between two normal, gabled wings and consists of a tower, screen walling, and two pavilions.

TOWNLEY HALL *see* BURNLEY, p. 82

9030   TRAWDEN

ST MARY. 1844–5 by *T. Chaffer*. Lancet windows and a thin w tower. A Commissioners' church (cost £1,400).

INGHAMITE CHAPEL. 1752. Three bays. Round-arched windows in two tiers. The doorways are from the N in bays one and three.*

WYCOLLER HALL, 1½ m. ENE. C16 to C17, with one window with arched lights.

4030   TREALES

CHRIST CHURCH, 1 m. N of the village. 1853 by *Sydney Smirke* for the Earl of Derby. Devoid of architectural interest, in spite of the polygonal SW turret. Nave and chancel; lancets. The adjoining SCHOOL has much more body. It is brick; asymmetrically Gothic. Architect *Hibbert* of Preston; date 1871.

6070   TUNSTALL

ST JOHN BAPTIST. The only church in North Lancashire which one can praise for never having given in to sweeping suggestions to restore windows and other features. How right Ruskin and Morris were! It creates a human appeal which cannot otherwise be roused. The church was rebuilt by Sir Thomas Tunstal about 1415, but the W and E responds of the N arcade have early C13 capitals, and the W lancets of the aisles are probably also C13. On the N side is a two-light Dec window. The two-storeyed porch is the finest piece of the C15 work. The Perp tracery of the S aisle and the Perp arcades are coarse. – FONT. C18 stone baluster with an elliptical marble baluster. – ROMAN ALTAR to Asclepius and Hygieia (NE window sill). – STAINED GLASS. The E window has Netherlandish late C15 and C16 glass from two different sources. It was brought from Flanders by Richard T. North (*see* below) before 1853. – PLATE. Chalice and Paten by *Richard Bayley*, 1708;

* There are Inghamite chapels also at Colne and one at Barrowford.

Paten by *Henry Jay*, 1709–10; Chalice inscribed 1713; Paten and Flagon by *Thomas Mason*, 1718–19. – MONUMENTS. Defaced early C16 stone effigy (S chapel), probably Sir Thomas Tunstal. – Many tablets, e.g. Lt. Miles North, 1837, with the relief of a shipwreck.

THURLAND CASTLE. Leland calls it an ancient castle; we would call it *Paley & Austin*'s. For though a substantial Dec doorway with ogee point survives and a great deal of ancient-looking masonry, though Sir Thomas Tunstal received licence to crenellate in 1402 and though *Sir Jeffry Wyatville* worked in 1810 for the North family and more additions were made in 1826–9, a fire in 1876 destroyed nearly all that, and in came Paley & Austin. They worked for Mr North North. Work took from 1879 to 1885, and the result was a superb semi-Elizabethan, semi-Gothic job, externally more impressive than internally. Internally the best room by far is the library on the upper floor, with the unexpected low, broad, panelled arch dividing it in two. The house is approached through a gateway and has preserved its fine moat.

TURTON

7010

ST ANNE, Chapeltown. 1840–1, perhaps by *John Palmer*. Smooth exterior. W tower with recessed spire. Windows with cusped Y- or cusped intersecting tracery. Thin octagonal piers; three galleries.

CHRIST CHURCH, Walmsley. 1839–40 by *Sharpe*. A sizeable church. W tower with big pinnacles. Paired lancets, triple lancets in the clerestory; transepts. Piers of the four-shafts-and-four-hollows section, arches with two sunk quadrants – i.e. archeologically accurate motifs. The transepts are two-bay-deep lower chapels. – FONT. C19; from Bolton parish church. – PAINTING. A Dutch(?) late C15 triptych of great interest. – STAINED GLASS. In the N and the S aisle one *Morris* window each, designed by *Burne-Jones*. Dates recorded 1872 and 1895. In each window two large figures and two small square scenes below.

ST MAXENTIUS, Bradshaw. *See The Buildings of England: South Lancashire.*

ST PETER, Belmont. *See* the present volume, p. 60.

UNITARIAN CHAPEL, Dimple. 1713. The sides have two tiers of small three-light mullioned windows. The front is altered. – BOX PEWS. – PULPIT in the middle of the side facing the entrance.

In the main street (No. 97) Humphrey Chetham's former house,
later a SCHOOL. But it looks a school. Central entrance, one
three-light window l., one r. The upper fenestration 3–2–3
lights. It makes a date before *c.*1660 or 1670 unlikely.

TURTON TOWER. Turton Tower is an L-shaped building,
originating in a pele tower, probably of the C15, with the remains of a spiral staircase in the NE corner and an Elizabethan
top storey. Blocked windows at different levels. About 1500
there was a separate building NE of the pele, running W–E. In
1596 this was remodelled and attached to the pele, i.e. a lower
range was added E of the pele to give more accommodation and
fulfil that function. The work of 1596 or a little later is partly
timber-framed, partly of stone. The large mullioned and
transomed windows of the pele belong to it. The S front of the
W–E range has its l. half ornately timbered *à la* Smithill's Hall
Bolton, Hall i' t' Wood Bolton, Speke Hall Liverpool (all South
Lancashire), and Samlesbury, its r. half lower and crowned by
a shaped gable. But that ornate timbering belongs entirely to
the work undertaken by Joseph Kay, a cotton spinner of
Preston, after he had bought the estate in 1835. However, the
shaped gable appears in an illustration of before his time. In
the pele on the first floor is a much restored Elizabethan ceiling
with pendants. Elizabethan also is the staircase with the flat
openwork balusters. The panelling in the dining room comes
from Middleton Hall and is of *c.*1700.

E of the house on a hill is a C17 SUMMER HOUSE with four
gables.

(The TURTON MODEL ESTATE is of the mid C19.)

CHEETHAM CLOSE STONE CIRCLE, close to the summit of
Turton Heights. This is a damaged circle of six surviving
stones with a diameter of 50 ft. 45 ft SW is a solitary standing
stone, and 60 ft beyond this the remains of a large RING
CAIRN, 72 ft in diameter. The bank is 4 ft wide and carefully
revetted on its inner and outer faces with upright slabs.

TYTUP HALL *see* DALTON-IN-FURNESS

²⁰⁷⁰

ULVERSTON

ST MARY. The W tower dates from shortly after 1540, when a
gale blew the previous tower down and 'utterly destroyed' it.
The S doorway is Norman, with one arch moulding of incised
zigzag and a surround which makes it certain that it is neither
in situ nor complete. The piers and arches and the clerestory

are Perp, the clerestory probably as late as the tower. The roof
has alternating hammerbeams and tiebeams and is of low pitch.
The rest of the church is by *Paley* of 1864–6, except that the
chancel was lengthened in 1904. Wide nave, no chancel arch.
– SCULPTURE. The kneeling child at a prayer-desk is by
Pasquale Romanelli of Florence. – STAINED GLASS. N and W,
partly after *Reynolds* (New College, Oxford), of *c.*1805–10. –
PLATE. Paten by *G.H.*, 1711; Flagon by *Gabriel Sleath*, 1737;
Chalice by *R.G.*, 1804. – MONUMENTS. William Sandys
† 1559. Recumbent effigies on a tomb-chest, the carving of
good quality. – Myles Dodding † 1606. Two brasses in a heavy
architectural surround of stone. – Myles Dodding † 1629.
Tablet with recumbent effigy between columns and with good
back decoration. – John Braddyll (of Conishead Priory) † 1727.
Signed by *Christopher Mason*. C17-looking cartouche. –
Thomas Braddyll † 1776. With a small bust. – W. G. Braddyll
† 1818. By *Blore*. A putto weeps into a big drapery.

ST MARY (R.C.), Victoria Road. 1895 by *Sinnott*. Red sandstone,
smooth walls. Mostly lancets, but also geometrical tracery.

HOLY TRINITY, New Church Lane. 1829–32 by *Anthony
Salvin*. A Commissioners' church (cost £4,978), with lancets
and flat buttresses. NW tower with plain spire. Severe rather
than merely plain. High octagonal piers inside. – WEST
GALLERY. – STAINED GLASS. In the N aisle one window by
Morris († 1887), the neighbouring one by *Kempe* (*c.*1905).

BARROW MONUMENT. On Hoad Hill, NE of the town.
Erected in 1850 in the shape of a lighthouse to commemorate
Sir John Barrow, the geographer and Secretary to the Ad-
miralty. By *A. Trimen*.

STANLEY HOSPITAL (the former WORKHOUSE). 1838, and
hence still entirely classical. Seven bays, two and a half storeys,
three-bay pediment.

In the SW corner of the MARKET PLACE a house probably once
the market house. It is dated 1736 and has quoins and an
arcaded ground floor no doubt originally open. Other pleasant
houses in the square and the adjoining streets, especially (to
the W) QUEEN STREET and PRINCE'S STREET. (In the latter
MAYFIELD has giant pilasters and a doorway with Ionic
columns. MHLG) Some attractive houses also in KING
STREET. NEW MARKET STREET has business premises
rather bigger than had until then been the scale of Ulverston.
MARKET STREET runs S out of the Market Square, and there
is here first the COOPERATIVE STORE of 1881 with very weird

details (pilasters with bases that are no bases and capitals that are no capitals), and then at the corner of UNION STREET the best building in the town, the SAVINGS BANK, dated 1845 on the substantial, but recessed short tower with cupola. To Union Street a three-bay front with rusticated ground floor and a three-bay pediment. Note the heavily Grecian cast-iron balcony, and also the two-light window with arched lights, typical of the 1840s. Off Union Street in FOUNTAIN STREET two pairs of early C19 houses with combined three-column doorways.

Ulverston was connected with the sea by a CANAL, 1¼ m. long. *Rennie* built it in 1793–6. It has long been disused, and Barrow has replaced Ulverston as a harbour.

(CHAPEL ISLAND, 2½ m. SE. On this island is the ruin of a chapel. The E gable with three lancet windows remains, says the MHLG. The VCH adds that part of the ruin was built as such by Col. Braddyll of Conishead in 1823. The chapel was built by the priors of Conishead for the use of those who crossed the sands.)

LEVEN VIADUCT, 2 m. E. 1857; 1500 ft long. An enterprise much admired at the time.

5000

UPHOLLAND

ST THOMAS. The magnificent scale of the interior is explained by the fact that this was the chancel of a Benedictine priory. The priory was founded in 1317–18 by Walter de Langton, Bishop of Lichfield. Ten or eleven years before Sir Robert de Holland had endowed a chapel, but this no longer exists. Of the priory buildings hardly anything remains among the walls of the houses adjoining on the S side. The present chancel is an addition of 1882–6, making the monastic chancel the nave. The broad W tower is late C15 or early C16 and stands where the crossing tower was intended to be. The priory church was apparently never finished. The W tower has quite a sumptuous portal with now defaced heads, figures, and fleurons. Externally, the splendour inside is heralded by the W walls of the aisles, which show the E crossing piers and the arches from the chancel chapels into the transepts. The aisle windows are Dec but Victorian and probably copies of the original windows. The projection on the N side contains the staircase into the crypt (cf. Warrington, South Lancashire, p. 411). There is nothing remarkable down there, but the nave interior is unforgettable with its tall and slender piers. The section is of four shafts and four hollows, more usual Perp than Dec, but the arches have a typically Dec section. Attractive plaster ceiling of 1752. – COMMUNION RAIL. With twisted balusters; late C17. – BENCH ENDS. A few, mainly 1635. They have simple curves at the top (cf. Standish). – CHURCHWARDENS PEW. Dated 1679 (nave w). – STAINED GLASS. Medieval bits in one S window, assembled as a pleasing jumble. – Several windows, e.g. E, by *Holiday*, 1883–4 and 1903–4. – PLATE. Chalice, 1706; Patens, 1720 and 1738; two Flagons, 1739; Chalice, 1817.

ST TERESA (R.C.), S of the college. By *F. X. Velarde*, 1952–7. Brick, but the top of the campanile with three tiers of round-arched openings of stone.

UPHOLLAND COLLEGE (R.C.). 1880–3 by *James O'Byrne*. Red sandstone, rock-faced, large. Additions of 1923–30 by *Powell & Powell*, including the chapel (by *Purcell* of Powell & Powell).

(UPHOLLAND COUNTY SCHOOL. By *Lyons, Israel & Ellis*, completed in 1959. Oddly broken outline with blocks projecting and receding irregularly. Brick cross-walls.)

NEWGATE FARM, ⅞ m. w. Dated 1707, but still with mullioned windows. Two gabled projections.

URSWICK

2070

ST MARY. The broad, squat w tower gives the impression of belonging to the C13, except for the Perp upper stage. The w doorway is small and single-chamfered with a segmental arch. The chancel must be C13 work too – see the one lancet. But it was lengthened in the C14; hence the Dec windows. The E window is very peculiar and looks as if it were composed of two different portions; yet it is said to be a facsimile of the original, made at the restoration in 1908. Nave and chancel in one and the tower as broad as both. – The distinguishing feature of the church is the WOODWORK with figural sculpture made by *C. R. Ashbee*'s Camden Guild in 1909–12. The figures belonging to the SCREEN are signed by *Alec Miller*. – The ORGAN CASE is also decorated with figures. – The SOUTH DOOR has the date 1909. – The delightful tester of the PULPIT is a thin shell supported by two putti. Its date is 1912. – There is also a PEW. – WEST GALLERY. Georgian, on two pairs of Tuscan columns arranged in depth. – PULPIT. A complete three-decker. – ALTAR PAINTING. Last Supper, by the local painter *James Cranke* Sen. (born 1707). – SCULPTURE. In the w wall of the tower high up a group of the Pietà, C15. – In the church part of an Anglo-Saxon CROSS SHAFT, with interlace, a runic inscription, and two men separated by a cross (Baptism of Christ ?). The scrollwork is Anglian in type, but the date is late, C11 according to Sir Thomas Kendrick. – Also a small interlace fragment. – PLATE. Chalice and Cover, London-made by *A.K.*, 1570–1; Plate, London-made, by *S.H.B.H.*, 1750–1. – MONUMENTS. Foliated coffin lid with inscription referring to Amicitia filia Johannis Francissi; C13. – A number of C18 and C19 tablets.

SKELMORE HEADS HILLFORT, ½ m. NNW. The defences enclose a roughly trapezoid area on the top of the hill. The univallate rampart is best preserved on the N. A single entrance occurs on the NW. Excavation revealed that the rampart was of rubble construction, some 8 ft thick, and was separated from a shallow ditch 4½ ft deep by a berm 12ft wide. This earthwork may have been preceded by a timber palisade.

ENCLOSURES, ½ m. NW of Little Urswick. There are two enclosures in this settlement, the W oval in plan and the E rectangular with an entrance on the SE. The latter site contains five hut circles. Excavation of these huts produced Iron Age pottery.

DRUIDS TEMPLE, on Birkrigg Common. This consists of two, non-concentric rings of stones, the outer 85 ft in diameter and the inner 30 ft in diameter. Within were five pits which contained cremation burials, one in a collared urn.

ENCLOSURE, on the NE slope of Birkrigg Common. The site is pear-shaped in plan and delimited by a rubble bank 10 ft wide. A single entrance occurs on the E. There are no surface traces of internal structures.

ENCLOSURE, 1 m. ESE of Little Urswick. The site is polygonal in plan and defined by a massive rubble bank revetted with large stone slabs. The foundations of two circular huts are visible in the interior. The settlement is unexcavated but is probably Iron Age or native Romano-British.

VICKERSTOWN *see* BARROW-IN-FURNESS, p. 59

WALMSLEY *see* TURTON

WALNEY ISLAND *see* BARROW-IN-FURNESS, pp. 57, 59

WALSUCHES MILL *see* HORWICH

WALTON-LE-DALE

5020

St LEONARD. Perp w tower and very low Perp chancel with a re-set E.E. priest's doorway. In between *J.P. Seddon*'s last work, 1902–6, a proud, very wide nave with open timber roof and double transepts. Blank Perp panelling above the low chancel arch. – MONUMENTS. Many tablets, mainly to Hoghtons.

ALL SAINTS, Higher Walton. 1861–4 by *E.G.Paley* (cost £6,000; Kelly). The steeple is of 1871. Broad tower, broach-spire. No aisles, but transepts, i.e. the pre-archeological tradition. Low polygonal apse. Late C13 forms. – STAINED GLASS. In the N transept 1877 by *Lavers, Barraud & Westlake*.

OUR LADY (R.C.), Higher Walton Road, ¼ m. SE of St Leonard. 1880 by *Pugin & Pugin*. Rock-faced, with a SW turret and a fancy W rose window. Apse. Forms of *c*.1300. Inside typical Pugin Jun. capitals, of a utilitarian, entirely un-period form. Corbels for the hood-moulds shaped on Exeter, i.e. big, long, and with naturalistic leaves.

St SAVIOUR *see* Cuerden.

Walton-le-Dale is the site of a ROMAN FORTLET overlooking the river Darwen. Occupation began in the late C1 with timber buildings, which were destroyed by fire. Subsequent C2 timber buildings were deliberately dismantled. The nature of the later occupation is uncertain.

WARDLE

9010

St JAMES. 1856–8 by *G.Shaw* of Saddleworth. It cost £2,700 (GS). Thin SW steeple outside the S aisle. Pairs and triplets of small lancets.

METHODIST CHURCH. 1874. Rich Italianate with a columned porch. Next to it its predecessor, probably of *c*.1830, and characteristically more modest.

WARTON

4070

1 m. N of Carnforth

St OSWALD. The oldest evidence is early C14: the S chapel SEDILIA (pre-1300 ?), the S arcade, if it represents original evidence (it is C19), and a S aisle window. Perp W tower, chancel, and N arcade. – In one PEW set-in shields – from older bench ends ? – Two BENCH ENDS, dated 1571 and 1612, are in the vestry.* – FONT. The base is typical of 1661, its date,

* In the rectory at the time of writing.

in the one elementary geometrical pattern. Also dated 1661 the lead interior, and this has much finer, indeed very delicate, patterns. – PLATE. Unmarked Chalice; Paten of 1716 by *S.L.;* Flagon inscribed 1802.

RECTORY. The rectory looks harmless enough, but behind it are two C14 structures, oddly unconnected, although adjacent. The large one is the hall of a manor house. It has its single-chamfered doorway, the roof-line of its porch, the three single-chamfered doorways to buttery, kitchen, and pantry, and the complete gable at the high table end with a quatrefoil window, the top and bottom foils of which are ogee arches. Immediately next to this end and part of the back of the rectory is a small structure of *c.*1300. The E window on the upper floor has cusped Y-tracery.

Warton has a main street with many worth-while houses.

WARTON CRAG HILLFORT, ½ m. WNW. The site occupies the S end of a promontory which is defended by three lines of widely spaced ramparts cutting off the end of the spur and terminating against the precipitous faces on the E and W. The innermost defences consist of a bank without a ditch enclosing a roughly rectangular area of 7 acres. A number of gaps exist in the rampart; that on the SE may be original. The middle and outer ramparts, which enclose an area of 15 acres, echo the plan of the innermost fortifications but are difficult to trace on the ground owing to the dense undergrowth in this area. The site is unexcavated.

₄₀₂₀

WARTON
3 m. WNW of Lytham St Annes

ST PAUL. 1884–6 by *Aldridge & Deacon.* Substantial and serious. Aisles with lancet triplets, the E window a group of five lancets. Round piers. The notable features are the large transeptal dormer on the S side and the chancel arch of three rounded orders, two of them starting corbel-like.

WATERFOOT *see* RAWTENSTALL

₃₀₃₀

WEETON

ST MICHAEL. 1843; enlarged 1852. Nave with bellcote and chancel. Lancets, not as tall as in the Commissioners' churches.

₆₀₇₀

WENNINGTON

WENNINGTON HALL. 1855. Of medium size, as C19 mansions go in this part of the county. Asymmetrical gabled façade with a castellated tower at the back. The picturesque STABLES are directly connected with the house and have their own lower tower.

WESHAM
¾ m. NW of Kirkham

CHRIST CHURCH. 1893–4 by *Paley & Austin*. Brick with red terracotta dressings. In 1894 only the nave was built. The rest is enlargement of 1927 – no doubt by *Austin & Paley;* for the whole is as personal as most of their churches. Wide nave and chancel. Brick facing. The aisles are replaced by low passages. Round stone piers, round brick arches. High clerestory. Dec motifs. Small SW steeple.

WESTBY *see* KIRKHAM

WHALLEY

The little town developed by the abbey, with the parish church just NW of the inner gatehouse.

ST MARY. The only certain Norman evidence is the S doorway with many-scalloped capitals; the arch, however, is E.E. Transitional may be the vestry E doorway, but if so, it is re-set. The E.E. style has left more than just a reminder in the chancel: five noble lancets in the S wall, the first a 'low-side' one, and a priest's doorway. The E window is a Perp replacement. Perp w tower, Late Perp aisle and clerestory windows. Inside, we are back at the noble E.E. The high and wide nave belongs to it; for both the N arcade with round piers and the S arcade with octagonal piers are E.E. Double-chamfered arches. The chancel SEDILIA and the PISCINA belong to the chancel build. The sedilia have detached shafts. Good nave and chancel roofs, that of the chancel earlier. The church is exceptionally rich in furnishings and especially woodwork. Pride of place belongs to the STALLS. They come from the abbey, and the20 initials W.W. on the abbot's stall date them to between 1418 and 1434. They are not at all in their original condition, but we have enough to say that essentially the shafts and the canopies, ribbed inside, are correct. On the N side is one poppy-head with two angels. The seats themselves, and especially the MISERICORDS, are well preserved, the latter one of the most rewarding sets in the country. They represent (S) a dragon, a man shoeing a goose (with an inscription explaining the story), vine and grapes (and the inscription: May they always rejoice who sit in this seat), a green man, an angel, Alexander carried to the sky by eagles, a pelican, pomegranates, and a lion and a dragon, and (N) Reynard the fox and a goose, St George and the dragon, two eagles feeding, a girl and a satyr (with the inscription: Think much, speak little), a plant, a rose, the *signum triciput*, a swine feeding on acorns, a husband beaten by his wife with the frying-pan.

The SCREENS to chancel, N chapel, and S chapel are all partly Perp. They have one-light divisions. – A pre-Reformation PEW (or a pew made up of dado panels of a screen) is immediately W of the rood screen. – The most spectacular PEW is ST ANTON'S CAGE. The inscription 1830 has of course nothing to do with the date of the pew. It has one inscription and date 1534 inside and another 1610. In fact the present elaborate upper parts belong to 1697. The date is inscribed too. – The PEW N of the cage is of 1702 and has fine carving. – At the W end the simple CHURCHWARDENS' PEW is dated 1690, and the CONSTABLE'S PEW 1714. – The BENCHES are almost complete. They have simple curly tops and one is dated 1638. – The splendid ORGAN CASE was made in 1729 for Lancaster church. – CHANDELIER. Of brass, C18, with three tiers of superbly scrolly arms. – FONT. Perp, octagonal, big and coarse. – SCULPTURE. Roman Altar. – STAINED GLASS. Designed by *Pugin*, 1847, and made by *Hardman* the S aisle E window. Three large figures, predominantly red. – By *Morris & Co.* the S aisle SE window. The date is after 1891. The three figures are rather soulless for Morris. – PLATE. Embossed Flagon, 1828–9. – MONUMENTS. Brasses to Ralph Caterall † 1515 with family. Small kneeling figures. – Mrs Elizabeth Whalley † 1785. By *Fisher* of York. Large tablet, very elegantly done. – Sir James Whalley Smythe Gardener † 1805. By *Westmacott*, but rather conventional. Sarcophagus and draped urn. – Dr T. Dunham Whitaker † 1822, by *Charles R. Smith* of London. Semi-reclining figure on a mattress. – Thomas Brooks † 1831. By *B. Baker* of Liverpool. Seated mourning woman by an urn. – In the churchyard are three ANGLO-SAXON CROSSES.

The churchyard has on its N side nice stone terraces, a pleasant, unobtrusive foil. The main street, KING STREET, is a traffic disaster. The prettiest building is the WHALLEY ARMS with a tripartite gable window halfway in shape between the Yorkshire C17 tradition and the Gothick of 1800. The house is in fact dated 1781. Nearer the bridge, i.e. the S end, a terrace of three-storeyed Early Georgian brick houses.

From certain vantage-points all this and the abbey premises are dominated by the brick railway VIADUCT, of fifty-three arches, built in 1850.

WHALLEY ABBEY. Cistercian monks settled at Standlaw in the Wirral in the 1170s. In 1283 they decided to move to Whalley and in 1289 received licence from the pope to build. This was soon temporarily revoked, and only in 1296 did they arrive. The first consecration dates from 1306. The church was begun in 1330. Licence to crenellate the premises was given in 1339. A burial in the church is recorded for c. 1345. The first mass was said in the church in 1380.

If one approaches not from the town but from the w one passes first through an OUTER GATEWAY, 300 yds W of the main entrance. It is of the early C14 and has very large double-chamfered outer arches on semi-octagonal responds. There is one upper window to the W, and one to the E, both deprived of their tracery. The passage is rib-vaulted in eight bays, with an intermediate archway after five bays. This archway is divided into a pedestrian and a horse, carriage, or cart entrance. The arches are segmental, the ribs single-chamfered.

The INNER GATEWAY was finished in 1480. It has diagonal buttresses and battlements. Fine wide arch on semicircular responds. One of the arch orders has two hollows. The N part of the interior is tunnel-vaulted. The vault is pointed, and the ribs are arranged like coffering. Can this really be pre-Elizabethan? Midway through the gateway is an internal division into pedestrian and vehicular passages. The latter has a round arch. That also points to a later date.

As one emerges from the gateway one has the house of the Assheton family opposite, the church to the W.

The plan of the CHURCH, of which not much is preserved, is laid out on the ground. It is typically Cistercian, with a straight-ended three-bay chancel with straight-ended chancel aisles, attached to each transept three straight-ended chapels, and a ten-bay nave with narrow aisles. The total length was about 260 ft. Of the S transept enough remains to show that it was vaulted. One respond in the S wall shows five stepped shafts. There is also one window jamb. The nave piers had eight groups of thin attached triple shafts. The aisles were vaulted too, see two corbels in the W bay of the S aisle towards the S.

The CLOISTER is easily recognized. In the E range was first the sacristy, whose doorway to the S transept is extant. In the W wall of the S transept and the sacristy are three recesses of the type in which abbeys kept their books. The chapter house entry has a fleuron order and the usual two-light windows l. and r. The doorway leads only into the vestibule. The chapter house proper lay to the E and has not been traced. Only the doorway is still indicated.* There follows the doorway to the parlour (with two hollow chamfers), then the doorway to the dormitory undercroft (in which in the C15 two-light windows and to the S a three-light window were put in, and also a fire-place). The dormitory was above and connected to the SE direct with the reredorter or lavatories, which were, as always, placed above a stream. All the remains here are C15 again. There are two big arches across. Then, round the corner, is the entry to the day stair. W of this was the refectory. Two doorways are recognizable, and one by the SW corner which led to the kitchen. The wide segmentally arched recess repre-sents the hand-washing place. The W range is C15 again. It had, as was customary, the stores on the ground floor. There are two doorways to the cloister. The seven surviving windows are Perp. The W wall is flush with the church W wall.

E of the E range of the cloister was an irregular manor-house-like building, earlier than the Assheton mansion. This and not the Assheton mansion may have been the abbot's lodging. But all that is not certain.

The Assheton house, considered the ABBOT'S LODGING, now looks predominantly c.1840, but there is a good deal more to it. The W part of the N front, with the round-headed porch and a second re-set porch, is later C17 – see the characteristic shaped gable with its horizontally set oval – but the masonry of this part and the whole N front and part of the E side dates from the C13, and probably a date earlier than the arrival of the Cistercians. Was it a manor house on the spot? The N window of two lancet lights is also re-set, but must have belonged to this work. At the S end of the E range was a chapel. PISCINA and AUMBRY remain, and Perp windows to E and S, the latter straight-headed of three cusped lights. Otherwise the E range has big Elizabethan windows with two transoms. The date 1588 appears on a buttress. There is also a two-transomed window (of five lights) in the E wall of the W range. The S end

---

* Medieval TILES in the vestibule

of the w range must again be older. It was the kitchen (see the three fireplaces) and may have been free-standing. The house apparently had no s range.

The OUTER COURTYARD, N of the house, is spacious. Its N range, by the gatehouse, looks Elizabethan.

(MORETON HALL, 1 m. SE. By *Webster*, 1829, Elizabethan, according to Mr Fleetwood-Hesketh.)

(CLERK HILL, 1 m. E. Charming Georgian, of several dates between 1715 and 1772, also according to Mr Fleetwood-Hesketh.)

PORTFIELD CAMP, 1 m. SE. The site lies on a slight, southward-facing promontory. Only on the NW are there clear traces of artificial defensive works consisting of a bivallate bank and ditch structure. Further defences may have existed on the E and SE, but no surface traces survive. Excavation revealed two phases of construction. The earliest consisted of a single, stone-revetted rampart without a ditch situated some 20 ft behind the present inner rampart. The first rampart was subsequently levelled and the existing inner rampart constructed. This was again revetted in stone on its inner and outer faces and had a clay core. It was separated from its ditch by a berm 20 ft wide. The outer bank and ditch also probably belong to this phase and may originally have had a slight counterscarp bank. No datable finds were recovered.

WHEELTON

6020

CLOCK TOWER. A memorial to the dead of the First World War. It looks like a left-over church tower, and a Victorian one at that.

PROSPECT HOUSE, ⅜ m. NE of the former. In the garden the top of the tower or bell-turret of the former Wheelton church (the present one is of no interest). It is a rotunda of six short columns carrying a cupola. The date 1776 is inscribed.

WHITE BORRAN CAIRNS see BLAWITH

WHITECHAPEL see INGLEWHITE

WHITTINGHAM

5030

MENTAL HOSPITAL. Built in 1869 etc., to the designs of *Henry Littler* of Manchester. Red brick blocks arranged radially round a centre. Many enlargements. The impression is of a whole town. The CHAPEL is of 1873, also by *Littler*.

WHITTINGTON

ST MICHAEL. Broad early C16 W tower with diagonal buttresses
rising with exceptionally many set-offs. Perp the arcades also,
of standard elements. But most of the church is of 1875, built
mostly at the expense of Col. D.C.Greene. It is a good job,
especially the varied grouping around the E end. – STAINED
GLASS. The E, the N aisle W, and the S aisle W and E windows
evidently by *Powell*, and evidently of *c.*1875. – In the S aisle
two windows by *Kempe & Tower*, very backward-looking. –
PLATE. Chalice by *W.R.*; large Paten and Flagon inscribed
1719. All three are silver-gilt.

WHITTINGTON HALL. Built for Thomas Green, it is said, in
1831. A gabled Tudor mansion of great ambition. A tower
rises behind the symmetrical façade. But can this really be
1831?

In the village street a number of instructive cottages. One is of
1658 and has on the upper floor windows of 4–2–4 lights, but
the doorway and the lower fenestration not yet in axis. Another cottage, of 1671, has this, except that the hall window is
still marked by one more light than symmetry would allow.
One of 1687 has a Yorkshire lintel with ogee motifs, and one of
1738 still has a Yorkshire lintel.

NEWTON GATE, 1½ m. S, is dated 1692 and is symmetrical and
moreover has above windows of three stepped lights and below
of six lights also with only one step, for the two middle lights.

WHITTLE-LE-WOODS

ST JOHN. 1880–2 by *Myres, Veevers & Myres* of Preston in
replacement of a Commissioners' church of 1829–30 by
Rickman & Hutchinson. Large, with a NE tower, a polygonal
apse, and a good transept keeping close to the tower.

ST CHAD. 1896. In an Italianate style, i.e. with arched windows
and a W tower with a low pyramid roof. Three-bay-long transepts, more or less like aisles. They go back to the predecessor
church of 1791. The arcade piers are granite columns.

SHAW HILL (Golf Club). The house looks *c.*1830. Ashlar, five
bays and two and a half storeys. Stone porch or veranda of
Tuscan columns and pillars, the centre part slightly projecting.
The mid-window is emphasized too, by a segmental pediment.
Round the corner a three-bay front with a big bow in the
middle and tripartite ground-floor windows.

LISIEUX HALL, ½ m. w. Early C19. Seven bays with a porch of Tuscan columns. At the back C17 with mullioned windows.

WHITWORTH

8010

ST BARTHOLOMEW. Away from the development of the village along the main road, up to the E, called first Church Street and in the end Whitworth Rake. An exposed position with views across to the moors opposite. 1847–50 by *Joseph Clarke*, and a remarkably mature work, large, serious, and archeologically entirely competent. Perp style – not 'Second Pointed'. w tower tall and with a taller stair-turret. Nave with clerestory. Long chancel. The buttresses are decorated with inlay of engineering bricks. Originally it was flint inlay. The interior, with octagonal piers, has less to offer.

ST JOHN EVANGELIST, Facit, also above the road. 1871 by *Medland & Henry Taylor*. s steeple, the stair-turret projecting semicircularly up to a certain height. Lancets and plate tracery.

(METHODIST CHURCH, Market Street. 1851. Three bays, angle pilasters, arched windows. Doric doorway. Opposite the SCHOOL – is it the original chapel? – dated 1811. Arched windows. MHLG)

(HALL FOLD CONGREGATIONAL CHURCH. 1849. Four bays, gabled front with rose window. MHLG)

WILPSHIRE *see* SALESBURY

WINMARLEIGH

4040

ST LUKE. 1876 by *Paley & Austin* (cost £2,100). Nave and chancel; very prettily (and subtly) detailed bell-turret near the E end. It has a boarded spire. Two transeptal chapels of two bays with separate pitched roofs. Nicely painted chancel roof – *à la* Bodley. – In the churchyard MONUMENT to the Reddaway family, a precinct with a blank Gothic back arch and against it a white marble figure kneeling and looking up to a cross. The monument dates from 1927. The Reddaways were at that time lords of the manor.

WINMARLEIGH HALL. Built by *Paley* in 1871 for John Wilson-Patten, Lord Winmarleigh, of Bank Hall, Warrington (*see The Buildings of England: South Lancashire*, p. 413). Red brick, with a four-storeyed tower and a cloister-like loggia below. There was a fire in 1927 and much rebuilding after that (e.g.

the centrepiece above the porch, and probably also the top
part of the tower).

WITHNELL

St PAUL. 1841 by *R. Towers*, a surveyor, says GR. With round-
arched lancets and a small w tower. Its top is octagonal, the
transition made by elementary broaches. Short concave-sided
spire.

WITHNELL FOLD FARMHOUSE, 1¼ m. NW. Three-bay front.
Dated 1736 and yet not symmetrical. The l. windows have
three lights, the r. ones four.

WOODFOLD HALL see MELLOR

WOODLAND
2½ m. NE of Broughton-in-Furness

CHURCH. 1891 by *J. W. Grundy & Sons* (GR). Nave with bellcote and apse.

ENCLOSURES, on Heathwaite Fell, 1¼ m. SSE. These consist of a
complex of seven conjoined enclosures, all irregular in plan,
defined by drystone walls 3–7 ft in thickness. The entrance to
the group appears to be on the S. In the vicinity of the settlement are large numbers of round CAIRNS. Many of these may
be the result of field clearance, but some were opened in the
C19 and proved to be sepulchral.

WOOD PLUMPTON

St ANNE. The great charm of this church is its s aisle, seen in
conjunction with the rest. The aisle is of 1748 but looks 1730
at the latest. It is low, six bays long and battlemented, and has
arched, keyed-in windows and doorways in the first and fifth
bays, with surrounds still decidedly English Baroque in treatment. A tower stands at the w end. It is not large, and has
a window with simplified Gibbs surround and an octagonal
cupola. The N aisle on the other hand is Perp, according to
masonry and windows, except that there is one window with
pointed-trefoiled lights and a rounded trefoil over, and that
must be of *c.*1300. Is it re-set? The arcades are Perp, both of
standard elements, but whereas the s arcade is all crude Perp,
the N arcade has capitals of different types, and one might even
be of *c.*1300. The church has no chancel arch. The roof with
its dormers is of 1900. There was a Norman church on the

site, as FRAGMENTS proved which were found in 1900 (and are now in the vestry). – MONUMENT. Henry Foster † 1831, navigator and astronomer, drowned in Mexico. Mourning man by a draped urn. Also a flag and an anchor.

ST ANDREW (R.C.), Cottam, 1¼ m. s. Built in 1790, for £335 5s. 4¾d., but how much, other than the walls and windows (minus their tracery), can be of that date ? The polygonal apse was added c.1860. What then is the date of the canted ceilings and the thin iron columns creating aisles ? The PRESBYTERY with the Tuscan columns l. and r. of the door would be convincing for 1793, but is of 1827.

WORDEN PARK see LEYLAND

WORSTHORNE

8030

ST JOHN. 1884–5 by *Lewis Vulliamy*. Lancets and thin buttresses. The chancel an addition of 1894, the w tower an addition of 1903.

HURSTWOOD. See p. 149.

WORTHINGTON HALL see STANDISH

WRAY
2 m. NE of Hawkshead

3000

Wray is the creation of Dr James Dawson, a Liverpool surgeon. He built WRAY CASTLE in 1840–7 to designs by *H. P. Horner*.[75] It is thoroughly towered and turreted, with machicolation and battlements everywhere, a vast porte-cochère, a central hall rising the full height of the main tower, and of course completely asymmetrical façades. Opposite the entrance jumbled-up artificial ruins. Wordsworth said it 'added a dignified feature to the interesting scenery in the midst of which it stands'.

ST MARGARET was built in 1845 also at the expense of James Dawson. It is a perfectly innocuous building of nave and chancel, with details of the late C13 to early C14, but the SE tower chimes in with the castle.

PULL WOODS (Huyton Hill School). 1890–1 by *G. Faulkner Armitage* for Sir William Crossley, engineer. A large mansion, Cheshire rather than Lake District, with its divers timber-framed gables.

WRAY
1 m. SE of Hornby

A specially pretty village street with the houses as continuous terraces and a Late Georgian three-bay house, white and black, as the *point de vue*. The village has also exceptionally many dated lintels.

HOLY TRINITY. 1840, with a chancel of 1880. Double bellcote. The sides with stepped triple lancets.

(At OUTHWAITE, 1¼ m. SE, the NMR records a cottage with a lintel of the C17 Yorkshire type and the surprisingly late date 1770.)

WRAYSHOLME TOWER see FLOOKBURGH

WREA GREEN see RIBBY

WRIGHTINGTON

ST JAMES, 1⅞ m. N of the hospital. 1857 by *E. G. Paley*. Nothing special. Nave with bellcote and chancel. Mostly lancets, but a W rose.

ST JOSEPH, E of the lake, by the hospital. 1892 by *Charles Clifton Dicconson*.

TUNLEY PRESBYTERIAN CHURCH (MOSSY LEE CHAPEL). Built in 1691. Plain rectangle. Most of the mullioned windows are restoration. The open cupola is not original either.

HARROCK HALL, 2 m. NW of the hospital. Later C17, and with a splendid façade. It has a central canted bay window of five sides of an octagon and two identical porch projections in the re-entrant angles of two somewhat projecting wings. Rounded crenellation. The windows are mullioned and transomed – of five lights in the walls between centre and porches. The wings have early C19 Gothick windows. Large l. extensions, also partly early C19. One would dearly like to know the original plan. Where was the hall? Did it have its hall-bay not at the high table end? And why two porches? The former STABLES have round windows, i.e. they are probably early C18.

WYCOLLER HALL see TRAWDEN

WYRESIDE HALL see DOLPHINHOLME

YEALAND CONYERS

ST JOHN. Outside the village. Built in 1838. W tower with clumsy battlements. Lancet windows and buttresses. Lengthened and provided with a new chancel in 1861 and 1882.

ST MARY (R.C.). 1852 by *Paley* (P. Fleetwood-Hesketh). Paid for by R. T. Gillow of Leighton Hall. Nave with bellcote and chancel. Lancets and plate tracery.

FRIENDS MEETING HOUSE. 1692. The windows in the typical pattern of e.g. Swarthmoor have later been sashed.

YEALAND MANOR HOUSE, opposite the former. 1805. Three widely spaced bays. Porch of pairs of Tuscan columns without a base, i.e. a decidedly 'modern' design.

BEECHFIELD, in the village street, is similar, but the columns are not so progressive. The village street altogether is exceptionally pleasant.

LEIGHTON HALL. The house, as one approaches it, forms[71] itself into a delightful picture of controlled asymmetry, thanks largely to *Paley & Austin*'s addition of 1870. The rest of the façade is Georgian, originally of c.1760, but gothicized with much gusto (and some cast-iron mullions and tracery) about 1810 or so for R. Gillow, the distinguished Lancaster cabinet-maker. The façade, of a very white local limestone, before the gothicizing had a centre and a link with a r. hand pavilion, but not the corresponding motif on the other side. The gothicizing is specially pretty in the link and the pavilion, with pinnacles and decorated battlements. The centre is treated more simply, with two turrets and a central porch. The back is largely still Georgian, but along one side are three mysterious buttresses, and in that part recently some Gothic arches have been found. So there is a medieval past still visible. Paley & Austin made their wing compact and higher than the rest and put into the re-entrant angle a yet higher tower. It is this that makes everything fall into place. The entrance hall leads through a screen of clustered Gothic shafts to a handsomely[72] curving staircase. The most interesting room otherwise is the dining room, originally the billiard room. Gillow is said to have been among the first to make billiard tables. Hence the oval skylight. On the walls decorative C18 panel paintings of landscapes with small figures.

NEOLITHIC SETTLEMENT SITE, 1¼ m. NW, on Storrs Moss. Excavations conducted in the peat at the edge of the moss recovered a timber floor consisting of brushwood surmounted by planks. This living platform was linked to drier ground by a causeway. The only artefact from the site was the rim of a large wooden bowl or trough, but radiocarbon tests suggest that it is Neolithic.

GLOSSARY

ABACUS: flat slab on the top of a capital (q.v.).

ABUTMENT: solid masonry placed to resist the lateral pressure of a vault.

ACANTHUS: plant with thick fleshy and scalloped leaves used as part of the decoration of a Corinthian capital (q.v.) and in some types of leaf carving.

ACHIEVEMENT OF ARMS: in heraldry, a complete display of armorial bearings.

ACROTERION: foliage-carved block on the end or top of a classical pediment.

ADDORSED: two human figures, animals, or birds, etc., placed symmetrically so that they turn their backs to each other.

AEDICULE, AEDICULA: framing of a window or door by columns and a pediment (q.v.).

AFFRONTED: two human figures, animals, or birds, etc., placed symmetrically so that they face each other.

AGGER: Latin term for the built-up foundations of Roman roads; also sometimes applied to the banks of hill-forts or other earthworks.

AMBULATORY: semicircular or polygonal aisle enclosing an apse (q.v.).

ANNULET: *see* Shaft-ring.

ANSE DE PANIER: *see* Arch, Basket.

ANTEPENDIUM: covering of the front of an altar, usually by textiles or metalwork.

ANTIS, IN: *see* Portico.

APSE: vaulted semicircular or polygonal end of a chancel or a chapel.

ARABESQUE: light and fanciful surface decoration using combinations of flowing lines, tendrils, etc., interspersed with vases, animals, etc.

ARCADE: range of arches supported on piers or columns, free-standing; or, **BLIND ARCADE**, the same attached to a wall.

ARCH: round-headed, i.e. semicircular; pointed, i.e. consisting of two curves, each drawn from one centre, and meeting in a point at the top; segmental, i.e. in the form of a segment;

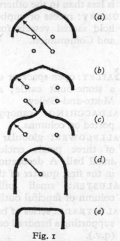

(a)

(b)

(c)

(d)

(e)

Fig. 1

pointed; four-centred (a Late Medieval form), *see* Fig. 1(a); Tudor (also a Late Medieval form), *see* Fig. 1(*b*); Ogee (introduced *c.* 1300 and specially popular in the C14), *see* Fig. 1(*c*); Stilted, *see* Fig. 1(*d*); Basket, with lintel connected to the jambs by concave quadrant curves, *see* Fig. 1(*e*).

ARCHITRAVE: lowest of the three main parts of the entablature (q.v.) of an order (q.v.) (*see* Fig. 12).

ARCHIVOLT: under-surface of an arch (also called Soffit).

ARRIS: sharp edge at the meeting of two surfaces.

ASHLAR: masonry of large blocks wrought to even faces and square edges.

ATLANTES: male counterparts of caryatids (q.v.).

ATRIUM: inner court of a Roman house, also open court in front of a church.

ATTACHED: *see* Engaged.

ATTIC: topmost storey of a house, if distance from floor to ceiling is less than in the others.

AUMBRY: recess or cupboard to hold sacred vessels for Mass and Communion.

BAILEY: open space or court of a stone-built castle; *see* also Motte-and-Bailey.

BALDACCHINO: canopy supported on columns.

BALLFLOWER: globular flower of three petals enclosing a small ball. A decoration used in the first quarter of the C14.

BALUSTER: small pillar or column of fanciful outline.

BALUSTRADE: series of balusters supporting a handrail or coping (q.v.).

BARBICAN: outwork defending the entrance to a castle.

BARGEBOARDS: projecting decorated boards placed against the incline of the gable of a building and hiding the horizontal roof timbers.

BARROW: *see* Bell, Bowl, Disc, Long, *and* Pond Barrow.

BASILICA: in medieval architecture an aisled church with a clerestory.

BASKET ARCH: *see* Arch (Fig. 1e).

BASTION: projection at the angle of a fortification.

BATTER: inclined face of a wall.

BATTLEMENT: parapet with a series of indentations or embrasures with raised portions or merlons between (also called Crenellation).

BAYS: internal compartments of a building; each divided from the other not by solid walls but by divisions only marked in the side walls (columns, pilasters, etc.) or the ceiling (beams, etc.). Also external divisions of a building by fenestration.

BAY-WINDOW: angular or curved projection of a house front with ample fenestration. If curved, also called bow-window; if on an upper floor only, also called oriel or oriel window.

BEAKER FOLK: Late New Stone Age warrior invaders from the Continent who buried their dead in round barrows and introduced the first metal tools and weapons to Britain.

BEAKHEAD: Norman ornamental motif consisting of a row of bird or beast heads with beaks biting usually into a roll moulding.

BELFRY: turret on a roof to hang bells in.

BELGAE: Aristocratic warrior bands who settled in Britain in two main waves in the C I B.C. In Britain their culture is termed Iron Age C.

BELL BARROW: Early Bronze Age round barrow in which the mound is separated from its encircling ditch by a flat platform or berm (q.v.).

BELLCOTE: framework on a roof to hang bells from.

BERM: level area separating ditch from bank on a hill-fort or barrow.

BILLET FRIEZE: Norman ornamental motif made up of short raised rectangles placed at regular intervals.

BIVALLATE: Of a hill-fort: defended by two concentric banks and ditches.

BLOCK CAPITAL: Romanesque capital cut from a cube by having the lower angles rounded off to the circular shaft below (also called Cushion Capital) (Fig. 2).

Fig. 2

BOND, ENGLISH or FLEMISH: see Brickwork.

BOSS: knob or projection usually placed to cover the intersection of ribs in a vault.

BOWL BARROW: round barrow surrounded by a quarry ditch. Introduced in Late Neolithic times, the form continued until the Saxon period.

BOW-WINDOW: see Bay-Window.

BOX: A small country house, e.g. a shooting box. A convenient term to describe a compact minor dwelling, e.g. a rectory.

BOX PEW: pew with a high wooden enclosure.

BRACES: see Roof.

BRACKET: small supporting piece of stone, etc., to carry a projecting horizontal.

BRESSUMER: beam in a timber-framed building to support the, usually projecting, superstructure.

BRICKWORK: *Header:* brick laid so that the end only appears on the face of the wall. *Stretcher:* brick laid so that the side only appears on the face of the wall. *English Bond:* method of laying bricks so that alternate courses or layers on the face of the wall are composed of headers or stretchers only (Fig. 3a). *Flemish Bond:* method of laying bricks so that alternate headers and stretchers appear in each course on the face of the wall (Fig. 3b).

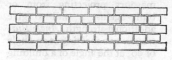

(a)

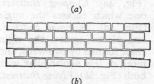

(b)

Fig. 3

BROACH: see Spire.

BROKEN PEDIMENT: see Pediment.

BRONZE AGE: In Britain, the period from c. 1600 to 600 B.C.

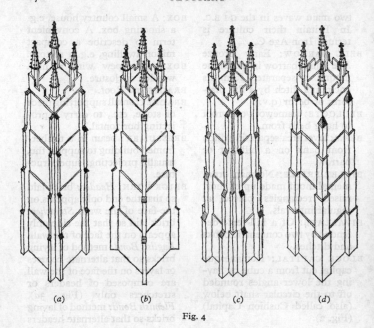

(a)   (b)   (c)   (d)

Fig. 4

BUCRANIUM: ox skull.

BUTTRESS: mass of brickwork or masonry projecting from or built against a wall to give additional strength. *Angle Buttresses:* two meeting at an angle of 90° at the angle of a building (Fig. 4*a*). *Clasping Buttress:* one which encases the angle (Fig. 4*d*). *Diagonal Buttress:* one placed against the right angle formed by two walls, and more or less equiangular with both (Fig. 4*b*). *Flying Buttress:* arch or half arch transmitting the thrust of a vault or roof from the upper part of a wall to an outer support or buttress. *Setback Buttress:* angle buttress set slightly back from the angle (Fig. 4*c*).

CABLE MOULDING: Norman moulding imitating a twisted cord.

CAIRN: a mound of stones usually covering a burial.

CAMBER: slight rise or upward curve of an otherwise horizontal structure.

CAMPANILE: isolated bell tower.

CANOPY: projection or hood over an altar, pulpit, niche, statue, etc.

CAP: in a windmill the crowning feature.

CAPITAL: head or top part of a column.

CARTOUCHE: tablet with an ornate frame, usually enclosing an inscription.

CARYATID: whole female figure

supporting an entablature or other similar member. *Termini Caryatids:* female busts or demi-figures or three-quarter figures supporting an entablature or other similar member and placed at the top of termini pilasters (q.v.). Cf. Atlantes.

CASTELLATED: decorated with battlements.

CELURE: panelled and adorned part of a wagon-roof above the rood or the altar.

CENSER: vessel for the burning of incense.

CENTERING: wooden framework used in arch and vault construction and removed when the mortar has set.

CHALICE: cup used in the Communion service or at Mass. *See also* Recusant Chalice.

CHAMBERED TOMB: burial mound of the New Stone Age having a stone-built chamber and entrance passage covered by an earthen barrow or stone cairn. The form was introduced to Britain from the Mediterranean.

CHAMFER: surface made by cutting across the square angle of a stone block, piece of wood, etc., at an angle of 45° to the other two surfaces.

CHANCEL: that part of the E end of a church in which the altar is placed, usually applied to the whole continuation of the nave E of the crossing.

CHANCEL ARCH: arch at the W end of the chancel.

CHANTRY CHAPEL: chapel attached to, or inside, a church, endowed for the saying of Masses for the soul of the founder or some other individual.

CHEVET: French term for the E end of a church (chancel, ambulatory, and radiating chapels).

CHEVRON: Norman moulding forming a zigzag.

CHOIR: that part of the church where divine service is sung.

CIBORIUM: a baldacchino.

CINQUEFOIL: *see* Foil.

CIST: stone-lined or slab-built grave. First appears in Late Neolithic times. It continued to be used in the Early Christian period.

CLAPPER BRIDGE: bridge made of large slabs of stone, some built up to make rough piers and other longer ones laid on top to make the roadway.

CLASSIC: here used to mean the moment of highest achievement of a style.

CLASSICAL: here used as the term for Greek and Roman architecture and any subsequent styles inspired by it.

CLERESTORY: upper storey of the nave walls of a church, pierced by windows.

COADE STONE: artificial (cast) stone made in the late C18 and the early C19 by Coade and Sealy in London.

COB: walling material made of mixed clay and straw.

COFFERING: decorating a ceiling with sunk square or polygonal ornamental panels.

COLLAR-BEAM: *see* Roof.

COLONNADE: range of columns.

COLONNETTE: small column.

COLUMNA ROSTRATA: column decorated with carved prows of ships to celebrate a naval victory.

COMPOSITE: *see* Order.

CONSOLE: bracket (q.v.) with a compound curved outline.

COPING: capping or covering to a wall.

CORBEL: block of stone projecting from a wall, supporting some horizontal feature.

CORBEL TABLE: series of corbels, occurring just below the roof eaves externally or internally, often seen in Norman buildings.

CORINTHIAN: *see* Order.

CORNICE: in classical architecture the top section of the entablature (q.v.). Also for a projecting decorative feature along the top of a wall, arch, etc.

CORRIDOR VILLA: *see* Villa.

COUNTERSCARP BANK: small bank on the down-hill or outer side of a hill-fort ditch.

COURTYARD VILLA: *see* Villa.

COVE, COVING: concave undersurface in the nature of a hollow moulding but on a larger scale.

COVER PATEN: cover to a Communion cup, suitable for use as a paten or plate for the consecrated bread.

CRADLE ROOF: *see* Wagon roof.

CRENELLATION: *see* Battlement.

CREST, CRESTING: ornamental finish along the top of a screen, etc.

CRINKLE-CRANKLE WALL: undulating wall.

CROCKET, CROCKETING: decorative features placed on the sloping sides of spires, pinnacles, gables, etc., in Gothic architecture, carved in various leaf shapes and placed at regular intervals.

CROCKET CAPITAL: *see* Fig. 5. An Early Gothic form.

CROMLECH: word of Celtic origin still occasionally used of single free-standing stones

ascribed to the Neolithic or Bronze Age periods.

Fig. 5

CROSSING: space at the intersection of nave, chancel, and transepts.

CROSS-WINDOWS: windows with one mullion and one transom.

CRUCK: big curved beam supporting both walls and roof of a cottage.

CRYPT: underground room usually below the E end of a church.

CUPOLA: small polygonal or circular domed turret crowning a roof.

CURTAIN WALL: connecting wall between the towers of a castle.

CUSHION CAPITAL: *see* Block Capital.

CUSP: projecting point between the foils in a foiled Gothic arch.

DADO: decorative covering of the lower part of a wall.

DAGGER: tracery motif of the Dec style. It is a lancet shape rounded or pointed at the head, pointed at the foot, and cusped inside (*see* Fig. 6).

Fig. 6

DAIS: raised platform at one end of a room.

DEC ('DECORATED'): historical division of English Gothic architecture covering the period from c.1290 to c.1350.

DEMI-COLUMNS: columns half sunk into a wall.

DIAPER WORK: surface decoration composed of square or lozenge shapes.

DISC BARROW: Bronze Age round barrow with inconspicuous central mound surrounded by bank and ditch.

DOGTOOTH: typical E.E. ornament consisting of a series of four-cornered stars placed diagonally and raised pyramidally (Fig. 7).

Fig. 7

DOMICAL VAULT: see Vault.

DONJON: see Keep.

DORIC: see Order.

DORMER (WINDOW): window placed vertically in the sloping plane of a roof.

DRIPSTONE: see Hood-mould.

DRUM: circular or polygonal vertical wall of a dome or cupola.

E.E. ('EARLY ENGLISH'): historical division of English Gothic architecture roughly covering the C13.

EASTER SEPULCHRE: recess with tomb-chest usually in the wall of a chancel, the tomb-chest to receive an effigy of Christ for Easter celebrations.

EAVES: underpart of a sloping roof overhanging a wall.

EAVES CORNICE: cornice below the eaves of a roof.

ECHINUS: Convex or projecting moulding supporting the abacus of a Greek Doric capital, sometimes bearing an egg and dart pattern.

EMBATTLED: see Battlement.

EMBRASURE: small opening in the wall or parapet of a fortified building, usually splayed on the inside.

ENCAUSTIC TILES: earthenware glazed and decorated tiles used for paving.

ENGAGED COLUMNS: columns attached to, or partly sunk into, a wall.

ENGLISH BOND: see Brickwork.

ENTABLATURE: in classical architecture the whole of the horizontal members above a column (that is architrave, frieze, and cornice) (see Fig. 12).

ENTASIS: very slight convex deviation from a straight line; used on Greek columns and sometimes on spires to prevent an optical illusion of concavity.

ENTRESOL: see Mezzanine.

EPITAPH: hanging wall monument.

ESCUTCHEON: shield for armorial bearings.

EXEDRA: the apsidal end of a room. See Apse.

FAN-VAULT: see Vault.

FERETORY: place behind the high altar where the chief shrine of a church is kept.

FESTOON: carved garland of flowers and fruit suspended at both ends.

FILLET: narrow flat band running down a shaft or along a roll moulding.

FINIAL: top of a canopy, gable, pinnacle.

FLAGON: vessel for the wine used in the Communion service.

FLAMBOYANT: properly the latest phase of French Gothic architecture where the window tracery takes on wavy undulating lines.

FLÈCHE: slender wooden spire on the centre of a roof (also called Spirelet).

FLEMISH BOND: see Brickwork.

FLEURON: decorative carved flower or leaf.

FLUSHWORK: decorative use of flint in conjunction with dressed stone so as to form patterns: tracery, initials, etc.

FLUTING: vertical channelling in the shaft of a column.

FLYING BUTTRESS: see Buttress.

FOIL: lobe formed by the cusping (q.v.) of a circle or an arch. Trefoil, quatrefoil, cinquefoil, multifoil, express the number of leaf shapes to be seen.

FOLIATED: carved with leaf shapes.

FOSSE: ditch.

FOUR-CENTRED ARCH: see Arch.

FRATER: refectory or dining hall of a monastery.

FRESCO: wall painting on wet plaster.

FRIEZE: middle division of a classical entablature (q.v.) (see Fig. 12).

FRONTAL: covering for the front of an altar.

GABLE: *Dutch gable:* A gable with curved sides crowned by a pediment, characteristic of *c.*1630–50 (Fig. 8*a*). *Shaped gable:* A gable with multi-curved sides characteristic of *c.*1600–50 (Fig. 8*b*).

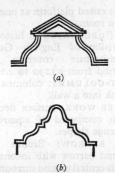

(a)

(b)

Fig. 8

GADROONED: enriched with a series of convex ridges, the opposite of fluting.

GALILEE: chapel or vestibule usually at the W end of a church enclosing the porch. Also called Narthex (q.v.).

GALLERY: in church architecture upper storey above an aisle, opened in arches to the nave. Also called Tribune and often erroneously Triforium (q.v.).

GALLERY GRAVE: chambered tomb (q.v.) in which there is little or no differentiation between the entrance passage and the actual burial chamber(s).

GARDEROBE: lavatory or privy in a medieval building.

GARGOYLE: water spout projecting from the parapet of a wall or tower; carved into a human or animal shape.

GAZEBO: lookout tower or raised summer house in a picturesque garden.

'GEOMETRICAL': see Tracery.

'GIBBS SURROUND': of a doorway or window. An C18 motif consisting of a surround with alternating larger and smaller blocks of stone, quoin-wise, or intermittent large blocks, sometimes with a narrow raised band connecting them up the verticals and along the face of the arch (Fig. 9).

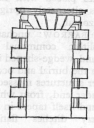

Fig. 9

GROIN: sharp edge at the meeting of two cells of a cross-vault.

GROIN-VAULT: *see* Vault.

GROTESQUE: fanciful ornamental decoration: *see* also Arabesque.

HAGIOSCOPE: *see* Squint.

HALF-TIMBERING: *see* Timber-Framing.

HALL CHURCH: church in which nave and aisles are of equal height or approximately so.

HAMMERBEAM: *see* Roof.

HANAP: large metal cup, generally made for domestic use, standing on an elaborate base and stem; with a very ornate cover frequently crowned with a little steeple.

HEADERS: *see* Brickwork.

HERRINGBONE WORK: brick, stone, or tile construction where the component blocks are laid diagonally instead of flat. Alternate courses lie in opposing directions to make a zigzag pattern up the face of the wall.

HEXASTYLE: having six detached columns.

HILL-FORT: Iron Age earthwork enclosed by a ditch and bank system; in the later part of the period the defences multiplied in size and complexity. They vary from about an acre to over 30 acres in area, and are usually built with careful regard to natural elevations or promontories.

HIPPED ROOF: *see* Roof.

HOOD-MOULD: projecting moulding above an arch or a lintel to throw off water (also called Dripstone or Label).

ICONOGRAPHY: the science of the subject matter of works of the visual arts.

IMPOST: bracket in a wall, usually formed of mouldings, on which the ends of an arch rest.

INDENT: shape chiselled out in a stone slab to receive a brass.

INGLENOOK: bench or seat built in beside a fireplace, sometimes covered by the chimneybreast, occasionally lit by small windows on each side of the fire.

INTERCOLUMNIATION: the space between columns.

IONIC: *see* Order (Fig. 12).

IRON AGE: in Britain the period from *c.* 600 B.C. to the coming of the Romans. The term is also used for those un-Romanized native communities which survived until the Saxon incursions.

JAMB: straight side of an archway, doorway, or window.

KEEL MOULDING: moulding whose outline is in section like that of the keel of a ship.

KEEP: massive tower of a Norman castle.

KEYSTONE: middle stone in an arch or a rib-vault.

KING-POST: see Roof (Fig. 14).

KNOP: a knob-like thickening in the stem of a chalice.

LABEL: see Hood-mould.

LABEL STOP: ornamental boss at the end of a hood-mould (q.v.).

LACED WINDOWS: windows pulled visually together by strips, usually in brick of a different colour, which continue vertically the lines of the vertical parts of the window surrounds. The motif is typical of c. 1720.

LANCET WINDOW: slender pointed-arched window.

LANTERN: in architecture, a small circular or polygonal turret with windows all round crowning a roof (see Cupola) or a dome.

LANTERN CROSS: churchyard cross with lantern-shaped top usually with sculptured representations on the sides of the top.

LEAN-TO ROOF: roof with one slope only, built against a higher wall.

LESENE or PILASTER STRIP: pilaster without base or capital.

LIERNE: see Vault (Fig. 21).

LINENFOLD: Tudor panelling ornamented with a conventional representation of a piece of linen laid in vertical folds. The piece is repeated in each panel.

LINTEL: horizontal beam or stone bridging an opening.

LOGGIA: recessed colonnade (q.v.).

LONG AND SHORT WORK: Saxon quoins (q.v.) consisting of stones placed with the long sides alternately upright and horizontal.

LONG BARROW: unchambered Neolithic communal burial mound, wedge-shaped in plan, with the burial and occasional other structures massed at the broader end, from which the mound itself tapers in height; quarry ditches flank the mound.

LOUVRE: opening, often with lantern (q.v.) over, in the roof of a room to let the smoke from a central hearth escape.

LOWER PALAEOLITHIC: see Palaeolithic.

LOZENGE: diamond shape.

LUCARNE: small opening to let light in.

LUNETTE: tympanum (q.v.) or semicircular opening.

LYCH GATE: wooden gate structure with a roof and open sides placed at the entrance to a churchyard to provide space for the reception of a coffin. The word lych is Saxon and means a corpse.

LYNCHET: long terraced strip of soil accumulating on the downward side of prehistoric and medieval fields due to soil creep from continuous ploughing along the contours.

MACHICOLATION: projecting gallery on brackets constructed on the outside of castle towers or walls. The gallery has holes in the floor to drop missiles through.

MAJOLICA: ornamented glazed earthenware.

MANSARD: *see* Roof.

MATHEMATICAL TILES: Small facing tiles the size of brick headers, applied to timber-framed walls to make them appear brick-built.

MEGALITHIC TOMB: stone-built burial chamber of the New Stone Age covered by an earth or stone mound. The form was introduced to Britain from the Mediterranean area.

MERLON: *see* Battlement.

MESOLITHIC: 'Middle Stone' Age; the post-glacial period of hunting and fishing communities dating in Britain from c. 8000 B.C. to the arrival of Neolithic communities, with which they must have considerably overlapped.

METOPE: in classical architecture of the Doric order (q.v.) the space in the frieze between the triglyphs (Fig. 12).

MEZZANINE: low storey placed between two higher ones.

MISERERE: *see* Misericord.

MISERICORD: bracket placed on the underside of a hinged choir stall seat which, when turned up, provided the occupant of the seat with a support during long periods of standing (also called Miserere).

MODILLION: small bracket of which large numbers (modillion frieze) are often placed below a cornice (q.v.) in classical architecture.

MOTTE: steep mound forming the main feature of C11 and C12 castles.

MOTTE-AND-BAILEY: post-Roman and Norman defence system consisting of an earthen mound (the motte) topped with a wooden tower eccentrically placed within a bailey (q.v.), with enclosure ditch and palisade, and with the rare addition of an internal bank.

MOUCHETTE: tracery motif in curvilinear tracery, a curved dagger (q.v.), specially popular in the early C14 (Fig. 10).

Fig. 10

MULLION: vertical post or upright dividing a window into two or more 'lights'.

MULTIVALLATE: Of a hill-fort: defended by three or more concentric banks and ditches.

MUNTIN: post as a rule moulded and part of a screen.

NAIL-HEAD: E.E. ornamental motif, consisting of small pyramids regularly repeated (Fig. 11).

Fig. 11

NARTHEX: enclosed vestibule or covered porch at the main entrance to a church (*see* Galilee).

NEOLITHIC: 'New Stone' Age, dating in Britain from the appearance from the Continent of the first settled farming communities c. 3500 B.C. until the introduction of the Bronze Age.

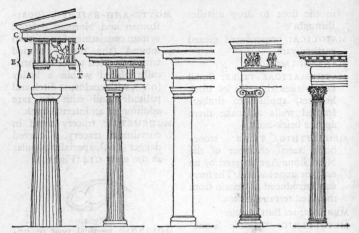

Fig. 12–Orders of Columns (Greek Doric, Roman Doric, Tuscan Doric, Ionic, Corinthian) E, Entablature; C, Cornice; F, Frieze; A, Architrave; M, Metope; T, Triglyph.

NEWEL: central post in a circular or winding staircase; also the principal post when a flight of stairs meets a landing.

NOOK-SHAFT: shaft set in the angle of a pier or respond or wall, or the angle of the jamb of a window or doorway.

OBELISK: lofty pillar of square section tapering at the top and ending pyramidally.

OGEE: see Arch (Fig. 1c).

ORATORY: small private chapel in a house.

ORDER: (1) of a doorway or window: series of concentric steps receding towards the opening; (2) in classical architecture: column with base, shaft, capital, and entablature (q.v.) according to one of the following styles: Greek Doric, Roman Doric, Tuscan Doric, Ionic, Corinthian, Composite. The established details are very elaborate, and some specialist architectural work should be consulted for further guidance (see Fig. 12).

ORIEL: see Bay-Window.

OVERHANG: projection of the upper storey of a house.

OVERSAILING COURSES: series of stone or brick courses, each one projecting beyond the one below it.

PALAEOLITHIC: 'Old Stone' Age; the first period of human culture, commencing in the Ice Age and immediately prior to the Mesolithic; the Lower Palaeolithic is the older phase, the Upper Palaeolithic the later.

PALIMPSEST: (1) of a brass: where a metal plate has been re-used by turning over and engraving on the back; (2) of a wall painting: where one overlaps and partly obscures an earlier one.

PALLADIAN: architecture following the ideas and principles of Andrea Palladio, 1518–80.

PANTILE: tile of curved S-shaped section.

PARAPET: low wall placed to protect any spot where there is a sudden drop, for example on a bridge, quay, hillside, housetop, etc.

PARGETTING: plaster work with patterns and ornaments either in relief or engraved on it.

PARVIS: term wrongly applied to a room over a church porch. These rooms were often used as a schoolroom or as a store room.

PATEN: plate to hold the bread at Communion or Mass.

PATERA: small flat circular or oval ornament in classical architecture.

PEDIMENT: low-pitched gable used in classical, Renaissance, and neo-classical architecture above a portico and above doors, windows, etc. It may be straight-sided or curved segmentally. *Broken Pediment:* one where the centre portion of the base is left open. *Open Pediment:* one where the centre portion of the sloping sides is left out.

PENDANT: boss (q.v.) elongated so that it seems to hang down.

PENDENTIF: concave triangular spandrel used to lead from the angle of two walls to the base of a circular dome. It is constructed as part of the hemisphere over a diameter the size of the diagonal of the basic square (Fig. 13).

PERP (PERPENDICULAR): historical division of English Gothic architecture covering

Fig. 13

the period from c.1335–50 to c.1530.

PIANO NOBILE: principal storey of a house with the reception rooms; usually the first floor.

PIAZZA: open space surrounded by buildings; in C17 and C18 England sometimes used to mean a long colonnade or loggia.

PIER: strong, solid support, frequently square in section or of composite section (compound pier).

PIETRA DURA: ornamental or scenic inlay by means of thin slabs of stone.

PILASTER: shallow pier attached to a wall. *Termini Pilasters:* pilasters with sides tapering downwards.

PILLAR PISCINA: free-standing piscina on a pillar.

PINNACLE: ornamental form crowning a spire, tower, buttress, etc., usually of steep pyramidal, conical, or some similar shape.

PISCINA: basin for washing the Communion or Mass vessels, provided with a drain. Generally set in or against the wall to the S of an altar.

PLAISANCE: summer-house, pleasure house near a mansion.

PLATE TRACERY: see Tracery.

PLINTH: projecting base of a wall or column, generally chamfered (q.v.) or moulded at the top.

POND BARROW: rare type of Bronze Age barrow consisting of a circular depression, usually paved, and containing a number of cremation burials.

POPPYHEAD: ornament of leaf and flower type used to decorate the tops of bench- or stall-ends.

PORTCULLIS: gate constructed to rise and fall in vertical grooves; used in gateways of castles.

PORTE COCHÈRE: porch large enough to admit wheeled vehicles.

PORTICO: centre-piece of a house or a church with classical detached or attached columns and a pediment. A portico is called *prostyle* or *in antis* according to whether it projects from or recedes into a building. In a portico *in antis* the columns range with the side walls.

POSTERN: small gateway at the back of a building.

PREDELLA: in an altarpiece the horizontal strip below the main representation, often used for a number of subsidiary representations in a row.

PRESBYTERY: the part of the church lying E of the choir. It is the part where the altar is placed.

PRINCIPAL: see Roof (Fig. 14).

PRIORY: monastic house whose head is a prior or prioress, not an abbot or abbess.

PROSTYLE: with free-standing columns in a row.

PULPITUM: stone screen in a major church provided to shut off the choir from the nave and also as a backing for the return choir stalls.

PULVINATED FRIEZE: frieze with a bold convex moulding.

PURLIN: see Roof (Figs. 14, 15).

PUTTO: small naked boy.

QUADRANGLE: inner courtyard in a large building.

QUARRY: in stained-glass work, a small diamond or square-shaped piece of glass set diagonally.

QUATREFOIL: see Foil.

QUEEN-POSTS: see Roof (Fig. 15).

QUOINS: dressed stones at the angles of a building. Sometimes all the stones are of the same size; more often they are alternately large and small.

RADIATING CHAPELS: chapels projecting radially from an ambulatory or an apse.

RAFTER: see Roof.

RAMPART: stone wall or wall of earth surrounding a castle, fortress, or fortified city.

RAMPART-WALK: path along the inner face of a rampart.

REBATE: continuous rectangular notch cut on an edge.

REBUS: pun, a play on words. The literal translation and illustration of a name for artistic and heraldic purposes (Belton = bell, tun).

RECUSANT CHALICE: chalice made after the Reformation and before Catholic Emancipation for Roman Catholic use.

REEDING: decoration with parallel convex mouldings touching one another.

REFECTORY: dining hall; *see* Frater.

RENDERING: plastering of an outer wall.

REPOUSSÉ: decoration of metal work by relief designs, formed by beating the metal from the back.

REREDOS: structure behind and above an altar.

RESPOND: half-pier bonded into a wall and carrying one end of an arch.

RETABLE: altarpiece, a picture or piece of carving, standing behind and attached to an altar.

RETICULATION: *see* Tracery (Fig. 20e).

REVEAL: that part of a jamb (q.v.) which lies between the glass or door and the outer surface of the wall.

RIB-VAULT: *see* Vault.

ROCOCO: latest phase of the Baroque style, current in most Continental countries between *c.* 1720 and *c.* 1760.

ROLL MOULDING: moulding of semicircular or more than semicircular section.

ROMANESQUE: that style in architecture which was current in the C11 and C12 and preceded the Gothic style (in England often called Norman). (Some scholars extend the use of the term Romanesque back to the C10 or C9.)

ROMANO-BRITISH: A somewhat vague term applied to the period and cultural features of Britain affected by the Roman occupation of the C1–5 A.D.

ROOD: cross or crucifix.

ROOD LOFT: singing gallery on the top of the rood screen, often supported by a coving.

ROOD SCREEN: *see* Screen.

ROOD STAIRS: stairs to give access to the rood loft.

ROOF: *Single-framed:* if consisting entirely of transverse members (such as rafters with or without braces, collars, tie-beams, king-posts or queen-posts, etc.) not tied together longitudinally. *Double-framed:* if longitudinal members (such as a ridge beam and purlins) are employed. As a rule in such cases the rafters are divided into stronger principals and weaker subsidiary rafters.

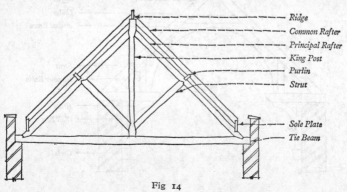

Ridge
Common Rafter
Principal Rafter
King Post
Purlin
Strut

Sole Plate
Tie Beam

Fig 14

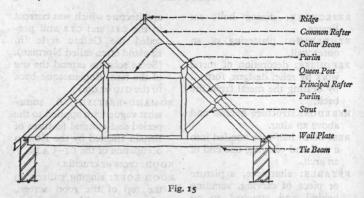

Fig. 15

Hipped: roof with sloped instead of vertical ends. *Mansard:* roof with a double slope, the lower slope being larger and steeper than the upper. *Saddleback:* tower roof shaped like an ordinary gabled timber roof. The following members have special names: *Rafter:* roof-timber sloping up from the wall plate to the ridge. *Principal:* principal rafter, usually corresponding to the main bay divisions of the nave or chancel

below. *Wall Plate:* timber laid longitudinally on the top of a wall. *Purlin:* longitudinal member laid parallel with wall plate and ridge beam some way up the slope of the roof. *Tie-beam:* beam connecting the two slopes of a roof across at its foot, usually at the height of the wall plate, to prevent the roof from spreading. *Collar-beam:* tie-beam applied higher up the slope of the roof. *Strut:* upright timber connecting the

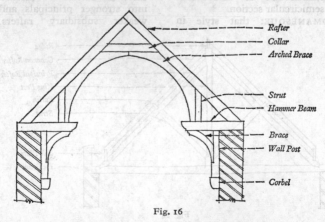

Fig. 16

tie-beam with the rafter above it. *King-post:* upright timber connecting a tie-beam and collar-beam with the ridge beam. *Queen-posts:* two struts placed symmetrically on a tie-beam or collar-beam. *Braces:* inclined timbers inserted to strengthen others. Usually braces connect a collar-beam with the rafters below or a tie-beam with the wall below. Braces can be straight or curved (also called arched). *Hammer-beam:* beam projecting at right angles, usually from the top of a wall, to carry arched braces or struts and arched braces. (*See* Figs. 14, 15, 16.)

ROSE WINDOW (or WHEEL WINDOW): circular window with patterned tracery arranged to radiate from the centre.

ROTUNDA: building circular in plan.

RUBBLE: building stones, not square or hewn, nor laid in regular courses.

RUSTICATION: *rock-faced* if the surfaces of large blocks of ashlar stone are left rough like rock; *smooth* if the ashlar blocks are smooth and separated by V-joints; *banded* if the separation by V-joints applies only to the horizontals.

S ADDLEBACK: *see* Roof.

SALTIRE CROSS: equal-limbed cross placed diagonally.

SANCTUARY: (1) area around the main altar of a church (*see* Presbytery); (2) sacred site consisting of wood or stone uprights enclosed by a circular bank and ditch. Beginning in the Neolithic, they were elaborated in the succeeding Bronze Age. The best known examples are Stonehenge and Avebury.

SARCOPHAGUS: elaborately carved coffin.

SCAGLIOLA: material composed of cement and colouring matter to imitate marble.

SCALLOPED CAPITAL: development of the block capital (q.v.) in which the single semi-circular surface is elaborated into a series of truncated cones (Fig. 17).

Fig. 17

SCARP: artificial cutting away of the ground to form a steep slope.

SCREEN: *Parclose screen:* screen separating a chapel from the rest of a church. *Rood screen:* screen below the rood (q.v.), usually at the w end of a chancel.

SCREENS PASSAGE: passage between the entrances to kitchen, buttery, etc., and the screen behind which lies the hall of a medieval house.

SEDILIA: seats for the priests (usually three) on the s side of the chancel of a church.

SEGMENTAL ARCH: *see* Arch.

SET-OFF: *see* Weathering.

SEXPARTITE: *see* Vault.

SGRAFFITO: pattern incised into plaster so as to expose a dark surface underneath.

SHAFT-RING: motif of the C12 and C13 consisting of a ring round a circular pier or a shaft attached to a pier.

SHEILA-NA-GIG: fertility figure, usually with legs wide open.

SILL: lower horizontal part of the frame of a window.

SLATEHANGING: the covering of walls by overlapping rows of slates, on a timber substructure.

SOFFIT: underside of an arch, lintel, etc.

SOLAR: upper living-room of a medieval house.

SOPRAPORTE: painting above the door of a room, usual in the C17 and C18.

SOUNDING BOARD: horizontal board or canopy over a pulpit. Also called Tester.

SPANDREL: triangular surface between one side of an arch, the horizontal drawn from its apex, and the vertical drawn from its springer; also the surface between two arches.

SPERE-TRUSS: roof truss on two free-standing posts to mask the division between screens passage and hall. The screen itself, where a spere-truss exists, was originally movable.

SPIRE: tall pyramidal or conical pointed erection often built on top of a tower, turret, etc. *Broach Spire:* spire which is generally octagonal in plan rising from the top or parapet of a square tower. A small inclined piece of masonry covers the vacant triangular space at each of the four angles of the square and is carried up to a point along the diagonal sides of the octagon. *Needle Spire:* thin spire rising from the centre of a tower roof, well inside the parapet.

SPIRELET: *see* Flèche.

SPLAY: chamfer, usually of the jamb of a window.

SPRINGING: level at which an arch rises from its supports.

SQUINCH: arch or system of concentric arches thrown across the angle between two walls to support a superstructure, for example a dome (Fig. 18).

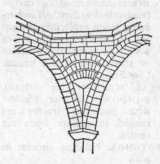

Fig. 18

SQUINT: hole cut in a wall or through a pier to allow a view of the main altar of a church from places whence it could not otherwise be seen (also called Hagioscope).

STALL: carved seat, one of a row, made of wood or stone.

STAUNCHION: upright iron or steel member.

STEEPLE: the tower of a church together with a spire, cupola, etc.

STIFF-LEAF: E.E. type of foliage of many-lobed shapes (Fig. 19).

STILTED: *see* Arch.

STOREY-POSTS: the principal posts of a timber-framed wall.

STOUP: vessel for the reception of holy water, usually placed near a door.

Fig. 19

STRAINER ARCH: arch inserted across a room to prevent the walls from leaning.

STRAPWORK: C16 decoration consisting of interlaced bands, and forms similar to fretwork or cut and bent leather.

STRETCHER: see Brickwork.

STRING COURSE: projecting horizontal band or moulding set in the surface of a wall.

STRUT: see Roof.

STUCCO: plaster work.

STUDS: the subsidiary vertical timber members of a timber-framed wall.

SWAG: festoon formed by a carved piece of cloth suspended from both ends.

TABERNACLE: richly ornamented niche or free-standing canopy. Usually contains the Holy Sacrament.

TARSIA: inlay in various woods.

TAZZA: shallow bowl on a foot.

TERMINAL FIGURES (TERMS, TERMINI): upper part of a human figure growing out of a pier, pilaster, etc., which tapers towards the base. See also Caryatid, Pilaster.

TERRACOTTA: burnt clay, unglazed.

TESSELLATED PAVEMENT: mosaic flooring, particularly Roman, consisting of small 'tesserae' or cubes of glass, stone, or brick.

TESSERAE: see Tessellated Pavement.

TESTER: see Sounding Board.

TETRASTYLE: having four detached columns.

THREE-DECKER PULPIT: pulpit with Clerk's Stall below and Reading Desk below the Clerk's Stall.

TIE-BEAM: see Roof (Figs. 14, 15).

TIERCERON: see Vault (Fig. 21).

TILEHANGING: see Slatehanging.

TIMBER-FRAMING: method of construction where walls are built of timber framework with the spaces filled in by plaster or brickwork. Sometimes the timber is covered over with plaster or boarding laid horizontally.

TOMB-CHEST: chest-shaped stone coffin, the most usual medieval form of funeral monument.

TOUCH: soft black marble quarried near Tournai.

TOURELLE: turret corbelled out from the wall.

TRACERY: intersecting ribwork in the upper part of a window, or used decoratively in blank arches, on vaults, etc. *Plate tracery: see* Fig. 20(*a*). Early form of tracery where decoratively shaped openings are cut through the solid stone infilling in a window head. *Bar tracery:* a form introduced into England *c.* 1250. Intersecting ribwork made up of slender shafts, continuing the lines of the mullions of windows up to a decorative mesh in the head of the window. *Geometrical tracery: see* Fig. 20(*b*). Tracery characteristic of *c.* 1250–1310 consisting chiefly of circles of foiled circles. *Y-tracery: see*

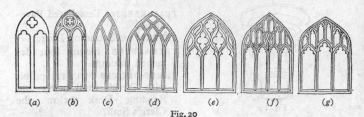

(a)　　(b)　　(c)　　(d)　　(e)　　(f)　　(g)

Fig. 20

Fig. 20(c). Tracery consisting of a mullion which branches into two forming a Y shape; typical of c. 1300. *Intersecting tracery: see* Fig. 20(d). Tracery in which each mullion of a window branches out into two curved bars in such a way that every one of them is drawn with the same radius from a different centre. The result is that every light of the window is a lancet and every two, three, four, etc., lights together form a pointed arch. This treatment also is typical of c. 1300. *Reticulated tracery: see* Fig. 20(e). Tracery typical of the early C14 consisting entirely of circles drawn at top and bottom into ogee shapes so that a net-like appearance results. *Panel tracery: see* Fig. 20(f) and (g). Perp tracery, which is formed of upright straight-sided panels above lights of a window.

TRANSEPT: transverse portion of a cross-shaped church.

TRANSOM: horizontal bar across the openings of a window.

TRANSVERSE ARCH: *see* Vault.

TRIBUNE: *see* Gallery.

TRICIPUT, SIGNUM TRICIPUT: sign of the Trinity expressed by three faces belonging to one head.

TRIFORIUM: arcaded wall passage or blank arcading facing the nave at the height of the aisle roof and below the clerestory (q.v.) windows. (*See* Gallery.)

TRIGLYPHS: blocks with vertical grooves separating the metopes (q.v.) in the Doric frieze (Fig. 12).

TROPHY: sculptured group of arms or armour, used as a memorial of victory.

TRUMEAU: stone mullion (q.v.) supporting the tympanum (q.v.) of a wide doorway.

TUMULUS: *see* Barrow.

TURRET: very small tower, round or polygonal in plan.

TUSCAN: *see* Order.

TYMPANUM: space between the lintel of a doorway and the arch above it.

UNDERCROFT: vaulted room, sometimes underground, below a church or chapel.

UNIVALLATE: of a hill-fort: defended by a single bank and ditch.

UPPER PALAEOLITHIC: *see* Palaeolithic.

VAULT: *Barrel-vault: see* Tunnel-vault. *Cross-vault: see* Groin-vault. *Domical vault:* square or polygonal dome ris-

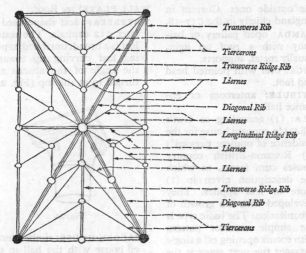

Transverse Rib
Tiercerons
Transverse Ridge Rib
Liernes
Diagonal Rib
Liernes
Longitudinal Ridge Rib
Liernes
Liernes
Transverse Ridge Rib
Diagonal Rib
Tiercerons

Fig. 21

ing direct on a square or polygonal bay, the curved surfaces separated by groins (q.v.). *Fanvault:* Late Medieval vault where all ribs springing from one springer are of the same length, the same distance from the next, and the same curvature. *Groin-vault* or *Crossvault:* vault of two tunnel-vaults of identical shape intersecting each other at r. angles. Chiefly Norman and Renaissance. *Lierne:* tertiary rib, that is, rib which does not spring either from one of the main springers or from the central boss. Introduced in the c14, continues to the c16. *Quadripartite vault:* one wherein one bay of vaulting is divided into four parts. *Rib-vault:* vault with diagonal ribs projecting along the groins. *Ridgerib:* rib along the longitudinal

10—N.L.

or transverse ridge of a vault. Introduced in the early c13. *Sexpartite vault:* one wherein one bay of quadripartite vaulting is divided into two parts transversely so that each bay of vaulting has six parts. *Tierceron:* secondary rib, that is, rib which issues from one of the main springers or the central boss and leads to a place on a ridge-rib. Introduced in the early c13. *Transverse arch:* arch separating one bay of a vault from the next. *Tunnelvault* or *Barrel-vault:* vault of semicircular or pointed section. Chiefly Norman and Renaissance. (*See* Fig. 21.)

VAULTING SHAFT: vertical member leading to the springer of a vault.

VENETIAN WINDOW: window with three openings, the central one arched and wider than the outside ones. Current in England chiefly in the C17–18.

VERANDA: open gallery or balcony with a roof on light, usually metal, supports.

VESICA: oval with pointed head and foot.

VESTIBULE: anteroom or entrance hall.

VILLA: (1) according to Gwilt (1842) 'a country house for the residence of opulent persons'; (2) Romano-British country houses cum farms, to which the description given in (1) more or less applies. They developed with the growth of urbanization. The basic type is the simple corridor pattern with rooms opening off a single passage; the next stage is the addition of wings. The courtyard villa fills a square plan with subsidiary buildings and an enclosure wall with a gate facing the main corridor block.

VITRIFIED: made similar to glass.

VITRUVIAN OPENING: A door or window which diminishes towards the top, as advocated by Vitruvius, bk. IV, chapter VI.

VOLUTE: spiral scroll, one of the component parts of an Ionic column (see Order).

VOUSSOIR: wedge-shaped stone used in arch construction.

WAGON ROOF: roof in which by closely set rafters with arched braces the appearance of the inside of a canvas tilt over a wagon is achieved. Wagon roofs can be panelled or plastered (ceiled) or left uncovered.

WAINSCOT: timber lining to walls.

WALL PLATE: see Roof.

WATERLEAF: leaf shape used in later C12 capitals. The waterleaf is a broad, unribbed, tapering leaf curving up towards the angle of the abacus and turned in at the top (Fig. 22).

Fig. 22

WEALDEN HOUSE: timber-framed house with the hall in the centre and wings projecting only slightly and only on the jutting upper floor. The roof, however, runs through without a break between wings and hall, and the eaves of the hall part are therefore exceptionally deep. They are supported by diagonal, usually curved, braces starting from the short inner sides of the overhanging wings and rising parallel with the front wall of the hall towards the centre of the eaves.

WEATHERBOARDING: overlapping horizontal boards, covering a timber-framed wall.

WEATHERING: sloped horizontal surface on sills, buttresses, etc., to throw off water.

WEEPERS: small figures placed in niches along the sides of some medieval tombs (also called Mourners).

WHEEL WINDOW: see Rose Window.

INDEX OF PLATES

INDEX OF ARTISTS

INDEX OF PLACES

NOTES